Signatures of Struggle

SUNY SERIES IN CONTEMPORARY JEWISH LITERATURE AND CULTURE

Ezra Cappell, editor

Dan Shiffman, *College Bound: The Pursuit of Education in Jewish American Literature, 1896–1944*

Eric J. Sundquist, editor, *Writing in Witness: A Holocaust Reader*

Oded Nir, *Signatures of Struggle: The Figuration of Collectivity in Israeli Fiction*

Signatures of Struggle

The Figuration of Collectivity in Israeli Fiction

ODED NIR

Published by State University of New York Press, Albany

© 2018 State University of New York

All rights reserved

No part of this book may be used or reproduced in any manner whatsoever without written permission. No part of this book may be stored in a retrieval system or transmitted in any form or by any means including electronic, electrostatic, magnetic tape, mechanical, photocopying, recording, or otherwise without the prior permission in writing of the publisher.

For information, contact State University of New York Press, Albany, NY
www.sunypress.edu

Library of Congress Cataloging-in-Publication Data

Names: Nir, Oded, author.
Title: Signatures of struggle : the figuration of collectivity in Israeli fiction / Oded Nir.
Description: Albany : State University of New York Press, 2018. | Series: SUNY series in contemporary Jewish literature and culture | Includes bibliographical references and index.
Identifiers: LCCN 2018000361 | ISBN 9781438472430 (hardcover   ) | ISBN 9781438472447 (pbk.   ) | ISBN 9781438472454 (ebook)
Subjects: LCSH: Politics in literature. | Nationalism in literature. | Israeli fiction—History and criticism. | Ideology and literature.
Classification: LCC PJ5030.P64 N57 2018 | DDC 892.43/609—dc23
LC record available at https://lccn.loc.gov/2018000361

10 9 8 7 6 5 4 3 2 1

In memory of my mother, Ayala Nir

Contents

Acknowledgments	ix
Introduction: Periodizing Israeli Literature	1
1 Prehistory: Zionist Hebrew Literary Realism, between *Altneuland* and *Khirbet Khizeh*	39
2 From Utopian Project to Utopian Compensation in 1950s Works by Yigal Mossinsohn and Nathan Shaham	65
3 Then as Farce: Naturalism and Disavowed Failure in 1950s Hebrew Novels by Hanoch Bartov and Yehudit Hendel	87
4 Is There Israeli Postmodern Literature? Orly Castel-Bloom, Yehudit Katzir, and the Vicissitudes of National Space-Time in the 1980s and 1990s	109
5 Disorientation and the Genres: David Grossman, Yehoshua Kenaz, and Batya Gur	143
6 Time in Hiding: Israeli Fiction and Neoliberalism	179
7 In Search of New Time: Renarrating Soldier, Pioneer, and the Tel Aviv Subject-to-Come	213
Notes	241
Bibliography	265
Index	277

Acknowledgments

An earlier version of chapter 1 ("Prehistory") was originally published in *Journal of Modern Jewish Studies* under the title "Literature at Work: Zionist Literary Realism between Utopia and *Khirbet Khizeh*."

Most of chapter 7 ("In Search for New Time") was originally published in *Prooftexts* under the title "On the Historical Imaginary of Contemporary Israeli Fiction, Or, Postmodernism's Aftermath in Novels by Lilach Netanel and Yiftach Ashkenazi."

Introduction

Periodizing Israeli Literature

One of the more nagging problems of writing a book in English about Israeli literature is a problem of audience: it is unclear whether one is writing for scholars of Israeli culture and literature, for people actually invested in Israel as a collective project, or for a larger circle of theoretically informed scholars. That this problem is symptomatic of a deeper problem of social mapping, or of having some stable mental representation of the way in which one's activity is inserted into the world, should be obvious. Yet, so quick of a plunge into a generalized social condition would be too easy. Much more difficult is another valence of this problem: the fast crumbling of the humanities academia, its institutional form undergoing a process of neoliberalization that eliminates the tenured positions on which its previous existence depended. It thus becomes unclear whether one can keep on writing as if the reader is the same academic professional, with its specific prejudices, habits, and sensitivities, or whether some new mode of writing, and new topics and new sets of preoccupations, should be developed. Complicating things further is that the position of more political academic work has always had an ambivalent relation to this institutional position. Indeed, a new realm of politicized writing has evolved in many new journals and other publication venues, one that does not depend on institutionalized academia and that does not follow its writing conventions (but is also different from the older lay publications, its interests sometimes echoing the narrow areas of specialization of the more academic kind of writing). One would be tempted to call such new forms of knowledge production neoliberal, even when the writing itself is completely antagonistic to the current hegemonic mode of social organization. That this book follows the conventions of the older academic style should be seen as itself somewhat of a utopian gesture—in the precise sense of evoking a social world that no longer exist—an ambivalent position if there ever was one.

But more practical problems result from this indeterminacy of audience, ones that have to do with more technical decisions on the composition of the following chapters, and which make introductions into more elaborate constructions than they were before. Thus, the introduction becomes something like a space in which one explicitly projects the book's expected audience, as if creating the readers in imagination. But the contradictions are not always easily solved on the level of the introduction's form itself. And so the crisis of the humanities—of which the devolving of theory from the lingua franca of the humanities into simply another hermetic field is surely another sign—is visible in the division of this introduction. In the first part, I provide an outline of the book's arguments. And to the second (and longer) part of it I leave the theoretical discussion of what this book is trying to achieve—placing its intervention not only within the world of theory but also in relation to the global study of literature, and with relation to the historiography of Israel and Zionism—for it should be clear that this book is no less about history and the theoretical problem of periodization than it is a book of literary criticism. In this latter part, I will briefly touch on the book's chapters again, as they relate to the theoretical issues raised. Any reader that has no interest in this more theoretical exercise of framing the book's intervention is welcome to skip the theoretical part altogether.

The present volume presents to the reader a new history of Israeli literature. To produce this new history I discuss three moments of transformation in Israeli letters: the 1950s, which are usually considered the moment in which Zionist realism gives way to the universalist "New Wave" of 1960s authors; the 1980s, which are usually taken to designate the moment in which Israeli literary postmodernism was born—with its accompanying multicultural valence; and the present moment (or rather a moment that began roughly in the middle of the first decade of the new millennium). This latter moment is usually not called anything in literary-critical commentary, for it is hardly discussed at all—a problem in its own right to which we will give due attention in the last two chapters of this book.

Even before the collapse of disciplinary boundaries, literary history has always been a strange creature—not entirely distinguishable from literary criticism, from the sociology of culture, or from history proper. So that this book forms new connections between literary and socioeconomic change should not be entirely surprising. And it is on this ground—of the mediation of social form into the realm of representation—that this book most clearly challenges existing histories of Israeli literature, and of Israel and Zionism generally. Most existing approaches, as the second part of this introduction will amply demonstrate, suffer from conceptual weakness, which is itself the result of the absence of a clear theory of mediation between the social and the cultural; but most also suffer from an impoverishment of the imagination, whose source is their commitment to the categories of the literary-historical paradigm established in the 1960s. It is the inability to go beyond this narrative in any substantial way that is the problem that is most forcefully tackled by this current volume. I hesitate to name the approach taken here a totalizing and a Marxist one, and not only because of the prejudices and confusions still associated with these labels (which seem to finally be on the wane, with the decline of Cold-War era liberalism). But also because to call the approach taken here a Marxist one is for many to commit to seeing it as one possible approach among many others, in some kind of irreducible multiplicity of interpretive options. But it is precisely this seeming universality whose particularity is challenged in this book. It is not possible to accept the narrative offered here alongside these other ones; the narrative offered here becomes incoherent if it is seen as existing alongside these other narratives, rather than as these very narratives' transformation or reworking. It is this latter point that has to be kept in mind if one were to call this present volume a Marxist history of Israeli literature.

Summary of the Argument

The first chapter engages what I am calling the prehistory of Israeli fiction—beginning somewhat arbitrarily with Herzl's *Altneuland* and continuing to the pre-statehood years of the first half of the twentieth century. I choose here to focus on the largely forgotten realist literature of the 1920s and 1930s, which is usually deemed to be nothing but Zionist propaganda. I argue that 1930s novels such as Yisrael Zarchi's *Barefoot Days* reproduce formal elements of utopian novels (represented for us in Herzl's *Altneuland*), in trying to imagine the overcoming the contradictions of the Zionist collective project in Palestine. As opposed to the mainstream narratives (Israeli-national; Post-Zionist), I use recent writing to see this collective project as one aimed at radical social transformation, but that is not necessarily aimed at an establishment of a capitalist state. The consequences of this position are that the establishment of the state is eventually the result of Zionism's failure, rather than its success, challenging the hegemonic literary-historiographical narrative established by Gershon Shaked (and inherited by all major commentators). The concluding section of this chapter, in which I address S. Yizhar's *Khirbet Khizeh*, will argue that it precisely this failure that is repressed socially, but becomes unconsciously registered in Yizhar's novella and in the literature of the 1950s. The more theoretical part of this introduction discusses in more detail the antagonism between this narrative and the Israeli-national one, but also its antagonism to the main Post-Zionist variants of this history (mainly, that the historical narrative presented here is a totalizing one).

The next two chapters explore the ways in which this repressed break between Zionism and the state is expressed in the literature of the 1950s. One of the more entrenched beliefs in Israeli literary criticism is that this period marks the beginning of a turn away from the "propagandistic" literature of the '30s and '40s to the more "universal" or "non-ideological" literature of the '60s. Shaked's "New Wave" is here universally accepted as the most important moment of rebellion against literature-as-midwife of the nation; the "Zionist metanarrative"—an empty pseudo-concept if there ever was one, as I hope to demonstrate in what follows—becoming the aim of literature's bitter critique, rather than supplying the latter's basic narrative forms. Chapter 2 sets itself the task of exploding this narrative, exploring works by Yigal Mossinsohn and Nathan Shaham, who are supposed to be some of the clearest examples of ideologically committed literature. I then show that in Mossinsohn, the invention of internality or the self is a way of successfully mediating between history and individual action (necessary precisely because the crisis of the Zionist collective project has entailed a crisis of historicity or this relation to history). In Shaham, the point of view of the *Palmach*'s soldiers is taken to emphasize precisely this crisis. The *Palmach* is here a perfect no-place: its sudden purposelessness as it nears its dissolution to form the national military removes social function from its members—and therefore becomes a convenient literary figure for the crisis of the Zionist project. The work of both authors, then, attempts to register this repressed crisis, and the interrogation of national-ideological motifs in both is a clear means to this end, and so is the ballooning of subjectivity and its antagonism to the social, under whose spell Shaked and other critics readily fall, as some imagined exit from ideology.

The next chapter then looks at the non-militaristic literary side of the '50s, by exploring works by Hanoch Bartov and Yehudit Hendel, giving particular attention to the latter's *Street of Steps*. Other thematizations of the same crisis, I argue, appear in the works of these two authors. In Bartov, a drama of integration of Jewish immigrants into a new Jerusalem neighborhood is modelled after the "settlement novel" of the '20s and '30s (in which rural agricultural settlements are established). I try to argue that a failure to narrate is formally embedded in this straightforwardly realist narrative: the intervention of an outside agency whose social position is never mapped (as opposed to all others) is needed for the national allegory to function. It is this "alien" help that betrays the presence of the same crisis of the Zionist project. In Hendel's much more complex novel, the failure to narrate becomes the formally dominant element (which is precisely the reason for the novel being so well-liked by the New Wave authors and critics). I address several thematizations of this narrative failure—the dissolution of time, the melancholia pervasive among Hendel's characters (and many other characters in 1950s fiction), and naturalist representation of relationships. All of these, I argue, are the result of the same historical crisis. What Shaked and Miron (and others) see as an anti-ideological turn to universal themes or some eternal truth of human existence is here instead explained as a historical result.

Chapters 4 and 5 jump thirty years ahead to the 1980s, which is the next important moment of transformation in Israeli literature—one Avraham Balaban called the "Other Wave" in Israeli letters, echoing Shaked's earlier "New Wave." To call it "postmodern" as we once did would be to ignore many newer commentators that try to persuade us that using that term was wrong in the first place. That claim becomes part of the problematic we will try to solve in these chapters. Three questions guide me here: Whether there ever was Israeli postmodern literature ("postmodernism" here implying a whole periodizing schema, rather than an (at the last instance, incoherent) usage of it as an ethical or aesthetic choice)? What social transformations are related to this aesthetic change? And, why do Israeli critics since the mid-2000s retreat from using the term to describe Israeli fiction? The latter question is mostly treated in the last two chapters (since its answer properly belongs in this later period rather than in the '80s and '90s). I then show that the works of Orly Castel-Bloom and Yehudit Katzir display all the characteristics usually associated with postmodern fiction. I argue that at the heart of these lies an unconscious crisis of social mapping and historicity—a dissolution of the ability to orient oneself in social space. Yet, the relatively early emergence of postmodernism in Israeli letters, I argue, make the immediate source of this crisis unique to the Israeli context: it is the overnight proletarianization of Palestinians by Israeli capital, following the 1967 war. After 1967, I argue, Israeli everyday reality becomes overwhelmingly produced by those who are not part of

Israeli social imagination—which results in the representational crisis that lurks behind the more playful tone of Katzir and Castel-Bloom.

I then turn to 1980s and 1990s writers who do not at all display Castel-Bloom's and Katzir's playfulness, and who therefore are taken as representative of the "non-postmodernists" of the period: David Grossman, Yehoshua Kenaz, and Batya Gur. I then proceed to show how the crisis of social mapping becomes the main problem that all three texts try to resolve in imagination. In Grossman's *The Smile of the Lamb* this crisis is expressed through attempting to reconcile politically committed literature with an aesthetic ideology in which collective meaning is impossible; in Kenaz's *Infiltration* this crisis is manifested in an encyclopedic pastichization of the 1950s self-representation; and in Gur's detective novels it is registered in the exploding of the agency of the detective in the final instance. I thus answer two of the three questions posed: Israeli postmodern literature does exist, we can say, as long as we remember the unique origin of this postmodernism in the results of the 1967 war.

Chapters 6 and 7 turn to the contemporary moment. My overarching claim in these chapters is that contemporary Israeli literature enacts a search for temporality or history. One should be careful to understand the specific difference of these texts from the previous, postmodern moment: these do not express some exit from or leaving-behind of postmodernity (a term whose specific significance I will address more fully in these chapters). Rather, the difference is one of coming-into-consciousness what was previously only an unconscious content: the disappearance of temporality and of historicity themselves—and the erosion of the possibility of mediation. These are no longer seen as freedoms (as they did in the postmodern moment), but are instead figured as problems to be solved, breathing life into a more utopian approach (or at least a more anti-anti-utopian) to the problem of a timeless present. Chapter 6 examines works by Ofir Touché Gafla (representing here the emerging Israeli SF) and Einat Yakir. Gafla's more speculative exploration of time in *The Day the Music Died* provides its readers with an unresolved contrast between a Fordist temporal world and the futureless present in which so many Israelis find themselves today. What is important here is that futurelessness itself must be contained by asserting its identity with previous generation's stable sense of the future. In Yakir's *Sand*, the search for time is enacted in a completely different way. The poor, precariously existing, family of ex-Soviet immigrants to Israel on which the novel focuses provides the occasion for a different temporal tension to emerge: that grating against each other of different modes of production typical in the experience of ex-Soviet immigrants into capitalism. Uneven development, we used to call this chafing of two systems of organizing social life, and a certain sense of progress—or of time—used to accompany their spatial juxtaposition: the development imaginary that separated the first world from the second and third. These little expressions of time are here recreated in Yakir's novel, as I hope to show, needing to find their place within a horizon of total contemporaneity inscribed by neoliberal capitalism.

But here too this book insists on the dialectical specificity of the Israeli "case" of neoliberalism (or the way in which it is precisely through its difference that the Israeli case is part of a totality). So I offer here a new model through which to imagine the entity that we call "Israel," one that offers its division into three "worlds," or three forms of social existence, only one of which is dominated by the neoliberalism of the more American kind. This trio, I suggest, does not form a whole in itself, but only through its relation to global capitalism. The novels explored in these last two chapters and the search for time which they enact, I argue, provide us with a glimpse only into the first of these three "Israeli" worlds. In the last chapter, then, I trace the search for time in three additional texts: Yiftach Ashkenazi's *Fulfillment*, Lilach Netanel's *The Hebrew Condition*, and Ron Leshem's *Beaufort*. Ashkenazi's novel presents its readers with an allegory of the collapse of historicity itself, tracing the development of the sensibilities and contradictions associated with it from the 1960s to the early 2000s. The specific causes or origins ascribed to it in the novel are less important for us than the attempt to generate historicity again, or a sense of the present as part of historical change, which was exploded in the previous postmodern moment. In Netanel's novel—if one can call it that—the search for temporality is expressed through the main formal element: the repetition with slight variation of different narrative segments. This is not a playful dissolution of history, of ideology, or of everyday reality, but the subsumption of all of these under a—now threatening—inability to narrate, which is finally contained at the end of the novel, as I try to show. Leshem's *Beaufort* is here viewed as the last instance in a genre which this book explores in the earlier two moments as well, in the works of Yizhar and Kenaz. What is unique to Leshem's novel is precisely again the staging of imaginary containment missing from the earlier novels—the dissolution of everyday Israeli life and of the possibility of telling history must here be dispelled. That, in turn, signals to us that both have become felt problems to be overcome.

It is neoliberal capitalism and its effects that are therefore registered and "solved" in imagination in all of these more recent works, which are thus given a historical and social background that distinguishes them from their predecessors. It is also the root cause of Israeli literary criticism's inability to identify this newness, and its gradual retreat from using terms such as "postmodernism," I argue in these last two chapters. The next section of this introduction explores in much more detail the theoretical background for the intervention performed by this book, mapping its relation to Israeli cultural historiography and to the theoretical problem of periodization more generally, as well as to Marxist theorizations of "peripheral literatures"—all these world literatures that do not belong to the core of global capitalism, assuming this last concept retains any coherence. Any reader that is not interested in these problems is welcome to skip over this next section and move on to the readings themselves. Yet this next section is necessary and urgent—and to defend this claim we must already move to the realm of theorizing.

Periodizing Israeli Literature, or Trying to Imagine the Present

This theoretical section of the introduction is divided into two parts. The first will deal generally with the problem of using a literary-critical tradition that has developed in the context of Western European and American literatures to discuss a peripheral literature. I will not focus here on the specificities of the Israeli case, but rather on the theoretical problem that can never be completely settled, namely, how Marxist literary criticism can be adapted to new social and cultural context. Our answer here would of course take us beyond these cultural specificities into that grand objective unity of the world under global capitalism. The second part of this introduction will be more strongly related to the subject matter of this book. I will here argue not only that a new history of Israeli literature is sorely needed, but also that the Marxist totalizing perspective—one that is able to relate cultural specificities to larger social structure and the history of form—is well suited to offer such new historical account.

Yet both of these depend on a more fundamental motivation that animates this project, one which has to do with a certain sense of being "stuck" historically, both in a narrower sense of what literary criticism of Hebrew literature offers us and in a broader sense of a lack of any transformative collective project beyond capitalism itself in a much more material sense. This is not to mean a lack of happenings, to be sure. But activity does not necessarily mean life, as Phillip K. Dick once said; and so it remains to raise in our imagination the possibilities of transformation at which this book is eventually aimed. The new history of Israeli literature offered here is thus also a new history of Israel in general, and the new way of imagining the past which it contains necessarily extends into a new way of thinking the future. And to answer the proponents of objectivity or "surface reading" that might frown at this explicit political horizon—we must bring out the old arguments again, to show that the horizon of all interpretation is political, whether one is conscious of it or not.

Yet to articulate the problem itself with any degree of clarity we need to take a detour through geopolitics and what it means to be a peripheral literature (in an entirely non-ethical way) for our analysis not to be an arbitrary application of concepts to matter. At the height of what used to be called the age of postcolonial theory, the organizing categories of our literary geopolitics were those of "The West" versus the rest of the world. These existed uneasily with an older division, that of the three-worlds paradigm, denoting the capitalist, communist, and what was neither of these.[1] If this trio became defunct with the collapse of the Second World (the Soviet Union and its allies), the former is also in rapid decline, with the falling out of vogue of postcolonial theory. It seems inadequate today to invoke "The West" in the same way as the postcolonials used it, when social strife seems to have reached out of the former colonies to infect the old empires. The newer distinction between "Global North" and "Global South," which to a certain degree inherited the old West-Rest distinction, rings false as well, mostly as it seems to be free from the ethical overtones and insistence on colonial past as the objective moment of origin of its problematic. Instead, the Global North-South divide seems to posit global inequalities as some matter for corporate intervention, a completely practical matter rather than one for revenge or revolution. Whatever the faults of the older categorical systems, their disintegration—or the absence of a stable frame to the way we think about geopolitics—puts us today in an even worse position. For, now our geopolitical imaginations seem to be ruled by a general indistinction—one that is inscribed either directly or through a nominalism in which there are just particular countries and no general categories can be applied. This synchronic indistinction is accompanied by a diachronic or historical one, in which imagined temporalities of development collapse. Gone is the imaginary operation that used to flatten the world into a linear sequence in which certain countries are more developed than others, making way instead for what Emilio Sauri and others see as a permanent contemporaneity.[2] One of the common examples of this tendency toward what we might call an empty difference (which by its own emptiness reverts to its opposite, sameness), is the notion of "alternative modernities," in which modernity no longer has any determinate content, but is rather exploded into an irreducible multiplicity of "experiences of the modern." We will return to this collapse of geopolitical mapping and temporality in what follows.

In this situation, the older critiques of these categories (modernity, development, etc.) from within the left become wholly unnecessary.[3] Yet there is one such geopolitical division that survives, I would like to suggest: the Marxist distinction between the global economic core and periphery, developed by Immanuel Wallerstein, but used in many other different Marxist theorizations of global capitalism, such as Robert Brenner's.[4] All of these hark back to Marx's own determination that "the tendency to form a world market is given in the concept of capital itself."[5] Thus, what unites the world into a single system is the global spread of capitalism itself, an expansion that historically takes place through colonialism and imperialism—but in which the colonized part of the world becomes no less capitalist than the colonizing one. But this spread of sameness is not inherently antagonistic to difference as such, but is rather the common grounds on which difference is allowed to develop. "One but unequal," is Wallerstein's formula for this unity of the world, in which the differences between countries is not reduced away, but explained through the different locations of each economy within the hierarchy of world capitalism—clearly dominated by the United States (and in the same breath one should add that dependence acts both ways in the totality of global capitalism—if anything, it is the master that depends on the cooperation of the slave more than the other way around).

The world is thus not relegated to sameness in this model, but rather to what is usually called "combined and uneven development," a term that already moves us from some purely economic register to one of social form. Crucial to this conceptualization of the world-system is the following observation: what (used to) seem to us like an imperfect economic development—thriving "economic" bustling not yet expanding into certain areas that seem backward—is actually produced and maintained *as underdeveloped* by the expansion of capitalism itself. As the Warwick Collective put it in their recent theorization of world literature:

> the imposed capitalist forces of production and class relations tend not to supplant (or are not allowed to supplant) but to be conjoined forcibly with pre-existing forces and relations. The outcome . . . is a contradictory 'amalgam of archaic with

more contemporary forms'—an urban proletariat working in technologically advanced industries existing side by side with a rural population engaged in subsistence farming; industrial plants built alongside 'villages of wood and straw'; and peasants 'thrown into the factory cauldron snatched directly from the plow' . . . The multiple modes in and through which this 'coexistence' manifests itself—the multiple forms of appearance of unevenness—are to be understood as being connected, as being governed by a socio-historical logic of combination, rather than as being contingent and asystematic.[6]

Thus, the "what" seems like a lag in development—the periphery of global capitalism lagging behind the core, displaying remnants of non-capitalist social structure—is in fact produced or reproduced by the global capitalist system. What is crucial for us to note is the shock of contemporaneity that thus becomes the antidote to some notion of imperfect or not-yet-complete development: the core's metropolitan skyscrapers and the periphery's slum cities and rural villages being complementary and necessary parts of the same capitalist world system.

Thus this Marxist conception of the becoming-one of the world system is antagonistic to any notion of alternative modernities as incommensurable realities (a special place should be reserved here for those "modernities" that took place, at least for part of their existence, precisely against and outside of capitalism—such as those of the Soviet Block, or that of China. It is only here that some true alternative to global capitalism temporarily exists, as Liu Kang notes for the case of China, even if these too ended up becoming part of the capitalist system in the end.[7] We will return to these cases in what follows). The title of Fredric Jameson's *A Singular Modernity* attests precisely to this Marxist position, whose explanatory advantage over its antagonist should be clear: the different modernities are here successfully seen as so many social experiences corresponding to different parts of the capitalist totality.[8] Put more dialectically, the difference of the periphery is precisely where their unity with the core resides.

It is this Marxist view of the historical formation of the capitalist world-system that becomes crucial for the kind of Marxist approach to peripheral literature followed in this book. The different literatures are related to the core and to each other by constituting so many imaginative responses to these local social conditions created by the global expansion of capitalism. This historical expansion is not just one critical content among many. Rather, as Nick Brown comments in his study of European Modernism and African Literature:

> The global expansion of capitalism, with all of its social, psychological, and cultural effects, is obscured when we speak of modernism as a product of "Western culture" and of African literature as "non-Western." Indeed, when the boundary between the two is bracketed, the differential movement of capital emerges not as one kind of content among many, but as the fundamental content of both modernism and African literature.[9]

What is important for us is not so much the critique of the category of "The West" as such, whose coherence and utility have diminished considerably as we said above, but rather a different point: that the expansion of capitalism as the referent (in the last instance) of both Modernism and African Literature is barred from being just another interpretation of both of them, alongside other readings—as in some non-antagonistic multiplicity of readings. Rather, this referent is either invisible (if we accept an insurmountable division between African literature and European Modernism), or it is the overriding referent of both, if we violate this division. It is in this sense that taking identity categories as our basic coordinates (rather than as ideologies or codes to be transcoded, excludes a Marxist reading, rather than supplementing it, or coexisting with it (and to be clear: a code of class is by all means also one of these transcodable imaginations). In other words, to see the validity of the global Marxist literary comparativism—that the different literatures are so many creative imaginary responses to different parts of a global capitalism—one has to accept that identity categories do not constitute endpoint or horizon of interpretation, which is to say that their existence in our mind is ultimately contingent and historically produced. This does not mean that they are secondary or derivative, but rather exactly the opposite: that they, among other figurative tools, are our only way of imagining resistance and transformation. To be sure, one could level the same accusation at the Marxist paradigm—that class antagonism as interpretive key can also be overcome (in thought and historically). And Marxists would be happy to agree: the dissolution of capitalism and social class as such have always been the ultimate goal of Marxist critique.

Alongside Nick Brown's work, other examples of the Marxist paradigm can be given. First, at a more general level, we have already mentioned that uneven development has meant the persistence of pre-capitalist hierarches and social forms alongside those of capitalism, to a certain extent even owing their continued existence to capitalist expansion. As Benita Parry and others argue, the coexistence of two (or more) radically different social systems accounts for all kinds of "irrealisms" or deviations from realist narration, a kind of splitting of the representational apparatus that a too-hasty reading would just identify with modernism.[10] Fredric Jameson similarly shows that literature that emerges out of these contexts, such as Latin American Magic Realism, "betrays the overlap or the coexistence of precapitalist with nascent capitalist or technological features." . . . The organizing category of magic realist film . . . is one of modes of production."[11] Yet the problem of peripheral literatures cannot really be resolved at this level of generality, but rather has to be posed and solved for each historical context anew, as Jameson and Brown themselves admit. Parry's "irrealisms" could serve as a good example for the unsatisfactory nature of such generalizations: the deviation from realist representational norms, even if it is common to all unevenly developed contexts, is too overdetermined by other causes to provide a good litmus test for peripherality. Franco Moretti's work well-known theorization of world literature, in which disruptions of narrative voice become the distinguishing mark of peripheral novels, is another example of such a generalization: no matter its value for defining world literature, it is certainly too general to become some kind of strict homologue of economic peripheriality.[12]

One should thus more closely examine theoretical accounts of specific literatures, of which Brown's discussion of African literature is a good example. Another example can be found in the writing of Roberto Schwarz on late nineteenth-century Brazilian literature. The problem of posed by the Brazilian conjuncture, according to Schwarz, is a peculiar meeting point of peripheral capitalism with imported liberal ideology. In the countries of the capitalist core, liberal ideology of individual freedom has explanatory (or, as some would say, orienting) value, at least in terms of the immediate experience of wage-laborer: competition between workers is the immediate condition encountered by workers in these economies. But this is not the case in Brazil. Here, according to Schwartz, the capitalist world market (for which Brazil is an agricultural exporter) depended on the continued use of slave labor in the late nineteenth century, rather than wage-labor. This entailed a rather unique adaptation of the function of the liberal ideology imported into Brazil, and its literary use. Schwarz's brilliant proposal for understanding of the relation between literature and social form in this context should be quoted at length:

Slavery was indeed the basic productive relationship, and yet it was not the social relation directly at work in ideological life. The key lay elsewhere. To find it, we must take up again the country as a whole. To schematize, we can say that colonization, based on the monopoly of the land, produced three classes of population: the proprietor of the latifundium, the slave and the 'free man,' who was in fact dependent. Between the first two, the relation is clear. Our argument will hinge on the situation of the third. Neither proprietor, nor proletarian, the free man's access to social life and its benefits depended, in one way or another, on the favour of a man of wealth and power [. . .] Favour was, therefore, the relationship by which the class of free men reproduced itself, a relationship in which the other member was the propertied class. The field of ideological life is formed by these two classes, and it is governed, therefore, by this relationship. Thus, under a thousand forms and names, favour formed and flavoured the whole of the national life, excepting always the basic productive relationship which was secured by force. Favour was present everywhere, combining itself with more or less ease to administration, politics, industry, commerce, the life of the city, the court, and so on. [. . .] Favour was our quasi-universal social mediation—and being more appealing than slavery, the other relationship inherited from colonial times, it is understandable that our writers based their interpretation of Brazil upon it, thereby unwittingly disguising the violence that had always been essential to the sphere of production.

Slavery gives the lie to liberal ideas; but favour, more insidiously, uses them, for its own purposes, originating a new ideological pattern. [. . .] Liberalism, which had been an ideology well grounded in appearances, came to stand for the conscious desire to participate in a reality that appearances did not sustain. When he justified arbitrariness by means of some 'rational' reason, the beneficiary consciously exalted himself and his benefactor, who, in turn, had no motive to contradict him, rationality being the highest value of the modern world. In this context, ideologies do not describe reality, not even falsely, and they do not move according to a law of their own; we shall therefore call them 'ideologies of the second degree.' Their law of movement is a different one, not the one they name; it honours prestige, rather than a desire for system and objectivity. The reasons for this were no secret: the inevitable 'superiority' of Europe, and the demands of the moment of expression, of self-esteem and fantasy, which are essential to favour. In this way, as we have said before, the test of reality and coherence did not seem to be decisive, notwithstanding its continuous presence as a requirement, recalled or forgotten according to circumstances. Thus, one could methodically call dependence independence, capriciousness utility, exceptions universality, kinship merit, privilege equality, and so on. By linking itself to the practice of what, in principle, it should criticize, liberalism caused thought to lose its footing. Let us not forget, however, the complexity of this step: inasmuch as they became preposterous, these ideas also ceased to mislead.[13]

The totalizing horizon of Schwarz's argument ("the country as a whole") here should be noted: his understanding of the uniqueness of late nineteenth-century Brazilian literature has to do with relating local ideology to the local economic base. The new social role of liberal ideology in this case emerges from the mismatch between imported ideology and a social form. It is only through this totalizing movement that Schwarz can conclude that Brazilian literature is wholly based in the "favor" social relation, which provides a simple but very powerful explanation for the curious pastiche-status of liberal ideology in the literary works he discusses (most notably, the work of Machado de Assis). But the national frame is not the absolute limit of this totalizing movement. The dialectical force and implication of the argument would be completely missed if we ignore that the difference of the Brazilian case is the form of appearance of its unity with the capitalist world system—which constitutes the final horizon of thought for Schwarz's argument.

The case of Israel and Zionism, on which we have not begun to touch, is too different from the Brazilian one to merit any direct analogies. What is important for my purpose here is to note the way in which the terms with which we do literary criticism become indirectly twisted in the periphery. To say "liberal ideology" in Schwarz's context is to be clear enough in terms of conceptual content. But, as Schwarz shows, it is to say something entirely new in terms of its social location and function—since the liberal subject is nowhere to be found, and liberalism does not function as an ideology in any familiar sense. As I will try to show throughout this book, the same is true of using imported terms in the Zionist and Israeli case—most importantly periodizing terms such as realism, modernism and postmodernism. Even if each of these, when invoked in Israeli literary criticism, designates the same specific determinate content that it has in the global core—the characteristics of a specific style or aesthetic principles—each functions in a manner entirely different within the contradictory totality of the development of Zionist and Israeli capitalist society. The antagonistic coexistence of realism and modernism in Hebrew literature from Palestine in the first half of the twentieth century is useful as a quick illustration here. For, what can we mean by "realism" and "modernism" when the latter does not supplant the former, but rather flourishes alongside it? If modernism is not seen as the result of some exhaustion of realism, in what sense is it modernism at all? Indeed, in what sense can one call "realism" an aesthetic branch that triumphed over its "modernist" antagonist—not today, in what seems like (but is exactly not) a revival of realism, as it were after the end of postmodernism—but in the early twentieth century?[14] That this strange situation makes one look for a model in the Soviet option, with its notorious doctrine of Socialist Realism, should in itself tell us that a radically different social state of affairs must exist to support such coexistence of "realism" and "modernism" (and it should be clear that the Soviet analogy is as problematic as the analogy to the capitalist core, since Socialist Realism was a representational strategy of hegemony, a position that was not available to early Zionism).

This book's exploration of three moments of transformation of Zionist and Israeli literature is precisely an attempt to make visible the dialectical difference of its subject matter, through its location within (or entry into) global capitalism. And the fate of Palestinians, as we will see, is absolutely central to this new historical mapping. The first moment is the 1950s, which should be seen as extending from the mid-'40s to the late '50s. This is precisely the moment of political triumph for capitalist social form in Palestine (which is not to say that capitalism first appears in Palestine in this time). The second moment is that of the 1980s, which was hailed as the coming of postmodernism to Israeli literature (a narrative which critics today seem reluctant to reproduce), which as I will try to show has to do with the economic results of the 1967 Israeli occupation of the West Bank and the Gaza Strip. The third moment is the current one, which can be characterized as the imperfect neoliberalization of Israeli society: the rolling-back of welfare-state social protections, and the heightened immediacy of subjects' relation to the forces of global capitalism, which seemingly paradoxically exists alongside the growth of a new "welfare state" in the occupied territories. To forestall the usual knee-jerk accusations of reductionism, it is important to emphasize how non-reductionist our Marxist readings will be (as any reading of the following chapters easily demonstrate): For, as Adorno's writing about popular music demonstrates, literature is here not at all "merely" an expression of the economic.[15] Rather, each text should be seen as constituting an original imaginative response to social contradictions, as a truly genuine creative effort to provide contradictions with perceivable figures and to imagine their resolution. For Adorno, 1940s American popular music retains its creative magic by mastering an outright impossible task: to reconcile the contradictory (social) demands of exhaustion and boredom. In a similar way, any truly Marxist understanding of cultural production must contain an account of its indispensable necessity as a separate realm in its own right (provided that culture does indeed still forms such a realm). Thus, it is only through offering a totalizing explanation—one that places culture within the force-field of a contradictory social whole—that the uniqueness of literature is preserved, rather than eradicated. And if "reductionism" is to be understood in a more temporal vein—as the explanation of the new wholly in terms of a preexisting explanatory schema—then a Marxist account is even more suitable to be a way of escaping reductionism into new and unfamiliar interpretive territory. As Walter Benn Michaels claims, our contemporary scholarly moment is overwhelmingly characterized by studies that focus on multicultural themes (racial, ethnic, sexual, etc.)—a judgment that can surely be extended to English-language publications on Israeli literature. A Marxist account thus undoubtedly offers a fresh, or non-reductive, analytical prism—one that as I argued above cannot be simply one among an irreducible multiplicity of marginal perspectives.[16]

But another short comment regarding multiculturalism or identity politics (which have dominated the critique of Israeli culture) is in order, if only to clarify that one does not need to imagine it to be absolutely antagonistic to Marxist hermeneutics. For one of the problems of accounts that stress the explicit appearance of race, gender, or class is that they are hermeneutically limited to an ethics of overt content. It should be clear that a morality tale about the misfortunes of the lower class is as non-Marxist as one about Mizrachis or an oppressed gendered perspective. Rather than championing such reified version of "class analysis," the hermeneutical model with which I work here is one of a layered model of interpretation, which can accommodate the antagonistic coexistence of multiple interpretive codes or levels (the most complete articulation of which exists in Fredric Jameson's *The Political Unconscious*, but has its predecessors in the works of

Lukács, Pierre Macherey, and the Frankfurt School, but also of Freud and Lacan). It should be stressed that it is entirely false that some interpretive levels are more primary or important than others in this model in any ethical sense; nor do any of them stand for a deeper "truth": the overt figure being completely necessary and vital, in that it is the only vehicle through which certain antagonisms can be become visible and usable in political struggle—and here, of course, the anti-reductionist primacy of representation in any Marxist account of culture is again asserted. A Marxist hermeneutic is therefore not to be preferred because it utterly replaces that of identity politics, but because it is the only one that can bring both codes together in a single interpretive effort, without it becoming some facile reconciliation.

It is here that we can finally approach one more specific charge of reductionism, namely, that seeing Israeli literature (or indeed any peripheral literature) through the prism of the global spread of capitalism ignores other historical narratives of this literature, as if declaring itself to be the real material transformation underlying what is essentially mere ideology. In the case of Israel, that would be the narrative of the development of Zionism and the Hebrew literature attached to it. We have two antagonistic types of narrative for these: the Israeli national narrative, and the Post-Zionist one. I would like to defer our detailed treatment of this history, or more accurately its rewriting, to the following chapters of this work. Here, I would simply like to address in more general theoretical terms the relation between this Marxist account of the spread of capitalism and narrating peripheral literary history using its own terms—briefly and schematically, but usefully so. I argue not only that the Marxist account is not reductive, but also that it can actually accommodate what seems initially to be irreconcilable narratives of the same period—those of national liberation, or even those of anti-capitalist collective projects as such. The case of China in Liu Kang's writing, which was mentioned above, is one such instance, and that of Zionism is another (and it does not matter for our present purpose whether one sees the essence of Zionism as oppressive or emancipatory). Anti-colonial struggles for independence are yet another. In all of these, to say that what counts is the integration into world capitalism of the specific peripheral area in question seems initially to ignore or discount those other narratives of struggle (which have their literary-historical equivalents—seeing the period's literature understood either as working in the service of this struggle or critical of it). In other words, it is worth elaborating further Brown's provocative assertion that

> The narrative of national independence, appearing spontaneously as complete in itself, in fact takes its historical meaning from what is excluded from it, namely the limitations placed on the liberation movements by their location in the world economy. Each of these countries, once independence was on the horizon, faced the same question: whether to dare genuinely to challenge the logic of capital and violently disturb property relations or, remaining within the context of a purely national liberation, to strike a bargain with the former colonizer (in the contemporary example of South Africa, with investment capital).[17]

It should be clear in today's political climate—in which what was previously the revolutionary "Second World" has long become thoroughly capitalist, and in which the massive protests of the Arab Spring mark the utter bankruptcy of the anti-colonial revolutions, we would do well to find a way of narrating these seeming historical openings—rifts that could have led to a different world—together with their final integration into global capitalism, without losing sight of either the possibilities opened up by the initial upheaval or that final incorporation into the global order. One should begin by noting that an anti-capitalist horizon actually did unevenly inform many of these struggles for national liberation. The more explicitly revolutionary cases of China and the Soviet Union are simply the ones that most emphatically pose the problem of such narratives: how to think together an anti-capitalist struggle (which sometimes even seems successful) with an ultimate integration into global capitalism. But ignoring this for the moment, rather than noting that capitalism is the unacknowledged limitation of national liberation narrative, I would like now to offer an explicit theorization of what Brown gestures toward by saying that "the narrative of national independence . . . takes its meaning . . . from the limitations placed on the liberation movements by their location in the world economy." In other words, what I will now argue is that the narrative of national emancipation is in fact preserved in the Marxist historical narrative of capitalism's expansion, rather than vanishing from it as some merely expressive illusion—a vulgar Marxist narrative if there ever was one.

So on the one hand we have an idealist narrative of national independence, and against it the vulgar Marxist narrative of the spread of global capitalism. It is worth noting at this stage that one of these narratives has to do with the economic base (spread of capitalism), while the other revolves around ideology or the superstructure (national independence). To understand both as part of the same historical moment I will use the Marxist appropriation of the Hegelian notion of the Ruse of Reason, or what Fredric Jameson calls the "vanishing mediator" in his essay on Weber's account of Protestantism and its relation to the birth of European capitalism.[18] The basic structure of historical transformation is understood here to have three moments, which take place along two axes: that of means (or material infrastructure) and ends (or ideological superstructure). The first moment in such transformation is the making-explicit of some goal that was implicit in the older superstructure. In the next moment, new means are elaborated in order to achieve this older goal, replacing older means which seem to have failed to serve their purpose. In the last moment, the older goal itself vanishes, leaving us with the new means, a new socioeconomic infrastructure. In Jameson's essay, whose subject matter is the rise of Protestantism and its relation to the "infrastructural" formation of capitalism, the first moment is that of Luther (in which the older religious goals are stressed and the existing means condemned); the second one corresponds to Calvin (in which the new rationalization of means is elaborated), and the third—in which religious goals disappear altogether, leaving us with nothing but the new means or infrastructure, capitalist social relations—is simply modern society. It is in these moments of historical transformation that the effectiveness of the superstructure is revealed, or as Jameson puts it: "Thus [in this schema], the superstructure may be said to find its essential function in the mediation of changes in the infrastructure [. . .] and to understand it in this way, as 'vanishing mediator,' is to escape the false problems of priority or of cause and effect in which both vulgar Marxism and the idealist position imprison us."[19]

It is this narrative structure that will now make it possible for us to think together the spread of capitalism and national or social liberation movements—even those that have a socialist element to them. For the first moment's old goal is precisely that of emancipation (which exists more or less implicitly on both the colonized and colonial side). And the second moment's new means that are introduced are precisely those of capitalist social form and the subjective set of behaviors needed to function in it, or a social form that would fit well into the unevenly developed economic position of each specific peripheral economy. In the third moment, the goal of liberation simply disappears or becomes tame and ineffective, leaving us with the new means that were created: capitalist society. Thus, the national liberation movement is here the ruse under which a transition into capitalist social form (or one of its stages) is made possible. It is in this way that national liberation struggle does not simply disappear from the narrative of capitalism's spread: the pursuit of these ideals of national liberation is not mere ideological window-dressing for the material transformation. Rather, As Slavoj Žižek emphasizes in his writing about the vanishing mediator, the pursuit of the old goal is a necessity for any transformation to happen at all, a step without which the material development (in our case, the specific incorporation into global capitalism) could never have been achieved.[20]

The vanishing mediator thus becomes a schema through which we can successfully narrate both the emancipatory moment and the transition into capitalism as part of the same transformation, which is precisely what the Marxist "perspective" makes possible, without resorting to any fetishistic opposition to power in general ("power corrupts," etc.). Yet there is one last objection that might be raised against this schema. For it would seem that while I have managed to narrate together national liberation and the spread of capitalism, this narrative sees historical transformation in terms of necessity rather than contingent intervention. The agents' misrecognition of the transformation taking place (into capitalism, rather than liberation) is precisely where this necessity resides, according to this objection. One should once again recall Žižek's writing on the vanishing mediator to see that it actually preserves contingency rather than eliminates it. As Žižek argues, the intervention itself—the renewed pursuit of the old goal using new means—is a purely contingent act, one that cannot be reduced to its conditions or context. But after this act has succeeded in giving birth to a new social form, it must lose its very contingency and becomes necessary, a precondition for the new reality.[21] In retrospect, the contingency of the contingent act that founded the new order must vanish, and the whole sequence must then appear necessary to us (resulting in historical narratives in which there always seems to be a missing link, as Žižek shows). It is in this way that contingency is dialectically preserved through its opposite in the resulting historical narrative. Which also implies that what appears to us retrospectively as utterly contingent is precisely what failed to produce historical transformation.

One should add another side-note here concerning the problems that this use of the vanishing-mediator argument helps us address, namely objections to what seem like prejudices of western Marxism, which have gained a new articulation in, for example, Harry Harootunian's *Marx after Marx*.[22] Very briefly, some of Harootunian's broad critical points are aimed at "western" Marxism's assumption of linearity of capitalism's development, and this Marxism's emphasis the cultural particularity of capitalism's ability to spread—the notorious Weberian instrumental rationality, taken up by the Frankfurt School and Georg Lukács. The dialectical structure of the vanishing mediator schema (developed by Jameson, incidentally, to deal precisely with Weber's "culturalist" account of capitalism's spread and his work's ambiguous location within Marxist thought) should make it clear now that these are simply pseudo-problems: the old goal (or cultural portion) of the vanishing mediator is radically different in different cultural contexts—the old goal under which capitalist social form will be introduced has to be picked up from local culture (thus, that old hierarchies remain in place alongside more familiar capitalist ones is not coincidental, but a residue of this process of transformation). And the developmental linearity should not be judged a-historically, as our brief discussion of the place of contingency demonstrates, but rather as receiving its significance form its historical moment.

But let us return to the argument about the interplay of oppositional histories. Narratives of national liberation (and their related literary histories) are therefore not unassimilable to that of capitalism's historical spread. The latter's successful colonization of the entire world depends paradoxically precisely on the truth of the former—the success national liberation and its literature is precisely that on which the spread of capitalism hinges. We can therefore say that both narratives are true, provided that we remember that "truth" is here defined historically rather than logically or empirically. But here we arrive at the last twist of our argument. In current theorizations of capitalism, the conception of uneven development that we have invoked in the beginning has been questioned. Emilio Sauri, for example, argues that the demise of national narratives of development in peripheral economies has completely eroded the imagined temporality that underpinned the way we used to relate peripheral economies to those of the core (the former always trying to catch up to the latter).[23] It is important here to emphasize the way in which uneven development becomes untrue today: it is not that material unevenness that becomes false (i.e., capitalism still produces slums alongside shimmering high-rises); rather, it is the temporality of development that disappears from our imaginations—the affluent world no longer appearing as the future of the poor regions (and one could argue that the pseudo-concept of "failed state" is designed to account for this loss of temporality). Thus, the uneven development argument no longer delivers the shock of radical contemporaneity that it did before, because the developmental temporal imagination has itself eroded away. It is precisely this radical contemporaneity that is many times associated with the operations of neoliberal capitalism—inscribing a permanent present where time used to exist. This loss of geopolitical temporal imaginary and its associated social mapping is strongly expressed in associating the revival of literary realisms today with a need to map the global social space, "taking seriously the possibility [. . .] of representing the world-system rather than thematizing its unrepresentability,"[24] as in recent writing by Christian Thorne, Sharae Deckard, Jed Esty, and Colleen Lye.[25]

It is essential to note that the vanishing mediator argument I put forth above results in the same global contemporaneity: it suggests that national temporalities of emancipation (the vanishing old goals) fade as the resultant capitalist social system emerges as their unintended result (which has here the advantage of marking the very material source of this illusion of contemporariness, rather than seeing it as a matter of pure preference). It can thus be suggested that instead of insisting on radical contemporariness of the world—through the unequal development argument or any variant of it—one should realize that this contemporariness is now inscribed by the system itself, and therefore our task is to start searching for new time, for any signs of a revival of some temporal imaginary. That these must first appear as voluntaristic illusions that have no new social form attached to them is not at all a problem. For we should recall here once again that being wrong in the last instance is a condition rather than a choice; we can only hope to be wrong in the right way. It is for this reason that the last two chapters of this book, the ones whose focus is contemporary Israeli fiction, constitute an effort to detect the reappearance of time in these works.

I here begin the second part of this introduction, the one that addresses explicitly a writing of a new Israeli literary (and non-literary) history. The need for such a new history is barely a matter of individual conviction, but rather of what presents itself objectively as a blockage of historical imagination. This blockage is itself not some theoretical stance, but rather emanates from the subject matter itself: it is Yigal Schwartz who brings up a lack of new historical understandings of Israeli fiction, dating this curious absence back to the 1980s. The new generation of 1980s critics, Schwartz argues, takes up a rejection of the "Zionist metanarrative" shared by its predecessors, and in this respect this new generation does not distinguish itself very strongly from its predecessors (despite its taking up of new methodologies—mostly those related to the perspectives of marginalized identities).[26] Both the 1960s generation of critics and that of the '80s see the task of literature as asserting the limits of national ideology, its brokenness and contradictoriness, its becoming useless or its always having been this way. The story of Israeli literature remains one that leads from commitment to political causes (namely, that of Zionism, understood as nation-building project), to an increasingly non-national horizon (or one whose usually implicit politics have to do with debunking the nation). Even if the stated agenda of this or that critic seems unique or new, it tends to project a similar historical understanding of Israeli literary history. Yitzhak Laor, for example, sees early twentieth-century Hebrew literature as simply the mouthpiece of the nation-building project (excepting, of course, several brave literary souls that object to this degradation of literature).[27] Dror Mishani's historical survey of Mizrachi writing reproduces the same narrative, and so is Michael Gluzman's exploration of Zionist and Israeli literature's relation to gender and sexuality.[28] Both take their cue from Gershon Shaked's writing on what he sees as early Zionist literature's degrading subservience to the goal of nation building. Another example is Yael Feldman's important history of women's writing in Israeli literature, a project which must map itself in relation to early Zionism's feminist goals. Feldman's solution in her introduction is to argue that this earlier Zionist feminism was never very serious about the liberation of women to which it payed lip service (a narrative solution at work also in some assessment of Zionism's socialist aspirations, as in Ze'ev Shternhall's).[29] Other examples abound. The result is, of course, precisely what Schwartz complains about: a reproduction of the larger historical narrative framework of the previous generation of critics (whose clearest representative is Gershon Shaked), in which the new literatures articulate so many resistances to the oppression of national collectivity.

Thus a certain collapsing into indistinction of two critical generation takes place on the level of literary history, one that does not rob these newer accounts of their otherwise important contributions to Israeli literary criticism. Yet it is this arresting of history's narration itself that concerns me in this book, a freezing of the way literary (and non-literary) Israeli history is told that might not seem all that problematic in the first place. Why should we expect the way history is told to itself change with the march of history? Is not our way of telling this history simply correct? Are not the older ways of narrating it simply false or mystifying? To answer these questions, one needs at this point to at least briefly defend the opposite position, namely, that historical narration itself must undergo transformation—a position not at all new, but which bears repeating in this new context. This position is inseparable from any minimal Marxism, setting it squarely against any conservative notion of some eternally true history. But another distinction is here necessary, this time from a more historicist camp: for, the transformation of the way history is told is not here arbitrary or voluntary (except in some immediate sense). Rather, as Marx put it, the narration of history is precisely one of those "ideological forms in which men become conscious of this conflict [in the economic base] and fight it out."[30] The telling of history is in this view part of a superstructural apparatus, which as we commented above cannot be reduced to the economic base, but rather always constitutes the attempt to resolve the latter's contradictions in imagination.

So the way we narrate history is related somehow to the moment in which we live in a completely objective way, which therefore sets Marxist approach to history against the idealist voluntarism implied by any historicist approach (i.e., simply choosing between available modes or styles of historical narration) and the politics of historical narration to which it gives rise.[31] And so the Marxist imperative to re-narrate history is different than both historicist relativism and conservative unchanging historical account. But a third position (and much more anti-theoretical one) must here be addressed, namely, the commitment to facts or to empirical investigation, one that seems to be a way to bypass the political altogether (insofar as the previous two positions connote a political stance). In this position, any renewal of historical narrative must be the result of some new empirical findings, and has nothing to do with politics—which is merely an external interference in a scientific process. What must be stressed against this position here is that the turn to facts always carries with it some political import, depending on the constellation of forces in which it is evoked, and is therefore not at all a way of going beyond politics, toward some story free from the latter. My position here is by no means a new one, but rather one that was already articulated a century ago by Georg Lukács (and is part of the Hegelian conception of the dialectical movement of history), namely, that facts are not some inert and neutral building-blocks which can be strung together into this or that narrative. Rather, each fact always signals to us the unnamed presence of some congealed narrative, or as Lukács put it, "the question of universal history is a problem of methodology that necessarily emerges in every account of even the smallest segment of history."[32]

It is therefore a matter of the form of the concept of fact as such that one cannot have fact without narrative or politics. One would thus do better to think of facts as moments of narrative resistance—the "information" contained in the fact as invoking some previous narrative with which the operation of new narrative construction has to come to terms. Facts are therefore the sharp protruding corners of form itself, which Adorno so brilliantly characterized as sedimented past content (and to say that facts are congealed narratives, is to say the exact same thing).³³ In other words, facts thus come to denote moments of incongruity or mismatch between narrative force-fields, each pulling one's imagination in a different direction, threatening to pull apart narrative continuity itself. The task of constructing historical narrative is therefore the task of confronting facts: but here the empirical test of truth is but a small and relatively trivial part of a much more difficult effort of the imagination, namely, to resist the older narrative that these facts so strongly evoke.

Turning to facts will therefore save us neither from political intervention, nor from the need to construct new historical narratives, and it should be clear by now that any such new narrative carries with it a universality, or that any minor narrative affirms some grand narrative, whether explicitly or implicitly. In other words, the so-called death of grand narratives is itself a grand narrative, a "fact" that one should always keep in mind. What is crucial to notice now is the following: what has previously appeared to us as a subjective interest or problem—the failure of newer Israeli literary criticism to produce a new historical account of its subject matter—has now reappeared as problem that resides in objectivity itself: a changed situation requires the revision of older narratives (and such revision takes place on some unconscious level regardless of one's intentions). In other words, "We cannot not periodize," as Jameson writes.³⁴ To make this objective need explicit and to try to outline one such possible new narrative is precisely the goal of this book. It is perhaps important to stress once more that the option of this narrative simply being one among other ones has become impossible here—since every such small or minor narrative, as we argued, carries with it a totalizing framework, even if this frame remains unacknowledged. Thus, the outline for a new history of Israeli literature presented in this book is consciously totalizing.

This totalization operation will necessarily constitute a reduction of its subject matter, an operation that I briefly defended above. More urgent at this point is to bracket the "literary" for a while, moving to the way in which the literary-historical trajectory outlined in this book constitutes a new totalizing historical understanding of Israel and Zionism themselves. This new history will inevitably clash with two previous (and antagonistic) totalizing understandings of Zionism and Israel, which in another context I named the national narrative and the Post-Zionist one, respectively.³⁵ Very schematically, in the national narrative, Zionism is seen as a redemptive nation-building project, whose success results in the establishment of Israel. In the post-Zionist narrative, Zionism is again seen as a successful nation-building project, but this time this success is judged negatively: as oppressive to Palestinians, to women and Mizrachi Jews.[36] The national interpretation of Zionism has been hegemonic in Israel from the 40s until the mid-'80s; the second had its brief moment in the sun from the mid-'80s to the early 2000s—but it still dominates academic writing, despite the emergence of what is sometime called "post-post-Zionism."[37] I have elsewhere sought to explain the decline of Post-Zionism, its persistence in the present no longer exciting or leading to any sense of newness or historical movement.[38] What is important to emphasize is that in both narratives, a continuity is asserted between Zionism and Israel, the latter being the culmination of the former: the state of Israel being the realization of the emancipatory dream in the national narrative; and in the post-Zionist one, the same state is the oppressive institutional form finally taken by Zionism's colonizing project. A recent example of this kind of post-Zionist assertion of continuity between pre-state Zionism and the state, in cultural analysis, is Uri Cohen's *Hanusakh habitchoni*. In that volume, culture becomes the means by which violence and war are promoted—focusing precisely on the moment connecting pre-state times to the 1950s.[39] Even if Cohen is hostile to the more theoretically sophisticated versions of post-Zionist critique (on which more will be said in what follows), the continuity of Zionist and state violence is implicit in his writing—very much like in Benny Morris's "The New Historiography," considered one of the founding essays of post-Zionist historiography.[40]

The new narrative proposed here suggests that we see the relation between the Zionist project and the capitalist state of Israel as one of historical break or antagonism, rather than seeing it in terms of continuity. But before I explore this narrative further, we must address one possible objection: that post-Zionism, at least some of its more theoretically sophisticated varieties, in fact takes aim at precisely such continuity between Zionism and Israel. For writers such as Hannan Hever and Adi Ophir, for example, Zionism is not itself a unitary, coherent project or movement, but a multiplicity of contradictory positions.[41] The presentation of Zionism as a uniform nation-building project is in their accounts precisely the national-hegemonic ideological operation—ignoring the rifts, contradictions, and material and symbolic acts of violence that constitute actually existing Zionism in order to form the illusion of continuity. Ophir thus emphasizes the voices within Zionism that opposed the establishment of a nation-state, while Hever brings back to view the silenced struggle over the Hebrew literary canon, from which the anti-state voices have been excluded, despite their prominent literary presence. Non-continuity is here prescribed by (a certain strand of) post-Zionism as an antidote to the national narrative's projection of a continuity between Zionism and Israel, and Ophir's essay goes one step further by incorporating this fragmentariness into its very form: Ophir's text is interlaced with a fragmentary, non-narrative, chronology of events that took place around the establishment of Israel, performing textually the non-continuity that it wishes to ascribe to its historical object. To these more established postmodern post-Zionisms, we can add many newer works, such as Shai Ginsburg's *Rhetoric and Nation*. What changes here is the urgency of the political commitment—the anti-national impulse no longer seeming very exciting—but the ideology of brokenness, the natural status of fragmentariness, remains unchanged. Or as Ginsburg puts it in his introductory analysis of a poem by Bialik:

> The national endeavor as a whole seems to hinge upon a reconciliation, that, nevertheless, remains elusive. The failure to achieve reconciliation both buttresses and unravels the key themes of the national project—language, territory, history, and aesthetics—for these depend on the reconciliation they are said to produce.[42]

Ginsburg's operation of revealing attempted imaginary reconciliations is not at all foreign to Marxist hermeneutic in general, of course. The difference is in the status of these failures. The ideological rather than historical nature of such failures to reconcile in Ophir or Ginsburg's work should be apparent: there is no mediation of such contradictions onto a plane of analysis in which their historical emergence can be accounted for; rather, textual contradictoriness is here a state of nature (or the end-point of analysis, one that cannot then be transcoded once more)—a Truth, with all of its metaphysical baggage. One can even read symptomatically, as Althusser used the term, the unprompted appearances of declarations of anti-totality and anti-closure in these works—a reading that could lead us directly from form to historical content carried over by this form: French theory's battle with Stalinism. To reproduce that moment once more is a conservative gesture today.

So this post-Zionist narrative variant (if it can be considered narrative at all) is very different from the Marxist reading I briefly introduce here, and this difference will become apparent as I present this latter option. As I suggested above, Hegelian Marxism makes it possible for us to think together in a single narrative national liberation and the historical expansion of capitalism, through the Hegelian ruse of Reason or its Marxist appropriation in the vanishing mediator schema (without relegating either to a status of mere illusion or vulgar materialism). In our case, I propose that we see Zionism itself as a vanishing mediator for the spread of capitalism into Palestine. As Tamar Gozansky's writing demonstrates, while the Ottoman empire's land reforms had already created the possibility for a transition into the capitalist mode of production, it is only with Zionism that new subjective practices (namely, the hegemony of wage labor over other forms of labor) more appropriate to capitalism are instilled in Palestine (among Jews and Palestinians alike).[43] As I mentioned above, the introduction of a new social form is performed under cover of an older goal in the vanishing mediator schema. This old goal is liberation or emancipation—which is, naturally, appropriated from Judaism itself (but also form a more general nationalist revival in Europe). Some post-Zionist criticism of Zionism's "false" appropriation of Judaism, such as Shlomo Sand's, finds here its more historicized and dialectical version: that such appropriations (repetition itself making them different) is actually part of any historical transformation.[44] At any rate, the schema proposed here does not attempt to avoid reduction a but rather offers a different reduction than the accepted ones. I propose that we "reduce" the multiplicity of Zionisms not simply to a nation-building project, but more generally to an emancipatory one, a collective enterprise whose goal has to do with an effort to shape lives and history. This "reduction" makes it possible to see different tendencies within Zionism as different solutions to the problem of autonomy, or self-determination, as I suggested elsewhere.[45] It is this emancipatory goal that serves as a ruse for the introduction of capitalism to Palestine in this vanishing mediator schema. And that the disappearance of the old goal after the transition has been completed is exasperating or frustrating is expressed in many ways in the late 1940s and the 1950s—on which we will have much more to say in what follows. Thus, in the version I propose here there is an antagonism or a discontinuity between these two moments, the Zionist one, in which the emancipatory goal is still alive, and the one of the state, in which this goal is rendered ineffective, moralistic, and generally toothless.

The important difference between this discontinuity (between Zionism and Israeli state) and the one posed by Ophir's strand of post-Zionism has little to do with the act of reduction itself, whose inevitability I already mentioned. Rather, it is the following one: in the schema proposed here, the contingency of the mediating agency, the irreducible intervention—an event, in Badiou's terms, or an act in Žižek's—is preserved, while in Ophir's it paradoxically disappears.[46] As I argued above, following Žižek, to remain faithful to the contingency of the intervention, one must recognize that this contingency must disappear from any retroactive view of the events: if the act has produced a new system, then it appears as a necessity from this later point in time. If on the other hand it failed to produce change, it is its failure that becomes necessary. What follows from this dialectical understanding of contingency is the following: that to understand the Zionism as a collection of contingent interventions means, from today's perspective, that precisely this contingency must disappear—for it is only through this disappearance that their status as contingent interventions is preserved.

It is here that the difference between the historical break posited here and that suggested by Ophir can be perceived. For, Zionism is precisely such contingent act that loses its contingency in the Marxist narrative that I am suggesting; while in Ophir's narrative, that contingency is elevated to a first principle in its own right. In other words, for Ophir and others, contingency and discontinuity themselves become a methodological necessity, as if it is a reality that lies behind any illusion of continuity (which, of course, should surprise no one: commitments to Foucauldian genealogies, for instance, are precisely such ideological "necessary contingencies"—ones that in fact have nothing contingent about them). (Indeed, in this a-historical understanding of the effects of fragmentariness, one is tempted to invert the terms by saying that the real possibility for textual subversion lies in showing how continuity is produced in them despite the tendency of all texts to fail to produce it). It is in this way that the Ophir's post-Zionist discontinuity between the Zionism and Israel is in fact a form of necessity and continuity themselves, even if these latter appear in the guise of their opposite. In other words: this variant of post-Zionism implicitly still asserts continuity between Zionism and the state—in both equally there exists a tendency to reconcile or to create "grand narratives" (even if it this operation fails in these accounts). Thus, with regard to this form of philosophically sophisticated post-Zionism, one could summarize the situation in the following formula: the national narrative ideologically forces continuity or reconciliation on the contradiction between Zionism and state; The (theoretically sophisticated) post-Zionist narrative forces discontinuity or eternal non-identity on the same subject matter (and thus, still, Zionism and statehood become each other's complement again). It is only in the narrative that is suggested here, I argue, that the Zionist antagonism to the state retains its vanishing contingency—the historical appearance and disappearance of contradiction.

And one can say a little more on the ideological status of such "failures to reconcile" in the postmodern accounts versus the more historical and dialectical ones proposed here. It should be clear that there is nothing wrong with finding failed reconciliations from a Marxist perspective. All imaginary reconciliations are ultimately failed ones—juxtapositions and impossible bringing-togethers that cannot but fail when put to a rigorous conceptual test. The problem is that the possibility of a totalizing reading is ideologically equated by Ginsburg, Ophir, and many others, with the failure of reconciliation. Totality in the Marxist sense is not a state of equilibrium or reconciliatory reproductiveness; it is rather a contradictory whole, a state of affairs whose contradictions or living antagonistic impulses are the engine of its historical transformation. What contradicts is thus always a future. And this alone should tell us that an antagonism must have existed between early Zionism and its future: the state of Israel. Therefore it is precisely not the nation as we know it today that should be used to imagine the struggle of opposed forces and their reconciliation in the earlier period. The totalizing operation—one which is certainly attempted in this book—does not block the detections of textual antagonisms. Rather, it shows how these imagined struggles are, in mediated form, what reconfigures the whole itself. Which is to say that it is radically a-historical to assume that this "whole" always remains the nation—even before the state was imaginable as anything more than a placeholder for utopia, and even when the argument is that the textual objects resist their national streamlining. Perhaps the most controversial argument put forth in this book is that to construct a totalizing account of the Hebrew Zionist literature of the 1920s or 1930s, and of later Israeli literature, one has to see that it is capitalism and its historical transformations that provides the horizon of the totalizing operation.

Even if no such historical-materialist account of Zionism exists to date, some of the more recent writing on the history of Zionism, such as Nitzan Lebovic's recent work, is arguable much closer to what the current book suggests. For intelligent idealism is to be preferred to any crude materialism, as Lenin once said. And Lebovic's attempt to rewrite the history of Zionism as a history of loss and melancholic attachment is precisely one such case of such idealism. It is beyond doubt that Zionist utopianism in Lebovic's account still plays the role of oppressive utopianism. But that alongside the Zionist utopian attempt to create newness, there exists a persistence of the old or a voice "refusing to accept the erasure of the past," allows a more dialectical movement to develop.[47] Zionism then becomes a constant failure to repress or return to an old way of life or goal—and it is in this way that something like a historical dialectic is reintroduced to fuel historical change. That Lebovic sees this melancholic position as a diagnosis for what is wrong with Israeli leftism is here even more important: it allows for a kind of real nostalgia (and with it, historicity) to return as a political force that can shape the present—a radical-leftist return to Zionism, which sounds like a paradox to any loyal post-Zionist, but in fact offers us a history that is on the move again in the place of the frozenness that pervades everything today. The narrative of Zionism offered here is different than Lebovic's not only in a nominal mediation to materialism, but even more importantly in admitting that forces such as nostalgia (the opposite of the dead historicism that so pervades neoliberal culture) offer precisely such utopian imaginaries that Lebovic's analysis still shuns, at least on its surface. A renewal of Israeli leftism, then, lies in the possibility of reviving this utopianism and its previous losses rather than rejecting it—as I have elsewhere suggested, in complete agreement with Lebovic's determination that "it is only when the loss of earlier hopes is acknowledged that the left can admit its responsibility and offer new ground for social and political transformation."

So our narrative is one in which Zionism is a vanishing mediator for the spread of capitalism into Palestine, and its emancipatory imaginary—very much informed by socialist ideas—should be seen as deeply antagonistic to the establishment of a capitalist state (which Israel undoubtedly was from its inception). It is here that we can finally bring this revised narrative of Zionism to bear on literary production. For, the Zionist literature (both its "genre" and "anti-genre" variants, terms that we will explore more fully in the first chapters) of the first half of the twentieth century is seen in this book to be a literature that tries to produce a figure of a historical subject, an act of radical imaginary creativity that is surely lost when we read this literature simply as subservient to Zionist ideology (or as opposing it). In the first chapter of this book, the Hebrew literature from Palestine of the 1920s and 1930s is thus radically estranged, framed through the properly Benjaminian rift in time in which it was produced. What our narrative brings back to the works of this earlier period is a sense of historical opening, of the great possibilities and potentialities of their historical moment—of experiments in social form and intra-Zionist political struggles, who in their moment cannot-yet be understood as certainly leading to the establishment of a capitalist nation-state, and to the oppression of Palestinians and others. Indeed, this sense of potentiality and very real opportunity for radical social change is almost completely lost in the writing of historians today—felt only in the unconscious margins of texts by David Za'it, Elkana Margalit, or Boaz Neumann and others, in which the multiplicity of social forms and emancipatory imaginaries at struggle are revealed.[48] This sense of historical opening or rift that is too quickly glossed over or missed in the conventional reading of this literature—as a literature committed to (or set against) the political goal of establishing a nation-state, which as I already claimed is a historical understanding accepted *tout court* today.

This new different understanding of early Zionist literature will then make it possible for me to provide a new reading for the literature of the late 1940s and the 1950s in two subsequent chapters as expressing precisely the foreclosure of potentialities and loss of radically transformative project (being the final moment of the vanishing mediator, to use the theoretical code on which I expanded earlier). As I will show, the formal implications of this loss provide an interesting lesson in the realism-naturalism-modernism nexus. But in the context of this introduction, it is perhaps more important that this new narrative of Israeli literature is a candidate for that newness whose absence was noted by Yigal Schwarz, which I had mentioned earlier. The new historical narrative that I propose here offers precisely the generational interpretive antagonism sought by Schwartz: for it has its sights on the reading of early Zionist literature which is common to Shaked and the 1980s critics. As I hope to show, Shaked's reading of late 1950s literature in ethical terms—as the transition from politically committed literature to one that is free from such commitment—is in my account rethought as a literature that manages to express a loss of utopian possibilities, a loss that was suppressed in conscious narration of the birth of Israel (and in which Shaked himself participates).[49] The Marxist history of Israeli literature proposed in this book, I argue, therefore offers a way out of the weakness of the Israeli literary-critical imagination that Schwarz detects (and that as I have argued constitutes an objective problem rather than simply a subjective position).

Yet to qualify as a new grand narrative of Israeli literature, this book must transform not only the historical understanding of early Zionist letters, but also of later moments, two of which are explored in what follows. The first has to do with what used to be called the '80s postmodern transformation of Israeli literature. I use the past tense since, as I mentioned above, in recent years several prominent critics have questioned the usefulness of "postmodernism" as a periodizing term in Israeli literature.[50] In the chapters dedicated to 1980s literature I thus try to provide a materialist framework for understanding Israeli literary postmodernism, whose early emergence (traced at times to Yaakov Shabtai's 1977 novel *Past Continuous*) should signal to us that the idealist explanatory model of Western influence might not work very well in this case.[51] I argue that the emergence of Israeli postmodernism is a surprising result of the 1967 war and the quick proletarianization of Palestinians by Israeli capitalism. It is this extension of social relations beyond the realm of relatively autonomous Israeli capitalist state that brings about a crisis of the social imagination, which is gradually registered in the literary imagination after the late '70s. The '80s literary works discussed here all try to imagine a solution for this crisis, each turning in different ways inherited literary forms into its figurative devices. Insofar as the term "postmodernism" designates a collection of styles or representational approaches, Israeli postmodernism surely exists, I argue. But one should keep in mind the very particular origin of this postmodernism as an aesthetic problematic.

But the 1980s chapters will have resulted in a new problem: why do Israeli literary critics tend to abandon postmodernism as a periodizing category? I will try to answer this question in the two last chapters of this book, which focus on contemporary Israeli literature. The dismantling of the Israeli welfare-state following neoliberal restructuring since the late 1980s will prove to be the decisive factor here, resulting in a socio-spatial division of Israel and the Palestinian occupied territories into three distinct parts, which I have already mentioned above. Conceptually, the analysis in this section will require a distinction between postmodernism as a style, and Postmodernity as a period; and both of these should be distinguished from neoliberalism, or that form of capitalist accumulation that is traced by David Harvey and others to the late 1970s.[52] This latter economic transformation is many times collapsed into some confused identity with that late capitalism, whose cultural logic is postmodernism. But we should remember that Jameson's notion of late capitalism in the title of the essay-turned-book is borrowed from Ernest Mandel's theorization of late capitalism, which has very little to do with the later development of neoliberalism (any identification of postmodernism and neoliberalism is thus a problematic one, relying on some cultural theme that is common to postmodern culture and neoliberal economic thinking, rather than on actual mediations between economy and culture). Neoliberalism should be considered, as other comment, as the "solution" capitalism found to its 1970s crises, which resulted from contradictions latent in the Bretton-Woods System.[53] "Postmodernity" becomes a useful term here to designate the period that started with postmodernism, but in which we are still present even if the style that characterized its earlier part is no longer hegemonic.

The cultural results of Israel's neoliberalization, as I try to show in the last two chapters, will not mean an exit from postmodernity, but more of an internal shift or coming into consciousness of what was only unconsciously expressed in postmodernism proper. The loss of temporal imagination and of historicity here becomes the conscious object of literary reflection, I argue, expressed in very different ways in works that belong to familiar genres of Israeli literature, but also in the emerging genre of Israeli science fiction (an emergence whose reasons I will explore alongside other meta-literary issues, such as the dwindling of Israeli literary criticism itself, and the "reaction" against postmodernism). All of these works, I hope to show, stage a search for time, or a search for an alternative to the eternal present of neoliberal time, on which many comment today. What is uniquely Israeli about this search is not only its particular contents—the specific themes and forms through which this search for time is taken up—but in the relation of this literature to social form itself. The neoliberalization of Israel means, as I will argue, the unique social splitting of Israel into three distinct social zones: Israel "itself," without the occupied territories, which offers us a familiar neoliberal landscape; the Jewish settlements in the occupied territories, which enjoy something like a welfare-state (and thus still enjoy the temporalities associated with it); and the Palestinian occupied territories, which constitute a wholly different social existence than the Jewish one, despite the geographical overlap of these two units (that a more "vertical" form of social separation takes place in the occupied territories is the subject of Eyal Weizman's *Hollow Land*, for example).[54] It is important to note that, taken together, these three social spaces do not form a social totality: none of these materially depends on the other two for its material existence. Rather, each zone makes sense only when considered an outcome of global capitalism's operations). The search for time articulated in the contemporary literary works that I explore in the last two chapters corresponds to only one of these zones, becoming quite alien to the concerns of the other two. It is thus no longer the loss of (or freedom from) national time to which these recent novels respond, but rather a different social problematic altogether. The seeming return of nationalisms on the ideological level becomes in this respect something altogether different than what they seem; rather, the erosion of national mediation of social form under neoliberalism makes these seeming ideological retrenchments into direct responses to neoliberal global capitalism, as I will argue in the last two chapters.

The three moments (or periods) of the resulting periodization certainly paint a bleak picture: the demise of a radically transformative social project; the playful collapse of national time and social mapping; a search for time under neoliberal absolute contemporariness. The history of Marxist thought is full to the brim with the elaboration of the opposition of principled optimism and pessimism—from Antonio Gramsci's formula of "pessimism of the intellect, optimism of the will" all the way to Adorno's equivocal declaration that one must have tradition in oneself to hate it properly. But that one can easily assume the posture of any of these positions tells us that this opposition has degenerated into an antinomy that does not allow thought to move forward—perhaps because the latter positions are simply frozen attitudes from a time of functional social imagination. If history is on the move again (generating, as I will argue, a different kind of Marxist theorizing of culture alongside the growing popularity of claims that the end of history has itself drawn to an end), it might be more useful to see this sequence of periods as part of the movement of history itself: the first moment is a negation of an emancipatory social project that leads into a capitalist Israel; the second moment is a second negation, this time of capitalist Israel itself; the third moment is not yet a fully-fledged positive term in its own right, but rather a becoming conscious of the second moment as negation or loss, rather than as liberation. That Israel is certainly not where the future of global capitalism is determined should not here disturb us; for the subjective mediation of transformation, or the assertion of agency in transformation is inevitable. To represent the development of capitalism as (partly) a local matter is therefore necessary. The controversial conclusion of this new periodization of Israeli letters search for time is thus that the mainstay of Israeli culture points toward a potential exit from capitalism through the double negation that it stages: the first moment leading into capitalism, the other negating that previous movement towards a yet undefinable horizon.

The near-absence of Marxist writing on Israel makes this book's political intervention not very easily mapable: it might seem to bring together political elements that in the current constellation of forces seem to belong to contradictory political positions. But then, again, it is always from a liberal perspective that being utopian and totalizing becomes synonymous with the right. The "confusion" of a leftist position that champions these is thus not in any sense real or some necessary fate, but is the result of the prejudices of a fast-shrinking liberal left. Indeed, the cannibalization of the past in liberal historicism makes necessary a kind of blindness and ignorance toward what utopia and/or totality actually are. As I hope will become clear, the narrative presented in this book is by far more conceptually and historically coherent than the nakedly defunct liberal one, which is neither a leftist one, nor historical in any real sense.

Significantly, one last point has to do with the status of Marxism itself in in relation to the contemporary ideological landscape. For the older anti-Marxists—still animated as they are by the Cold War and the rejection of Stalinism—will surely see it as completely equivalent to all other forms of liberatory ideologies today, being just another false promise, offering just another harmful utopian vision, or of totality being indistinguishable from totalitarianism. It is not clear at all that one should actually still answer this liberal ideological nexus of fears, whose representatives are already fast disappearing: liberalism's post-ideological "end of history" having nothing to offer in terms of historical problem-solving any longer, even to the rich. On the one hand, therefore, the seething with utopian energy of society is a sign that history is on the move again—despite the best efforts of neo-liberalism to convince us otherwise—and that some radical action, some radical dislocation of the state of things, is required in order to fight over the future, because the liberal status quo has simply led us to the brink of self-annihilation (which is simply another way to say that it is precisely the liberal order that led to the rise of the right, or even that fascism is a necessary logical conclusion of capitalism, and not an aberration in it, as both the Frankfurt School and Žižek insist).[55] The proliferation of utopian visions is in this sense a necessity rather than of tasteless choice for most people—the becoming unbearable of social contradictions requiring the appearance of some death-drive, or a drive toward radical renewal.

And therefore it is in the making-equivalent of all these utopian options that bourgeois impulse truly resides, since it is this equivalence that makes it possible to reject them all in the name of the an existing "sane" state of things (which exists for almost nobody anymore). It is this identification that should be completely rejected, and the distinctions between different political streams and options be explored—an itinerary that is the core of the form of utopian novels, as I will argue in the following chapter. And that the Marxist "option" is, of course, different and unique in its totalizing operation, one in which the present state of things is not the result of timeless ethical choice but of historical agency under conditions not of one's choosing. It is surely beyond the scope of this introduction to discuss this difference of Marxism at any length. But it should be acknowledged that with the decline of the liberal end-of-history, this discussion is becoming more urgent than it has been in a while.

1

Prehistory

Zionist Hebrew Literary Realism, between *Altneuland* and *Khirbet Khizeh*

One cannot write a literary history without having an implicit or explicit prehistory in mind, or at least some state of affairs that existed prior to the historical period under discussion, the latter receiving its significance and force from its break or difference from the former. I here, therefore, present one such "prehistorical" narrative of Hebrew literature from Palestine from the first half of the twentieth century—but one which would strike anyone familiar with the literature of the period as strange: for it deals with the dark and forgotten side of the Hebrew literature of the period—the forgotten Zionist realists on which very little is written anymore. Indeed, realist Hebrew fiction of the 1920s and 1930s has not fared well in literary critical circles since the 1960s, and seems to have been all but forgotten. In contrast to the Hebrew literary modernists of the period, the realist alternative today seems to designate a degraded form of literature. Gershon Shaked, to cite a prominent example, argues that "its literary quality was not the highest," as it tended to make literature subservient to ideological strictures. It is hardly surprising that Shaked and other prominent literary critics and scholars of his generation almost unanimously dismiss the realist writers of the 1920s and 1930s as inferior.[1] As Nurit Gertz reminds us, the literary critics who rose to prominence in the 1950s and 1960s were part of a conscious effort to move away from this realist tradition, a move that was strongly tied to the growing prominence of the writers of the State Generation (*Dor hamedina*).[2] Yet, even in Gertz's own account, the literary realism of the 1930s is seen primarily as the main aesthetic branch of literature written in the service of the Israeli nation-building project, which Gertz (and many others) contrasted to the contemporary modernists' insistence on the autonomy of art, or its subservience to nothing but itself.[3] Thus, in Gertz's account as well, 1930s literary realism remains a degraded form of literature, insofar as it is seen as consciously serving a political agenda. This view of the realists seems to be shared across political divides as well. Yitzhak Laor, for example, who is identified with a more leftist political position than that of Shaked or Gertz, also argues that the Hebrew realists were only ideological mouthpieces for the national enterprise.[4]

The problem persists even in sympathetic accounts. For instance, in his recent book Todd Hasak-Lowy goes to great lengths to show that Hebrew literary realism of the first half of the twentieth century is born out of a shift in the status of literature: it is part of a larger transformation in which writing literature becomes an inseparable part of a new effort to give shape to Jewish history and identity.[5] Yet, the history being made in this account is still assumed to be that of the Israeli nation-state. An inevitable linear progression is thus again implicitly drawn from the Zionist collective project to the establishment of Israel. From this perspective, we encounter the same problem in a different form: if the history-making aspect of Zionist realism has to do only with the national project, then it becomes uninteresting for us, for its historical task has certainly been completed. Noticeably, the writers who, according to Hasak-Lowy, express ambivalence toward nation-building and are therefore made interesting (such as Y. H. Brenner, S. Y. Agnon, and S. Yizhar), are precisely those usually not considered part of the realist "hardliners." Must we therefore consign the realists of the 1920s and 1930s to the dustbin of history? Have writers such as Ever Hadani or Yehuda Burla, who did not display the ambivalence associated with Brenner or Agnon, according to critics, produced nothing but propaganda?

In this chapter I attempt to offer a different reading of Hebrew literary realism from the '20s and '30s, more broadly placing it within a literary-historical trajectory that challenges its knee-jerk association with nation-building. I would like here to posit a hypothesis whose full examination must remain outside the scope of this short prehistory, but that would immediately change the way in which one approaches this period in Hebrew literature. Namely, that the works of the period—whether realist or not—are all preoccupied with one urgent task: the attempt to provide a figure for a subject of history: an attempt to fuse together, as in the Freudian operation of condensation, the different subject positions onto one imaginable figure of an agent, a subject that affect the course of history.

But in this chapter I would like to focus on a narrower thematization of this larger problem of figuration, one that will have to do, as we will soon see, with the representation of everyday life in the Zionist settlements and the historical imaginary governing them. As a starting point, it is important to notice a certain tension within the critical literature we have just mentioned. On the one hand, realism, taken at its most naïve understanding as verisimilitude, purports to describe its present. On the other, as both Shaked and Hasak-Lowy agree, the realist corpus is highly speculative: it tends toward an idealization of Zionist settler vanguardism, and of the settler's—the *halutz*—life.[6] Or, if we follow Hasak-Lowy, these works try to imagine historical transformation, thereby having somehow to represent the past or the future. This paradox can be said to reside even at the moment of origin so important to Shaked's critical enterprise—Brenner's distinction between "genre" literature, which Shaked characterizes as realist, and "anti-genre" literature, which Shaked associates with modernism, but which according to Brenner is good at representing reality "as it is," as if doing verisimilitude better than realism. Of course, invoking more dialectical understandings of realism (such as that of Georg Lukács, but also the oppositional views of Ernst Bloch), could, of course, help us resolve this apparent paradox.[7] But this would miss the point altogether, since we are here interested in a contradiction internal to Israeli literary criticism itself, for which the problem of such realism is precisely that it is (simplistically) realist but also that it is at the same time not realist enough. How are we, then, to understand this fusion of realist adherence to what exists with its speculative negation? As a way into the speculative moment, we will start our discussion with what is surely one of the most speculative literary genres: the utopian novel.

The Structure of Literary Utopia

The following brief discussion of the form of utopian novels is not designed to generate a detailed understanding of that form, which is undoubtedly alien to the corpus of Hebrew realism from the 1920s and 1930s. Rather, it will enable us to develop our approach to that corpus in two ways. First, the structure of the utopian novel will allow us to note the literary use of contradiction in trying to imagine a transformative social project. Second, it will help us to gain insight into the historical tendency to lose sight in retrospect of the open-ended, transformative core of literary utopian programs (or, in other words, it will help us explain why past utopian novels seem to be ideologically dogmatic) today.

In his study of the relationship between utopia and nation-building, Phillip Wegner defends the radical speculative openness of the form of utopian novels.[8] According to Wegner, utopian narratives attempt to orient their reader in a new social space. Thus, utopian narration consists in "pedagogical practices [. . .] that enable us to inhabit, make sense of, orient ourselves within, and act through any particular space. This [. . .] is the domain of architecture, urban planning, nation building, and social engineering."[9] The orienting function of utopian narratives is expressed through what Wegner calls, following Louis Marin, "the refusal of non-contradiction."[10] Simply put, the utopian narrative advances by refusing to reconcile contradictions, continuously displacing them instead. As Wegner and others argue, it is this refusal of reconciliation that puts the utopian novel in direct opposition to the operation of ideology, which in Althusser's formulation, attempts to produce precisely this imaginary reconciliation.[11] Again, we should emphasize that it is not the case that some eternal opposition exists between ideology and utopia: that the utopian in general finds its way into ideology is one of the thematic centers of gravity of Marxist cultural critique. What Wegner's formulation seeks to establish is that when read in their historical context, utopian novels do not present us with a closed ideological system, but rather refuse ideological reconciliation.

In order to demonstrate what the utopian novel's refusal of non-contradiction means, we will briefly examine Michael Gluzman's reading of Theodor Herzl's *Altneuland*, published in 1902.[12] *Altneuland* follows the general structure of utopian novels. The protagonists, both disillusioned with their lives ("sunk in the depth of depression"), decide to travel to a remote island, away from a society in which they cannot find their place.[13] After spending twenty years in solitude, they decide to visit Europe, and stop on their way in Palestine (in what would be the future from the novel's contemporaries' perspective). Much to their surprise, the country has undergone a radical transformation following massive Jewish settlement and the foundation of *Altneuland*. Here we encounter the familiar structure of the utopian narrative—the travelers explore the country and learn about the structure of the utopian society with the help of local guides.

Gluzman's analysis focuses on the way in which *Altneuland* imagines a transformation of gender relations (and in particular the masculine body). According to his reading, Herzl's utopian society contains a contradiction. On the one hand, in imagining the new society, the novel seeks to transform weak-bodied and weak-willed diaspora Jewish men into strong and assertive ones,[14] (the anti-Semitic ideological stereotyping of diaspora Jewish men as weak and effeminate was common in Herzl's circles).[15] On the other hand, the same process is intended to create gender equality: women can (and are free to) perform any task that men can, an ideal derived from the influence of socialist ideas on Herzl.[16] Herzl's mobilization of these ideas thus leads to a contradiction: men are cured of their femininity, yet they are equal to women. This, for Gluzman, is a damning contradiction. Here, however, we can assert that the contradictoriness that Gluzman detects is rather precisely the point of the utopian structure: it is part of the process of the constant displacement of contradictions, or the refusal to resolve them. One need not subscribe to Herzl's ideology of the healthy masculine body to see this process at work here. Initially, the novel diagnoses a contradiction between the weak and parasitic diasporic Jewish existence and the assertiveness and strength needed for the utopian project. By ridding the Jewish man of his weakness, the contradiction is displaced onto the one detected by Gluzman: the new, strong, Jewish man is both equal and non-equal to Jewish women. This new contradiction thus awaits the further elaboration of the utopian constructive process, which potentially can go on indefinitely, mapping something like a Lacanian fantasy space. It is this continuous displacement of contradictions that constitutes the radical openness of the utopian novel. And, as we will see below, it is this insistence on keeping contradictions open that constitutes an important formal element of the literary realism of the 1920s and 1930s.

This openness is lost when *Altneuland* is read today. While we cannot here discuss the novel's reception at any length, we can suggest that readings of it can roughly be divided into two camps. The first sees the novel as "painfully naïve," or condescendingly claim that its transformative vision was always unachievable.[17] The other interpretive line sees it as constituting an oppressive program, not only toward Palestinians but toward Jews as well.[18] Common to both readings is the disappearance of the open-endedness of utopian novels. Indeed, losing sight of utopian novels' radical openness in the eyes of their contemporaries is by no means specific to *Altneuland*; nor should we chalk it up to a postmodern incredulity toward utopias in general. As Wegner remarks, narrative utopias are vanishing mediators, "cultural interventions that in retrospect appear as bridges over the 'holes in time' between different organizations of social life, and whose particular effectivity disappears once these transitions have been accomplished."[19] And as I will show in what follows, the openness of the realist writing of the 1920s and 1930s disappears in a similar fashion.

The constant displacement of contradiction has one more effect that will prove important to us in our discussion of the Hebrew realists of the 1920s and 1930s. By weaving together transformations of body, human desire, social structure, and history, the utopian narrative becomes a totalizing one, in the sense that Lukács and Jameson give the term.[20] The complex structure of mediation between history and individual that, according to Jameson, science fiction—of which utopian narratives are part—enacts, is what narrative utopias generate in mediating between bodily transformations, desire, the structure of collectively and history.[21] It is this totalizing imaginary, in which no realm of human existence escapes the refusal-of-non-contradiction's constant operations, that is important for us here, and that we will see reproduced in the realism of the '20s and '30s.

From Utopia to Realism

In order to see how the structure of utopian novels informs the literary realism of the 1920s and 1930s, we will have to take a brief detour through history. For it is only through reconstructing, however minimally, the structure of feeling dominant in the Zionist settlement project that we will be able to challenge their being read as inferior propaganda. The background for the realist writing is the imaginary of the *halutzic* movement, or the settler vanguard of Zionism. For Shaked and others, this ideological structure can be summarized as a "Zionist metanarrative," whose telos has always been the establishment of Israel.[22] Here, however, we will have to complicate this picture by delving a little deeper into the particularities of the *halutz* imaginary. According to Boaz Neumann, at the center of this imaginary is an immense desire for laboring toward a radical transformation of the self and its social, material, and natural surroundings.[23] We should note that "labor" is not to be taken metaphorically here, but rather refers to actual agricultural work in the Zionist settlements, expanded into a transformative project. The ideological world and the structure of feeling that this transformative labor entails is a strongly spatialized one, and (as utopian imaginaries tend to be) very self-contradictory: it is both a conquest or harnessing of natural forces (through technology and conscious efforts) and a complete merging with nature. In it one can take control of one's life, and at the same time become immersed in historical forces oblivious to individual agency.

Significantly for our purposes, the intimate connection with the land formed through this notion of transformative labor, a connection strongly eroticized in the *halutzic* imaginary, is wholly antagonistic to ownership; it cannot be acquired in the market as property but only achieved through productive labor, as Neumann argues, discussing the writing of some of the main ideologues of the movement:

> Berl Katznelson defines the [*halutz* imaginary] as total self-control, man's conquest of his world, and his control of this world. For Katznelson, the uniqueness of the Zionist *halutz* movement among its contemporaries lies in the fact that it does not revolve around leadership or a pre-defined program, but is rather centered on man's life and labor [. . .] the *halutzim* do in their lives what the collective will do in the future. They are soldiers, and as such their role is to conquer. Not a violent conquest, but a subduing and harnessing of land and labor. It is their job to take on agricultural labor [. . .] construction, agricultural industry and other tasks.[24]

"Conquest" in this context, as Neumann hastens to emphasize, designates something like taking control, learning how to master a skill or a space of human activity, and not military conquest. Furthermore, it is this project of agricultural labor, in the center of which stands the interaction between human and land that then spills over, as it were, into other realms: from that eroticized fascination with the landscape and the creation of an almost mystical connection with it (substituting to a certain degree a religion), to larger social projects that involved education, creating an egalitarian and non-alienated social structure with corresponding politics and subjective change (both bodily and ideologically). Thus, labor transforms land, history, society, and subjects in interconnected ways, and allows for a sense of historicity to emerge—a sense of the present as part of a transition from past to future in which one's immediate surrounding is all charged with a sense of agency. In the *halutz* imaginary, we can see a textbook example of how a mediated relation (relating the human to the land through labor) ends up reconstructing a lost immanence, or becomes its own reason and cause, in the becoming-one of human and nature, much as in Marx's definition of "species-being."²⁵

We should also note the totalizing nature of the *halutz* imaginary. As was the case of the totalizing structure of the utopian novel discussed above, the *halutz* project presented its subjects with a multilayered structure of meaning, with labor acting as the great mediator between the levels of meaning. Bodily transformation (the molding of Zionist bodies, both masculine and feminine), was related through labor to radical social restructuring (the formation of egalitarian agricultural settlement and its institutions), which was then imagined to reeducate desire itself (the formation through labor of a love of the land, landscape, and other workers), and to exert agency over the course of history (bringing about Jewish—if not universal—emancipation).

It is this imaginary structure that led to tension with the real development of the Zionist enterprise, creating, in some cases, confrontations between different *halutz* movements—such as the Young Guard (*Hashomer hatza`ir*)—and the dominant institutions of the Zionist movement in Palestine, particularly the Labor Unity movement (*Ahdut ha`avoda*) and the General Federation of Labor (the *Histadrut*) which it controlled. As David Za'it and others show, the Young Guard's vanguardism was strongly ambivalent about the notion of *national* emancipation.²⁶ Rather, the Young Guard's approach to the *halutzic* project strongly linked it to a Marxist understanding of social revolution, or of the working class becoming the author of its fate.²⁷ The writing of Ber Borochov, and Borochov's ideas' appropriation and further elaboration by figures such as Meir Ya`ari, demonstrates this ambivalence toward the national project, which they regarded as essentially a bourgeois project, or one that leads to the formation of a dispossessed working class.²⁸ The problem faced by movements such as the Young Guard, and the Labor Brigade (*Gdud ha`avoda*) was therefore the following: how to imagine a social revolution without immediately jeopardizing their settlements? What kind of experiments in social form could lead to a solution to the problem of autonomy, to the ability of workers to exert agency over the course of their history, if the establishment of a capitalist nation-state cannot but fail to achieve that?

As the 1920s were drawing to a close, the leadership of the Young Guard realized that private capital and rapid urbanization were dominating the settlement project, forcing more and more workers into capitalist wage-labor.²⁹ Moreover, animosity between the Jewish and Palestinian population was growing, as economic crises and the accelerated creation of landless Palestinian workers heightened competition between Jewish and Palestinian laborers—the division between them existing to a large extent due to the General Federation of Labor's discrimination of Palestinian workers. Indeed, cooperation efforts were actively discouraged (if not blatantly prevented) by the General Federation of Labor and other bodies.[30] Thus, the project toward which large segments of the *halutz* movement was working, was in danger of unravelling. Our argument here is that the realism of the 1920s and 1930s speaks precisely to this tension between the *halutz* imagined emancipatory project and the actual material conditions in which workers found themselves. Indeed, the primary preoccupation of the period's realists, as we will now see, is to map the contradictions between imagined goals and encountered conditions (which is a thematization of that bigger goal that we mentioned earlier—providing a figure for a subject of history), rather than to regurgitate some ideological dogma. This need to map the contradiction in concrete terms is the reason for the wandering of the protagonists of realist works by Zarchi, Aricha, Burla and others who—just like the protagonists of utopian novels—spend their time moving between different social surroundings (primarily those of the egalitarian agricultural collectives, those of the *moshava* (capitalist agricultural settlements) and urban settings.

Thus, for example, one of the central thematic threads of Yisrael Zarchi's 1935 novel *Barefoot Days* (*Yamim yehefim*) is the tension between utopian aspirations and the lives of the workers. The novel narrates the journey of Yosef, the worker-protagonist, through different social spaces. Yosef's wandering is mostly a result of a constant search for work (for labor is always temporary, particularly in the rural capitalist settlements and the cities on which the novel focuses). Right from the start, the novel sets up the multilayered structure of meaning that was briefly described above. For the narrator, immigrating to Palestine contains a promise of transformation on several levels: recovering from chronic illness that plagued him throughout his European childhood;[31] worker camaraderie that contains the seeds of a different social structure; a love affair with Rimona, a woman worker who shares his ideas; and finally, the narrator is trying to write a novel about the life of Jewish workers, an act of authorship that becomes symbolic of authoring history itself in the novel.[32] Thus, the drama that unfolds throughout the protagonist's travels has to do with his attempt to realize his dreams, or have the utopian promises fulfilled.

Yet very early in the novel the protagonist's expectations are thwarted. The long workdays at the winery at the opening of the novel (and later) seem to hinder his work on the novel, rather than provide the subject matter for it, as he had hoped.[33] The tension between his intellectual aspirations and everyday life is formally registered throughout the novel, through the interruption of his thoughts about his writing by mundane external details:

> Could he form a complete image of a simple person's life, with its toils and doubts, an image weaved also of bonds of fraternity and friendship, those wonderful strings that still exist among human beings, whose weaving will make up life's future tapestry?
> —Quick! The barrels are already full!
> His entire being, the entirety of his soul turned now toward that wonderful and precious thing: literary creation. Not a row of pale protagonists, utterly alienated from reality, would populate his future work, but broad swathes of life full of work and suffering, drenched in sweat and sorrow, with only a few sparks of joy shooting here and there from under the blows of life's hammer. All his senses were finely attuned to absorb the complicated weave that we call human life. But would his powers suffice?
> —Red beet juice, cheap today![34]

The reference to "pale protagonists, utterly alienated from reality" is an obvious reference to the "anti-genre" (or modernist) heroes of the works of Brenner and U. N. Gnessin which constitute the main cultural opposition to the realism of the 1920s and 1930s. It is important to note that this tendency to disrupt the protagonist's idealistic train of thought runs throughout the novel. For example, when the narrator Rimona is speaking about problems of gender relations, enthusiastically agreeing that "whatever measures we take to fix the situation, the first condition for success is honesty between the genders,"[35] their conversation suddenly stops when Yosef's friend Avraham crosses their path. Avraham's sudden appearance reminds Yosef that his relationship with Rimona is based on a betrayal of his friendship with Avraham, who was previously in love with her. Thus, the repressed act of betrayal disrupts the utopian talk of gender equality and honesty. It is this disruption by the conditions of everyday life, the gap between material conditions and the possibility of realizing emancipation, which constitutes the central contradiction around which the novel is constituted.

Thematically, the challenges to any emancipatory project are apparent everywhere in the novel: from the petty competition between wage-laborers at the orange-packing plant preventing class cooperation,[36] all the way to the attitudes taken by landlords, land owners, and other representatives of the emerging bourgeoisie, whose need for profit pushes them to exploit the workers and become cynical about any non-capitalist collective project.[37] Most important in terms of thematic tension is the relationship between Yosef and his worker friend Avraham. In the novel, Avraham's character presents the reader with an opposite pole to Yosef's idealism, as he sneers at the latter's utopianism: "For what is our life? A farce and nothing else. No more than eternal competition. To better ourselves? To change human character and heal it? Can medicine cure prosthesis? Nonsense!"[38] Avraham's shattering of the picture of the "future woman" hanging in Yosef's room—another symbol of the latter's utopian aspirations—is probably the best expression of this tension between the characters.[39]

As the novel progresses, we learn that Avraham's cynicism, his thieving, lying, and sexual predations, are all a result of the dispossession and poverty of the workers' lives. Yet, by highlighting Avraham's knowledge of the conditions of life of the workers, it becomes possible to see his actions not only as a result of social circumstances. Rather, they reveal the moment of truth of his character: while Yosef tends to turn a blind eye to his life's conditions, focusing instead on the hazy hope of a better future, Avraham's actions are no less expressive of a utopian impulse. His thefts, his little acts of corruption and sexual exploits, are attempts to appropriate all those things that he is socially denied and that have essentially been stolen from him, through the capitalist appropriation of surplus-value (and thus, one can say, each of the two characters represents one possible response to the conditions of life). Perhaps most interesting in this regard is Avraham's admiration of modernist art and contempt toward Yosef's more realist artistic sensibilities.[40] By associating Avraham and his sense of alienation from reality with modernist abstraction, Zarchi draws our attention to a common argument in the Marxist analysis of modernism, namely, that the feeling of alienation and loneliness so prevalent in modernist art (as in the protagonists of Brenner, mentioned earlier) is not simply a matter of subjective artistic taste or personal belief. Rather, these are aesthetic expressions of the increasing objective alienation of subjects from the forces that produce their world under multinational capitalism, as Jameson argues.[41] The "problem" with Avraham becomes paralleled in this way to the "problem" with realist art under what Lenin famously called the stage of monopoly capitalism—the cause of both of these problems resides outside their bearers (Avraham and realist literature, respectively). Both are the result of capitalism's violent expansion onto a global scale, stretching relations of production beyond what can be easily represented in a realist novel.

For our purposes, the point to be emphasized about the antagonism between Yosef and Avraham is that neither the idealism of the former nor the cynicism of the latter are vindicated in the novel—no easy morality tale is hidden in the pages of *Barefoot Days*, even if Shaked's critical writing creates the opposite impression. Avraham ends up sailing back to Europe in an attempt to escape the drudgery of life of workers in the *moshava*. Yosef, after a period of seemingly successful integration of creative work and physical labor, during which his relationship with Rimona thrives, is subject to a worse fate. His novel is denied publication for economic reasons,[42] his childhood illness—that he previously thought to be cured—returns to plague him,[43] and his relationship with Rimona ends.[44] The momentary reconciliation thus turns out to be a false one. Thus, the contradiction between the emancipatory goal and actual conditions, which takes numerous forms throughout the novel, is never reconciled. Rather, the novel follows what we called above the utopian refusal of non-contradiction, in which antagonisms are never resolved, but rather mapped and reworked in the different social spaces through which the protagonist moves. It is in this sense that Zarchi's novel remains radically open to transformative possibilities, neither proclaiming the veracity of a smooth, unproblematic, "Zionist metanarrative," nor denying the possibility of a collective transformative project.

The ending of the novel emphasizes this point. Yosef, barely recovered from his latest bout of illness, writes the following to Rimona:

> A person standing at the helm of his life must join the effort for the betterment of all life, for a transformation of values. We must advance one step after another, even if our hands are bleeding [. . .] Let us be as those hardier plants that thrive despite horrible heat waves. The vulnerable young sapling withers and dies. But man, like a deep-rooted, broad branched, tree, breathes deeply and rises up again. It has weathered another calamity, and emerged hardened and strengthened. He is gathering forces for new life!
>
> This is my first triumph. My triumph over myself.[45]

Rather than a sudden reaffirmation of an ideal Zionist narrative, Yosef's assertion that he has triumphed over himself has two meanings. First, it signifies a recognition of his past idealistic intentions to be too-quick reconciliations, ones that tend to ignore the very material obstacles that have to be overcome by a more sophisticated and collective of a project than a simple act of individual will. Second, it signals to the reader that his probably imminent death should not be interpreted as a condemnation of the collective project as a naïve illusion; rather, it calls for a continuation of the struggle for it, as the beginning of the quote makes clear. The tragic ending is thus not some triumph of a cosmic, "truer," principle of failure or human nature (as Shaked would have it, but also as Nitzan Lebovic's work on Zarchi implies).[46] It is rather an assertion of the historical openness of the collective enterprise: neither promising a sure success nor settling for its certain failure. The opposition between individual fate (which must be a tragic one) and that of collectivity (whose horizon remains open) is one of the ultimate formal elements of this realist corpus's commitment to non-reconciliation.

The structure and themes of Zarchi's novel are not unique. Other realist or "genre" literary texts, such as Yosef Aricha's 1933 novel *Bread and Vision*, follow the same general structure, in which the narrator's travels map the contradictions of the settlement project, again mostly staying within the spaces of the rural capitalist *moshavot* and the cities.[47] Even though we will not be able to address Aricha's work here in any detail, it is worth noting briefly that Zarchi's reflection on creative literary work is largely absent from Aricha's novel, which instead focuses on violence and bodily transformation and their relation to labor in the settlements, and an even more detailed exploration of gender relations than in Zarchi's novel. The drudgery and precarity of manual labor in the *moshavot* pushes the narrator toward the end of the novel to explore the collectivized agricultural settlements, the description of which is far from idealized (hard work and poor conditions are apparent everywhere).[48] Even though Aricha devotes very little space to this part of his journey, the radical openness of the *halutzic* project is wonderfully captured in two instances. The first has to do with a plan of action that one of the characters puts together in response to the precarity of wage-labor in the capitalist settlements. This is how the plan is presented in the novel, the initial phrase evoking biblical language:

> And thus spoke Gideon:
> – – – – – – – –
> – – – – – – – –
> – – – – – – – –
> – – – – – – – –
>   [49]
> – – – – – – – –

This puzzling quoting of empty lines becomes a bit clearer if we remember that the same gesture appears in Nikolai Chernyshevsky's utopian text *What is to be Done?*, after which Lenin named his well-known essay elaborating his revolutionary program.[50] The attempt to capture a sense of openness, of things yet be defined and fought over, should be clear. The other instance of a clear expression of potentiality laden openness appears in the novel's ending lines: "A young man whips the mules, and they start moving towards the field. The vegetation glimmers with dew drops. The plow's first furrow blackens. Its fertile earth shimmering in the sunlight."[51] The open furrow is here symbolically charged with open potentiality or promise, rather than prescribing a linear narrative that leads as if automatically or unproblematically to the establishment of a nation-state.

It is in Ever Hadani's 1930 *The Wooden Cabin* that we get a glimpse of the collectivized agricultural settlement, the *kvutza*, later to become the more familiar kibbutz.[52] The novel, usually considered part of the realist corpus, presents us with a very different interpretational problem than that of Zarchi's works. Most of the novel cannot be called realist in any formal sense, since very little actual narration takes place. Almost every chapter revolves around a single event in the life of the settlement, usually unrelated in any causal way to other chapters. Just as in the cases of Zarchi, in which the narrator's travels are partly an instrument to orient the readers with social settings unfamiliar to them, the descriptions of life in the collectivized settlement had a familiarizing function for its readers. Since, as Neumann argues, relatively few Jewish immigrants actually joined the *halutz* settlements, literature became a means for readers to become acquainted with them.[53] The construction of some common subject of history is, of course, also implied by this familiarizing gesture. This, to be sure, explains the strongly didactic tone of many passages, such as the following:

> A person travelling through the Khula in the rainy season would not have his wagon pulled by only two oxen, but rather use two pairs or sometimes three, because the swamp is large and the beasts' legs may sink in the mud to their stomachs [. . .] Most dangerous of all is the creek that stays dry through the summer, but in rainy days is sometimes filled with a sudden flood of water, rushing down angrily from the mountains. If a wagon stands in its way this kind of flood would wash it and its people away.[54]

Rather than recognize the simple orienting function of these passages for their 1930s readers, later critics and writers mock their didactic tone and preoccupation with technical details, seeing these mostly as coded "ritualistic" adherence to an idealizing literature in the service of nation-building.[55] Even if this orienting function (which again should invoke for us the function of utopian narratives discussed earlier) is largely uninteresting for today's reader, its misunderstanding by critics clearly illustrates the knee-jerk tendency to read the period's literature in terms of nation-building.

More interesting for our purposes is another formal feature of *The Wooden Cabin*: the usage of the poetic vignettes (*reshimot po'etiyot*), a form inherited from Gershon Shofman and other writers, according to Gertz. In these passages, detailed descriptions of natural landscape and agricultural work are interwoven with a character's internal musings, as Shaked puts it.[56] As Gertz argues, the adoption of these long descriptive sections was common to the realists, who sought to imbue the settlement enterprise with a sense of stability.[57] This is evident in the descriptions of agricultural labor in *The Wooden Cabin*, whose rhythms seem to merge with natural ones almost seamlessly:

> Indeed, in working the land there is something of the sublime joy of the only enslavement that is natural to mankind: being shackled to the sun, to the rain, to the wind, and to the annual cycle of life in the summer, the fall, the winter, and the spring. In the field a peasant ploughs his land with his pair of oxen—while the other pair rests [. . .] And so it goes for days, generations, and centuries.[58]

If writers such as Shofman used the poetic vignette to create a sense of individual alienation from one's surrounding, the opposite is true of its usage by the realists who used it to affirm the collective ability to mold their surroundings. Understanding the poetic vignettes in this way, it becomes possible to problematize Gertz's conclusion, according to which the poetic vignette was used by the realists to "impose the national on the universal."[59] For what becomes universal (or natural) here is the very malleability of nature, landscape and individuals by the collective project. Rather than a stricture or an imposition, this transformative potential is experienced as freedom.

This freedom is expressed through the layered structure of meaning that we mentioned above, in which transformations in human body, social structure, desire, and history come into tension with one another. The moments in which *The Wooden Cabin* celebrates the workings of this structure are those in which it indeed seems to idealize the collectivized agricultural settlement: its people are the strongest and most skilled;[60] its social structure allows for flexibility in adapting to everything from raising children to bad agricultural seasons; the love of the land and camaraderie not natural or spontaneous to the settlement's people, but rather traits that are materially learned; and the totalizing teleological orientation toward future prosperity.[61]

Yet, as the novel progresses, contradictions arise that threaten the success of the enterprise. If in Zarchi's novel the central contradiction, thematized in a multiplicity of ways, was the one between abstract utopian aspiration and real conditions, Hadani's novel thematizes the element that resists the utopian project through highlighting problems of historical transformation. First, the workers of a stone quarry abandon the collective because they cannot handle the hard work without proper machinery, which the small settlement cannot afford without external capital.[62] Second, despite an awareness of the gendered division of labor, its emotional effects, and the need to transform it, one of the settlement's women becomes chronically depressed and commits suicide.[63] Third, the settlement's growing dependence on urban centers, despite the settlers' largely negative view of their capitalist logic, slowly erodes the unalienated image of their lives.[64] This dependency is both material (the settlement depends on the cities as markets for its goods in order to be able to purchase from urban factories all kinds of materials and machines that the settlement cannot produce) and ideological (urban centers, with their upheavals and mysteries, seem to attract the younger generation away from the settlement.[65]

These failures make the celebration of the settlement's life seem increasingly unjustified as the novel progresses. At the beginning of the novel, the narrator forgivingly condescends to the younger workers when they proclaim that the life of the settlement will have to change soon: "With youth's arrogance and confidence they say: our generation is not one in which life is built on love and naive belief, but a generation of revolution, industry, and machine . . . You will turn the dairy farm into a machine for milk, the land into a machine for seed, and the field into a machine for vegetables."[66] The mechanized is presented, of course, as antithetical to the feeling of an unalienated relationship to nature through transformative labor. However, at the end of the novel, it turns out that it was the narrator that was wrong all along, turning a blind eye to historical processes. The novel ends with a delirious hallucination experienced by the protagonist, a narrative device that enables a transition into historical speculation. In the hallucination, an engineer prophesies the end of the small agricultural settlement and its non-alienated relation to nature, precisely as the young workers had predicted: machines will handle the hard work, and "the sheep will no longer be sheep for the farmers, but rather a little factory for wool, milk, and meat."[67] Again, the presence of the mechanical should not be read only as a progressive eventuality, but also as something that carries with it the alienating threats of the city into the settlement. Ending the novel this way, Hadani refuses to reconcile the historical contradiction, its challenges to the *halutzic* project and its structure of meaning—just as in the utopian novel. Furthermore, rather than celebrating some overarching Zionist narrative, Hadani's thematization presciently echoes the concerns of the Young Guard, in recognizing that what resists and threatens the collective emancipatory project is not to be found within the collectivist settlements, but rather in forces external to them—namely, their failure to free themselves from the growing power of capital.

What the realist works have in common with the utopian novel is a refusal to reconcile the contradictions that arise between a utopian goal and material conditions. Just as in the utopian novel, imagined ideological solutions to real problems are elaborated, only to be constantly disrupted, their resolution constantly thwarted. What threatens the collective project remains threatening, thereby expressing the radical openness of their historical moment in which the continuation of the transformative project envisioned by the *halutz*—which does not necessarily lead to establishing a nation-state—hangs in the balance. It is important for our purposes to notice that two imagined resolutions to these contradictions are possible. The first is the one suggested by Gertz and Shaked: idealizing the settlement project and narrating its victory at every point. We have already shown that the realists refuse this narrative solution. The second is the negation of the first: to narrate the failure of the project as inevitable, claiming that some alienation or imperfection of human nature will always stay out of its reach. The realists refuse this ideological resolution as well: Zarchi's cynics or alienated characters are never vindicated. In other words, we might suggest that the realists dialectically perform a Hegelian negation-of-the-negation, in which the contradictions stay open for future development.

But the utopian formal openness, that refusal of non-contradiction, is a more objective or external way of thinking about these '20s and '30s works. It is perhaps easier to address the hackneyed charges of repressing individuals and their desires by rewriting our interpretation in terms of desire itself, in a way that will create a structure of mediation between internality (or the subjective realm) and externality (the objective one). The openness that we detected in this realist corpus can be formulated through Lacan's notion of the *objet petit-a*, or the object-cause of desire. As Slavoj Žižek argues, the *objet petit-a* is not some material object in reality, but it is rather responsible for the production of a stable reality itself, the creation of a fantasy space in which the pursuit of desire is mapped, and things become meaningful by their relation to this pursuit. It is important to emphasize that the *objet petit-a* does not distort preexisting reality; rather, there is no stable reality prior to desire's ordering of it:

> If we look at a thing straight on, i.e., matter of factly, disinterestedly, objectively, we see nothing but a formless spot; the object assumes clear and distinct features only if we look at it 'at an angle,' i.e., with an 'interested' view, supported, permeated, and 'distorted' by desire. This describes perfectly the *objet petit a*, the object-cause of desire: an object that is, in a way, posited by desire itself. The paradox of desire is that it posits retroactively its own cause, i.e., the object *a* is an object that can be perceived by a gaze 'distorted,' an object that *does not exist* for an 'objective' gaze. In other words, the object *a* is always, by definition, perceived in a distorted way, because outside this distortion, 'in itself,' *it does not exist*, since it is *nothing but* the embodiment, the materialization of this very distortion.[68]

In this Lacanian schema, it is not the satisfaction of desire that constitutes the ultimate end (which is a first version of a reconciliation of contradictions); nor is it denying desire the object of its pursuit (which would be another form of reconciliation, one in which the lack becomes its own solution). Rather, the purpose of desire is the reproduction of the pursuit itself, as Žižek emphasizes, and in this way openness itself is what must be preserved—that lack constitutive of desire—a preservation that cannot ever be abstracted from its subject matter. It is easy to see the identity of Marin's more spatial "refusal of non-contradiction" with the production of reality as Lacanian fantasy space, in which the lack itself must be preserved, a contradictoriness that keeps history moving, so to speak.

That the operation of the *objet petit-a* is a totalizing one—that all of reality exists by its relation to the movement of contradiction, mediating constantly between the subject and social world—is important with regard to these realist literary works. For it is in this way that a unique narrative option becomes available to them: moments of "closure" that are at once radically open, but in a way that renders this radical openness not threatening but rather invigorating, not disabling but calling to action. As we will see in the next chapters, this is the last time in Hebrew literature from Palestine in which this narrative option is imaginable (recent attempts to reproduce this peculiar narrative option, such as in Eshkol Nevo's *Neuland*, fall short of reproducing this effect—not of any fault of the novels themselves, of course, but because of the context of their production, which we will discuss extensively in our two final chapters).[69]

It is this openness of the Zionist realism of the 1920s and 1930s that makes the corpus interesting, and which is lost when it is read as a mere mouthpiece for the nation-building project. Again, just as in the case of the utopian novel discussed earlier, once the potentialities of their moment are foreclosed, this realist works' openness itself becomes invisible. As Fredric Jameson has argued in another context, it is precisely this historical foreclosing of the possibilities undergirding the realists' literature that makes their work seem inferior or childish.[70]

Khirbet Khizeh and the Crisis of the *Halutzic* Transformative Imaginary

The following discussion of S. Yizhar's well-known 1949 novella *Khirbet Khizeh* as the endpoint to the trajectory we have been charting (from *Altneuland* through the realists) is meant to further support our argument that the realism of the 1920s and 1930s should not be read as simplistic propaganda for the establishment of a Zionist nation-state.[71] As we will see, Yizhar's novella unconsciously expresses a deep crisis of the *halutzic* transformative imaginary that animated the realism of the '20s and '30s. The historical potentialities associated with this imaginary are lost in the '40s.

Shaked and Gertz see the realist literature of the 1940s and 1950s largely in terms of a smooth development from their 1930s predecessors,[72] a literary-historical claim echoed by other critics.[73] In order to problematize this claim, we have to note the historical developments that separate the late 1940s from the 1930s. The *Mapai* party and the General Federation of Labor had by the '30s risen to a clear hegemonic position within the settlement project. As David Za'it and others argue,[74] this development led to the failure of the Young Guard and its settlement movement, *Hakibbutz ha'artzi*, to create an urban analogue to their collectivist rural settlements, and actively prevented any substantial cooperation with Palestinian workers (as well as to the failure of other movements that supported class struggle against the hegemony of the Mapai).[75] The rural collectivist settlements became strongly dependent on the emerging capitalist economy, which meant that the *halutzic* socially transformative project was slowly disintegrating. Labor in the kibbutz suddenly became ordinary work, completely equivalent to wage-labor, becoming dissociated from the transformative imaginary it possessed in earlier periods. It is for this reason that in this period the realist camp begins to produce damning critiques of kibbutz life, as in David Meletz's 1945 *In Circles* or Yigal Mossinsohn's 1953 *The Way of a Man*, some of which we will discuss in the following chapters.[76] Even in the case of sympathetic works, such as Moshe Shamir's 1946 novel *He Walked through the Fields*, life and work in the kibbutz are not imbued with the social potentialities associated with them in the 1930s novels.[77]

Most important for our purpose is that the 1948 war marks a significant challenge to the way the *halutzic* movement narrated the tension between reality and utopia. Instead of purchasing land, the Zionist settlements now took it by force. The Jewish armed forces grew considerably in the 1940s, and a few weeks into the war, over 12 percent of the Jewish population of Palestine was on active military duty (80,000 out of 650,000), according to Ilan Pappé.[78] It is this shift that acts as the background for *Khirbet Khizeh*. The novella narrates the occupation of a Palestinian village by a group of soldiers and the subsequent deportation of its inhabitants. Yizhar's canonical standing in modern Hebrew letters, and his background—having grown up in an environment suffused with *halutz* ideology—is important for us. It is here that we find a clear dramatization of the encounter between the *halutzic* imaginary, based on transformative labor, and a challenge that it cannot overcome.

It is on the grounds of form, rather than content, that Yizhar's story stands out in the realist corpus. Yizhar's narrator begins by addressing the readers directly, professing an inability to forget certain events:

> True, it all happened a long time ago, but it had haunted me ever since. I sought to drown it out with the din of passing time, to diminish its value, to blunt its edge with the rush of daily life, and I even, occasionally, managed a sober shrug, managed to see that the whole thing had not been so bad after all, congratulating myself on my patience, which is, of course, the

brother of true wisdom. But sometimes I would shake myself again, astonished at how easy it had been to be seduced, to be knowingly led astray and join the great mass of liars—that mass compounded of crass ignorance, utilitarian indifference, and shameless self-interest—and exchange a single great truth for the cynical shrug of a hardened sinner. I saw that I could no longer hold back, and although I hadn't a clear idea of where its telling will lead, it seemed to me that, instead of staying silent, I should, rather, start telling the story.[79]

What this beginning immediately suggests is that the narrator is facing a problem of narration, or of not knowing exactly how to recount the events. This problem of narration is further highlighted in the passages following this one, in which the narrator considers several starting points for telling the story, not quite being fully satisfied with any of them.[80] The "broken" form of the novella highlights the problem of narration even further, foregrounding the narrator's dissatisfaction with the narrative and stubbornly insisting that something troubling fails to be articulated. Thus, for example, after the narrator describes the soldiers' mission in a tone belittling the importance of the actual details (and therefore raising the question of why describe them in the first place) we read the following passage:

That was what waiting had been like. But on this glorious winter morning, upon the luxuriant hill, when everything around was green and watered, it was nothing more than a picnic on a school outing, when all you had to do was be happy and celebrate the pleasant hours and then go home to your mom . . . everything that we had been ordered to do on this mission wasn't worth a thought, that village over there, the infiltration within it, and whatever else the devil might put together here . . .

Apart from all sorts of things, all this might only be one further piece of evidence that this war had gone long enough, as was commonly agreed, in fact too long . . . .[81]

The attempt to describe the mission as easy and meaningless fails to capture "all sorts of things" that bother the narrator yet fail to be articulated. The transition into the hackneyed "this war had gone on long enough" only further emphasizes this inability to articulate something important. This effect is generated countless times in the novella, hinting time and time again that the most important point had been missed, or that "underneath it all there was something vague, accumulating in the air."[82]

In order to understand why the protagonist finds it so difficult to narrate the events of the military operation, we have to turn to the novella's narrative background, or to what is represented in it but never takes center-stage (a hermeneutic operation that we will discuss further in what follows). As Kna'ani and others of Yizhar's early critics note, it is to the *halutzic* imaginary that Yizhar's narrator turns for solace, for a momentary escape from the disturbing failure to convey what is taking place.[83] The landscape descriptions, the constant imagining and re-imagining of agricultural labor and its temporalities, and the familiar social relations associated with it—all immediately connote the *halutzic* imaginary with which Yizhar had intimate familiarity. Not only does the narrator find relief in it, but some of the other soldiers as well. For example, when the soldiers encounter a wild colt, one of them tries to befriend it, wanting to "raise it to be a great horse," instantly suggesting familiarity with farm work and the taming of wilderness so central to the *halutzic* imaginary.[84] But perhaps the most striking example of the narrator's escape into the *halutzic* imaginary is when the fields of the occupied Palestinian village are reimagined from the perspective of a settler:

> We examined the entire agricultural plan of the village and its fields, we fathomed their purpose in selecting places for planting, and we grasped their reasoning in the layout of the vegetable plots; the purpose of the field crops, the fallow land, and the crop rotation became clear to us, it was all so evident (even if you could have planned something better suited to our tastes, and we had already started to do so, without realizing it, each of us in his own mind) and all that was needed was for them to come and carry on with what they were doing. Some plots were left fallow, and others were sown, by design, everything was carefully thought out [. . .].[85]

The continuous attempt-and-failure to narrate the events is thus contrasted throughout the narrative to the stable *halutzic* imaginary.

The broken form of *Khirbet Khizeh* therefore dramatizes the irreconcilability of the contradiction between the experience of military conquest and the settlement imaginary. The *halutzic* imaginary, centered as it was on transformative labor aimed at social emancipation, simply could not contain the experience of conquest and expropriation. Thus, we can suggest that the crisis of narration in the novella expresses the historical crisis of the *halutzic* project, or the foreignness of the experience of military conquest to any notion of transformative labor (and we should not assume that such irreconcilable antagonism is natural, or revealing a pacifist Truth—but that it is precisely a way of expressing the disintegration of the *halutzic* project). It is important in this regard to contrast the disintegration of the settlement imaginary in Yizhar's novella to its treatment by modernists such as Brenner. For the latter, the *halutzic* imaginary is doomed right from the start, taking on the status of an idealization of reality or a convenient illusion, from which the protagonist is alienated. In contrast, in Yizhar's novella, the *halutzic* imaginary is the one in which he feels at home, made clear by his repeated attempts to find refuge in it from the events that refuse to be narrated.

Even if we are not able to do justice to the novella's many interpretations, it is important to note briefly how the reading proposed here relates to some of its more influential readings. Many of the novella's earlier critics judge the protagonist ethically, either praising him for joining in the conquest and deportation despite his doubts, or condemning him for the same doubts, now seen as moral weakness.[86] The problem with these readings is that ethical strategies of narrative containment—either legitimizing the action or condemning it—are just some of the containment strategies considered by the narrator itself, only to again prove unsatisfactory. Here is one example:

> I was ill at ease. Where did this sense come from that I was being accused of some crime? And what was it that was beginning to press upon me to look for excuses? My comrades' calm behavior only intensified my own sense of distress. Didn't they realize? Or were they just pretending not to know? [. . .] I clung to that famous phrase in the operational orders "operatives dispatched on hostile missions." I conjured up before my eyes all the terrible outrages that the Arabs had committed against us. I recited the names of Hebron, Safed, Be'er Tuvia, and Hulda. I seized on necessity [. . .]. I once again contemplated the mass of people, seething indistinctly and innocently at my feet—and I found no comfort.[87]

Thus, in interpreting the novella to be passing ethical judgment on the events, critics subscribe to an ethical resolution that *Khirbet Khizeh* itself refuses. Even the ending of the novella, in which the narrator seems to convince himself that the deportation of Palestinians should be seen as exiling them, is riddled with signs of a failure to comprehend or narrate the events.[88]

In a more psychological vein, other critics suggest that the novella demonstrates the need to repress trauma, either the soldiers' personal trauma of experiencing violence, as Amos Oz has it, or a collective need to repress systematic violence against Palestinians to legitimize national ideology.[89] In the case of the soldiers' purely personal trauma, we can suggest that what is manifested psychologically on the individual level is extended to the social level by the interpretation suggested here—the individual trauma is expressive of another, social trauma—the loss of transformative potentialities with the death of the *halutzic* project. The second option, that of collective repression of ideological needs, seems to incorrectly recognize the content being repressed. For it is not exactly the violence committed against Palestinians that is being repressed in Yizhar's novella (as long as we understand repression along Freudian lines, as making some content absent and then having this absence manifested through formal symptoms).[90] The foregrounded appearance of the occupation and deportation in the novella should themselves signal to us that whatever repressed content floats into consciousness here, it has very little to do with the overt drama. All that goes to strengthen the interpretations suggested here: that the repressed content that haunts *Khirbet Khizeh*'s anxious narrator is the crisis of the *halutzic* emancipatory project, or the gap separating the realists' collective imaginary of the 1920s and 1930s from its crisis in their work of the late 1940s. Yizhar's novella therefore testifies precisely to this act of repression of the break that separates Zionism from state, or the literature of the '30s from that of the late '40s. Not a literary continuity is registered in the works of the latter period, but a dramatic historical break and its repression.

Finally, we can now explain why the Zionist realist writers of the 1920s and 1930s are seen merely as ideologues for the national project. The smooth linear narrative connecting them and the *halutzic* project to the establishment of the state of Israel depends on the repression of the rift separating the 1920s and 1930s from the late 1940s, or the crisis and ultimately the death of the radically transformative project imagined by the *halutzic* movement. As we have tried to show, it is this rift that makes its symptomatic appearance in Yizhar's novella. We have therefore transformed the way in which the realist literature of the period is to be seen. But our initial trajectory will prove important for the following chapters too—for it will allow us to show how the same crisis is registered in all of the literature of the 1950s, like a fault-line testifying to the passing of some prehistorical tremor.

2

From Utopian Project to Utopian Compensation in 1950s Works by Yigal Mossinsohn and Nathan Shaham

The last chapter's prehistory of Israeli literature has provided us with the contours of a new historical hermeneutic for it. The new interpretation has two layers, one has to do with the expansion of capitalism into Palestine, and the other with the open-endedness of the Zionist transformative project in the first half of the twentieth century. Recalling the introduction, this duality has to do with that structure of historical change that we called a vanishing mediator: the transformation in social form (spread of capitalism) brought about by a reinvigorated pursuit of an old goal (Zionist pursuit of emancipation). Our prehistory emphasized the latter level, arguing that the vanishing of the *halutzic* transformative project has been itself repressed, and that the traces of this repression can be found in S. Yizhar's writing. The next two chapters, whose subject matter will be the literature of the late 1940s and 1950s, will demonstrate the interpretive power of this new hermeneutic, which will make possible the emergence of a new account of the relation between the literature of the period and its socioeconomic realities. For, the readings in these chapters will not constitute mere illustrations of a preconceived theoretical account; rather, each reading will insist on the imaginative newness of each literary work, or each of their different attempts to solve in imagination some real historical problem—a problem which we still have not solved—and which at the last instance is always the problem of revolution. For, as these readings will hopefully make clear, Israeli literature of the "long Israeli '50s" (which includes the late '40s as well as the '50s), constitutes as a whole nothing less than a representational problematic of the relation between the material infrastructure and its accompanying superstructure, a problematic that we should designate by the term "naturalism," as we will see at the end of the next chapter.

Our more immediate concerns in this chapter are the late 1940s and the 1950s works of Nathan Shaham and Yigal Mossinsohn, both considered representative of the 1948 war (or, the *Palmach*) generation's writers. To argue that there is something interesting about these works today is no easy task. For, critical hegemony—represented again in this case by Gershon Shaked's established interpretative line—tends to see these authors mostly as the inheritors of the much-maligned "genre" writing. At their worst (in the case of Shaham, according to Shaked), they simply constitute a continuation of "genre" writing's idealization of some so called Zionist "metanarrative"; or at their best (in Mossinsohn's case), it is literature of little aesthetic value, that nevertheless presents its readers with a slight deviation from this "metanarrative," one that paves the way for the more complete rebellion of the 1960s, as Shaked has it.[1] Again, this interpretive line is reproduced by critics who seem to share very little with Shaked in terms of their intellectual project or critical sensibilities. Thus, for example, Yael Feldman almost reproduces Shaked's exact words when she deems Mossinsohn's 1949 *In the Negev Prairies* as a "simplistic and melodramatic play,"[2] whose only function was a cathartic one for Israelis following the death toll of the 1948 war.[3] This tendency to read Mossinsohn's work as melodramatic (or as Shaked puts it, "a literature of heightened emotive effects") misses, in the reading presented here, the repression that makes the appearance of the symptom so strongly a-signifying or emotional—much like in an interaction with an hysteric.[4] Instead, we will try here to recapture what has made the play (and Mossinsohn's other writing) so interesting for its contemporaries, who far from being melodrama-addicted dupes, were drawn precisely to the way in which Mossinsohn's writing approached the repression of the death of what we called the *halutzic* transformative collective project.

The only existing alternative to Shaked's line of interpretation seem to be that of what we might call "establishment" critics, who resist the characterization of '40s realism as propagandistic in their celebration of the *Palmach* generation's literature (and who are completely ignored by Shaked's liberal camp).[5] We will not explore this critical position here at any length, yet it should be noted that what is implicitly registered in their writing is something like the erosion of any stable sense of committed or propagandistic art, noticeable in Nurit Govrin's "folding" of national values into individual autonomy—arguing that there is nothing propagandistic or committed about the work of an author who truly believes in the "values" he celebrates.[6] At any rate, we will not take up here the critical position whose main goal is to celebrate for some national purpose the late '40s and the '50s realist literature. We will, however, show that the true preoccupations of these works are very different than is commonly claimed by Shaked and his critical followers.

Each of our authors will provide us a way into one central critical point of interest. Mossinsohn's *Way of a Man* will make it possible for us to address what is usually thought about in terms of a conflict between individual and collective, common to this period's literature and culture.[7] I will try, however, to de-reify the common Hobbesian view of this conflict—in which one invariably ends up legislating a compromise between abstract individual freedoms and collective needs. Instead, I will insist that rather than seeing as individuality constituting an independent antagonist to society, individuality itself should be seen as an imaginary social construction—which does not imply that it is not real and effective. It is therefore what this construct makes possible in Mossinsohn's novel that will be of interest to us in what follows. As we will see, rather than a reified subject of liberalism we will be able to see the rise of subjectivity as making possible an imaginary solution to a very real social problem of the '50s.

The other overarching issue, one that we will address in our reading of Nathan Shaham's work—the novella "Always We" and the short-story collection *The Gods are Lazy*—will be that of the clear nostalgic tone of much of the *Palmach* literature, and which is also clearly expressed in '50s works not directly associated with the 1948 war, such as Hendel's *The Street of Steps*, as we will see in the next chapter.[8] As Michal Arbell notes, the clear nostalgic tone is evident in Palmach generation's literature even before the 1948 war—its first appearance traceable according to Dan Miron to Yizhar's first short story, *Ephraim Goes Back to the Alfalfa*, published in 1938.[9] This, of course, prevents us from explaining this strong nostalgic overtone, as Shaked does, as expressing a sense of disappointment of that generation with the state's alienating realities following its establishment.[10] Seeing the state's establishment as the moment after which disappointment and nostalgia become pervasive is not unique to Shaked. For example, Netiva Ben Yehuda, one of the conspicuous spokespersons for the *Palmach* generation since the early 1980s, expresses something similar in claiming that "we had the state stolen from us right under our noses."[11] The temporal gap that annuls this narrative—nostalgia setting in a decade before the 1948 war—demands that we account in a new way for these nostalgic yearnings, whose appearance in the writing of writers in their twenties and thirties is indeed very odd.

Michal Arbell's writing on nostalgia and masculinity in 1950s literature constitutes another attempt to account for this nostalgia. According to Arbell, it is a result of a contradiction internal to *halutzic* masculinity itself: becoming men means staying an ever-moving youth, as opposed to "mature masculinity [that] requires stopping."[12] The nostalgic yearnings are in Arbell's account simply the result of fear of losing movement itself in the movement to adulthood. Yet, this account remains tethered to a middle-class or bourgeois ideology of adulthood as a stopping point, after which no radical transformation takes place in one's life. This model, assumed universal by Arbell, has nothing to do with the *halutzic* revolutionary or utopian adulthood (both masculine and feminine), in which maturity itself cannot be associated with constancy but rather with a continuous pursuit of change. It is for this reason that Arbell's account as well does not offer us a satisfactory solution for the clear nostalgic tones of *Palmach* literature.

In what follows we will offer a different explanation for this nostalgia. If both Shaked's and Arbell's accounts end up seeing nostalgia as a result of a fault in the subjective attitude of the *Palmach* writers' *halutzic* outlook, our narrative will constitute an inversion of these accounts: rather than merely subjective fault—*halutzic* naïveté becoming sentimentalism after an encounter with harsh reality, as Arbell puts it (i.e., discovering that the state is a rather more alienating and bureaucratic entity than what the "idealists" had imagined it to be)—our narrative will recognize the cause of nostalgia in a fault in objective reality itself. Rather than condescend to *Palmach* writers for their misrecognition of reality, our narrative will expose the moment of truth of their nostalgia—a rupture in reality that they unconsciously tried to articulate against a repressive effort, one that is entirely missed by the liberal readings of Shaked and Arbell.

Individuality as the Preservation of Historicity: Yigal Mossinsohn's *The Way of a Man* and the Crisis of the *Halutzic* Revolutionary Project

Mossinsohn's *The Way of a Man* is easily misread today simply as articulating the author's own political journey—a disillusionment with kibbutz life, leading to an abandonment of so-called socialist kibbutz "values," and an embrace of the political Right (which in the '40s meant insisting on the primacy of the individual over some reified notion of collectivity, and action against the British mandate).[13] The novel's reception—establishment critics deploring the novel's attack of national symbols such as the kibbutz—supports this political contextualization of the novel. One of the points of critique of the kibbutz that the novel shares with others of its period is a developing antagonism between collectivity and the individual—the kibbutz represented more and more as a bureaucratic machine, completely alienated from human desire or need, driven by petty individualist politics only masquerading as collective will. To be sure, many passages in the novel do indeed seem to indict the kibbutz in this manner. For example, Yosef's request for a prolonged vacation becomes in the kibbutz's general assembly into something like a parody of a battleground between different organizational representatives, with reified ethical positions used to thinly veil egotistic affirmation—ignoring completely Yosef's urgent need for the vacation.[14]

Yet this reading is a very limited one, in restricting the novel's interpretation to a kind of correspondence between its explicit content to its immediate political context. Of course, that the novel is a work of art rather than a political position-paper is completely missed when the novel is read in this way. When one ignores completely the novel's aesthetic dimension, as Shaked does, there could be little wonder that the interpretation thus produced condescendingly sees little aesthetic value in the novel.[15] Instead of reading the novel as if it were a political manifesto, we should notice that individuality is staged also in the novel's dominant formal feature—that highlighting of the tension or antagonism between subjective interiority and its surrounding world, registered in the authors use of two sets of fonts: one reserved for characters' interior monologues and the other for the narrator's own voice. This visual signaling of a change in narrative perspective is not unique to Mossinsohn. It appears in Shaham's work as well, usually through his utilization of parenthesis to signal the transition to "interior" narration.[16] (whenever Shaham refrains from giving his readers any signal—neither narrative nor visual—that narrative perspective has changed, as in "Always We," the overall effect is quite disorienting, which is to be sure an intentional move whose purpose we will address below). This peculiar need for visual signaling for change in narrative perspective will return in the postmodern novels of soldiers' experience, Kenaz's *Infiltration* and Shimoni's *A Room*, but this time as a pastiched formal feature, a phenomenon that we will address in the following chapters.[17]

It is not the distinction of narrative perspectives itself that is peculiar, but that it is visual rather than the usual narrative cues for the transition (such as "she thought that . . ."). Mossinsohn (and Shaham) thus highlight a kind inhospitability of the external narrator to individual consciousness, or simply its complete disregard for it. Interiority therefore appears, almost literally, in the "cracks" or gaps that exist in-between portions of objective or "external" text. Our discussion in what follows will address precisely this dominant formal device of the text, which other critics have completely ignored despite its obvious relevance for any consideration of the antagonism between individual and collective—an antagonism that liberal critics love to invoke in any discussion of the Israeli 1950s.

Our de-reification of this antagonism in Mossinsohn's novel will now be made possible through this formal device. For, what is important here is not only the antagonism between the different portions of the text belonging to subjectivity on the one hand and society or exteriority on the other. Rather, we can now consider subjectivity not in the usual reified manner—as some irreducible primordial essence that exists prior to, and independently of, the social order and clashes with it. Instead we can see it as no less of a social construction as the other, "external," part of text, yet one which designates a completely new textual level, one that makes possible a new interpretation of the "objective" or "external" or "social" text, a textual historical development whose importance is paramount for Marxist literary analyses.[18] In our de-reified view of it, therefore, individuality will somehow decipher the objective or external text, making explicit a kind of meta-commentary on it, as we will now see. We should, however, not gloss over the important social development of which this formal device is itself symptomatic: that previous realist writing does not perform such a strong separation between subjective interiority and its outside makes this development in Mossinsohn and Shaham important—for it now marks the potential unmooring or abstraction of subjectivity from external reality, gaining something like a semi-autonomy from it.

What we can now finally argue is that what the text of interiority makes possible in Mossinsohn's novel is everything that is for some reason blocked or unattainable in the text of the exterior or the social—wish fulfillment, critiques of kibbutz social and cultural realities, expression of all manner of suspicions and fears, and most importantly to keep a living sense of contradiction open where external narration seeks to resolve it. The first two of these are perhaps the easiest to discern. Here, for example, is the narration of the novel's protagonist's thoughts when he returns to the kibbutz after having escaped British imprisonment:

From Utopian Project to Utopian Compensation 71

> Rafael is walking between the trees. An expectation of happiness pervades him when he enters, anticipatory but cautious, to the dining hall. What would the kibbutz members say? Joy and pleasure thaw in his limbs. It is better to draw out moments of surprise, handshakes and shoulder squeezes: "how did you manage to escape?" Just so. It wasn't that difficult. "You exaggerate, Rafael. You exaggerate. No mines went off? [. . .] "Oh, you're such a responsible comrade. I wish we had more like you. So, what do you say, Shoshana? What do you think about your Rafael?" [. . .] She stays silent and puts a soft hand on the back of his neck, and her grey eyes, with their brown specks, rest on him with love. She will be proud of him, to be sure [. . .] and Reuven Bloch standing to the side watching everything [. . .] At the edge of the tall hedge, where light washed over, Rafael stopped and filled his lungs with air [. . .] No one greeted him when he entered the kibbutz. He saw people walking between the wooden cabins, but they didn't notice him, apparently [. . .] It seemed that whoever crosses his path is intentionally ignoring him.[19]

The point, of course, is not simply that Rafael is surprised by the cold, suspecting, welcome—as the "objective" narrative admits as well—but the details of this expectation that are important: that he is treated as a hero by the kibbutz members, loved by his wife, Shoshana, and that Reuven Bloch—who he has been suspecting is having an affair with Shoshana will be witnessing his moment of glory. Thus, the way interiority functions in this case, and in many others in the novel, is as making possible imagining wish fulfillment—mapping what Slavoj Žižek calls "fantasy space" following Lacan, which we have seen in the last chapter to be an important formal feature of *halutzic* realism.[20] As Žižek has it, the fantasy space is a kind of mapping of desire, an imagining of the obstacles that have to be overcome to achieve the object of desire. We should not however read this imaginary space as of purely psychological consequences. Rather, in our context, Rafael's fantasy space does not simply map his way to seeming brave in the eyes of other kibbutz members and be attractive to his wife, but is rather more ambitions than that: it imagines a resolution for the problems that are plaguing reality itself, a reality that in the novel seems "stuck" or aporetic, or for whose problems no one seems able to imagine a satisfactory solution. What the passages of interior monologue provide in the novel, in a way completely absent form earlier "genre" literature, is a kind of imagined utopian compensation for what is lacking in reality.

It is precisely in this way that we should see the "critiques" of the kibbutz that appear in the novel (and that usually appear in the passages of interior monologue)—as so many attempts to understand what is wrong with reality, attempts that always somehow miss their target. The dialogue between Yosef and Nachum in the beginning of the novel, that revolves around kibbutz corruption and carelessness toward individual needs. As Yosef himself realizes during the discussion, voicing these critiques publicly will not lead to a transformation of kibbutz reality, but rather play into the hands of those trying to destroy the kibbutz as a social form altogether, and lead to his ejection from the kibbutz. On the other hand, staying silent is almost unbearable for Yosef, who is also suspecting his wife for having an affair with the same Reuven Bloch. Nachum, the writer who discourages Yosef from voicing his critiques, simply retreats into his private affairs in order to not confront reality's problems (a retreat into the private sphere that mirrors Mossinsohn's own use of it in the novel).[21]

Thus, Yosef finds himself in a situation for which he cannot imagine a solution, and whose diagnosis seems more like a displaced frustration with his personal life than a convincing recognition of a social problem. Corruption of the kibbutz and state institutions, a theme that runs through all of 1950s literature (which is related to the nostalgic yearnings for a "pure" or uncorrupted past, which we will address below), is therefore presented here as a failed containment strategy—an attempt to represent a social problem that leads to an aporia, or falls flat, or is unconvincing. It is here that we can finally start relating the interpretation to Yizhar's text with which we ended the last chapter. For, this explanatory failure, or failure of containment strategies, is precisely what we encountered in Yizhar—and what was used as a figuration of the crisis of the *halutzic* revolutionary imaginary. Of course, that what fails to be accounted for convincingly in Mossinsohn's novel is the problems of the kibbutz is indicative of the fact that we are faced here with the same figuration of the death of the *halutzic* collective project. We should notice the multiplicity of explanatory schemas invoked in the novel—from that of corruption, to the dissolution of the nuclear family, to a kind of an inarticulable generational imperfection, to the persistent threat of degeneration into weak European Jews—all of these are invoked but always somehow fall flat.[22] This explanatory failure is perhaps expressed most clearly in Yosef repeated claims that "a hidden force, much greater than me or my wife, is making us do all this."[23] It is even made unclear if adultery can be named the source of the Yosef's and Rafael's restlessness. For, contrary to Shaked's elliptical description of the novel, it remains undecided whether any adultery has taken place—the readers are constantly given hints that this is not the case after all, making Rafael's and Yosef's suspicions that their wives are having affairs into yet other explanatory schemas that fail.[24]

It is in this way therefore that interiority is opposed to external narration in the novel: it makes clear that there is a problem in external reality, something that has gone wrong and that for some reason cannot be articulated. Even if interiority does not provide the characters with a convincing diagnosis of the problem—all attempts to contain the problem fail—it does allow for antagonisms and hidden desires to be expressed, ones that are glossed over or silenced in "externality" or objective narrative. It is for this reason that interior monologues in the novel sometimes seem to teach the reader to read the external narrative symptomatically, as in the following passage:

> Humans only want to be their private selves. Only a few lucky ones actually get to be themselves. And those that don't find release in sexual adventures. Those that are courageous, or that are not afraid of public opinion, might still find their way eventually [. . .] And out loud he asked: "So you think that the family as an institution is falling apart in the kibbutz"?[25]

The interior monologue is here used to as if interpret the external conversation as symptomatic—as indicative of some hidden repressed content, whose meaning can only be given in interiority. To teach its readers to read external narration symptomatically, rather than for its direct content, is the goal of many passages of interior monologue. Even seemingly unimportant details ("Rafael sighed. It was a deep, but light, sigh") are decoded to indicate some hidden unresolved problem by the passages of interior monologue that precede or follow them.[26]

Thus subjective interiority transforms external narrative into a realm of the symptomatic, of where problems are somehow both expressed and unacknowledged (or, to use the Althusserian formulation, objective narrative becomes the scene for the appearance of questions for unarticulated questions or problems).[27] It is here that we can finally relate the formal expression of the opposition between individual and society to the text's explicit individualistic ideology. For, if kibbutz society is somehow problematically "stuck," in a way that cannot be named and over which no one seems to be able to exert agency, individuality is a different story altogether. For, one's agency is still effective with regard to more private, immediate desires in Mossinsohn's novel. It is here that the novel elaborates something like a Nietzschean ideology of personal desire and its authentic pursuit—with a clear emphasis on bodily desires and those of power, against any sense of social morality that opposes it, a pursuit that does not require any rational explanations, but is rather celebrated in all of its irrational arbitrariness.

What is important for our purposes is not the ethical condemnation or celebration of this individualist ideology and its opposition to the state, but rather the way that it functions in the novel. For, the structure of the novel's plot revolves precisely around the workings of individualism. The novel can be divided into three parts. In the first part, which takes place in the kibbutz, individuality or interiority simply helps register the flaws in reality, add an overt critical voice where objective narration stays silent, and imagine all manner of immediate wish-fulfillment—as discussed above. In the second part of the novel, Rafael has been arrested by the British with other members of his kibbutz. His presence in the makeshift jail allows for something like a loosening of the kibbutz's grip on his life, or a neutralization of the day-to-day kibbutz-related activities.[28] It is here that individual desire is allowed to develop, in the absence of the structure given to life in the kibbutz. It is here that the textual passages of interiority disappear almost completely—formally expressing the fact that no "escape" from the outside into imagination is necessary here, in the "no place" of jail that allows for clearer reflection. In the third part of the novel, Rafael escapes British captivity—an act through which he tries to regain agency symbolically over his own life, his first authentic pursuit of individual desire—and returns to the kibbutz only to discover how greatly he is (and has been) alienated from it.[29] After Rafael's cold welcome (in the quote above), we discover that the kibbutz does not even recognize his act as an attempt to regain individual agency—kibbutz members see his escape as irresponsible, as disobeying the kibbutz's figures of authority in the jail, and puts him on trial.

It is precisely this non-recognition of his individual agency that, in the ideology of the novel, pushes Rafael to murder Reuven. Even in this case the kibbutz tries to deny agency from Rafael—labeling the killing of Reuven an accident, despite Rafael's almost explicit desire to be recognized as a murderer.[30] Thus, as in the first part, the kibbutz objective reality is one of denial of its problems, according to Mossinsohn's text. The only difference is that in the third part Rafael is much more sharply aware of this "repression," which finally drives him out of the kibbutz.

It is the ending of the novel that reveals what individualism finally allows the novel to imagine, beyond the critique of the kibbutz. For, what is enacted in the ending is a reconciliation of subjective desire and historical agency—one that could not take place before the "awakening" of subjective desire in Rafael. In the kibbutz, according to Rafael, "one could imagine that nothing else exists in the world except the kibbutz,"[31] expressing a certain sense of alienation from "big" historical events—the confrontation with the British, the aftermath of World War II, etc. In contrast, after he leaves the kibbutz, the pursuit of subjective desire—captured in his love affair with the right-wing Atalia—can make possible a regaining of a sense of historical agency. Several levels are here paralleled: a worldwide effort to establish a Jewish state, represented in the newspaper articles that Rafael is reading; the struggle against the British mandate in the city itself, constantly present in the periphery of the events narrated; and Rafael's love affair with Atalia, who is aligned with the right-wing Jewish guerilla organizations. The final scene, in which Rafael resists his British interrogators, is emblematic of this imaginary reconciliation of subjective desire and historical agency—of a state in which one can imagine one's actions as participating in the making of history.[32] It is for this reason that for Rafael the dawning day finally signifies transformation: "a new day, different than all that preceded it, and a new truth," in which he can finally take pride in his subjective agency.[33] Thus, in the kibbutz one's desire has to find outlet in personal sexual adventures, since one is completely alienated from exerting agency over one's life. In contrast, outside the kibbutz, the following of one's subjective desires means simultaneously exerting agency over history—in joining the right-wing guerilla war against the British oppression of Jews in Palestine.

Therefore, in the last instance it is not individual existence or life whose preservation is the goal of the individualistic ideology in Mossinsohn's novel. It is rather a revival of historicity, or the possibility of imagining subjective agency in history—which is unavailable in the kibbutz for unknown reasons in the novel—that is its goal. Individuality in Mossinsohn's novel is therefore not an entity or category that exists independently of collectivity and comes into contradictions with it. Rather, it is clearly an element of the social itself, one that allows for Mossinsohn to imagine a revival of agency over history. It is here that we can return again to the interpretive framework we established in the previous chapter. The reason for which the kibbutz does not provide this sense of historical agency any longer, a sense of historicity which therefore has to be sought elsewhere, is precisely the breakdown of the *halutzic* collective project throughout the 1940s. If the latter, as we discussed, provided a whole series of mediations between subjective action and the making of history, the 40s saw the slow demise of the *halutzic* project and its final absorption into the newly found state. That Mossinsohn's characters cannot account for this loss of historicity in the kibbutz is the result of its repression—through the national narrative that presented the establishment of the state as the success of the *halutzic* project, rather than recognizing that the opposite is true.

In attempting to imagine a reconciliation of subject and history, Mossinsohn's work marks yet another important transformation, this time one that has to do with the social location and function of literature and culture itself. If the writing of the realists of the 1920s and 1930s could be considered something like revolutionary self-representation, or an attempt to imagine the challenges to the transformative *halutzic* project, in Mossinsohn this function is no longer present. Instead, literature becomes the site in which utopian compensation is imagined—a compensation for subjective experience that is no longer related, as in the *halutzic* imaginary, to radically transformative possibilities. We will have more to say on the entry into capitalism which according to Fredric Jameson accompanies this transition—from utopian project to utopian compensation—in the next chapter.[34] It is only after the demise of the collective project that culture takes on this compensatory role, that which makes national ideology, as Hannan Hever puts it in the Israeli context, always act to reconcile contradictions.[35]

The loss of the revolutionary or utopian collective project is registered across Mossinsohn's late-1940s and early-1950s writing—the entirety of which is dismissed by critics. Another brief example is the play *In the Negev Prairies*, considered by Yael Feldman to be simplistic and melodramatic, of only slight interest insofar as it acknowledged the feeling of personal loss and sacrifice—in opposition to the national celebration of heroism—in the 1948 war.[36] For Feldman, the focus of the play is ideological rather than ethical (which is code for saying that the play is of poor aesthetic quality) in that it revolves around the question of authority to command death, or sacrifice, rather than challenging the sacrifice of individual life in the name of the nation altogether. Feldman's analysis relies on the reified, and de-historicized notion of an opposition between individual and collective, whose relevance for understanding Mossinsohn's writing we have questioned above. What is important to emphasize is that what Feldman deems an ideological question actually masks what we have called a failure of historicity. For, in this question lies the tragic kernel of the play—in which a father finds himself sending his own son to his death in battle. It is precisely this strongly tragic tone of the play that brought about its stormy reception, described by Shaked.[37] What we can now say is that it is not merely personal sacrifice, or deciding on the death of one's family members, which makes Mossinsohn's play intolerable (for self-sacrifice, as critics tirelessly repeat, seems to be a "value" shared by almost all *Palmach* generation writers). Rather, what makes the individual deaths of *In the Negev Prairies* difficult to accept is that the affirmation of a collective transformative horizon that used to accompany such deaths in "genre" literature (as we have seen at work in *Barefoot Days* in the previous chapter) drops completely out of sight—revealing an absence of relation between individuals' deaths and the making of history.

The same dialectical tension between individual and collective is true about *The Way of a Man* as well. That an individual's life must end with death and is therefore essentially a tragedy is recognized in the final scene of the novel, in which Rafael keeps thinking about the future ("A new day, different than the one that preceded it"), unable to recognize his imminent death. Yet, since Mossinsohn's novel has by this point reimagined a reconciliation between individual desire and history, the tragedy of the individual is coterminous with the comedy of the collective, to use Kim Stanley Robinson's terms.[38] In other words, the dialectical tension between individual and collective is maintained, but at the price of the reification of collectivity into national ideology—since the collective project now is no longer that revolutionary *halutzic* one that was based on transformative labor, but rather a nationalist one based on masculine bodily prowess and its equivalent national might. Thus, it is in Mossinsohn's literature that the contradictoriness of the *halutzic* project, always kept open for further imaginings of historical movement, turns into a compensatory reconciliation—from utopian project to utopian compensation. It is in this way that the Israeli capitalist national-hegemonic culture would always require a compensatory supplement (since the worker is can never be given agency over her own life under capital's reign), or an imagined reconciliation. What makes Mossinsohn's novel interesting for us today is precisely its desperate attempt to save historicity—an imagined relation between subjective agency and the movement of history—a problem for which we still undoubtedly have no solution, as the concluding chapters of this book will demonstrate.

The *Palmach* is not a Place, or Alienation from History in Shaham's "Always We"

If Mossinsohn's novel registered the failure of the *halutzic* project by attributing to the kibbutz a general failure of historicity, in Nathan Shaham's work the same failure is given a wholly different thematization, as we will see in what follows. Shaham was particularly prolific in the late 1940s and throughout the 1950s, producing numerous short stories, plays, and novels. We will focus on his novella "Always We"—not because the novella is unique among Shaham's works, but because it is the one that Shaked deems one of Shaham's worst works.[39] Again, rather than seeing the novella's meaning as limited to some narrow ideological debate, as Shaked does, we will see that the novella finds a brilliant way to unconsciously thematize the breakdown of the *halutzic* project and the transition into capitalism. If Mossinsohn's "solution" for the problem depended on elaborating a whole ideology of subjective desire and interiority, Shaham's protagonists will find their way back to history through ethics, as we will see. Indeed, rather than simply reflecting some neutral transformation of values, as Rivka Gurfein's positive assessment of the novel suggests,[40] We will see how the ethical becomes for Shaham the realm through which one responds to historical transformation that seems completely divorced from one's agency.

The plot of "Always We" takes place in an unnamed kibbutz toward the end of the 1948 war, after the perceived immediate danger to the existence of the state has already been ostensibly removed. The novella focuses on several soldier characters that belong to the Israel military's forces stationed in the kibbutz. What divides some soldiers from others is their previous belonging to the *Palmach*, a militarized force established in the early '40s, ostensibly to help the British effort in the Second World War. Since the more utopian or transformative valences of the *halutzic* project were disappearing, joining the *Palmach* quickly became a substitute for it since—through its involvement in the Second World War and later in the struggle against the British, it provided a practical way of imagining agency over history, as Mossinsohn's novel demonstrates (that most of the volunteers for it were members of kibbutzes also attests to this "flow" of utopian energies from the revolutionary *halutzic* imaginary to the *Palmach*). The *Palmach* was disbanded in 1948, as the Israeli military was forming. Shaham's choice of presenting the perspective of ex-*Palmach* soldiers in the new national military is arguably the most important feature of the novella. Rather than simply expressing petty political struggles of its time,[41] the perspective of the ex-*Palmach* soldiers functions here as a point of view external to the social order, a kind of "no place"—like that famed "non-placeness" of the sea and its travelers in realist fiction—from which an imagined detached observation of the social itself can take place.[42] This "outsider" effect was generated precisely because the *Palmach*'s dismantling, its absorption into a professional national army, stripped from all the socially transformative aspirations that survived into the *Palmach*. The ex-*Palmach* soldiers in the new national army thus suddenly felt purposeless, as if suddenly serving no historical purpose.

The sudden dislocation from the social order is precisely what makes it possible for Shaham's ex-*Palmach* characters to recognize—just like Mossinsohn's kibbutz members, and Yizhar's soldier—that something is wrong with the new reality being formed, but never be satisfied with any explanation offered up for it: "something is bothering you guys, but you don't know what exactly," as Landau, one of the novel's characters, puts it.[43] This is precisely where we find what we called before the staging of failure of containment strategies, which we will specify in what follows. What is important for us in this stage is simply to emphasize the suddenness with which Shaham's characters find themselves in a social "no-place," whose narrative advantages—the detached construction of abstract explanations—become a kind of compensation for social alienation that made the perspective possible in the first place.

It is here that we can address Shaham's characters' hyper-intellectualism or almost obsessive self-reflection, often viewed negatively by the novella's early critics, such as Baruch Kurtzweil.[44] What is missed is that rather than some aesthetic flaw, this is rather precisely the point—the rise of subjective interiority as a response external reality that no longer makes sense makes its appearance in Shaham's writing in an even more pronounced manner than it did in Mossinsohn's novel. The second story of the collection *Hay and Lead*, for example, is made up of its protagonist's thoughts almost entirely, having the unimportant plot events recede completely into the background.[45] Again, this magnification of subjectivity (which we will address more fully in the next chapter), should signal to us that the containment strategies evoked by the characters are not themselves the point, but rather the intractable problem in reality that gives rise to them in the first place. In other words, rather than reading them as ideologically dogmatic explanations, as Kurtzweil does, their appearance is precisely symptomatic again—the fact that they are uncalled for, that they are so numerous and self-contradictory—should signal to us that their staging is the important point rather than their ideological content.

Provided that we keep in mind their status as symptoms, we can now finally address some of the more common explanations or containment strategies evoked by the characters. These are important not only because of their "contextual" weight—the fact that they were part of the political discourse of the time—but also because they include some of the critical attempts to understand the novella and 1950s literature generally. For example, Netiva Ben Yehuda's and Shaked's claim that the sense of disillusionment was a result of the corruption of the state apparatus, is one of the common ways through which the characters try to capture what is wrong. The ex-*Palmach* characters often say in the novel that what is wrong with the new military is that "those for whom ethics isn't exactly their strong suit easily made their way into officers' ranks, due to the fast growth of the military [. . .] they were given through administrative means the respect and trust that they could not gain by the power of their personality."[46] That self-serving opportunism is at the root of the problem, corrupting what has so far been an ethically pure collective project serves here to distinguish the ex-*Palmach* officers from other ones, or effective commanders from non-effective ones. But here we have almost imperceptibly moved to another field of containment, as it were—a utilitarian discourse that tries to understand the current transformation through the effectiveness of the new military. One example is Landau's utilitarian approach, one which he uses against the ex-*Palmach* group:

> Honestly, I'm sick and tired of all this talk about the *Palmach* and its spirit, and all that monkey business. [. . .] so some talented guys were there? All right. They'll leave the military? Others will replace them. These will have better training, they'll study abroad, they'll practice more comprehensive maneuvers [. . .] in short, they'll learn to command a military, and not just a bunch of training platoons that provide labor for kibbutzes that poorly planned their economy [. . .] Just stop it with all that howling of yours—killing the spirit? Are you the spirit?[47]

Landau's utilitarian approach is here meant to de-mystify talk about some ineffable "spirit" of the *Palmach*, trying to reduce the transformation to one that is only about the effectiveness and professionalism of the military.

However, just as talk about corruption produced slippage into a utilitarian field of meaning, Landau's words produce slippages as well. One of these has a strong sociological class-analysis valence—seeing the *Palmach* as nothing but a thinly veiled source of labor, something needed only to "solve the seasonal work problems in the unplanned economy of some kibbutzes,"[48] as Landau puts it elsewhere. But if for Landau this is an argument against the talk of the *Palmach* spirit, this valence is used by others to diagnose the problems of the new military in terms of an emerging class difference. Thus, for example, one of the soldiers, Shlomi, says that "the oh-so-good Israeli youth is destined to form a class-conscious bourgeoisie, very much willing to give up the freedom of the working class for its own security. You will be shocked when you realize how quickly the 'good guys' will become corrupted [. . .] it will be a class confident in its superiority."[49] This more direct invocation of class is accompanied by a commodification of political goals and the labor needed to achieve them, or a sense that "the government will have to prioritize the duties that it values [. . .] through that old measure, *money*. Higher wages for holier duties. So that things will get confused and whoever is richest will also be the most loyal patriot."[50] And, of course, Shlomi is not alone—and emerging class antagonism is invoked multiple times to try to contain the sense of loss, or the suspicion that something in reality itself is wrong, rather than a subjective problem with this or that particular person or incident.

This "class analysis" seems in its turn to slip back into talk about corruption, as in Shlomi's words above, but also to yet another field of meaning, that of the "spirit" of the *Palmach*, dominated by a dichotomy of culture and barbarism (whose successful reconciliation only exists in the *Palmach*'s spirit, according to some). Ram's character is an important figure in this regard. He more-or-less consciously tries to embody some kind of reconciliation of the of the two—foregoing as assignment as an officer and participating in the war while at the same time being a university student, seeing himself as an "ideal of a Hebrew fighter," that aims to inspire by setting an example.[51] The letters he writes from the frontline to his professor, in which he reports, excitedly, about his new discoveries about the flora and fauna of Palestine, while fulfilling his duty as a soldier, attest precisely to this attempt at reconciliation.[52] Yet, we quickly learn that Ram's attempt is received with contempt. As Avi, one of Ram's friends puts it, "you're funny [. . .] you're very fortunate that no one has figured out what kind of comedy you're acting."[53] Important here is to notice that Ram tries to impossibly weld together what has already been torn asunder by history—the *halutzic* imaginary, that we described in the last chapter, in which knowledge of the landscape was part of transformative labor's remaking of human and nature alike. By the late 1940s, both the study of landscape and the bodily prowess were abstracted—in the sense of their removal from their original context—and made into autonomous "professional" expertise: the scientific endeavors of the university professor and those of the soldier, under reifying influence of capitalism, which Georg Lukács described extensively.[54] It is precisely in this way that Ram's impossible reconciliation of the two "realms" is an unsatisfying anachronism, one that only inspires cynicism. We will address the true content of Ram's nostalgic imitation and the longing that underscore it in what follows.

The cynicism with which Ram's reconciliation is received leads to yet another slippage into a different realm of meaning, and toward the last containment strategy that we will discuss. For Ram's attempt to reproduce this past ideal is always suspected of being self-serving in some way, echoing the more ethical accounts, or those of corruption, that we discussed earlier. But here we must again turn this perspective on its head. For, in the case of Eliyahu, the ex-*Palmach* commander of the military forces in the kibbutz, retiring from public activity toward private life is revealed to be a defensive retreat into the private sphere from a public one that he can no longer affect in any clear way. Eliyahu's long monologue toward the end of the novella is a long apologetic explanation of his decision to retire from the military after the war, choosing to focus instead on his family matters and those of his kibbutz. Eliyahu emphasizes his non-agency in the larger social developments again and again:

> [. . .] Knowing our patriotism, they knew that to make sure we don't lose the war, we will obey any order that goes against our convictions. But after the war I will not be able to stay in the military. Party squabbles will become personal conflicts. And I don't have the energy for that. I can fight against the enemy, but not against yesterday's friends. A workers' party whose core is common memories rather than ideology, will become a variation on a bourgeois theme, one that possesses plenty of good will but little freedom to act [. . .] I'm too old to get into sordid fights with contemptible people. There's no point in it.[55]

Eliyahu's retreat into the private sphere is thus yet another way of containing or explaining social problems, one which, again, constantly enacts slippages into other fields of meaning.

Thus, the constant slippages between different containment strategies dizzyingly presents what seems initially as selfish or evil as simply one bad response to a given situation among other bad ones. In other words, no individual response to the situation seems satisfactory as the novella draws to a close; each offering neither a convincing account of the transformation, nor agency over it that is more than passively letting the new reality set in. If ethics is abstractly defined as legislating what should be considered an appropriate individual course of action in a given situation, Shaham's novella can be said to stage an utter collapse of the ethical (rather than prescribing an ethical course of action, as Gurfein argues),[56] since no individual response effectively remedies the situation. (also echoed here is seeing the subjective realm in these 1950s works as making possible some kind of new interpretation of an objective reality that seems unable to offer its own diagnosis, which we discussed in the case of Mossinsohn above). What is important for our purposes is that rather than simply articulating a political position within its immediate context, as Shaked argues (context always being a poor replacement for history), the novella is structured around a series of slippages between different positions, none of which are deemed satisfying or the "correct" party line. It is in this way that Shaham's novella is very similar to Yizhar's *Khirbet Khizeh*, which as we have seen is also dominated by the staging of a failure of containment strategies—the ethical being simply one of these, rather than some overriding factor.

And it is precisely in this manner that Shaham's novella does "perceive the social processes [. . .] and the historical dynamic within which his protagonists act," as opposed to Shaked's claims.[57] For, Shaham's formal staging of unsatisfactory solutions articulates some kind of search for historicity, or articulates the latter's loss. To this more formal articulation of loss we can now add its expression in the content of the novella—the omnipresent nostalgia for the *halutzic* past expressed by many of the characters. That "things aren't like they used to be" or the longing for the volunteering "spirit" that seems all but replaced with self-interest—or the present corruption of some pure past—is a sentiment expressed by many of the ex-*Palmach* characters in the novella.[58] We can now finally assert that the true lost object of these longing, the cause of the constant slippage from one containment strategy to another, is the repressed breakdown of the *halutzic* collective project. The loss of the socially transformative project, and its substitution with state-run capitalism is precisely what causes the secularization of work which seems to be at the center of this nostalgia—from its first appearance in Yizhar's story "Ephraim Returns to the Alfalfa" (first published in 1938), articulated very strongly in Shaham's story collection *The Gods are Lazy* all the way to

Landau's character and others in his "Always We."⁵⁹ Labor simply ceases to constitute the imaginary center of a project whose purpose is revolutionary, and becomes monotonous wage-labor under capitalism.⁶⁰

The important point for us is to emphasize that the nostalgia of the *Palmach* generation writing is for us not simply some kind of subjective error (an idealization of the past, or the remainder of a past naïveté's clashing with a harsh reality, as Shaked and Arbell argue). Rather, its moment of truth is in its stubborn insistence that something in objective reality itself has been lost, even as it misrecognizes this object, as Walter Benjamin argues in a completely different context. The inability to capture the true lost object—in our case the revolutionary project—is expressed precisely in the constant slippage between the different explanations of the loss that as we have seen is constantly enacted in the novella—a rejection of all explanations as unsatisfactory that charges the nostalgic longings with strong irrationality. It is important to note that this failure to capture the lost object is not any particular fault of Shaham's novella—not one which could have been avoided. Rather, we should emphasize that this failure is itself a result of the same social transformation that it fails to capture—the absorption of the *halutzic* settlements into a bigger capitalist economy. That the representational forms associated with the previous social form go into crisis as they are no longer able to map the social—the explanatory failures in Shaham being only one expression of this crisis—should be of no surprise. Thus, the clear thematization of a failure of containment in "Always Us" constitutes an unconsciously capturing of the historical dynamic of its time, one that presents it as a problem that is still alive and interesting for us today—how to imagine a return to the lost revolutionary collective project.

What our reading of "Always We" is still missing is a component whose presence we have emphasized in the case of Mossinsohn's novel and which alerted us to a transformation in the social function of literature itself, namely, the emergence of the literary function of utopian compensation. The '20s and '30s "genre" literature, as we argued in the first chapter, was constantly busy mapping the challenges to collective transformation. In the literature of the '50s, on the other hand, an imaginary compensation for the non-transformative existence under capitalism is made necessary. If in Mossinsohn's novel that compensatory moment was the imaginary reconciliation between subjective agency and historical change, it is completely of a different nature in Shaham's novella. Here, it is precisely the tragic accident that ends the novella—the death of the soldiers that go on the relatively safe reconnaissance mission—that constitutes this compensatory moment.⁶¹

It is that accident that stands as the most irrational figure for the nostalgic refusal to accept any of the explanations or containment strategies for the flaws in reality offered up by its immediate political context. The explosion thus stands in for a Freudian death-drive, an imagined destruction of the emerging capitalist reality—a strong moment of unconscious wish-fulfillment, the more general utopian valences of which are typically explored in genres such as the post-apocalypse as Evan Williams notes, which are completely foreign to Shaham's writing.[62]

We have therefore shown how the 1950s writing of both Mossinsohn and Shaham is to be understood historically as responding to the breakdown of the *halutzic* project and, as a result, of the realist writing that constituted part of that project. In the next chapter we will expand further our survey of '50s literature toward those authors who are less identified with the *Palmach* and the experience of the 1948 war—Hanoch Bartov and Yehudit Hendel—showing how their writing as well attempts to imagine a solution to what should be seen as a triumph of capitalism over the revolutionary Zionist project. Before we leave behind the writing of Shaham and Mossinsohn, we should note that their work, as well as that of Yizhar, inaugurates a genre that is unique to Israeli literature, one for whom the soldier is a clear figure for the nation. It is important here to see the soldier as a much more suitable figurative device for subjectivity under capitalism than the *halut* ever was. The latter was never very effective in taking on the meaning valences of urban existence; another problem is the fact that the *halutz* is tied down to a small piece of land—making it difficult for him to become a figure for a subject of history that has to have condensed in itself different types, personalities, or geographical areas. The soldier, on the other hand, is much more useful for representing wage-laborers who are not tied to a specific place (one of whose conditions of existence is the "freedom" from the means of production, as Marx famously said, land being one basic component of these means). The soldier thus becomes a much more convenient representational vehicle for the collective subject's figure, and therefore takes over the role of figuring the collective, precisely at the point in which the anti-capitalist potentialities of this collectivity are foreclosed.

We should emphasize two things in anticipation of our discussion of more recent works in the genre that revolves around the figure of the soldier. First, that the genre should be distinguished from war literature—the events of war are marginal or even absent from the more recent novels. Even Shaham's "Always We," which is ostensibly taking place at the end of the 1948 war, features the events of the actual war very marginally. The uniqueness of the genre resides precisely in this distinction from war novels. The second point has to do with how we think about the first. That the genre of soldiers' experience is clearly allegorical should not lead us toward a reified postmodern rejection of allegories—as solely expressing some pre-known ideological content. Rather, as we have seen in this chapter, we should emphasize Benjamin's view of allegories, which allegory's postmodern critics always missed: that living allegories (as opposed to reified older ones) never simply reiterate what is already known or never simply illustrate a point; rather, they constitute a preconceptual working-through of a narrative for which we do not yet have a concept or a name, and which only in hindsight will seem like superfluous illustrations of familiar narratives or concepts, as Louis Marin puts it in the context of the "allegorizing" process of utopian novels.[63] It is therefore only in hindsight that allegories seem to simply tell us what we already know. As is the case with the writing of Shaham and Mossinsohn, each instance of the genre addresses the deepest representational and social problems of its time, always trying to come up with new solutions to what hurts, which is history itself.

3

Then as Farce: Naturalism and Disavowed Failure

1950s Hebrew Novels by Hanoch Bartov and Yehudit Hendel

The breakdown of the *halutzic* collective project and its mediation into the literary realm has provided for us an interpretive framework though which we were able to dialecticize our understanding not only of "genre" realist literature, but also of the war literature of the late 1940s and early 1950s. As we argued in the last chapter, the emergence of the literary soldier as a figure that bears the marks of collective transformation should be seen as both the most complete articulation of its "realist" predecessors, and as the same time as something already altogether different—as marking the birth of a new genre, one which comes to take the place of the realist-utopian "genre" writing, and on which we will have much more to say in the following chapters. What this chapter aims to do is to broaden the scope of our survey of '50s literature beyond the realm of representations of the 1948 war itself, into social spaces more familiar to readers of realism, in Hanoch Bartov's *Each has Six Wings* and Yehudit Hendel's the *Street of Steps*.[1] The historical work of the previous chapter now makes it possible for us to move faster through the prevailing "historical" evaluation of these works. We will use our revised historical narrative to make problematic, again, the assessment of both novels in terms of their adherence to the so-called "Zionist metanarrative."[2] As we have argued in the previous chapters, earlier realism had very little to do with simply affirming some nationalist cause. Thus, if the work of Bartov and Hendel is different from those earlier realisms—displaying greater affinity with Shamir's *He Walked Through the Fields* or

Megged's *Sea Winds* than with realist literature from the '20s and '30s—we will have to construct some alternative explanation for this difference, which we can no longer characterize in terms of greater attention to individuality and subjectivity and an abandonment of national ideology.[3]

How, then, are these two novels different from their realist predecessors? Our overarching critical theme of narrative failure will become crucial in trying to answer this question. For our argument will be divided into three general parts. The first two will highlight how our two novels take failure—particularly the failure or dissolution of older realism—as their subject matter. As we will see, not only do these two novels express in this way the dissolution of the *halutzic* collective transformative project; they also try to imagine resolution to the contradictions and antagonisms that constitute their explicit content. The third part of this chapter will place the disintegration of realism in Israeli 1950s literature in a wider theoretical context, arguing that these '50s works should be seen as naturalist rather than realist. The dissolution of realism in both novels will be used here to tie them to the Marxist view of naturalism: the erosion of an ability to narrate a contradictory totality expressing capitalism's destruction of smaller social totalities and the rise of an increasingly multinational capitalism. As we will see, Hebrew '50s literature will allow us to reaffirm in a wholly new and unexpected way this Marxist view of naturalism.

Each has Six Wings and the National *Deus ex Machina*

Our discussion of Bartov's novel will be the shorter of the two, mostly since it is designed to demonstrate a very clear instance of narrative failure, which has generally elided commentators. As Dan Laor argues, the novel should be seen in the context of the massive immigration into Israel after the 1948 war and the national literary effort to document the efforts to integrate them into Israeli society.[4] This literary agenda is strongly reflected in the reception of Bartov's novel: established critics such as Ukhmani and Gurfein praising Bartov's tackling of the burning social issues of the time.[5] Yet, Laor and others frame their reading in terms that we have already problematized. According to Laor, we should see Bartov as partaking in the "national and Zionist pathos" in representing the massive immigration's social integration as a national success story—a deplorable authorial choice, in Laor's eyes, that is nothing but a convenient national illusion or private wish-fulfillment.[6] This framework for reading the novel—shared by all contemporary critics, even in cases where they choose to question the novel's commitment to the national literary cause[7]—all contrast an adherence the literary adherence to national ideology to the more anti-ideological modernist literature. We have already argued in the first chapter that reading 1950s Israeli literature through this dichotomy represses the historical break around which much of that literature revolved.

In contrast, we will here affirm that Bartov's novel indeed performs an imaginary reconciliation of contradictions in the name of the nation. Yet, this reconciliation will not constitute for us the end-point of the interpretive effort, or some ethical sin. Rather, as we will see, the novel's moment of ideological reconciliation, when read historically, is a moment of narrative failure. This failure will then be understood as the equivalent of similar moments in the work of Yizhar, Mossinsohn, Shaham, and Hendel—as at once expressing the breakdown of the *halutzic* collective project, and trying to imagine its resolution.

The main figure for the newly arrived immigrants in the novel is the family of Noah and Gitl Klinger, who is assigned housing in a Jerusalem neighborhood that was occupied in the war and whose houses stand empty, its Palestinian inhabitants now absent—deported to behind enemy lines. The realist core of the novel is composed of the difficulties the family encounters in trying to make a life for themselves in the neighborhood. It is important to note that the scale of the problems they encounter expands as the novel progresses. Early in the novel, the relationships of the family itself and their immediate living spaces that poses problems: the crucial challenges have to do with connecting the family's new house to running water and generally making it inhabitable, and with opening a functional shoe-repair shop.[8] All of this then leads to making new acquaintances in the neighborhood, and to a realignment of the relationships between the members of the family.[9] As the novel progresses, the scale of problem-solving is enlarged: Noah Klinger finds himself becoming the center of life in the neighborhood, acting as an arbiter in conflicts between the different newly arrived immigrants, and helping newcomers with their housing and income problems.[10] Toward the end of the novel, the Klingers' agency reaches beyond the scale of the neighborhood—toward the municipal center itself. We will return to this final enlargement of scale later in our discussion. Throughout, the tendency toward resolving contradictions or conflicts emphasizes the coming-together of people of different ethnic backgrounds (some are Mizrachis and others Ashkenazis), and the unification of older residents and "Sabras" (those born in Palestine) with the newly arrived immigrants. The representative of the "Sabras" in the novel is Rakefet, for whom becoming something like an organic intellectual of the neighborhood provides a way out of a personal crisis she experienced after her boyfriend's death in the 1948 war.[11] It is here, therefore, that the figurative effort of the national allegory, and its dynamic of reconciling a differentiated population into a collective, is plainly visible.

Contrasting *Each has Six Wings* with its realist predecessors will make it possible for us to see again the newness of Bartov's novel, or what made it interesting for its contemporaries. The need to adapt "genre" writing to an urban setting is Bartov's biggest challenge—since urban spaces always tended to be "genre" writing's threatening Other, a kind of chaotic Lacanian Real, charged with ominous, utopian allure. As others comment, Bartov falls back on representations of Jewish eastern-European *shtetls* or small towns.[12] We will briefly touch on the significance of this choice in what follows. At the moment what is important for our purposes is to notice the contradiction Bartov is facing in looking to adapt the challenges faced by characters in the rural collectivist settlement to urban setting.[13] As Gertz observes, the traces of this adaptation are clear in the novel. For example, the first challenge faced by the Klingers—connecting the house to running water—is an adaptation of the *halutzic* digging of a well in the rural settlement, often portrayed as one of the first acts in establishing a settlement.[14]

Yet this adaptation presents a bigger challenge as the plot progresses. For, as we have seen in the previous chapter, what the realist plot of the 1920s and 1930s made possible is a sense of collective self-determination, or a sense of mapping individual agency onto a larger collective purpose. It is for this reason that at the start of the novel we are frequently reminded of the fact that Noah Klinger is "a man of action" who "as he walks, he takes note of those things that need to be addressed, fixed, or changed" in the neighborhood at large.[15] We should however emphasize that the urban setting in its capitalist form presents a major challenge to this representational goal. For, a subject that can plausibly carry with it the potentialities of the *halutz* is not readily available. On the one hand, urban wage laborers, who do have a sense of collectivity, cannot entertain even a semblance of the autonomy and self-governing logic of the rural, class-neutralizing, *halutz*—since their fates are largely determined by capital. On the other hand, the urban bourgeoisie, which does enjoy a sense of autonomy and self-determination (however reified this sense might be),[16] is excluded from any sense of cooperative collectivity that concretely produces its life, as opposed to the *halutzic* rural settlers.

It is here that the petit-bourgeois characters—the shoemakers, bakers, painters, and barbers—that populate Bartov's novel present themselves as an effective representational solution. It is a class that in its everyday life can entertain—however minimally—a sense of autonomy and self-determination (the one generated by the reified freedom that accompanies being one's own boss and other ideological tropes). At the same time, since the poor immigrants are not really yet an established petit-bourgeoisie but an emerging one, common infrastructural needs and other preconditions for their existence still have to be negotiated collectively. It is for this reason that the novel stresses the Klinger's social role in resolving conflicts—through it the collective dimension of the emerging petit-bourgeois life remains constantly visible. Only an emerging petit-bourgeoisie makes possible, therefore, a unification of collectivity and self-determination in the urban setting, one that can, at least to a certain degree, echo the rural *halutz*. In the process, of course, the revolutionary kernel of the *halutzic* project drops out of sight.

The tendency toward reconciling contradictions can here shed light on the contours of something like narrative failure. As Gertz notes, the threats to the emerging order, the contradictions that manifest themselves and that have to be reconciled seem not very threatening or menacing.[17] It is here that we can recall Bartov's reliance on the realist representation of the eastern-Europe Jewish town, particularly those of Mendele or Shalom-Aleichem. For it is in their work that highlights something like an imperfect realization of bourgeois social roles, particularly gendered ones, in the Jewish towns. Men are not good providers for the household, but are many times just lazy and weak; and women's femininity is as much disrupted as men's masculinity—they are many times strong physically, and shrewd in dealing with affairs outside the household. In a similar fashion, Gitl's femininity is a disrupted one in *Each has Six Wings*, her temper and demeanor many times seeming non-feminine. Early on in the novel, for example, her motherly instincts are questioned when the reader is informed that "pedagogical principles were not exactly her strong suit."[18] Later, after Gitl decides to take on some work outside the household—cooking and doing laundry for others—her husband Noah becomes upset over the disruption of the gendered division of labor. Against his complaints, "Gitl argued that not of his hand she lives, and that she'll do whatever she pleases. Not a slave she is to him, and if she'll only will it she'll cook and do others' laundry. And also: he should not put on the airs of a prince, when her home is too poor to even keep them alive."[19] Hints of Gitl's non-feminine appearance are also everywhere in the novel.[20]

What is important for our purposes is to notice that Gitl's disrupted femininity does not pose a threat to the (capitalist) social order in the novel in any way. Rather, Bartov adopts a half-humorous attitude toward these "imperfections," again following Shalom-Aleichem's and Mendele's work.[21] If in Mossinsohn's *Grey as Sack* or Shamir's *He Walked Through the Fields*, femininity and its reworking posed a threat to the ideological reification that associated masculinity with the nation, Bartov's novel on the other hand simply diffuses these threatening valences.[22] Thus, the social antagonisms staged in the novel are somewhat eroded, becoming not as socially pertinent as they used to be, as a result of the older literary form that Bartov uses. This erosion of contradictoriness—highlighted by the staggering number of reconciliatory moments in the novel—is precisely a sign of narrative failure, or of the fact that something has been missed in this representation: the novel as it tries to compensate for the relative emptiness or reified status of each contradiction by increasing the frequency of reconciliatory moments.

However, where narrative failure makes its most decisive appearance is in the novel's *dénouement*. After a newly arrived immigrant couple is denied the license to open a bakery in the neighborhood, the residents decide to protest the decision.[23] This is the moment of final enlargement of scale, and the final test of the neighborhood's ability to function as a collective—which as we have argued is the urban parallel, in the novel's imagination, of the rural collectivist settlement. The final success here—that the license is finally obtained and the immigrant couple starts a family—is the most important moment of national-ideological reconciliation, as other critics argue.[24] Yet what critics seem not to notice is that it is actually not clear at all that the demonstration had any effect on the decision to grant the license. Rather, it was the result of a political power-struggle taking place behind the scenes of realist representation: a journalist who is not a resident of the neighborhood had threatened to blame a politician for the protest if the latter would not use his influence to grant the license.[25] Thus, it remains unclear of the demonstration itself—which is the figurative embodiment of the neighborhood's collective will—had any affect beyond the merely theatrical expression of that will. The journalist's intervention here functions as a classic *Deus ex Machina*—sweeping in and providing narrative resolution even though it was never part of the initial balance of forces.

Thus, narration fails in *Each has Six Wings* at the moment of ideological reconciliation: reconciling the neighborhood to its "outside" (municipal and national institutions, and the intelligentsia as figured by the journalist) comes at the cost of not being able to determine if the neighborhood's autonomous will, their molding of their own life, had really prevailed. We must distinguish this narrative failure from the open-ended contradictoriness of the ending of the realist novels of the '20s and '30s that we explored in the first chapter. The latter had no qualms about representing the *failure* of its protagonists to transform their lives—as was the case in *Barefoot Days*—as long as the struggle for transformation was kept alive. In contrast, Bartov's novel does not present failure or success exactly, since the reader simply cannot tell whether its protagonists succeeded or failed. And this explanatory failure is not a chance one, but a necessary formal component of the novel: only in this way the agency of the neighborhood can be affirmed—obeying its parallel to the rural collective—while at the same time staging the neighborhood's reconciliation to the nation. It is in this way that the moment of decisive ideological reconciliation of contradiction is at the same time a moment of narrative failure.

This moment in Bartov's 1950s novel should be of no surprise to us by now. As I argued above, these moments that appear across '50s Israeli literature should be read as cultural symptoms of the repressed failure of the utopian Zionist collective project. What is different in the case of each writer or novel is the way they imagine the resolution of the contradiction through which this repressed rupture is thematized: if in Mossinsohn's work, the contradictions are resolved through a new ideology of masculinity; and if in Shaham's it was morality that is evoked to lay narrative antagonisms to rest. Bartov chooses a different route: a burgeoning petit-bourgeois sense of entrepreneurship and camaraderie. We will now turn to what is surely the grandest summing-up of all possible stagings of narrative failure, that of Yehudit Hendel 1950s novel, the *Street of Steps*.

The Political Secret of Nostalgia in Hendel's *Street of Steps*

> What were the new things? Empty Dreams. Objects, merely objects. The shaky barracks, there in Galilee, were filled with the sense of time. But what was there in those square white houses that Gavriel was building? Time lost its meaning there.[26]

It is in Yehudit Hendel's masterful *Street of Steps* that the erosion of previous realisms or the notorious "genre" writing receives its fullest articulation. As before, our argument here will hinge in the possibility of destabilizing not only the localized interpretation of the work, but also on seeing its new reading as inextricable from a completely new understanding of the historical reality that produced it. It is Dan Miron's reading of the novel that we can take here as the most canonical one, or as a reading that serves as an interpretive key that is later taken up and developed by other critics.[27] Miron reads the novel as taking up the realist literary norms of its time in order to subvert them, resisting a process of national meaning-making associated with the realist tradition.[28] This subversion, according to Miron, is a result of Hendel's own artistic preferences, which conveniently enough coincide with what can be only described as Miron's own literary ideology. The latter emerges when the distinction between Miron's voice and what the novel's narrator believes is blurred, such as in the following passage: "In Hendel's work, it is [one character's] implied conception of reality that is dominant in terms of the truth it contains. This is a truth according to which life is a collage of moments, situations, events, and pauses, in which no single piece is more important than any other one [. . .] this is the more important truth in Hendel's conception of reality."[29] Thus, if realist or "genre" writes create hierarchies between characters, meanings, and moments in the service of national ideology, Hendel reveals these to be mere illusions, according to Miron, who seems to share the view that he ascribes to Hendel's novel.

Virtually all recent writing on *Street of Steps* follows Miron's lead in seeing Hendel as knowingly subverting the realist literature of her time and its ideological mission, paving the way to the prose of the 1960s (which is seen as far less ideologically driven than its 1950s predecessor). This consensus is echoed in, for example, Lily Ratok's claim that "as opposed to many writers of her generation, the majority of whom were committed to giving form to the 'Zionist metanarrative' [. . .], Hendel represented to figures who were marginalized from hegemonic Israeli discourse."[30] To see Hendel as writing against a Zionist myth or illusion—this ideological subversion registered in both the form (anti-realist modernism) and content (representing marginal figures) of her writing—seems to be the starting point of any discussion of the novel.[31] In all of these readings, the "Zionist metanarrative"—an expression coined by Gershon Shaked, as I mentioned in the previous chapter—is seen as an illusion or useful lie, covering up an existentialist abyss that Miron takes to be an eternal truth of human existence—an armchair existentialism, one that has lost any remnants of shock-value and has completely been absorbed into hegemonic discourse, by the time Miron writes these lines.

What our reading will do, in contrast, is to insist that *Street of Steps*'s expression of alienation from the nation is deeply historical, rather than expressing the author's voluntary rejection of national ideology in the name of some eternal existentialist truth (a position which is obviously no less ideological than that against which it sets itself). To return to the argument of the previous chapters, we will see how the explosion of realism in Hendel's novel, perhaps the fullest articulation of this explosion in all 1950s Israeli literature, is an expression of the failure of a Zionist utopian collective project that falls apart in the 1940s, as argued in the first chapter.

The plot of Hendel's novel takes place in the years following the 1948 war. Avram, a young Mizrachi man from one of Haifa's poorer neighborhoods, becomes romantically involved with a young Ashkenazi woman, Erella, of the emerging national bourgeoisie. The social tensions typical to a love affair that straddles ethnic and class boundaries were a common subject matter in the literature of the period. Yigal Mossinsohn's popular play *Kazablan* was also centered around an Ashkenazi-Mizrachi love affair, and novels by Moshe Shamir and others (including *Each has Six Wings*) also featured lovers whose pairing defied social divides, their attempt almost always leading to a tragic end—one shared by Avram and Erella.[32]

If in *Each has Six Wings* used relatively few devices to express the falling apart of its realist predecessors—the explanatory failure highlighted at the novel's *dénouement* and the pastichization of conflicts common to "genre" writing—Hendel's novel offers us an entire arsenal of dissolutions, aporias, and other forms of failure, as we will see. Our reading of the novel will be divided into three main parts: first, we will address the purely formal ways through which *Street of Steps* marks its distance from its realist contemporaries. We will then discuss the novel's treatment of temporality, which will allow us to move from the discussion of the novel's form to the treatment of its content. Finally, by addressing the novel's content, it will become possible for us to reconnect it to its historical context and to a larger historical transition.

One of the novel's more conspicuous formal devices is that of fragmentation, or, to put it in more temporal terms, its tendency toward fragmenting the more properly realist narratives. This formal feature is perhaps clearest at the novel's second part, "Avram" which is composed of fragments of moments from Avram's life, ordered chronologically.[33] Some of the fragments narrate what seem to be significant events, while others are mostly detailed descriptions of the common or the habitual, of no particular value except in showing the reader what the experiences of poverty or war are like; some are narrated by a third-person narrator, while some are clearly narrated from Avram's perspective and consciousness or from that of another character. The earlier sections in this part are the ones in which fragmentation is most strongly emphasized, having the effect of turning events into almost tangible objects:

> The delusions of poverty-stricken mothers. The hopes hanging like transparent veils on windows and doorways, and turning into daydreams. The muttering of mothers, during anguish-filled nights, in dark corners of the house, worrying about the endless days, in poverty.
> "Make him strong, God."
> "When you grow up you'll do something good, my son. You'll amount to something."[34]

It is important to notice that Hendel's extensive usage of fragments in this chapter is not completely novel, but a radicalization of the same tendency in novels by Hendel's realist contemporaries. Moshe Shamir's *He Walked Through the Fields*—probably the paradigmatic realist novel of the period—makes use of the same formal device to portray past moments.[35] Yet, what in Shamir's and Megged's work is still merely a secondary device, subservient to a linear realist plot, turns in Hendel's novel into a primary formal characteristic. The succession of fragments thus becomes a kind of literary montage which precludes precisely realist narration, instead imbuing the events with a familiarity that as if makes narration unnecessary. Nowhere else in the novel does Miron's assertion of the explosion of old representational hierarchies, the making of all moments of equal value, become clearer than here.[36] What is important to emphasize is not simply the use of more "modernist" literary device of fragmentation, but that this tendency is precisely a development that emerges out of the older realisms themselves, who we tend to see as entirely alien to it.

Not only a tendency toward fragmentation distinguishes Hendel's novel from her realist predecessors and contemporaries. Although we will not be able to discuss these at any length here, one could argue for the existence of a naturalist Hendel, based on her extensive usage of detailed descriptions throughout the novel, but most conspicuously at the beginning of chapters. We will return to the characterization of Hendel—and of most Israeli literature of the 1950s—as naturalist in the last part of this chapter. To Hendel the naturalist one must add Hendel the modernist, clearly implied in highlighting her works' affinity to Agnon's or to that of the "anti-genre" writers.[37] The tendency toward fragmentation is here joined by Hendel's extensive usage of stream-of-consciousness, and free indirect discourse.[38] Even though we will not focus on these latter formal features here, it should be briefly noted that these, just as in the case of fragmentation, should be seen as dormant possibilities existing within realist narration, which then turn hegemonic in *Street of Steps*. The naturalist Hendel and the modernist both betray, as Lukács has argued in a completely different context,[39] the tendency toward a greater abstraction of individuals from their social world—an argument to which we will return later.

It is on the novel's treatment of temporality that our reading here now hinges. For one of the great achievements of *Street of Steps* is the figuration it gives to the dissolution of a temporal imaginary—the ability to imagine self-identity over time[40]—that comes about with the disintegration of earlier Hebrew realisms. Fragmentation itself can now be seen as a new light—as a formal figuration of the disintegration of former realism's temporality. This fragmentation (or feeling of time out of joint) is not only highlighted in the second chapter discussed above, but also, for example, in Ovadia's thoughts,[41] which highlights the unmooring or abstraction of certain moments from a temporal sequence. But beyond the tendency toward formal dissolution of time, Hendel's novel incorporates in its content the feeling of temporal dissolution. The first example of this sense of time's dissolution appears in the quotation with which we opened this section, in which Erella's grandfather complains about the disappearance of a sense of time that used to exist in the "shaky barracks, there in the Galilee."[42] This is a reference to his *halutzic* past, contrasting the temporal imaginary once made available by the utopian collective project to the timelessness of his present. But this sense is clear in other characters' thoughts too. Avram's fragmented memories are but one example of this dissolution of time. For one of Avram's neighbors, Malka, time stands still—every day is the four-year anniversary of her son's death. As Ovadia—Ram's uncle—puts it, "Nothing makes a difference [. . .] There's summer, there's winter, there's morning, there's evening—it's all the same to her."[43] Or, for Avram's brother Nissim change or transformation become completely incomprehensible, as he is contemplating the possibility that Avram will leave their house:

> It was coming. What is expected sometimes comes and sometimes it doesn't come. What is expected can suddenly start a pounding in your head, whether it comes or not [. . .] The expected and the unexpected. The illusions. The passing time. And, now, Avram was about to leave home, the street, and him.[44]

Nissim's tendency to see the difference between movement and sameness as illusory, to argue that "life is the same everywhere," is what leads him to conclude even now that "nothing will change when he leaves. Of course. Nothing will change."[45]

Nor does this disjointedness of time belong only to the poor residents of the Street of Steps. Erella's failure to understand the transformations in her life in her character's long stream-of-consciousness section is another expression of time being out of joint in the novel. Perhaps more significantly, even Ella's father, the bourgeois real-estate dealer, who supposedly enjoys the greatest degree of agency in the novel, is having trouble with time. This is made clear in his almost aggressive avoidance of any talk of the past, and his attempt to materially and spatially repress it through his construction projects:

> [Erella] remembered her mother dying of malaria in grandpa's house when they still lived together in the small colony in Galilee. But she could not remember what her mother had looked like [. . .] Small houses were scattered about at great distances from one another when Dad came with her to the mountain from the colony, and Dad had said it was neither a village nor a town, and she played alone in the courtyard [. . .] Later, it took her a long time to learn to play with children. But Dad said it didn't matter, that there would be a city here [. . .] Dad only shrugged his shoulders when reminded of those days. He loved the city that had been built, but he never liked people who lived on memories. Dad said that the few old houses on the main street always looked faded and that they hurt his eyes, for they seemed transplanted from somewhere else or belonged to a different period.[46]

The father's radical presentism—his constant erasure of the past—again ends up forestalling the possibility of imagining temporality and something like identity and its transformation over time. This repression has to do with the death of Erella's mother, and with a bigger sense of loss that is associated with strong nostalgic tones—an important point that we will address in what follows.

That this sense of time-out-of-joint is common to all of the novel's characters deserves a quick pause in the argument we have been pursuing, for it seems to support the interpretive line that we are questioning, namely, that the novel simply expresses a general existentialist stance, or that some basic loneliness or alienation are the core of human existence (as Miron has it).[47] What should be emphasized here very briefly is that even though this might be the novel's general philosophical stance, we should provide a more historical interpretation of *why* this stance could gain credence in 1950s Israel. We will do precisely that in what follows. Here we should simply say that, as many commentators remind us, Hendel's novels usually focus on the lives of the socially marginalized—in our case, Mizrachi urban poor, and women.[48] That these never had identified with the *halutzic* imaginary and its temporalities, and therefore were always "timeless," is not surprising. What is crucial to understanding 1950s literature is that with the disintegration of the *halutzic* imaginary, even those who could imagine themselves sharing the temporalities of the collective project—mostly Ashkenazi men—suddenly found these temporalities ineffectual. Thus, the absence of temporality typical of marginalized perspectives suddenly becomes generalized after the dissolution of the utopian project: it is now shared by everyone, not only those who were previously marginalized. It is for this reason that the absence of an ordered temporality becomes a universal truth—holding true for all characters in the novel—at this historical moment (and not, as we have been emphasizing, because it is some eternal truth about human nature).[49]

We will return to the novel's relation to history below. The discussion of the novel's treatment of temporality allowed us to move from the purely formal characteristics of the novel to its content: the sense of temporal disjunction formally is expressed in fragmentation finds its explicit expression in characters' avowal of their disjointed temporal experience, or of a temporal failure. We can now expand our exploration of the ways in which the novel thematizes failure in its content. The countless incidents of explanatory and communicative failure in the novel can serve as good examples here. Common among these are "no-exit" explanatory loops of couples' psychological dynamic, one that recalls the naturalist dialogues of Strindberg plays, as for example in the interaction between Tilda and Mussa, a glimpse of which we get in the following passage:

> "Sure, my heart went out to you [Mussa] once, but you think I can remember all my life? How I used to stand and watch you walk. [. . .]" "It's not so bad, Tilda, and in the meantime you can let me finish eating." "Eating?" she shouted [. . .] "You don't need anything, only eating" [. . .] he looked at [Tilda]

triumphantly, and with a strange hatred, in which there is both betrayal and fidelity.[50]

What is important for our purposes is that the text highlights the impossibility of understanding the forces that brought Mussa and Tilda together, and how a vague feeling of disappointment turns into a never-ending fight in which everything is also its opposite: victory and defeat are achieved in the same act, as are fidelity and betrayal.

These moments of explanatory and communicative failure happen throughout the novel, as in Avram's inability to communicate his frustration to the state officials or to Erella's father, Gavriel, who opposes their relationship;[51] or in Ovadia's linguistic struggle to explain life in the poor neighborhood to Erella;[52] or the frustrated communication between Avram and Erella themselves.[53] These instances of failed communication many times take an additional valence—something like an inexplicable blockage of enjoyment, an alarming absence of joy where one expects to find it. This is the case, for example, in the long description of Avram's night out with Erella and her friends (who belong to her social milieu). That enjoyment had been somehow foiled is also very clear in the case of Rivka—whose unreciprocated love for Avram drives her to the brink of madness. Her desire is constantly frustrated, as every plan she devises to attract Avram's attention fails,[54] and plans to pursue one's object of desire become useless or unmoored from reality: "I'd iron [Avram's] shirts every day, Ma, I'd buy him socks with stripes and checks. I'd dress him in pretty clothes, and I'd cook him everything he likes, and at night we'd go to the movies or take a walk." It is important to emphasize here is not merely Rivka's unrequited love, but that a whole fantasy-space suddenly becomes unhinged or exposed as dysfunctional.

Hendel's novel, then, constantly exposes dysfunctional structures of enjoyment, or those Lacanian fantasy spaces: that elaboration of desire into an entire structure and ordering of actions and identifications that serve to "orient" desire itself, whose imagining, as we argued, was one of the primary roles of the early realisms.[55] As Žižek writes, it is precisely the existence of collective imaginary structures of enjoyment and identification that make possible this mapping of desire.[56] The point to be made here is the following: the unmooring of structures of enjoyment in *Street of Steps* is yet another indication of the dissolution of the *halutzic* or utopian collective project that we discussed in the first chapter. Again, the pervasive loneliness and alienation of all the characters, which in the novel's own ideology is some basic human condition, is in fact a historical result of the crisis of the *halutzic* project.

What must still be addressed in discussion of the thematization of failure in the novel is the pervasive sense of melancholia and nostalgic loss expressed so strongly by both Erella and Avram. Their experience of the 1948 war is central to this nostalgic melancholia, both characters are acutely aware of the irrationality of this nostalgia for the war, in which, as they constantly remind us, so many of their friends die.[57] It is Tamar Marin's brilliant psychoanalytical reading of the novel that will help us here, for it will permit us to show how psychic effects are at the same time mediated historical ones (which, as we argued in the introduction, does not mean a reduction of psychology to social forces). Marin points out that both Erella and Avram lost their mothers at an early age, and that their melancholic longing for the past is precisely the result of this loss. She draws on the Freudian understanding of melancholia as the imagined internalization of the lost object—in this case the mothers of both characters. Marin then reads this loss through the Lacanian notion of the mirror stage, in which the child learns to distinguish itself from its mother. According to this reading, in Erella's and Avram's case the loss of their mothers means that the mirror stage was never completed, implying an interrupted or incomplete sense of selfhood.[58] Thus, Erella and Avram's love is actually a displaced search for missing mothers and selfhood. Yet here we will suggest a different historical mediation to this interpretation than the one Marin herself proposes, which draws strongly on Miron's reading of the novel that we have been problematizing. Marin ends up generalizing the mother's loss to Hendel's entire generation, following arguments by Shirav and Arbell that this loss can be read as expression the marginalization of women's roles in the 1948 war and the newly formed nationalist discourse.[59]

Rather than identifying a symbolic absence (marginalization of women from national war discourse) with an actual loss of the mother (as in the cases of Erella and Avram), our reading of the melancholic-nostalgic attachment to the war and the pre-war past, will draw on the argument that we have been developing in this book. This attachment to the war is completely in line with the similar irrational attachments that abound in the works of Mossinsohn and Shaham that we discussed in the previous chapter. What we can now suggest is that the loss of the mother is the subjectively mediated form of a different collective repression: the repression of the loss of the utopian collective project of the 1920s and 1930s is what gives birth to the melancholic nostalgia of the characters of *Street of*

Steps, just as it animated the nostalgia of Nathan Shaham's early works,[60] and just as it had been the absent cause of the tragedy in Mossinsohn's *In the Negev Prairies*.[61] The inability to express some ineffable loss, the failure to articulate a bothering point—just like in Yizhar's 1949 stories—is the only trace of protest against the dissolution of the collective project and the temporalities or futures it contained, and its replacement by a wage-labor in a capitalist state. It is this disintegration of this project that "universalizes" the breakdown of temporality (so that it holds for everyone and not only the excluded). And it is the same collapse that accounts for the sudden dissolution of explanatory schemas and structures of enjoyment.

We should notice that our interpretation serves several purposes. First, we have related the multiple articulations of failure in *Street of Steps*—explanatory failures and sense of nostalgic loss, formal fragmentation and abstraction, and breakdown of temporality and structures of enjoyment—to a historical transformation the death of the *halutzic* collective project, in what we should see as a crisis of what Jameson calls cognitive mapping.[62] Second, since the utopian valences of that collective project are what fueled the realist "genre" literature, the end of the *halutzic* project also explains the movement away from the realist tradition in *Street of Steps*. It is not that this realism is simply revealed to be a convenient illusion, but rather that the collective project animating its imaginary structures has vanished. Last, we have challenged the accepted reading of *Street of Steps* and of the literature of the 1950s in general. Literary transformation is not here merely a change of fashion or taste (which is not an explanation at all), nor is it conceived idealistically as a movement from illusion—Zionist myth or propaganda—to truth, some version of universally true existentialism as human nature (as Miron, Shaked, and their followers would have it). Rather, we have presented a historical materialist understanding of this transition: it is the result of the falling-apart of previous collectivities and the way individuals in them had imagined their relation to their conditions of existence, to quote Althusser's "positive" definition of ideology,[63] to be replaced by national ideology proper. *Street of Steps* protest against national ideology is therefore not performed from the stance of a modernist aesthetic autonomy, or art's freedom from "ideology" (itself an ideological stance if there ever was one); nor is it only taking up the cause of the marginalized against a hegemonic "Zionist metanarrative" (a concept whose coherence we have exploded in the first chapter). Rather, the novel's resistance to national ideology is an unconscious protest against the breakdown of the transformative collective project, a breakdown that was the condition of possibility of the establishment of the Israeli state in the first place. What *Street of Steps* offered its 1950s readers, therefore, is a grand allegory of this breakdown and its related aesthetic project, the realism of the "genre" writers.

To conclude our discussion of Hendel's magisterial 1950s novel, we will show that it does not merely register the repressed failure of the *halutzic* project—not merely express a transformation that took place outside literature—but also attempts to imagine a resolution to the contradictions that it opens up. For, as many critics comment, Hendel refuses the imaginary resolutions prescribed by national ideology.[64] Hendel also refuses to leave contradictions open—as we have seen was the case in '20s and '30s realism and in Yizhar's case. Instead, Hendel dialectically turns the problem into its own solution: the communicative and explanatory failures, disjointed time, the inexpressible loss and the alienation that all characters suffer from—are not historical results in the novel's own aesthetic and existential ideology, but simply human nature: loneliness is a basic human condition, as Nissim has it, everyone's life seem somehow not right, and communication must always fail. This is how the novel "solves" the problems that it detects. These dominate human experience simply because they are its essence, according to the novel. Or as Miron has it, Hendel's novel revolves around human "defective being that is beyond any national effort to mend it."[65] It could thus be argued that Hendel paved the road to the becoming-hegemonic of this strategy of containment in the '60s and '70s, one which we will not be able to address here.

Of course, in contrast to Miron, we need not adopt the novel's ideology to affirm its unconscious observations about social reality. That alienation becomes generalized in the 1950s, as we have tried to argue, is a historical result of the collapse of the *halutzic* project rather than an eternal truth. *Street of Steps*'s "solution" to the contradictions it conjures is of particular importance for our purposes, because in contrast to Shaham's or Mossinsohn's imaginary resolutions, it becomes the hegemonic literary ideology in Israel in the late 1950s, one whose proponents quickly become cozily ensconced in national academic institutions (in stark contradistinction to the literary "national ideologues" of the 1920s and 1930s that they look down upon).[66] It is precisely in this sense, then, that Hendel is a forerunner to the literature of the 1960s and 1970s. In *Street of Steps* she finds an aesthetic ideology that makes natural or a-historically true what is actually a result of repressed historical transformation: the sense of alienation and temporal disjunction that appear with the breakdown of the collective project that preceded the state. It is precisely in this sense that Shaked's and

Miron's "anti-ideological" literary agenda paradoxically ends up constituting the starkest case of national ideology: its sentencing of "genre" literature to oblivion performs an essential service to the nation, for it gives the appearance that the establishment of the capitalist state is the natural outcome of the Zionist collective project, rather than the forceful foreclosure of the radical historical possibilities opened by the *halutzic* movement.

Realism's Demise, Materially

Even though 1950s literature includes works that traverse the whole formal "spectrum" that stretches from realism to modernism (and maybe even some an embryonic postmodernism), there is a good reason for referring to it as naturalist literature, as I will try to argue in this short section. We should emphasize at the outset that "naturalism" in this context will not designate a set of formal characteristics—lengthy and detailed physical descriptions, for instance. Rather, we will use it to designate a specific relation between a literary formal transformation and transformation in social form. As we will see, the Israeli literary 1950s offer a surprising corroboration and de-reification of the Marxist theorization of the transition from realism to Modernism, and the equivalent expansion of capitalism onto a truly global scale.

It is in the writing of Georg Lukács that we get the first systematic theorization of the parallel between the formal literary transformation and the history of capitalism, which constituted the terrain of much debate between Lukács, Bloch, Adorno, and others.[67] Lukács's usefulness for us here resides in his dialectical understanding of deep connection between naturalism and the different modernisms, arguing that

> they all take reality exactly as it manifests itself, to the writer and the character he creates [...] they fail to pierce the surface to discover the underlying essence, i.e. the real factors that relate their experiences to the hidden social forces that produce them. On the contrary, they all develop their own artistic style—more or less consciously—as a spontaneous expression of their immediate experience.[68]

What naturalism shares with modernism according to Lukács is a failure to go dialectically beyond immediacy toward what we should call the mediated, rather than "essence," in order to prevent any confusion of the totalizing operation Lukács is describing from some assignment of unchanging "essences" to phenomenon. Lukács's uncompromising dialectical approach sees the tendency toward descriptive detail in naturalism as completely in line with modernism's tendency to focus on subjective experience, deeply suspicious of any attempt to relate it to the external world. It is in abstraction that both meet: the detailed descriptions of naturalism in their abstraction from the invisible forces that produced them; the modernist subject considered in abstraction from social forces.[69]

Thus, what Lukács makes possible for us is to theorize the relation between the different "Hendels" that we described above: the naturalist and the modernist (and we can even add a proto-postmodernist Hendel to this list).[70] Common to all are the operations of abstraction itself—the disintegration of a totalizing representation, in which subjectivity, time, and the spatial-objective world are still somehow dialectically held together. The pervasive temporal out-of-jointedness is perhaps the strongest expression of this abstraction: different moments in time are pulled out of an imagined continuum and allowed to "thingify" or become objects in their own right, which can now be moved to other places in the text at will. We should note in this context that the *Street of Steps*'s second chapter's literary montage has a double function in this respect: on the one hand, it is failure to go beyond immediate experience; on the other, the mere juxtaposition of different life-moments acts to highlight the problem of totality as such.[71]

It is precisely this failure to produce realist totalization, or to move beyond immediacy in some determinate way, that unites Hendel with the other authors of the 1950s that we have been examining in the last three chapters. Yet we should resist the tendency to see this "failure" of realism as an ethical choice of the author, or as reflecting some eternal reality. It is important in this respect to recall Žižek's dialectical notion of ideology:

> When some procedure is denounced as "ideological par excellence," one can be sure that its inversion is no less ideological. For example, among the procedures generally acknowledged as "ideological" is definitely the eternalization of some historically limited condition, the act of discerning some higher Necessity in a contingent occurrence (from the grounding of male domination in the "nature of things" to interpreting AIDS as a punishment for the sinful life of modern man; or, at a more intimate level, when we encounter our "true love," it seems as if this is what we have been waiting for all our life, as if, in some mysterious way,

all our previous life has led to this encounter . . .): the senseless contingency of the real is thus "internalized," symbolized, provided with Meaning. Is not ideology, however, also the opposite procedure of failing to notice the necessity, of misperceiving it as an insignificant contingency (from the psychoanalytic cure, in which one of the main forms of the analysand's resistance is his insistence that his symptomatic slip of tongue was a mere lapse without any signification, up to the domain of economics, in which the ideological procedure par excellence is to reduce the crisis to an external, ultimately contingent occurrence, thus failing to take note of the inherent logic of the system that begets the crisis)? In this precise sense, ideology is the exact opposite of internalization of the external contingency: it resides in externalization of the result of an inner necessity, and the task of the critique of ideology here is precisely to discern the hidden necessity in what appears as a mere contingency.[72]

What is important here is to resist Miron's and other's identification of the collapse of mediation in Hendel as corresponding to some reality that lies behind the illusions of the so-called "Zionist metanarrative." The critic's position is here no less ideological, in the Žižekian sense. What must be exposed, as Žižek would have it, is the contingent nature of this "nature" that Miron and others ascribe to reality. It is important then that we resist the urge to see the explosion of literary totalization as more "real" than its opposite number.

At any rate, we cannot here take up the question of Lukács's own position on the topic at any length. For, on the one hand, Lukács's defense of critical realism many times ends up constituting precisely an ethical commitment, one whose role to the representational function and social role we cannot address here.[73] On the other, Lukács seems very much aware, just like many of the critics debating him,[74] not only that the disintegration of totality is an objective phenomena caused by capitalism, but also that the imaginary reconstitution of that totality in literary representation is not at all an obvious possibility in the early twentieth century, no matter how committed the author is to the totalizing operation.[75] In other words, the erosion of the possibility of going beyond immediate experience to reconstitute a totality of social relations is itself the result of capitalism's expansion. Perhaps it is true, as Lukács argues, that modernism fails to go beyond subjective experience (even though, as Adorno comments, that might only mean that what used to be the external world is now reflected in that new subjective interiority). But it is also true—and this is a point that Lukács never addresses—that realist novels contains moments of representational failure whenever the system of social relations to be given representation is stretched beyond national borders, as Christian Thorne argues.[76]

For our purposes it is important to emphasize that the failure to totalize (regardless of intention) is here not to be judged ethically but rather be understood as the result of the expansion of capitalism onto a multinational scale. It is precisely this point that is at the center of Fredric Jameson's notion of "cognitive mapping."[77] As Jameson argues (echoing an older Lukácsian argument about the spread of capitalism and the ensuing breakdown of social units) capitalism's stretching of social relations onto a global scale produces a crisis of social "cognitive mapping," or individuals' imaginary relation to the real conditions of their existence. European subjects' everyday life was increasingly produced elsewhere, as significant parts of productive processes took place in colonies.[78] Thus, the breakdown of realism—first in naturalism and then in Modernism—reflects precisely this objective crisis of cognitive mapping. Or, in other words, modernist authors are right to insist on the fragmented nature of existence, on a sense of alienation as inseparable from modernity itself, and on the difficulty of reproducing social totality in representation—since these are precisely the ways in which the expansion of capitalism is registered in subjective experience.

So the breakdown of realism is not a matter of subjective preference, or of literary taste, but an aesthetic result of an objective transformation. Yet this all might sound like a "reductionist" explanation, one that construes aesthetic changes as merely the expression of an economic one. What drops out of sight is the social mediation of this process (which is actually an inseparable part of Lukács's or Jameson's theoretical account), that would bring back agency and the making of history back into the picture. This is where Israeli 1950s literature becomes important for us, for it will help us reaffirm the Marxist account from a surprising perspective. As we have been arguing, the work of Hendel, Shaham, Mossinsohn, Yizhar, and other 1950s authors registers the collapse of the *halutzic* radically transformative collective project, whose literary counterpart was the realist "genre" writing. In this case, the dissolution of realism corresponds to the end of the autonomous, self-governing settlement project, and the integration of these settlements into something like a national economy.[79] The relatively economically autonomous settlements allowed for a clear "cognitive mapping" to develop—the *halutzic* imaginary, which tied individual experience to the system governing it. This sense of social mapping disintegrated when activity in the small settlements was no longer a means to creating collectively defined use-value, or the furthering of the utopian project, but rather became commodity production for the market—be it national or international. It is precisely the becoming-subjective of use-value, and becoming objective of exchange value (or that becoming of exchange value the principle that governs productive activity) that designates the moment of entry into capitalism, or what Marx would call formal subsumption.[80]

Thus, the integration into a proto-national economy in the 1940s is what deals a death blow to how collective agency is imagined. In the small settlements, individuals could imagine how their work takes part in making history, or how it contributes to a collective effort to change the shape of life itself. This is precisely the sense in which Jamesonian cognitive mapping involves the mapping of individual experience onto a larger system (or what in other instances Jameson calls historicity, or the possibility of imagining the present as part of an open making of history).[81] As argued in the previous chapters, "genre" writing could be thought of as the revolutionary self-representation of the *halutzic* movement, in the sense that in it, the obstacles to the collective project, the different contradictions that arise within it, are thought through. Thus, when the activity of the collectivized settlements becomes wage-labor that produces commodities for a capitalist market, historicity itself, or agency over history as it was imagined in the *halutzic* imaginary falls apart.

Thus, that Hebrew realism goes into crisis in the late 1940s, giving rise to a host of figurations of failure (and imaginary solutions for it) is a reaffirmation of the Lukácsian-Jamesonian formula—for it is precisely a result of the breakdown of the social form of the autonomous settlements and their integration into a capitalist national economy (and to global capitalism in general). It is for this reason that we might want to term the literature of the 1950s a naturalist literature, since it designates the collapse of an easily mappable social totality and its contradictions; and in the dust one can already see the shadows of a much broader system, that of global capitalism itself, which makes its appearance in those shady, dangerous, and confusing areas of exteriority in the literature of the '60s and the '70s, which we will not address here.

4

Is There Israeli Postmodern Literature?

Orly Castel-Bloom, Yehudit Katzir, and the Vicissitudes of National Space-Time in the 1980s and 1990s

Confusingly perhaps, it used to be much easier to demonstrate the existence of a postmodern turn in Israeli literature. One does not need to look too hard to find 1990s pronouncements of postmodernism's conquest of the literary center stage in Israel, be these pronouncements more or less celebratory, as in Yossi Gurevitz's once-influential book, or negative critiques of postmodernism's appearance, as in Ortsion Bartana's reading of it as a harbinger of something like a cultural apocalypse.[1] Indeed, any discussion of Israeli postmodernism—which will be the object of the next two chapters—must come to terms with the growing reticence among Israeli critics of characterizing the literature of the 1980s and 1990s as postmodern. It is for this reason that our discussion in this chapter will operate simultaneously on three interrelated registers. First, we will set out to determine whether "postmodernism" names a distinct body of '80s and '90s Israeli literary works. This will inevitably include an evaluation of specific literary works' postmodern-ness. Yet, as with any periodizing schema, its usage will quickly become a not only a matter of its truth but instead mostly of usefulness and its political adventures: in other words, in our second interpretive register we will try to account for the historiographical transformation itself, for the strange fact that critics of Israeli literature today, as opposed to their '90s counterparts seem to be dissatisfied with postmodernism as a periodizing concept—one which is too vague or general, if to mention Yaron Peleg's objection.[2]

In this second interpretive register we will inevitably touch on factors external to the literary-critical in trying to account for transformations in the latter. Thus, our discussion will have moved to a third level, one in which the two previous registers will be dialectically subsumed. Here, we will suggest a wholly new theory for the transformation of Israeli literature in the '80s, one which will bring together socioeconomic, literary, and literary-critical changes, a "synthesis" in which the previous moments of our analysis will find their place.

We must begin however by providing some minimal definition of postmodernism, one that will frame the following literary discussion and our invention in the critical debate around Israeli literary postmodernism. It is Fredric Jameson's influential account of postmodernism that we will borrow for the purposes of our discussion.[3] Jameson's conception of postmodernism has the singular merit of characterizing its object on multiple levels: it provides a dialectical account of its aesthetic characteristics, as well as the historical institutional-social, and economic transformations that undergird this set of aesthetic traits—generating a theoretical account in which postmodernism appears as a set of symptomatic cultural attempts to "solve" in imagination late capitalism's socioeconomic contradictions. We will not discuss at length the "aesthetic" characteristics most identified with postmodernism, for the simple reason that for the most part these formal features are the ones that critics (including Israeli ones) do seem to remember and reiterate (such as interpretive flatness, the dissolution of unified subjectivity, the dissolution of hegemony, etc.). Instead, what is important to emphasize for the purposes of our discussion are the forgotten social and economic mediations that Jameson associates with these aesthetic transformations. In particular, what immediately troubles any existing discussion of Israeli postmodernism, as we shall see, is that the latter designates, according to Jameson, an institutionalization of previously resisting modernisms.[4] Rather than being a "style" that can be picked up at will, the formal features associated with postmodernism can always be found in one once-resisting modernism or another. postmodernism's distinction is thus taken out of the realm of authorial choice (of this or that aesthetic feature), residing instead in the social location of cultural production: their absorption into existing capitalist culture, rather than being situated outside this institutional framework—as with many modernisms.[5]

To the institutionalization or domestication of modernisms we should add another commonly ignored level of mediation, namely, that postmodernism is the universalization of a crisis of social imaginaries, or cognitive mapping, registered in modernism. It is the stretching of the social relations of production over the entire globe which launches previous social imaginaries (most famously those of the nation-state) into crisis—creating a kind of social disorientation whose source is precisely that the simple matters of everyday life come to be produced at an unimaginably other place across the ocean, rather than in the national backyard.[6] It is at this level that the loss of historicity so central to Jameson's notion of postmodernism is of course traced to its core cause. As we will see in the following two chapters, this understanding of the sociocultural conditions of postmodernism's emergence constitutes the major challenge with which any theory of Israeli postmodernism will have to grapple.

Any discussion of Israeli postmodernism should therefore, first and foremost, not focus solely on the reproduction of this or that abstracted aesthetic trait (for these will always, as we just claimed, confusingly collapse into the aesthetic features of modernism). Rather, any claim to the existence (or nonexistence) of Israeli postmodernism must address these extra-literary questions, ones that pertain to the location of culture—to the ways in which cultural object are structured around the figuration of social contradictions. If Israeli postmodernism exists, it is not simply because it shares abstracted aesthetic features with its Western counterpart; rather, it is because it performs the same imaginary labor with respect to the social that its Western counterpart does. We will address these questions fully toward the end of these two chapters.

What our short detour through the theorization of postmodernism makes possible is to begin developing the historiographic interpretive register that we mentioned earlier—peculiarly before we even address the literary texts and postmodernism itself. Recent critical attempts to move away from postmodernism as a periodizing term in Israeli letters can now be seen as insufficient—both in the ways these different attempts characterize postmodernism, and in the alternative periodizing terms suggested. One candidate for such revisionist historiography is Smadar Shifman's attempt to see Israeli postmodernism as simply an outgrowth of modernism, utterly reversing her older evaluation of writers such as Orly Castel-Bloom as postmodernists.[7] Shifman's understanding of postmodernism identifies the latter with an eschewing of a "search for meaning," a criterion according to which even works such as DeLillo's postmodern *White Noise* would can begin to seem non-postmodern. What is of course the essential problem here is that to be postmodern becomes in Shifman's analysis a matter of the individual author's ethical and stylistic choice. As we already argued above, this psycho-ethical understanding of postmodernism has no choice but to be unable to distinguish postmodernism from modernism—since the "aesthetic" features of each of these can be found in the other.

Yaron Peleg's writing on Israeli culture in the 1990s—"between two intifadas"—constitutes another attempt to sideline postmodernism as a periodizing term in Israeli literary history. Arguing that "observations about literary diversity and postmodernism are expansive and somewhat vague," Peleg opts instead for seeing '90s fiction in terms of a formal and thematic focusing on the "romantic duo," a first-person dual narrative that emerges particularly in the cultural enclave of Tel Aviv, and that acts as an alternative to collectivity or the solitary "I":

> Keenly expressive of the profound changes Israeli society underwent in the last two decades of the twentieth century, [the] four writers [discussed here] struck a new narrative voice. Instead of the common Zionist 'we' of previous generations or the individual 'I' who rebelled against it, Keret, Taub, Weil, and Amir adopted an unaffiliated Me and You, an alternative romantic narrative that focuses on coupling and privileges personal love over communal and national attachments.[8]

Peleg's more creative approach to literary periodization, and notwithstanding the brave attempt to pair a critique of commodity culture with his periodization of the '90s, remains somewhat unsatisfying as well. First, the "romantic duo" as an imaginary realm of utopian escape is far from being a hegemonic narrative device is in the literature of the '90s, for it is simply one of the literary figures that many prominent '90s authors (such as Orly Castel-Bloom, as we will soon see) assiduously dissolve and problematize, as Peleg himself admits. But the second and deeper problem for our purposes has to do with Peleg's brave foray into mediating culture with society. The "profound changes Israeli society underwent," which constitute the extra-literary cause for literary transformation in Peleg's account suffer from a conceptual problem: the "bourgeoisification," the adoption of Western values, of consumerism to which Peleg alludes throughout his introduction—all of these, according to other critics, are not exactly new in the late '80s, but rather start appearing in the late '60s and early '70s.[9] As we will see below in our literary analyses, the appearance of Western (or more particularly American) consumerism is an important figurative node for the writers of the late '80s—but it is definitely not its first appearance in Israeli literature by that time. Nor is the adoption of a critical approach to "Zionist ideology" (read: national ideology), the cultural undermining of Israeli nationalism, as many critics have it, and the retreat from it to the personal realm is of course not special to the late '80s.[10] The well-known literary "new wave" of the '60s, the one championed by Shaked, is premised precisely on this rejection, as we have seen in previous chapters (we will touch on the more historically grounded "post-Zionism" labeling of this literature in what follows). In fact, critics seem to designate too many starting points as causes of the drift away from national hegemony. Where, then, does social Westernization and the turn away from national ideology make their decisive appearance? In the late '60s, under the influence of Western counter-culture? After MAPAI's historic loss in the 1977 election? Or with the arrival of malls to Israel in the late '80s? Or is it war-weariness after the 1973 *Yom Kippur* war? Is it the 1982 Invasion of Lebanon that triggered this weariness of the nation and its narratives? Or was it, after all, the war of 1948 that should be seen as the starting point for all such talk of war-weariness? The infinite collapsing-back of the interpretive thematic threads would make anyone dizzy. Westernization and the turn away from nationalism thus turn out to be something like pseudo-concepts here: ideologemes that can be invoked to "explain" literary transformations in the '60s and in the '80s equally, without actually explaining anything. Thus, current revisions of Israeli literary history and its grounding in social and political transformations, despite its truly laudable attempt to provide a framework of mediation between social and cultural registers, is ultimately unsatisfying, both in the causes of transformation it suggests, and in the alternative it poses. Toward the end of this chapter, we will have constructed a clear theoretical account of the ways in which economic transformation is connected to the sea-change of Israeli literature in the 1980s.

But there is one other type of revisionist periodization that tends to isolate the emergence of multicultural literature in the '80s as the decisive factor, ignoring altogether the relation between postmodernism and the explosion of multiculturalism. In Adia Mendelson-Maoz's account, for instance, the '80s are seen as an era in which "alternative narratives and cultures were rising to the surface, shaping a multicultural picture, with different national, ethnic, and religious attributes," challenging what was until then a nationally homogenizing culture (the latter of course viewed by Maoz as essentially oppressive, having completely lost the utopian-transformative significance it possessed in the 1930s).[11] Maoz is, of course, not alone. Dvir Abramovich's account of the 1980s literary transformation is an even more celebratory account of the rise of a multiplicity of literary identities and perspectives, signaling the dawn of what sounds like no less than a liberal utopia of multiplicity and variety (indeed, one can imagine Israel to be a utopian space, if all one knows about it came from Abramovich's propaganda). If postmodernism as a term is considered at all by Abramovich, it is only as surrogate for the birth of multicultural literature, bringing about the end not only of literary political engagement, but of all ideology as such and whatever hegemonic public sphere used to support it.[12]

To make such narratives problematic, it would suffice to recall once again Jameson's definition of postmodernism in terms of the institutionalization and domestication of once-threatening modernisms. The same rule of thumb can be applied to the different "cultural" perspectives opened up: if previously Mizrachi or women's literary voices had been silenced, their representations always being intolerable to the hegemony, in the 1980s these voices lose any sense of symbolic resistance: the gestures of symbolic resistance to national ideology no longer being counter-hegemonic; these moments are rather the consensus of a new cultural hegemony—although it is hardly clear that such narrow and negatively defined common ground could even function hegemonically in the Gramscian sense in any substantial sense. We might therefore be able to return a peculiar sense of shock to Abramovich's narrative: for we must realize that the institutionalization of what had previously resisted is taken here to be a real triumph, rather than part of a critical analysis in which this institutionalization makes consciousness seek a new symbolic language through which resistance can once again be expressed. Thus, Abramovich's narrative should be seen as that of a new "hegemony," in which the search for oppositional language is itself abandoned, replaced with a celebration of an institutionalization of gestures of symbolic resistance. To the degree that today's Israel is very far from being a liberal utopia, free from social antagonisms, this narrative is highly unsatisfying.

Yet the more important objection to this narrative of the rise of multicultural literature is one articulated briefly by Yigal Schwartz, an objection whose psychoanalytical and social significance has not deserved the attention it surely deserves. According to Schwartz:

> Many of the literary studies in [the late '80s] use models from the field of minority discourse, and feminist and queer theory, to explore narratives of social and national groups that have hitherto been silenced, marginalized, or that have disappeared

altogether. Women's narratives, those of Mizrachis, Arabs and others, all of whom are "Others" within the new Hebrew culture [. . .] all of the newer critical projects take a clear oppositional stance towards the metanarrative produced by Zionist historiography. And in this respect—and this in my mind is a point of weakness—theses new literary historians are strongly connected with their predecessors' metanarrative, both in terms of critical themes and methodologically.[13]

What is thus puzzling about the 1980s multicultural turn is that it does not in fact constitute a "turn" or a break in any clear sense, because its predecessors—Miron and Shaked in criticism, Oz and Yehoshua in literature—are just as committed to undoing the "Zionist metanarrative" as this newer multicultural wave. The easiest but ultimately unsatisfying narrative solution is to argue, as Abramovich and Maoz do, that the multiculturalist turn is simply an intensification of the older anti-national tendency, again making the break seem much more like a continuity. Here of course we have come full circle: Shifman's collapsing of Israeli literary postmodernism to its modernist predecessor, with which we have started our discussion, turns out here to be not a matter of Shifman's personal critical preference or moral stance, but rather a general historical indistinguishability of the literary '80s from its predecessors. Schwartz's quick diagnosis does not itself lead him to replace this '80s critics' failure-to-rebel with a clearer conceptual distinction of '80s literature. Instead, he opts for seeing Israeli literature in terms of an irreducible Lyotardian narrative multiplicity—itself a postmodern end of history that again does not mark an antagonist position against its historiographical patriarchs.[14] It is this failure to distinguish '80s literature from what came before it that is the most pressing problem that we face, one that is not limited to Schwartz's account or that of the multiculturalists, but raises its head whenever critics try to distinguish '80s literature's relation to national politics: this latter clearly seems to ironically and critically distance itself from political issues, just as in the previous generations. Invocations of the newer literature's "post-Zionism" or greater disinterest in politics does little to dispel what is essentially an identity;[15] Oz's literature's late-'60s overt stance toward the national narrative being the same as Castel-Bloom's late-'80s one.

Thus, existing attempts to provide a periodization of Israeli literature that avoids or bypasses postmodernism as a term seem to falter, and the nagging intuition that '80s literature is somehow different than what preceded it remains bereft of a clear conceptualization. Yet simply returning to an older periodization (one that includes postmodernism as a period) would be tantamount at this point to an act of repression, a repetition that is—whether we admit it or not—altogether different than the original gesture. Instead, we should again reiterate one of the three questions with which we started: what has caused postmodernism to become an unsatisfying periodization term? This problem, as we will see, will open an arc of inquiry that we will only resolve in the last two chapters of this book, for it deals with what is essentially a matter of contemporary sensibilities rather than those of the '80s, the discussion of which we reserve for the last two chapters. Deferring the treatment of one question, we are still left with answering the other two: the "empirical" question of whether or not postmodernism can after all be used to describe an Israeli literary period, and the question of the extra-literary transformations that produce this (supposedly) postmodern sensibility. That we are blocked from simply returning to older periodizations will necessarily make our answers here take surprising routes. We will answer these questions through our literary discussions.

Adopting the Jamesonian understanding of postmodernism as the domestication of previously resisting modernisms inevitable leads us into the realm of problems of periodization more generally, which we have discussed in the introduction. For we here must acknowledge the connection of this understanding of postmodernism to Jameson's conceptualization of modernism itself. Modernism for Jameson has two periods: high modernism, with its energetic political rebelliousness, and late modernism, from which the political energies are drained, leaving us with an "aesthetic" or formalistic modernism.[16] It is late modernism that then "serves as a transitional space, a kind of vanishing mediator in the ultimate emergence of postmodernism," as Phillip Wegner observes.[17] If Israeli postmodernism is to be an exact reproduction of this trajectory, we find ourselves having to posit the existence of an Israeli late modernism—in which the political transgression of older modernisms is tamed and institutionalized. We will not be able to discuss the literature of the '60s and '70s in any detail, but a few brief remarks on it are in order to address the existence of an Israeli late modernism that is itself somewhat of a precondition for the appearance of postmodernism. We can briefly say that the literature of the '60s and '70s seems to be a good candidate for Jamesonian late-modernism: Oz and Yehoshua, for all their critique of the national establishment, being the darlings of precisely this establishment, as Nurit Gertz and others comment.[18] The earlier modernism of Brenner or Gnessin was animated by political impulses of Jewish (or more generally human) emancipation, aimed against either at powerless exilic Jewish existence or at the British or other oppressors, or even at the oppressiveness of tradition itself. This early modernism was not part of "high" literature, but defined itself against that culture—the latter embodied in the affluent domiciles populating Gnessin's work, or the romantic petit-bourgeois Zionist illusions against which Brenner's writing was aimed. The situation is altogether different in the case of Oz and Yehoshua's writing, whose criticism of Israeli national ideology aspires to be adopted as "high culture" and is performed from within national institutions, which their writing in no way aims to abolish, but rather to naturalize. It is in this sense that Israeli literature of the '60s and '70s can be seen as late-modernist in the Jamesonian sense, opening the way to seeing the literature of the '80s as postmodern.

From this perspective—the existence of an Israeli late modernism—1980s Israeli literature begins to seem as indeed postmodern in the general Western sense. Our attempt to answer our last question—the inquiry into the origin of the '80s turn—will however provide us with a dialectical negation here: it will help us distinguish Israeli '80s literature from Western postmodernism and to see it as a unique transformation in its own right. In our literary discussions to follow, both the identity and difference of Israeli '80s literature from postmodernism will be grounded in part in historical comparison. We will use Oz's writing—particularly his early novels *Elsewhere, Perhaps* (1966) and *My Michael* (1968) as well as works by Yehoshua and Amalia Kahana-Carmon as comparative backdrop to '80s and '90s works we will be discussing.[19] It is this historical depth that will make it possible for us to suggest a clear conceptual framework for the difference of the '80s and '90s works from their predecessors—a task which remains an open challenge in Israeli literary history, as argued above. The works discussed in this chapter are Orly Castel-Bloom's *Where am I?* and Yehudit Katzir's *Closing the Sea*. The next chapter will continue our exploration of Israeli literature of the '80s and '90s, focusing on works by David Grossman, Yehoshua Kenaz, and Batya Gur. This division is somewhat arbitrary: this chapter focuses on more playful works, whose status as postmodern used to be widely accepted. The next chapter's group of authors is in contrast far less playful in its writing—and arguing that they should be seen as part of a the general '80s "postmodern" turn is far more controversial, considering existing evaluations. Yet it is only in their writing that some of the 1980s author's clearest distinctions fully emerge, as we will see.

Playful Disorientation in Orly Castel-Bloom's *Where am I?*

The early evaluations of Orly Castel-Bloom early 1990s writing as paradigmatic Israeli postmodernism as recently found their exact parallel in recent denunciations of these texts' postmodernism. And not that anything was ever so clear cut, in what seems like critics' unacknowledged nagging doubt on whether postmodernism, a term borrowed as it is from Western cultural criticism, can be so unproblematically applied in the Israeli context. It is for this reason that influential '90s critics such as Adi Ophir or Gurevitz, while generally seeing Castel-Bloom as paradigmatic of Israeli postmodernism, insist on the "imperfection" of her writing's postmodernism in blatantly unconvincing ways: a postmodern celebration of meaninglessness that is "nonetheless still attentive [. . .] to the great myths that make up Israeli identity and the 'Israeli place.' Even if this 'identity' is constantly dissolved into contradictory currents [. . .] the process itself has a healing moment to it. . . ."[20] It is in this way that the evaluation of Orly Castel-Bloom as imperfect postmodernist becomes nonsensical as literary judgment, instead becoming a disavowed site for an imaginary reconciliation of the universal and particular—in this case universal Western cultural criticism and Israeli particularity. For it is of course nonsensical to see postmodernism merely in terms of meaninglessness and a search for meaning. Not only because it is precisely this tension that dominates many modernisms, but also because Gurevitz and Ophir seem to simply not be able to decide whether Castel-Bloom's writing does one or the other, ending up attributing both qualities at once to her early writing, collapsing any clear conceptualization of what each of these means textually.

It is here that contemporary revision intervenes, simply shifting the emphasis between these two poles, making the "non-postmodern" qualities of Castel-Bloom more strongly apparent: Shifman, as we already mentioned above, seeing Castel-Bloom's writing as imbued with a strong search for meaning, and thus opting for her being a form of modernism; or Uri Cohen's vehement insistence that her writing has never been postmodern and that postmodernism is generally impossible in the Israeli context—simply intensifying Ophir's position.[21] Thus, we have already paved the way to what usually follows the debunking of Castel-Bloom's postmodernism, which is attributing to her writing this or that political position. For example, Cohen argues that "Castel-Bloom's writing's political effect was to disrupt the drumbeats of authors who see themselves as guardians of the Israeli nation," joining Shifman, Peleg, and Hasak-Lowy in seeing Castel-Bloom's writing as an attack on national-ideological themes and forms.²² It is indeed not difficult to find passages in which Castel-Bloom's first novel seems to mock national motifs, such as the passage in which the heroine boards a bus from Tel Aviv to Jerusalem:

> "Excuse me," I addressed the driver. "Is this the bus to Jerusalem?"
> "Yesssss"
> "So where is the road to Jerusalem?"
> "I'm doing the Forty-Eight route"
> "Forty-Eight?" I was shocked. "That's the bus line that goes form Ra'anana through Hertzlia, Ramat Hasharon, Neot Afeka, to Tel Aviv [. . .]"
> "I meant nineteen-forty-eight, the year."
> "What do you mean?"
> "So that these tourists that don't care about this country can see what went on here in forty-eight."
> [. . .] I took the driver's spot. Some cars started chasing the bus. Behind me a Fatah terrorist poked a gun in my back and said stop or I'll take out your terrorist cell. I tried to stop. I tried and tried, but couldn't. The police were chasing after the bus. I heard the sirens. "don't stop or I'll shoot," he changed his mind suddenly." [. . .] I drove the bus into the central bus station and everyone got off and went their way, some headed for the tunnels, some to other buses, some to get a hotdog with mustard."²³

This passage invokes a number of familiar national-ideological tropes, but only in a playful manner, as if using them incorrectly: the 1948 battles over the old road leading from Tel Aviv to Jerusalem as familiar symbols of national heroism and triumph, and busses being a preferred target for terrorist attacks. Identity confusion ensues, when the terrorist uses military lingo, lost here in translation in "take out your terrorist cell" or when the protagonists uses the official-sounding term "man of Fatah" in her gossip-like narrative. That the protagonist is not clearly on the side of the terrorists or of the police is another instance of playful identity switching. And finally, closure and ideological reconciliation is itself playfully sabotaged when the whole affair does not culminate in some significant witnessing and judgment by a Lacanian Big Other—the hotdogs standing in for the mundane and mediocre non-event, or even for easy enjoyment. It is in this way that

Castel-Bloom does seem to be criticizing national ideology—staging the failure of figurative process associated with the latter.

A special place is reserved here for the debate over Castel-Bloom's feminism: several seeing her as a critic of bourgeois monogamy, marriage as an institution, and gender identities which constitute something like subjective mediation of national figuration. Thus, for example, Shai Rudin argues that the protagonist's failed marriages in *Where am I?* "emphasize the impossibility of romantic coupledom, or as the heroine declares, every marriage ceremony 'separates couples forever.' "[24] If Rudin's reading remains on the ethical level—its horizon of interpretation being that the novel expresses a feminist stance that Rudin himself seems to share—others take the feminist reading beyond the ethical horizon. Thus, for example, Tamar Hess sees Castel-Bloom's feminism in going beyond the previous generation of writers (such as Amalia Kahana Carmon). Whereas the latter's heroines always seem to suffer because of their individual husbands from which they do not break free, Castel-Bloom's critique is more systemic. Here, argues Hess, what seems like an individual fault is externalized and presented as a universal (patriarchal) condition from which escape seems generally impossible—since no subject position seems to liberate Castel-Bloom's protagonist from the clutches of patriarchy.[25] Castel-Bloom's heroine does not affirm this or that moral stance in relation to femininity or marriage in this reading—for no such moral stance seems to liberate from the system. Rather, as Shifman, Hess, and others point out, it seems that when the heroine is at her most anti-patriarchal rebelliousness that she finds herself reproducing precisely the stereotypes she has been trying to escape all along.[26] We would therefore do well to designate this movement of the text as aporetic—as reproducing an antinomy which seems insurmountable with available imaginative devices, and which echoes Derridian deconstruction or the self-undoing of textual closure, just as much as it seems to designate the inner limits of a system we have somehow failed to grasp from the outside. We will return to these aporetic moments in what follows.

Yet what makes each of these positions—Castel-Bloom as critic of national ideology or of patriarchy—problematic is that both fail to contend with the underlying playfulness of Castel-Bloom's approach to the history of literary representations: that pastichization of past representational forms that is so prevalent under postmodernism, as Jameson argues.[27] We will now have to address the history of Castel-Bloom's evocation of national or feminist tropes, for it will not do to quickly and triumphantly declare that Castel-Bloom "refuses to adopt the linear realism that characterizes Israeli literature,"²⁸ since of course modernism has made its appearance in Hebrew letters approximately a century before Castel-Bloom's novel—and our brief discussion of attributing the status of late modernists to Oz and Yehoshua will prove particularly pertinent here. Consider for example the following passage from Oz's 1968 novel *My Michael*:

> I lie in bed, holding a novel by John Steinbeck which my best friend Hadassah brought me when she came to visit me last night [. . .] A fly dashes itself against the windowpane. A fly, not a sign and not an omen. Just a fly. I am not thirsty [. . .] At nine o'clock the radio announced: Last night the Israeli Defense Forces penetrated the Sinai Desert, captured Kuntilla and Ras en-Naqeb [. . .] A military commentator explained. While from the political point of view. Repeated provocations. Flagrant violations of the freedom of navigation. The moral justification. Terrorism and sabotage. Defenseless women and children. Mounting tension. Innocent civilians. [. . .] Keep calm. Stay indoors. Blackout. No hoarding. Obey instructions. The public is requested. No panic. The whole country is a front. The whole nation is an army.²⁹

The reification of national ideological discourse into premade meaningless formulas is of course clear here, not unlike in the passage from Castel-Bloom's novel. Oz's earlier novel *Elsewhere, Perhaps* stages even more clearly this reification of national ideology. The sense of the linguistic automation or highlighting its status as a series of clichés, which Dan Miron identifies as the central formal characteristic of Castel-Bloom's writing, is of course strongly present in this passage from Oz (even if in Oz's case this reification is still circumscribed, limited to some areas of life, rather than becoming universal as in Castel-Bloom).³⁰

Nor is the confusion of identities present in Castel-Bloom's *Where am I?* foreign to Oz's novel, where in countless dreams or hallucinations Jerusalem is being invaded, and it is not at all clear if the protagonist is alarmed by the invaders or is in fact on their side. The aporetic moments of Castel-Bloom's novel: those that join impossibly together rebellion and conformity, are also present in Oz's heroine, for whom the threat of destruction or oppression is very much also a source of allure.³¹ We will touch below on the obvious Freudian valences of this contradictory impulse—the proper name for which is the death-drive, in what follows. And of course, the critique of heterosexual coupledom and bourgeois monogamy is central to

Oz's novel (and to Kahana-Carmon's 1971 *And Moon in the Valley of Ajalon*, with its heroine's proclamation that "in every married woman something is broken"—Hess's critique notwithstanding).[32]

Not only therefore is Castel-Bloom's "refusal to adopt linear realism" present in her predecessors, but also the precise coordinates of women's oppression, the tracing of the intricate antagonism between liberation and desire, is charted in these earlier works. That the novel's protagonist's great escape from her second husband to Be'er Sheva and then to Eilat ends up simply with her helpless surrendering to his will is therefore a trajectory of failure with which Israeli literature is already familiar by the time Castel-Bloom's novel is published. And we need not stop our search for historical precedents with Oz's and Kahana-Carmon's canonical novels. One can trace many of the figurative devices that oppose subjective desire to political goal to the literature of the 1950s: for example, the role of personal desire in Mossinsohn's novel that we discussed in previous chapters, or in the familial tensions present in Shamir's *He Walked Through the Fields* and the association of enjoyment in general for both with the corrupt city—even if the latter belong to the much-maligned realist Israeli tradition (which in the '50s becomes naturalist, as argued in previous chapters), rather than being Oz's modernist predecessors.

What is crucial for our argument is that when all of these make their appearance again in Castel-Bloom's novel, we are dealing with a repetition which nonetheless constitutes something completely different, in the Hegelian sense of such repetitions.[33] For in Castel-Bloom's narrative these national or feminist tropes are pastiched, or offered up as representations rather than as figures for living social contradictions. This formal and thematical pastiche of older literary representations is not a satirical gesture, as critics claim; rather, it is the '60s and '70s writing of Oz, Yehoshua and others that these moment constitute genuine satire. The reappearance of Oz's treatment of national ideology in Castel-Bloom's novel is rather, as in Jameson's account of postmodernism, the moment in which pastiche eclipses satire. If in Oz's late modernism there is still a hegemonic voice to be opposed, a Symbolic order that reconciles contradictions and makes a national community imaginable, this hegemonic Symbolic order is in full crisis in Castel-Bloom: its "code" becomes simply one more style among others, losing its hegemonic status. It is for this reason that what looks like a debunking of national ideology or like a making-visible of women's oppression in *Where am I?* is in fact only the imitation of symbolic gestures of resistance found in Castel-Bloom's predecessors' writing, or in other words, only pastiche that is no longer a figure for real social antagonism.

That Castel-Bloom's tone is so playful speaks precisely this transition from Oz's late-'60s high-minded existential critique to its playful recreation as dead style. It is important for our purposes to emphasize that no ideological recourse to the primacy of the individual, or the private sphere would do here—imagining a collapse of politics from which authors find refuge in the realm of subjectivity, as some critics tend to argue. For, as we have argued in the first chapter, subjectivity is always-already entangled in the figuration of collectivity, the literary construction of individuality always in some way already an interpretation or a figuration of historical processes—the theorizations of this enmeshment attempted by thinkers as varied as Michel Foucault, Judith Butler, and Georg Lukács, all the way to the Lacanian inclusion of the Other as a constitutive part of supposedly private desire, their attempts all related to the emergence of the semi-autonomy of the private sphere from the public one, which characteristically appears with capitalism's becoming a dominant mode of production. Rather than simply speak about the dissolution of this or that idea of collectivity and literary retreat from it into subjectivity, we would do better to insist on the dialectical relation of the two, which can be discussed in terms of mediation: how does the narration of the subject present us with a level of interpretation of a social situation, or constitutes a response to this situation ethically or psychologically? (a question whose centrality to Marxist literary criticism is crucial to understanding why the latter are not simply another critical "perspective" alongside other ones, but rather dialectically contain these other critical moments, from the Lukácsian definition of literary individuals as the dialectical interaction of social conditions and class, to the Althusserian formula for ideology as subject's imagined relation to real conditions of existence, and all the way to Jameson's allegorical levels of *The Political Unconscious*).[34]

The total dissolution of actually existing structures of mediation between the individual and social situation is precisely what Castel-Bloom's literature revolves around, rather than simply the death of ideology, and herein lies its difference from its literary predecessors. In the quote from Oz's novel above, what is dramatized as a failure of such mediation: the clear national victorious narrative and its interpellation of Israeli subjects ("Keep calm. Stay indoors.") failing to relate to the heroine's private life (in which disarray and non-agency abound). In Castel-Bloom's case, in contrast, these failures are not threatening anymore; their pastiching instead signaling the absence of a hegemonic center to rebel against. Karen Grumberg's analysis of the failure of relation between private and public in Castel-Bloom—ingeniously focusing on the role of balconies as mediating space in *Where am I?*, holds true with relation to Castel-Bloom's predecessors rather than to her novel, in which these threats are no longer threatening and can be approached playfully.[35] This different figurative role of the failure of these structures of mediation is clear in the following passage:

> My brother Arthur told me that his friend Omri is visiting from the US after so many years of studying aeronautics, and that he's planning to explore the northern part of the country in a hot-air balloon, and that I'm welcome to join. [. . .] We entered a cloud. The hot air balloon was rocking a bit, as if it was at sea. "Were you ever on a ship"? Asked Omri kindly. "I paddled a boat once or twice in my life." We emerged from the cloud. I looked down into the valley, an everyday of rural villages. I waved at Shraga who was fixing a tractor's engine. "What brought you to Israel?" I said. "You did." We flew over a field of doughnuts [. . .] we passed above a field of blueberries. We started: "sometimes I go cherry-picking with a little basket." "Sometimes I eat grapes and swallow their seeds." "Sometimes I want someone to stop me in the street to ask me a practical question." "Sometimes I feel like being in charge of a radio show." "Sometimes I feel like marrying again. Like being a man's wife. Like being the wife of a successful executive." "Sometimes I feel like mumbling umm umm I love you."[36]

The convention mediating social and subjective is here of course the paralleling of the romantic involvement with acquiring knowledge of the land, both processes achieved through the trip—a mediating mechanism that was common in Zionist realist literature. (Zarchi's novel discussed in the introduction, for example, makes use of this device, as well as the much later works by Shaham and Mossinsohn, in which it already loses some of its suggestiveness and vitality as an imaginary device.) What is clear in Castel-Bloom's case is that the failure of mediation—the non-relation that holds between the social and the psycho-ethical (or the subjective) is merely a matter for play—betrayed by the repetition of the "sometimes I . . ." declarations and sheer nonsense ("field of doughnuts"). In Castel-Bloom, this failure of mediation is not menacing anymore, as it had been in Oz's contrasting of personal life and national imagination; in place of the neatly demarcated spaces of Oz's *Elsewhere, Perhaps*, which allow an actual (bourgeois) satire of national discourse to develop, in Castel-Bloom we have a pastiche of this failure: the imitation of the modernist insistence on the irreconcilability of the social contradictions that national ideology attempts to reconcile.

The playful pastiching of structures of mediation between subject and society dominate much of Castel-Bloom's novel. Examples abound, importantly for our purposes including the moments of seeming rebellion against marriage or patriarchal domination. One instance revolves around the protagonist seeking to avoid attending university, despite her husband's insistence that she do so:

> When the campus lawns turned grey, I knew I had to choose: Either I'm loyal and obedient to my second husband, and then I'm fully committed to my studies, Or I start neglecting my studies, and to lie to this cute paratrooper, who is—as far as I can tell—a good person, that is, driven by sound moral judgment, considerate of others' well-being, etc. [. . .] On a stormy day, I flowed outside against the current of students going to class. I was ejected into University Street, and I went toward the sea. [. . .] I was looking for a good spot to go down to the beach. Soft earth everywhere. I found a path. The rain grew stronger. The sea was dancing with joy, and I was wondering why. The sea was trembling with laughter, and I was wondering what's so funny [. . .] And then I felt a need to talk to the sea. To make it speak, to dance the tango with it. I've never danced the tango, neither with a sea, nor with a man. I've never danced at all. But the sea didn't give my dance even a small chance. Its strong, inconsiderate movements. I'm not surfing—let me go! Enough! But the sea pulled me into its depths. I can't swim! Enough! [. . .] I must have lost my consciousness. When I woke up [. . .] I was pulled up into a fishing boat. They were amazed to see a first-year history student, and helped me. [. . .] They took me in and I lived with them for many days. We fished for a living. I weaved fishing nets and roasted fish. They were out fishing whole days, morning to night.[37]

The self-destructive drive—the death-drive—that dominates the protagonist's relation to her second husband, is manifested also in the threatening allure that the sea holds for her. Oz's *My Michael* can be used here again as instructive comparison. Oz's protagonist, Hannah, is identical to Castel-Bloom's in this respect: a strong contradictoriness is present in her relation to her husband, who is a source of attraction to her only insofar as he is far from being a paragon of national masculinity. Hanna's desire is thus a self-destructive one, a subject position in which desire is paradoxically premised on non-agency or indirect agency. The allure of the Arab other for Oz's female protagonists has of course to do with its being forbidden or beyond the pale of the nation—imagined as possessing a savage agency, unencumbered by social divisions and regulations. Thus, Hannah's fantasies about the Arab twins have to do precisely with breaking a national taboo—a death-drive that here mediates subject and nation (or more precisely indicates the failure of mediation, insofar as Hannah and her husband are failed national subjects).[38] Castel-Bloom's passage here toys precisely with this mediating structure and its conventions, evoking the contradictoriness that dominates the protagonist's relation to her husband, and the Arab other as the object of perverse desire. Yet here the threat posed by this other is no longer real, but is simply pastiched and presented to us as imaginary convention. It is for this reason that the story ends with a gesture that confusingly reconciles the protagonist with the Arab fisherman—a gesture that playfully sabotages the hermeneutical code or the mediating literary structure, suddenly drained of its goal (either national or, in Oz's case, anti-national) when what must be contained or repressed—the romantic union with the Arab other—suddenly becomes a gesture of bland reconciliation. The failure of mediation that was threatening in Oz's literature thus becomes non-threatening in Castel-Bloom's playful pastiching of these failures.

It is therefore not critique anymore but rather its eclipsing by pastiche that is staged in Castel-Bloom's novel. Countless times the reader is cued to expect a hermeneutical process by the invocation of familiar mediating tropes of national ideology; but each time the cue turns out to be a false one, as what ensues is a playful variation on a national theme, rather than any exploratory project. The result could be said to be pure meaningless textuality, which seems according to some critics many to constitute the newness of Castel-Bloom's writing and that of other '80s and '90s authors. Again, here it could at first glance seem that we have escaped the political altogether through the nonsensical and the playful—which seem quite foreign to the seriousness of Oz's (and his contemporaries') writing.[39]

What is crucial here is to recall that nonsense is a strictly psychoanalytical phenomenon—akin to coincidences and accidental slips, on the significance of which, as symptoms, Freud famously insisted.[40] This narrow psychological conception can easily be transcoded to the more properly textual Derridian notion of being "under erasure," designating the ill-fitting yet necessary word or phrase (which forms part of Derrida's general critique of the Heideggerian metaphysics of presence).[41] To qualify Castel-Bloom's texts as nonsensical would here mean the putting under erasure (or disclosed denial) of the text's participation in the process of signification itself—a symptom without a cause, or "detective services without a case, a murderer without a corpse, a murder weapon without a victim," as the novel itself puts it.[42] Yet we should avoid adopting the novel's interpretation of itself, for it is typical of symptoms to consist partly of a denial of their status as such. It is useful to contrast Castel-Bloom's self-effacing symptom to those of Oz's protagonist, Hannah, who insists in the quote above that "a fly dashes itself against the windowpane. A fly, not a sign and not an omen. Just a fly."[43] Here, the denial only works to amplify Hannah's thoughts' status as symptoms, and the symptomatic reading of Oz protagonist is part of a hermeneutical edifice in which subjective psychopathology is strongly opposed to national discourse. It is precisely this contrasting in Oz of private drives and public discourse that lead Shaked and others to see Oz and his generation in terms of the rise of the individuality, as our discussion in previous chapters has shown. What is important for our purposes is that in Castel-Bloom, nonsense—or self-effacing symptom—is again the pastiche of such constructions in the literature of the 1960s and 1970s. The signs of an absent cause are manifested, as it were, but the depth antagonism between subjective interiority and public discourse that underpinned this symptomaticity seem to have completely vanished.

Nonsense in Castel-Bloom's novel is thus the pastiche of earlier literary constructions of symptomaticity: an imitation of figurative cues that no longer fulfills the critical modernist function but is rather presented to us playfully as representational trick. Our reading of Castel-Bloom strongly hinges on her pastiching of previous representational forms, an imitation of dead figurative devices that no longer fulfil a social-figurative role—problematizing most critical claims about the politically critical content of her work. This seems to place Castel-Bloom's novel squarely within what we defined above as postmodernism. Yet—and this is a point that must be emphasized about all postmodern works—that the figures evoked are pastiched does not mean that Castel-Bloom's novel is bereft of a figurative dimension or an allegorical interpretation. That an allegorical level of interpretation persists (regardless of a text's own aesthetic ideology) is an often ignored-point about Jameson's conception of postmodernism, one that is highlighted in, for example, Phillip

Wegner's study of '90s American culture mentioned earlier. Rather than simply being a representation of what is already known or easily articulable, according to Wegener, who takes his cue from Walter Benjamin, "allegories enable complex or abstract historical processes to take on a concrete form. Indeed, allegories often offer figurations of these historical movements before the emergence of a more proper conceptual or theoretical language."[44] We should thus resist critics' tendency to fall under the postmodern spell of their object—seeing allegory as nothing but unconvincingly illustrative of something already known—and instead pose the question of what social tension exactly is being allegorized through the process of pastichization of older figurative devices in Castel-Bloom's novel.[45] We will answer this question toward the end of the chapter, after we trace the adventures of pastiche in the work of yet another playful writer of the early '90s, Yehudit Katzir. As we will see in what follows, in Katzir's novellas pastiche operates somewhat differently—allowing an allegorical juxtaposition of the '80s to earlier periods to develop. For now, however, it should be noted that we seem to have answered at least one of the questions with which we started: The central role of pastiche in Castel-Bloom's writing seems to make her writing irrevocably postmodern, all those "searches for meaning" or political stances being playful imitations of previous representations.

Closing the Sea and the Affirmation of the Allegorical

The prevalence of pastiche in postmodernism undoubtedly makes critical attempts to read allegorically particularly challenging—as one's mind tends to be drawn to the figures that are pastiched, away from the living process of figuration actually taking place. Yet what remains bothersome in this case is that the literary text seems only to repeat what is already known, already fully conceptualized: literature becoming simply a mode of imperfect illustration of what has been already abstracted by thought. Substituting dead figures for the actual process of figuration thus results in making literature unnecessary—a kindergartner's "concrete" substitution of what all of us easily grasp conceptually. As an illustration of this or that idea, literature becomes strictly moralistic or moralizing, demonstrating the righteousness of a certain behavior or chain of events—literature becomes, in short, the loyal blind follower, or precisely what the enemies of allegory usually seek to escape, reconstituting critical writing itself as a sterile vicious circle. Discussing Katzir's four novellas of *Closing the Sea* will provide an opportunity to demonstrate the ways in which literature becomes indispensable again when our reading insists on transcoding itself allegorically, going beyond what has already reified into exchangeable ethico-psychological stances toward the figurative process that makes newness appear: the first seedlings of things not yet known or imagined. That anti-ideological contrast of so-called concrete details with the allegorical—seeing the concrete detail as exposing the allegorical as inherently illusory, so common to '80s and '90s critics,[46] is therefore its most ideological moment, one which Žižek named cynical ideology.[47] It nonetheless might be Lukács again who can provide us here with a critique of the more literary version of this ideology of the concrete detail, one that we have already mentioned in our discussion of '50s Israeli naturalism: the literary detail according to Lukács being governed by the logic of abstraction—in the sense of being abstracted from (and considered separately of) the web of social relation that produced it—which then of course leads one to recognize in the literary subject matter the same remove from reality that one thought to have already overcome by banishing the allegorical.[48] We will touch further on the persistence of the allegorical in works that aim to disrupt its very possibility in our discussion of Kenaz's *Infiltration* in the next chapter. What is important for us at this juncture is simply to emphasize that our reading of both Castel-Bloom and Katzir's early '90s works as postmodern does not entail any abandonment of the allegorical. Rather, we will return to the question of what exactly these allegorize toward the end of this chapter.

What perhaps unifies all four novellas of *Closing the Sea* is the central place of nostalgia and what used to be called kitsch before the advent of postmodern pastiche. The dead world of the aging film director of "Fellini's Shoes"—in which *yiddishkayt* and Western cinematic allure surprisingly meld with each other—is one example. Descriptive details are paramount here in generating the longing for a lost world:

> We went to the southern part of town and stopped at one of the old streets, opposite a small theater. The wall next to the box office was covered with peeling posters for Yiddish shows. We went in the back door and down a long corridor with neon lights. Faded black-and-white pictures of actors in costumes and heavy make-up were hanging on the walls where big water spots had the shape of strange moldy-smelling animals. My director walked in front of me with big strides of his polished shoes and opened the door at the end of the corridor. We went into

a dim room. The air was dusty and I started sneezing *Wer ist dort?* Screeched a women's voice from the depth of the room. *Dos bin ikh*, answered my director. *Ah, Spielman, ikh kum shoyn*, said the woman. I didn't understand a word. Spellbound, I walked around the room, which looked like they held the dance of the dead there. Long gowns of shiny cloth were hanging along the walls, next to suits, long black jackets, and Styrofoam heads with wigs and top hats and big crinkly hats trimmed with plastic flowers that stared with blind eyes on the shelf above them [. . .][49]

Representation itself—pictures, posters, costumes—becomes the realm from which the nostalgia-evoking bric-a-brac is drawn, as in the other novellas: "masks,"[50] Herzig calls them, denoting their ambivalent role in reproducing nostalgia and somehow going beyond it (toward an allegorical imaginary that we have not yet discussed). We will return to the central role of representation in what follows, as it will allow us to distinguish Katzir's nostalgia as a specifically postmodern one. If here the specter of the Holocaust is not directly invoked as *yiddishkayt*'s tragic point of termination, it makes its appearance in the first novella, "Schlafstunde." Here, the Holocaust's shadow hangs above every reminiscent invocation of Jewish life in Europe. The spaces of the grandparents' lives act in the novella as secret reproductions of a dead Jewish-European way of life, existing almost invisibly alongside national spaces:

> In the afternoon we went down, as always in the first day of vacation, to eat in the Balfour Cellar, and the tall thin waiter, who looked like a professor, and Grandfather told us that many years ago he really had been a professor in Berlin, wearing glasses in a silver frame and a beard the same color and a black bowtie, gave a little bow because he knew us, and especially Grandfather, who was a regular costumer, and pulled out the chars for us to sit down, and quickly put menus in front of us and said, What will you have, Herr Green, even though Grandfather always ordered the same thing, roast with puree of potatoes and sauerkraut, and a bunch of purple grapes for dessert, and the regular customers around the tables knew us, and smiled and waved at us with napkins [. . .] and once you told me that the restaurant had a secret cellar right underneath us and that was why it was called the Balfour Cellar, and in the cellar there were lots more barrels

like those and all of them were full of sauerkraut that could last a long time in case of another Holocaust [. . .][51]

Thus, the Holocaust is used in the first novella as a central hermeneutical key, a rich enough code through which all life can be deciphered, at least from the perspective of the grandparents' generation (we will touch on the perspective of the child-narrator in what follows). And this code makes possible a stubborn fidelity to a lost existence which is entirely unreproducible within national culture (or indeed an existence that Israeli national culture before the mid-'60s always presented as abject and degenerate, as Idith Zertal shows).[52]

Yet, as Ziva Shamir comments, the nostalgic tone strikes one as somehow false, as "fake kitsch" that seems to be nothing but a decoy or red herring for some other process taking place.[53] It is precisely the persistence of the allegorical that will become crucial in what follows for unearthing that other process animating Katzir's novellas. For now, however, we should register that the figures of nostalgia act in these texts as something like enjoyment detectors: mapping whole areas of past enjoyment and old articulations of desires. Old Jewish songs, old movie theaters, old movie stars, old food, American consumerism: the detailed world of enjoyments and taboos is clearly demarcated in every novella. Thus, for example, the family friend—and a love interest of the protagonist's mother—in "Disneyel" is clearly contrasted to the protagonist's father: the former standing for imported enjoyments drawn from the sphere of culture and representation, while the father is associated with national politics, responsibility, the unglamorous, and the realities of the Israeli welfare-state that are increasingly lacking affective charges. Collectively organized national enjoyment—holidays, for example, are here drained from fun, while everything foreign (or, the representation of foreignness) becomes highly charged with it. Temporality itself is organized according to this new logic of enjoyment: older national rhythms and unique events (holidays and Ben-Gurion's death) recede into meaninglessness, the passage of time given quality instead through the different postcards sent by the family friend from abroad: each year remembered by the specific postcard received and its "aesthetic" qualities.[54]

Crucial here is the shocking association (but not really shocking anymore, even in 1990) of the breaking of taboos with desire, of transgression with furtive enjoyment: that allure of otherness of "exilic" Jewishness or the non-national spaces of desire in "Schlafstunde," laden with threats of degeneration, strongly associated with forbidden homosexuality and incest taboo; those urban excesses that defy the national ascetic ideals, related to what was seen at some point as the hedonistic aspects of a creeping Western consumerist culture in "Disneyel"; the forbidden love affair of the young protagonist with an older married man in "Closing the Sea," and implicit homoeroticism of the young women couple; all the way to the thrill of anti-institutional crime as such—the aging director of "Fellini's Shoes" robbing the movie theater in a desperate attempt to finance his film, an uncompromising insistence on making art that defies some reified aesthetic mores of "social responsibility." All of these sites of prohibition are mined in Katzir's novellas for the way in which desire latches on to prohibition in its cycles self-perpetuation, to use the Lacanian formulation.[55]

So it is clearly with the collapse of national hermeneutic that pleasure is so strongly associated in Katzir's novellas, a falling-apart of national meaning-making that is omnipresent in them: In "Schlafstunde," for example, the encounter with "degenerate" exilic Jewishness not exactly producing a threat against which a proper national subject must guard itself; abandoning one's (nationally symbolic) job as teacher to go on a shopping spree, as in "Closing the Sea," is not to be shunned and contained but is rather related to some personal world of meaning.

It is here that the turning point in our argument will take place, for it is precisely all these transgressions that are clear cases of literary pastiche rather than living figures of the social, which is quickly revealed in even a brief look at literary history. Consumerism, with its valences of urbanity and hedonism (and even of modernist artistic sensibilities), would do well as an example here. Mossinsohn's 1946 *Grey as Sack* contains a clear figure of the threat of urban consumerist allure, in the figure of the kibbutz members' antagonism to the urban artist and his allure, a source of attraction that is clearly marked in Shamir's *He Walked Through the Fields*, and in many other '30s and '40s works (which is related to a more general representational problem posed by the city in the period, as we mentioned in earlier chapter).[56] If in the early '40s consumerism can still be thought of as a threat to a collective project, the situation is very much reversed a quarter century later: one could recall here that shopping is a common symptom of Hanna's predicament in Oz's *My Michael*, already here posing a legitimate alternative hermeneutic to the national one, against which it is squarely asserted.[57] The publication in 1970 of Amos Kenan's hugely popular *Book of Pleasures*—introducing Israelis to all manner of hitherto frowned-upon consumerist pleasures—signaling of course that consumerism was no longer perceived as a threat to the nation (S. Yizhar's fulminations against the "espresso generation" as early as 1960 has by the end of the '60s already seeming old-fashioned, and Kenan himself, a symbol of resistance to the Israeli establishment in the '50s, being absorbed into the institutional framework that was once threatened by him well before 1970).[58] Thus, by the time Katzir's work is published in 1991, consumerism and the hedonism with which it was associated was no longer seriously feared or imagined as a threat. The reproduction of this threat in Katzir's novellas is therefore pastiche of former representations.

Other hermeneutical forms can be shown in a similar manner to be pastiche of former representations: an imitation that no longer has any real social content. The Holocaust as what produces national hermeneutic or mediation between subject and collective is one such pastiched organizing thematic. Even the aging director of "Fellini's Shoes" and the mother's love interest in "Disneyel" have their precedents—for example, in the burlesque show producer, a European-Jewish relative who seduces the kibbutz-born young heroine of Oz's *Elsewhere, Perhaps* (a figure that will reappear in contemporary literature in a surprising new way, as we will see in the concluding chapters of this book).[59] Here, too, what still holds some satirical or resisting power in Oz's novels becomes pastiche in Katzir's work, a no-longer-threatening figuration of social antagonism. Another important literary-historical thread has to do with nostalgia itself, on whose function in Katzir's work we will have more to say in what follows. In 1950s literature, as we have seen, nostalgia for pre-statehood and for the 1948 war was a symptom of the repressed failure of the Zionist utopian collective project— an expression of an unconscious fidelity to former revolutionary goals. The nostalgia of Katzir's work is not a direct pastiche of these: the novellas are certainly not populated with ex-soldiers wanting to go back to the war (as in Hendel's *Street of Steps*) or back to the pre-war *Palmach* operations and *halutzic* days (as in Shaham's '50s works). Rather, this nostalgia is associated with enjoyment in some way that is no longer accessible.

The exploration of Katzir's nostalgia will now make it possible for us to demonstrate the preponderance of the allegorical in a literature that thinks itself to have left allegory behind altogether. First, we must note that the spaces of pleasure traced in Katzir's work belong to the past: the transgressive libidinal investments are old ones, belonging to older generations or at least to a foregone childhood—no longer holding their power in the present. The parental drama of "Disneyel"—the antagonism between the mother's love-interest and her husband standing for an antagonism between imported enjoyment and national existence—clearly belongs in the protagonist's past, losing its clarity and vitality by the time she is sitting at her dying mother's side. Or in "Closing the Sea," the furtive transgression of the young heroine's love affair with the married man or indulging in consumerist pleasures hold true for the protagonist's past, but fail her in her present: pretending to be sick to avoid her (symbolically nationally-responsible) work as a teacher and her visit to the Tel Aviv mall clearly fail to reproduce the same transgressive satisfaction:

> Ilana walked out of the shop with slow careful steps because the hem was so tight. People passed her quickly, men in suits, older women in blouses buttoned up to the neck and tied with a ribbon, and young girls in jeans and sneakers. She froze. Nobody was dressed as she was. Everyone was looking at her, their eyes like slivers of a shattered mirror. Her body a long black tube, and bony white legs with a red puff above them like a ridiculous clown's rear end in a target contest where nobody loses. Tears filled Ilana's eyes, as on the school playground during gym in third or fourth grade.[60]

The older transgressions thus clearly fail to produce the same pleasures, and a sense of disorientation sets in—one that constantly mixes in unstable ways the spheres of enjoyment and national subjectivity that are so neatly mapped and opposed to each other in the borrowed representations of older times. In "Fellini's Shoes," this contrast between the old and the new is played out partly through affective details: those belonging to the aging director's world, as we have seen in the quote above, all harmoniously add up to a once-functioning structure of prohibitions and desires. The affective details of the protagonist's world function provide a telling formal contrast:

> I looked out the window and saw the sea swell and overflow the shore. A salt wind whistled in awful nasal rage, and wet-rag dirty clouds choked the light, and the green water rose higher, and waves high as mountains invaded the patio of the swimming pool and the tennis courts, sweeping rackets and green balls and chaise longues and parasols and bottles of suntan lotion and Scandinavian tourists with their paperback Agatha Christie murder mysteries and sunglasses and towels and beach clogs and Walkman sets and an inner tube with a duck's head and a little boy in it, and a lifeguard and his whistle. Now with their white

tongues the waves are devouring the windowpanes and bursting in and flooding the chairs of the lobby and the rugs and the chandeliers, and the pots fill with water and sink with a plop, and decorated plates and cups float and collide with the ping of china, and spongecakes sponge up water and also sink, and knives and forks and spoons sink too, and packets of instant coffee and sugar and saccharine and mint-flavored or cinnamon-flavored toothpicks and furs and whimpering society ladies [. . .][61]

What starts as an apocalyptic hallucination—apocalyptic in the accurate sense of cueing the reader to expect some great revelation—ends up with a three-page-long enumeration of details, remnants of human pleasures that clearly fail to add up to any representational order, in contrast to what happens in the case of the director's lost world. This sense of disorientation in the present, and its contrast to the older stability or ordered spheres of life, is manifested throughout the novella. Present disorientation—one that makes true enjoyment impossible—seems thus to be contrasted to a stable, mappable past in which pleasure is to be had subversively, by violating prohibitions and taboos.

And here we finally come to the heart of the allegorical in Katzir's writing. For we must recall in this juncture that nostalgic representations of the past are new representations of it: to even invoke the empiricist notion of nostalgia as a lie or an illusion means that the past's representation has been altered, that it has been packaged anew to address some new situation. The political force of nostalgia, as Benjamin's musings on nineteenth-century Paris intimates, is thus by no means necessarily conservative. Rather, the horizon of this new representation of the past could very much be a utopian or transformative one, as it is, again, in the case of Benjamin's imaginary return to Paris. We can now finally understand what distinguishes Katzir's nostalgia: rather than a new representation of the past, it evokes the past's own already existing self-representations, or generates longing for these representations (evident if one considers the kinds of objects that evoke the "past" in the novellas: pictures, films, costumes, posters, songs—all representational objects). What distinguishes these stereotypes of the past is their stable spaces of human existence: both the sense of some national sensibility and subjectivity, and the pleasures to be had from breaking its taboos and tasting those forbidden fruits—Jewish-European otherness, consumerism, non-heteronormative sexualities, etc. This stability is wholly robbed, as we have seen, from the protagonist's present. Thus, as in what Jameson calls postmodern nostalgia films, pastiche (or the past's self-representations) is here used to present an allegorical encounter or contrast between a present that does not have a clear perception of itself, and a past that did.[62] The allegorical kernel of Katzir's work resides in providing a figurative expression for a present state of disorientation—a crisis of the social and historical imagination that Jameson's theoretical account of postmodernism called alternately a crisis of historicity and one of cognitive mapping. The present is bereft of historicity, while the self-representations of the past betrays its existence: the stable mapping of social spaces of Oz's work and in the work of his predecessors, no matter how much they subjected that mapping to critique, is wholly absent from Katzir's world; pastiching the past's self-representation and contrasting it to a present state of disorientation is an allegory of precisely what we can now, in hindsight, call a crisis of cognitive mapping or historicity. While Castel-Bloom registers this disorientation mostly spatially, Katzir can be said to provide us with a more temporal or historical understanding of it (although, of course, spatial disorientation is not absent from Katzir, nor is the dissolution of historical imagination absent from Castel-Bloom's work). Thus, what Herzig sees as Katzir's deep ambivalence to the "myths" of the past, at times falling under their spell, at times dispelling them as mere illusions, is precisely the result of a sociohistorical disorientation.[63]

We should counter two possible misunderstandings at this point before exploring further the significance of this allegory, which distinguishes Katzir's writing from her predecessors.' First, that the generalized crisis of historicity registered in Katzir's allegory is not an ethical stance that can be avoided or the result of stylistic choices (living allegorical process, in other words, always takes place beyond the ethical and psychological interpretations of a work). Rather, as we will see in the following chapter, it is a state of affairs that is registered in all literary texts of the '80s and '90s regardless of their aesthetic taste and sensibilities. The literature of the period—and that is an argument that will be better established after the next chapter—can all be seen as responses to this predicament, as different attempt to solve it or come to terms with it, using various imaginative strategies. Even to write "realistically" in the late '80s, as we will see in our discussion of Batya Gur's detective fiction, inevitably registers this crisis of the sociohistorical imagination. Second, we should also note that this allegorical reading does not preclude the ethical or psychological readings of the same texts. Rather, these should be understood as coexisting alongside each other—yet with an irresolvable antagonism. In other words, the point is not that Castel-

Bloom or Katzir are not committed to feminist ethics or an anti-national one; but that the continuous process of contrasting pastiche to the present keeps betraying a mismatch between the two—a failure to imagine the present in terms of these older representations. Thus, readings that stop at the level of ethicopsychological critique are always an antagonistic part of the multi-layered allegorical reading we are proposing here, rather than precluding each other.

We this seem to have an initial answer to one of the questions with which we have started this chapter: the literature of the 1980s and 1990s, at least to the degree that Castel-Bloom and Katzir are representative of it, seems to be postmodern indeed. It is a postmodernism with Israeli characteristics: not in the sense that some existing political problems cannot allow postmodernism to flourish truly, as Adi Ophir and others claim, in what is essentially a misunderstanding of postmodernism as a periodizing category. Rather, the pastichization of the role of American consumerism and representational culture as designating a realm of enjoyment that stands against the nation, for example, is not a trope of American postmodernism (although it appears in European ones). Pastiching the Holocaust as realm of abjection but of desire as well is another example. Yet, as our answer to the second question—why does postmodernism take root in Israeli letters?—will demonstrate, it is somewhat misleading to simply speak of the literature of the '80s and '90s as postmodern, for it glosses over the real socioeconomic circumstances of its emergence. What our analysis of Castel-Bloom and Katzir makes possible now is to rephrase the question in the following way: why does Israeli literature from the '80s and '90s display a generalized crisis of the social imagination? For it is not only Katzir and Castel-Bloom's writing in which we find this sense of disorientation, but also in the work of other authors, more "serious" and "anti-postmodern" ones, such as Kenaz and Grossman, as we will see in the next chapter. What, then, makes these allegories of the dissolution of the cognitive mapping, taking up again Jameson's terminology, so pervasive in the literature of the period?

We should briefly revisit Jameson's definition of cognitive mapping now, for it holds a slightly modified approach to understanding the rise of Modernism and postmodernism, one that emphasizes the socioeconomic transformations—those of the mode of production—rather than aesthetic characteristics. What is crucial for our argument is that the crisis of cognitive mapping associated with postmodernism (and with Modernism before it) is the result of the gradual development of capitalism onto a global scale: the stretching of capitalist relations of production beyond national boundaries pose a challenge to existing imaginaries of collectivity.[64] It becomes too cumbersome and complex for national ideology to make imaginable in any detailed way these new social sites—overseas colonial and imperialist ones usually—in which the production of the material of metropolitan everyday life takes place. Put differently, what Modernism insisted on (politically at first, then benignly) was the growing failure of the national subjects' ability to imagine their relation to what surrounds them materially: a relation that becomes only more strongly mediated by the absent colony, in which raw materials and cheap labor abound. The institutionalization of Modernism that we call postmodernism thus means the normalization of this crisis of the social imagination, its turning into a human nature or some basic unalterable reality. To argue that Israeli literature from the '80s and '90s is postmodern is therefore to argue that Israeli political economy moved historically in a similar way.

Now, the political-economic history of Israel diverges in key aspects from that of the United States or Western Europe, to be sure, and therefore makes any hasty importation of this trajectory problematic. The problem we are facing is thus twofold. First, one should understand Israel's location in the general history of the global system of combined and uneven development (a problem which is still yet to receive its full treatment by historians of political economy). The second facet of our problem has to do with unique events in the economic history of Israel—ones that might add a dimension of particularity to the more general placing within the global system. On the first problem we will have very little to say here. In its first two decades, Israel definitely depended on global surplus extraction, even if not so much directly, but through international aid it received from the empires, which according to existing research made possible Israel's ability to maintain a relative autonomy within the world market, protected as it was by the superpowers, as Jonathan Nitzan and Shimshon Bichler argue (and which saved Israel from the fate of structural underdevelopment characteristic of exploited postcolonial third-world countries).[65] It is this relative autonomy that made the formation of stable national ideology in Israel possible and maintainable at all, one could argue. That Mizrachis, women, and Arab Israelis appear as Others in the literature of the '60s and '70s can still therefore be seen as a result of their status as proletarians (or alternately as utterly excluded from wage-labor) in the relatively autonomous Israeli economy.

Yet one result of this narrative is that it requires us to address the particularities of the Israeli economy, if we are to account in any way for the appearance of a cultural crisis of cognitive mapping within this economic relative autonomy (remembering here that we trace the appearance of Israeli postmodernism to Shabtai's 1977 *Past Continuous*). The neoliberalization of the Israeli economy would not do here, for it happens too late—usually traced to 1985 by Michael Shalev and others—to account for a cultural phenomenon that appears in the late 1970s.[66] That Israeli postmodernism thus appears almost simultaneously with its American counterpart also disrupts any easy notion of Israeli authors simply imitating Western postmodern trends.

We can begin tracing Israeli particularity by noting the difference in the emergence of a so-called middle class in Israel, traced in the West usually to the 1950s and postwar Keynesian reconstruction. In Israel, surplus-value availability and distribution did not allow for a significant middle class to develop until the early 1970s, as Nitzan and Bichler and others note.[67] (Tellingly, the '60s and '70s intellectuals of Oz's texts or of Yehoshua's are noticeably poorer than the suburban professors of American postmodernism, but also far from being able to enjoy the thrills of European bohemian existence). Now, the development of a middle class is not in itself an indication of a deep change within a capitalist economy. Yet, the period's heavy economic protectionism of Israel by external powers does not lend itself very easily to an explanation of this transformation. Unless, that is, we register the economic effects of the 1967 war, which usually go unmentioned (critics choosing instead to focus on the ethical implications of the 1967 occupation). As Emmanuel Farjoun and others note, the 1967 occupation marked a dramatic expansion of Israeli capital's exclusive domain of operation: a new captive market for its products and imports, the size of which was 30 percent of the existing Israeli one, and perhaps more significantly, a new large (in proportional terms) Palestinian workforce.[68] The advantage of this captive workforce was twofold for Israeli capitalism: First, labor laws could be completely disregarded in its employment, since Palestinians are not considered Israeli citizens. Second, the 1967 war had done a great service for Israeli capitalism in breaking apart these workers from their prior workplaces (some West Bank agriculture a notable exception), intensifying their dependency on Israeli-related economic enterprises.

What allowed for the development of an Israeli middle class in the 1970s is therefore the proletarianization of the Palestinians at the hands of Israeli capitalism following the 1967 war. And it is precisely this development, I argue, that causes the crisis of social imagination that makes its first appearance in the late '70s (the delay, of course, has to do with the time it takes such economic transformations to be mediated socially and then culturally). For with the proletarianization of Palestinians everyday Israeli reality becomes increasingly produced by others that are absent from political and cultural view—or who have no place in the cultural imaginary. Subjective relation to everyday built and social environment goes into crisis as a result, as existing ideology becomes ineffective in mapping Israeli subjects' relation to their everyday life. Thus, it is those Palestinian workers in the lettuce fields of Ramat Hasharon, casually mentioned by the narrator in David Grossman's 1983 novel *The Smile of the Lamb*, whose integration into the Israeli economy results in a deep crisis of the Israeli social imagination.[69]

What the writing of Castel-Bloom and Katzir offers us are allegories of the dissolution of the social imagination. If the late-modernism of Oz and Yehoshua worked—in their own "depoliticized" way—to expose the irreconcilable contradictions at the heart of national existence, these gestures of rebellion are themselves pastiched in the works of Castel-Bloom and Katzir. The borrowed imaginary antagonisms that these writers of the '80s and '90s adopt from their predecessors are no longer charged with social content, but are instead dead representations, the shadows of former contradictions: the threats of consumerism, of non-heteronormative sexual desires, of the failure to become appropriate national subjects—all of these are no longer threatening when reproduced in the works not only of Katzir and Castel-Bloom, but, for instance, also in the popular works of Yoel Hoffman, Meir Shalev, Avraham Heffner, Ronit Matalon, Etgar Keret. In Matalon's fiction, for example, the appearance of script in bold stages an attempt at narrative mediation (as in '50s works that we discussed), that nonetheless fails.[70] While in Keret's "Missing Kissinger" the Freudian drama itself in not where active social content resides; rather, it is in the collapsing of allegorical level—the literalization of what is supposed to be an interpretive code—that the crisis of representation is enacted.[71] The playful parade of the past's own representation of itself in '80s and '90s literary works should be understood in two different interpretive registers: first, as a form of ideological (or ethico-psychological) reconciliation—the crisis of social imagination appearing as its own solution by presenting itself as a new freedom from previous illusion. This is an operation that is perhaps clearest in critics' tendency to adopt the explicit ideology of their object (something done peripherally in most critical texts), as in Uri Cohen's declaration that Orly Castel-Bloom's work rebels against "the Zionist method, for which the seemingly biological fact (being Jewish) takes precedence over that irrevocable human indefiniteness (being human)."[72] It is not the attack on Zionism that concerns us here—we have already discussed the status of this critique as pastiche in Castel-Bloom work—but rather the "irrevocable human indefiniteness" that Cohen advocates here by way of Castel-Bloom's writing. That falling under the spell of one's object is in itself a problem is not of particular concern to us here—we will return to this tendency in the next chapter, in our discussion of Kenaz's *Infiltration* and its critical reception. Instead, what is important for our purposes is that "indefiniteness," or the failure to produce a stable imaginary of the world, functions here as a reconciliatory gesture—signaling that we have as if arrived at some truth of human nature, and thus making the search for historicity itself unnecessary. In this way, what even in late-modernists such as Oz was still a gesture of ideological non-reconciliation—of keeping the figuration of contradictions open, driving narration forward—turns in Cohen's commentary and in work of the Israeli postmodernists into a gesture of ideological reconciliation. On the ideological level, then, the works of the '80s and '90s perform the task of ideological imaginary reconciliation—no matter how fervently critics announce these works (and their own) leaving-behind of "ideology." It is on this ideological level that different works creatively respond to the historical situation in which they are produced, rather than being a mere reflection of it.

Second, alongside this effect of ideological reconciliation or closure exists the more deeply allegorical interpretation, which is the more important interpretive register for our purposes, insofar as it captures the social-representational crisis itself—the inability to produce a stable mapping of the Israeli social world—a crisis whose cause we traced to the proletarianization of Palestinians at the hands of Israeli capital after 1967. The antagonism between the two interpretive registers consists in the fact that what is registered as irresolvably contradictory in this allegorical interpretation is then rewritten ideologically to produce a reconciliation. And it is here that we can finally return to our questions about the postmodernism of Israeli literature of the '80s and '90s. What we can now coherently argue is that these texts can be labeled postmodern as long as we remember that the origin or cause of their postmodernness is the proletarianization of Palestinians after 1967. Palestinians become the absent mediator between Israelis and their everyday environment—social and physical—after 1967, and this absence is precisely what brings about the crisis of cognitive mapping allegorized in the works of the '80s and '90s. The situation changes again following the first *Intifada*—armed Palestinian resistance—that began in 1987 and caused Israel to free itself from any dependence on Palestinian workers (replaced by globally available migrant workers). This later transformation, one that has to do with the dismantling of the Israeli welfare state and its neoliberalization will be discussed extensively in the last two chapters. In the next chapter, we will strengthen further our understanding of the crisis of cognitive mapping present in '80s literature, extending it to authors of the period who usually are not considered postmodern ones by Israeli critics.

5

Disorientation and the Genres
David Grossman, Yehoshua Kenaz, and Batya Gur

The previous chapter made it possible for us to establish the basic coordinates of the understanding of Israeli postmodernism developed in this volume: that the condition of social disorientation with which all Israeli 1980s and 1990s literature wrestles is a result of the massive proletarianization of Palestinians following the 1967 war. It would be somewhat misleading therefore to label this cultural turn a postmodern one, since the latter seems to signify for most Israeli critics simply the adoption of a Western cultural trend (a narrative for which we would have to ignore the too-close temporal proximity of Israeli postmodernism to its Western counterpart, if we still take Shabtai's 1977 *Past Continuous* as the marker of the former's emergence). Yet to the degree that Western postmodernism signaled the normalization and universal spread of a similar condition of social disorientation, we can still call the Israeli equivalent by the same name, provided that we remember the very local catalyst—if not cause—of this state of affairs. Indeed, what is interesting about the literary works of the '80s and '90s is not that they express a non-literary transformation such as the proletarianization of Palestinians and the sense of social disorientation thus produced. Rather, that these non-literary problems are then reworked as aesthetic problems to be solved by literary works—this is where imaginary newness lies, and where the analysis of '80s and '90s culture remains interesting.

The late-'80s works that we will explore in this chapter were chosen for the radically different ways in which they translate this problem or contradiction into the aesthetic realm. The previous chapter's authors—

Castel-Bloom and Katzir—were both characterized by the playful handling of pastiched representational contents and forms—parading the latter as so many abstracted fragments of representations once-laden with historicity. In contrast, playfulness is almost absent from the novels of this chapter: David Grossman's *The Smile of the Lamb*, Yehoshua Kenaz's *Infiltration*, and Batia Gur's *The Saturday Morning Murder*.[1] These make it possible for us to demonstrate that there is no necessary relation between postmodernism and playfulness, against all kind of Israeli exclamations about the very serious issues that prevent a full development of Israeli postmodernism.[2] Consider the seriousness of political and ethical convictions in Grossman's novel, the hermeneutical earnestness of Kenaz's, and Gur's detective's indefatigable search for truth—all of which, as we will see, are thoroughly postmodern and yet thoroughly serious.

We should also briefly discuss the different forms of what I call in this book "ideological reconciliation." Following the Marxist tradition of Althusser, Macherey, and Jameson, I argue that that ideological drive toward problem-solving should be seen as universal, at least under capitalism and its relegation of art into a sphere opposed to utility (and in which hyper-commodification of art—as in recent Hollywood movies—which seems to imply a new connection of art and usefulness, is not a return to some non-alienated usefulness of art but rather the substitution of exchange for use, as in the classic account of the commodity as production "for the other," to use Nicholas Brown's terms).[3] At any rate, what is of prime importance for an understanding of postmodernism is that what seems in it to constitute a non-reconciliation of contradictions—a leaving-open of oppositions—is itself a form of reconciliation, as Jameson once remarked. That such reconciliatory "non-reconciliation" is met with love and admiration by the market is, of course, one of the signs of this reconciliatory function of what used to be a modernist insistence on non-reconciliation. Contemporary horror films are perhaps the realm in which this phenomenon is clearest: the ending in which the monster or demon is not contained (killed or captured or at least forced into temporary rest) is today the figure of reconciliation rather than its opposite: the delight in constant danger (and its flipside's horrific realities of precarity under neoliberal capitalism) is what becomes gratified in this reconciliation-through-its-seeming opposite. Analysis of these movies that celebrate their leaving-open of contradictions therefore work with a reified version of reconciliation itself: imagining that the containment of the monster is always its moment.[4]

Yet it is not the case that one cannot escape reconciliation, or that whenever it seems to be avoided, it is always an illusion. Rather, as our context of the transition from Modernism to postmodernism already implies, reconciliation should be understood historically: what is at first a leaving-open of contradictions becomes at a later moment its own solution—signifying an imaginary resolution rather than an antagonism to be addressed. Thus, what in Modernism designates a burning problem that remains unresolved becomes naturalized in postmodernism as something that never needed reconciliation in the first place (and in the process the original oppositions are drained of social meaning, becoming pastiche). Phillip Wegner's recent writing on Greimas's rectangle and historical transformation demonstrates perfectly this process in which what was once the contradictory-utopian is transformed in a later moment into one or (usually) more possible solutions for the problem it once designated.[5]

Any theorization of the ideological work being performed in literature should thus always keep in mind the historical essence of any notion of ideological reconciliation. This observation will become pertinent in our discussion of the three novels by Grossman, Kenaz, and Gur.

The Smile of the Lamb and The Pursuit of Peace

Commentary on Grossman's early novels has tended to focus on his less-directly political works, such as *See Under—Love*, or *Book of Intimate Grammar*.[6] This is not surprising, considering that their publication took place in a critical atmosphere in which the political signifies the anti-literary, at least since Gershon Shaked's declaration of the arrival of the 1960s "New Wave." For once the dialectical relation between the spheres goes unrecognized, one has very little to say about a political novel: it seems wholly unnecessary to drag complex figurative devices simply in order to argue for a political position, be it new or old. The '80s transformation changed little in this respect: politically committed novels remained anathema to critical sensibility, as Yaron Peleg claims, even as literary critique itself was once again allowed to discuss literature politically.[7]

It is precisely in this context that Grossman's *The Smile of the Lamb* becomes important for us. For it will allow us to demonstrate that post-modernism is not a matter of choice, but rather a historical condition to be negotiated and solved in imagination. Demonstrating that will become in what follows a matter of rereading the novel through a seemingly small displacement of the way in which it is usually read. Most commentators focus on Grossman's political commitments—celebrating, like Yisrael Barma, Grossman's demonstration that "politically engaged writing does not need to be simplistic or flat."[8] In contrast, we can now recognize that it is precisely on this ideological level that the operation of reconciliation is performed, which does not annul its creativity and newness in its context. Thus, rather than understanding all political interpretive frameworks as simplistic (a notion with which the novel as an artistic form in general is intimately related—as in Stendhal's famous declaration that discussing politics in a novel is like shooting a gun during a concert), we should remember that explicit historical and political context is many times relegated to the representational periphery of novels—be they the ideologically committed ones of '20s and '30s, or in A. B. Yehoshua's "Facing the Forests," which will become more important for us below, and in which the post-'48 war context and national temporality appears constantly at the fringes of the work.[9] Thus, Grossman's novel can now be seen as recreating this novelistic relation between political periphery and personal center-stage, but in the context of Israeli post-'67 occupation of the West Bank. Thus, the challenge that Grossman successfully tackles is to reconcile—and this is an ideological reconciliation if there ever was one—the late-modernist crisis of mediation of system and individual (in which ethics seem to always fail or falter), with the historical and political context of the occupation as such—which seems to demand such stable ethical code.

Our reading will proceed in three steps. We will first see how, for each of the four main characters, the late-modernist-turned-postmodern failure of narration takes place in a different way. We will then see how this failure, dramatized on an ethico-psychological register, becomes welded with its historical context. Finally, we will be able to set our sights on the antagonism between the two as such, tracing the way in which it becomes, as we just discussed, its own solution or reconciliation—its newness finally inhering in making the new subject matter—Israeli military rule over the Palestinian West Bank—fit Oz's and Yehoshua's paradigmatic structure of narrative failure.

That the failure of mediation or understanding is strongly present in the case of all characters in the novel is plainly visible, taken by the novel as a truth of some human condition. Here it is, for example, in the opening pages of the novel, narrated by Uri, one of the central characters of the novel:

> [E]verything is not understood. Shosh said once that what we think we understand, the bits of information we draw, are like

the least fit members of some imaginary herd. "Darwin's law of consciousness," she called it: that's what the herd uses against the deadly effects of human intelligence, leaving us with the poorest meat, and not much pleasure in the hunt.[10]

Or a few pages later:

> But drive on. Lies, all lies. The menfolk's square you're passing now, for instance, with its skeleton of a car that probably dates back to the Ottoman empire, this square, too, is a lie, and so is everything that is supposed to have happened here, such as Khilmi flying overhead like a quiet old bird; I mean, that's preposterous, and so are the other things, like Katzman's father imprinting his memories in Katzman's mind, or Shosh lecturing me so eloquently on the morphology of lies; and Zussia isn't the only abstruse sort of hero, as Abner calls him, who mustn't be pushed too far. We're all *kan-ya-ma-kan* ["there-was-or-there-was-not," O.N.] around here, the only real thing about us is the pain we bring.[11]

The crisis of communication or meaning thus becomes one of the central axes around which the entire novel revolves, in a much more explicit way than Oz's characters' Freudian denials or symptoms that we discussed in this previous chapter. Another important difference from Oz or Yehoshua is that in these authors' work, characters' descriptions of external reality are still necessary to dramatize formally the failure of mediation—the fly repeatedly hitting the glass in Oz's *My Michael* that we quoted in the previous chapter is one straightforward example of this usage of external reality (and, of course, the forests in Yehoshua's important short story, which we will discuss further later, are another). In Grossman, much fewer descriptions of the narrator's immediate reality can be found, as the novel is mostly made up of recollections and the telling of past events, which of course prevents such formal use of external reality, which simply recedes from the visible realm altogether.

This attitude to communication, which we can call the romantic paradox—meaning being lost in the moment of its expression—is one of the main ideological devices through which the failure of mediation is figured in the novel. We should notice this paradox's intimate relationship with that tendency to develop private languages or forms of expression in Grossman, which is only present in *Smile of the Lamb* in embryonic form, and which will be much commented upon after the publication of *The Book of Intimate Grammar*. As Avidav Lipsker-Elbak comments, the creation of private languages holds an anti-national impulse, in its challenging of the nation as that imagined community of unified language (and so strongly in the case of the Zionist revival of Hebrew).[12] Private languages become associated with the familial and other immediate interpersonal connections, their origin in precognitive embodied relationships, as Elbak comments, and they become the markers of these easily perceivable social groups that are wholly antagonistic to the national "repressive canonization." The communicative romantic paradox is expressed in the inevitable corruption of what begins as unalienated language when it becomes disembodied, semiotic, and denotative, a language that can only guarantee its continued life as long as it works to "continuously expose new private orders that have not yet been petrified by lexicons of conventional signs."[13]

Yet the cause of this imminent betrayal of language in Grossman is not really meat-eating, as Elbak suggests, but is rather much more mysterious and difficult to find. Its pervasiveness endows it with the status of a natural phenomenon, a kind of immutable "language-nature," as should be clear even from the early stage of development of this textual ideology in *The Smile of the Lamb*. It is only in the immediately personal realm rather than the mediated one that languages bear any meaning—and it is for this reason that the entire novel is made up of personal reflections. Here it is, for example, in the case of Shosh's character:

> Only I can't believe [Abner] or the pain behind his words anymore. Because now I know that the human inclination to deceive will use anything, even love, as a lethal weapon, and a passion for one person can be translated into the body language of another, nothing is ever in and of itself. And we are as empty signs, and if we have any meaning, we recognize it only according to our temporary place in a word that is being deleted in the moment of its writing.[14]

Thus bodies speak behind consciousness's back, and understanding becomes a matter of an inarticulable instant. Or consider the following, also in Shosh's words:

> . . . and look at this from a more humorous and story-like perspective, because, you see, this too, is a modern art of the

lie, the art of simultaneity, that demands a humorous side, and a tolerable side, and one that will be justifiable in well-formed arguments, even in the most painful and gruesome cases, and that we can always know that we speak the truth when at another place in our body someone lies, and that one thing always stands for something else and one person is always the tool of another, and nothing is in and of itself, so that my passion for Katzman could be diverted to Uri, and my desire for Uri was cruelly translated into my language with Mordy.[15]

Here the failure of narration or mediation is associated with the kind of naturalism that we have seen at work in Hendel's *Street of Steps*, whose additional formal similarities to *Smile of the Lamb* should not go unnoticed: each chapter narrated from a different consciousness and is completely immersed in that consciousness's recollections and stream of thought. The aporetic simultaneity of good-and-bad, the inability to control social exchanges and the substitutions of desire—are all here related to a failure of communication or linguistic expression that is much more developed in Grossman than in Hendel's novel. Yet if in Hendel's case the failure of expression still holds a certain threat to national cultural hegemony, this is of course no longer the case in Grossman's 1980s novel—in which this literary "attack" on national language is old news, borrowed from the literature of the '60s and '70s and becoming almost a natural state of things. What in Hendel is still perceived as an imagined threat or alternative to national language becomes a condition of all communication for Grossman's novel.

Yet we should not here conclude that Grossman's novel is primarily a 50s pastiche. That its subject matter is drawn from the post-67 war context is of course important in this respect, signaling to us that the treatment of this new material must inject some kind of newness into the representational frame. That newness takes us immediately into the realm of politics or course, and the marginal appearance of historical context in the novel: it is tempting here to suggest that Grossman's novel's relation to the '67 war stands is somehow analogous to Hendel's *Street of Steps* relation to the '48 war: in both cases an irrational feeling of loss, failure, and a collapse of mediation is contrasted to the celebration of victory. Yet one should be careful with analogies such as these. First, Hendel's novel is published against the reigning feeling of elation and national mission sentiment prevalent at the time.[16] Grossman's 1983 novel, on the other hand, represents the period following the 1967 war from the perspective of a much less semiotically effective national imaginary—strongly visible after the '82 war and public responses to it. As we said in the previous chapter, what has been a gesture of resistance in Hendel's case becomes in Grossman's 1983 novel a stance of the literary center.

Thus the new representational content introduced by Grossman's novel makes it into more than a pastiche of previous allegories; yet the novel is blocked from, in some way, performing a simple "updating" of these allegories with new content—since the dissolution of national discourse no longer functions as a threat to some living hegemony. We would now do well to address this newness, which has much to do with the representation of Arabs and the political context. It should be clear that the normalized crisis of mediation is equally present in the case of Khilmi, the central Palestinian character of the novel:

> It was Shukri Ibn Labib who revealed to me that just as the characters of script are dead, lacking a life of their own, begetting neither joy nor sorrow until they meet and touch, so it is with people and dogs and the books of the Koran, or grapes upon the vine . . . what are these but dead markings, the writing of an invisible hand? So it is, Shukri instructed me, the white hairs on his craggy nose fluttering in the breeze like a horse's mane, they are only dead markings, and the pain and joy we beget upon each other pass understanding. Perhaps, shutting his eyes as in dark meditation, only a madman can understand these children born of travail. Perhaps only a mute can suffer them, rejoice in them, perceive them like glass needles inside: perhaps only a blind man can read them in the seven shades of white inside his eye.
>
> But I could not say this to the youth [Yazdi, Khilmi's son, O.N.] who sat before me . . . .[17]

The reduction of language to the body, the separation from which immediately evacuates it from meaning, is plainly clear here. The excesses of descriptive details ("the white hairs on his craggy nose") are not exactly the result of some naturalist fidelity to what exists, but of so many indecipherable signs of "pain and joy" that "pass understanding." That the failure of language itself cannot be communicated—that Khilmi cannot convey even this inability to his son Yazdi, seals the paradox: the failure of language itself belongs on the plain of the inexpressible, one cannot even proceed safely even by trying to express this failure, thus sabotaging Khilmi's very attempt to express it.

What is important for our purposes is that here we encounter formal newness: Khilmi is made completely equivalent to the non-Arab characters in the novel by ultimately getting caught in the same failure of mediation that engulfs their consciousness. It is this equivalence of the Arab to the non-Arab characters that is paramount in Gilead Morhag's 1986 account of the '80s transformation of the representation of the Arab in Israeli literature. The equivalence of Arab and Jewish character marks for Morhag a break from a tradition in which Arab figures help articulate transgressive desires or moral injunctions.[18] Yochai Oppenheimer's much later and more extensive survey of the representation of Arabs in Israeli fiction reproduces Morhag's narrative in this regard, arguing that the uniqueness of Grossman's novel is to be found in its "ability to present the figure of the Arab as having a fascinating internal world rather than simply a foreign (or exotic) one, and as possessing a language that expresses a struggle with both external and internal oppression (the occupation and nationalist ideology)."[19] Both critics seem to share the ideological stance that they ascribe to their object: praising psychological depth and generally contrasting older use of Arab figures to think through Zionist desire and ethics to "real" subjectivity. Grossman thus gives us the "real" Palestinian, as it were.

Therefore, the equivalence that we have detected between Arab and non-Arab in *Smile of the Lamb* is usually taken as a secularization of older representations in which Arabs are merely the appendages of Jewish subjectivity. Yet it is always the case that to imagine a step out of ideology is precisely to fall under its spell, to use Žižek's formulation.[20] We will now therefore rewrite this narrative through a quick exploration of a well-known precursor of Grossman's novel, A. B. Yehoshua's "Facing the Forests," first published in 1963. In Yehoshua's well-known novella, an academic takes a job as a forest-fire watchman. His work brings him into daily contact with an old Arab and his daughter, who provide him with food. He soon finds out that the forest covers the ruins of a forgotten Palestinian village, the forest clearly acting as a national erasure of previous Palestinian presence, one that is symbolically revealed once a fire actually erupts—as a result of the actions of the watchman and the Arab.

The Arab in Yehoshua's short story clearly stands for a resistance to national ideology, as Oppenheimer maintains, a resistance that we have come to expect from the late modernists of the 1960s.[21] Here, the scholar's muted sense of alienation from his social reality converges with the erasure of Palestinian presence from the landscape—both condensed into a monstrous threat to national ideology. The Arab figure thus clearly becomes a figure for Jewish desires and fears, rather than acting as a full-blown subject. Hannan Hever takes this observation that the Arab is used as figure for Jewish desire one step further—seeing Yehoshua as actually staging a preservation of national ideology, rather than its critique, in allowing a Jewish protagonist to assume a minoritarian stance or voice (that of the Arab) in relation to dominant ideology.[22] Yet the problem that Hever is trying to solve using this formula is the paradox that while Yehoshua's story seems to be challenging national ideology, it is actually celebrated by Israeli national hegemony. We have already suggested a solution to this problem: seeing the late modernists of the 1960s as the defanged inheritors of the real threat posed by the "anti-genre" or Hebrew literature modernists of the early twentieth century. The real abject notion to the national hegemony of which Yehoshua is undoubtedly a part is, as argued in previous chapters, the repressed failure of Zionism—the discontinuity or break between the utopian enterprise and the capitalist nation state that replaced it. We do not need, therefore, to follow Hever's attempt to turn Yehoshua's seemingly resistant stance to national hegemony into a reinforcement of it.

Rather, we can see it for a (defanged) resistance in which the strange combination of Jew and Arab can be seen as something like what Freud called condensation: in which different and often contradictory valences are somehow fused together into a single figure. And it is the meaning of this condensation that we must then uncover—a meaning that exists on a different plane altogether than the Jewish-Arab antagonism through which it is expressed.

Thus it should be observed that temporality and history constitute the deeper subject matter of "Facing the Forests," our scholar-protagonist being a historian, and the story taking place—vaguely but significantly—after the 1948 war. The narrator's alienation from anything national needs no emphasizing, of course. However, what should be observed is that an antagonism of temporalities dominates the story formally: the repetitive or frozen time of the watchman contrasting sharply with a national temporality of victory and progress, punctuated by national commemoration that reaffirm it—the forests themselves being a matter of national pride and often used as staging for remembering national time, toward which the watchman feels nothing but detachment:

> Ceremonies. A season of ceremonies. The forest turns all ceremonial. The trees stand bowed, heavy with honor, they take on meaning, they belong. White ribbons are strung to delimit new domains. Luxurious buses struggle over the rocky roads, a procession of shiny automobiles before and behind . . . Little by little they assemble, crush out cigarettes with their black shoes and fall silent—paying homage to the memory of themselves. The fire-watcher, too, participates in the ceremony, from afar, he and his binoculars. A storm of obedient applause breaks out, a gleam of scissors, a flash of photographers, ribbons sag.[23]

Thus, the watchman's eternal present—a waiting for something to happen that is not even punctuated by the rhythms of the day anymore, as he can't fall asleep fearing a fire might start—is constantly formally contrasted with a national time of progress.

This formal dominant makes it possible for us to argue that it is alienated wage labor that is actually the social experience that is unconsciously expressed in the repetitive, unchanging temporality inhabited by the watchman, and that contrasts so violently with an imagined temporality of national progress. Utopian is here precisely the burning of the woods, the act that is imagined as eradicating the eternal, repetitive, rhythm of wage-labor, before its postmodern turning into "career." The Arab and the destroyed Arab village also inhabit this temporality—the erased village eternally awaiting revelation—divorced from and set against Israeli national time. Thus, what the Arab in "Facing the Forests" helps figure is, however feebly, wage-labor itself and the threat of revolution. We can here now notice that we have transcoded the interpretation of the figure of the Arab in pre-'80s literature: on an ethico-psychological level, Arabs remain non-subjects in this literary period, useful as simple figurative vehicles for expressing Jewish desires and their transgressions. But on a deeper level of historical interpretation—that of the history of the modes of production, to use Jameson's terms—the Arab is part of the figuration of labor under capitalism as such. These two interpretations are not antagonistic to one another—one does not have to choose between them. Rather, they belong to two different interpretive spaces: what is sayable using the terms of one is inexpressible in those of the other.

We can now finally return to our discussion of *Smile of the Lamb* and register the implications of our quick rereading of the representational history of the Arab in Israeli fiction. The equating of Arab and Jewish subjects performed on the novel can now be reread as a loss: the loss of the possibility of figuring the otherness and resistance of labor and the proletariat that the Arab had made possible before. The inclusion of the Arab as a subject equivalent to Jewish-Israeli ones thus, at the same time, marks a loss or a weakening of our imaginative power here: from revolutionary non-subject the Arab becomes another reified bourgeois consciousness, entailing a degradation of possibility of imagining an alternative to existence under capitalism. Again, one should emphasize that this interpretation does not cancel out the previous one: the inclusion of the Arab as a subject is at the same time a weakening of Israeli literature's ability to figure the rhythms of labor.

Thus, the failure of mediation between subject and social world inherited from the late-modernists is universalized in *Smile of the Lamb*. This failure is everywhere in the novel presented together with the everyday realities of the Israeli oppression of Palestinians, at least in the narratives of the three male figures: Uri, Katzman, and Khilmi. Uri's pursuit of an "enlightened occupation"—seeking constructive cooperation between Israeli authorities and Palestinians is constantly frustrated—the corpse of a donkey in the middle of the Palestinian town serves here as a figure for the persistent contradiction or tension that no one can solve:

> And so began the donkey days . . . The air was heavy with the stench, and at first I just sat there covering my nose with bits of soap on a handkerchief. The donkey had burst open, and its coiling intestines poured out into the dust . . . day after day. The neighborhood folks grew used to me and no longer crowded around my jeep or asked me questions, because they realized I wasn't going to answer them. But they also got used to the donkey. The women walked right past it with babies in their arms . . . and the children played stickball up and down the lane, their shouts blotting out the stench somehow, and I watched, I had decided not to make a move until I understood . . . Even now I feel a ripple of rage, even now when it's not important anymore . . . I barged into [Katzman's] room without knocking and stopped there before him, red faced, perspiring, and trembling with rage, Get the donkey out of there, Katzman, get it out of there! . . . Katzman . . . said, The donkey stays. One of my men was wounded in that lane, and two months ago something similar happened there, and if they refuse to turn in the culprit, when we're sure we know who it is, let them choke.[24]

The displacement or transference of violence from the killing of the soldier to Katzman's insistence that the donkey corpse remain where it lays, a form of punishment to which Uri objects, is of course one of the dizzying transferences and substitutions that human desire inexorably and imperceptibly enacts, according to the novel's ideology of language—which we have discussed earlier. The confrontation between Uri and Katzman itself undergoes one such transcoding: the fight over the donkey corpse suggestively acting as substitute for another fight between the two, over Katzman's affair with Uri's girlfriend, Shosh.

To Uri's desire's entanglement with the social realities of the occupation in some unbreakable knot we can add Katzman's—his past as a child in Europe during the Holocaust also somehow responsible for his contempt for what he sees as Palestinians accepting or servile attitude toward their Israeli oppressors.[25] Here, too, belongs Khilmi's conviction that there exists a mystical symmetry of violence, or that "the Jews are not a stupid race and they have probably realized by now that the conqueror is also the conquered, and that injustice has teeth in his tail," which mirrors his general reclusiveness and inaction, also a result of his personal history.[26] The same can be argued for Shosh's character, in whose life the occupation is not directly present, becoming instead metaphorized through her relations to the other characters and to the subjects of her work. In all of these cases, the Israeli occupation of Palestine becomes part of a personal psychological drama in which it never becomes clear if social realty is a cause or an effect. It is important to underscore the difference between *The Smile of the Lamb* and the social mapping of early Zionist realism, one that we addressed in the first chapter: in the 1920s and 1930s, one sees clear causal connections between social form and subjective experience. In Grossman's novel, no such causal connections are allowed anymore—only weak analogical substitutions suggest themselves only to be canceled a moment later, in what is an absolute fidelity to the failure of mediation of the late-modernists.

And so we have a pairing of a political context—the post-'67 war Israeli occupation of Palestine—with the subjectivities of the four main protagonists, for which, as we have seen, no mediation from the personal to the social is possible. That the novel ends with a grotesque satire of an attempt to end the Israeli occupation of Palestine—Khilmi's kidnapping of Uri, demanding that the Israeli military withdraw from all Palestinian lands—attests precisely to this inability to imagine a mediation from the personal to the social. (Another way of putting it would be the collapsing-together of two levels of interpretation: personal and collective allegories—the grotesqueness of Khilmi's act reminds one very much of Etgar Keret's fiction). The Israeli liberal left's conviction that "the occupation" somehow corrupts the inner life of Israelis is thus demonstrated.[27] And it is this juxtaposition of the two that is precisely the operation of ideology in the novel: a kind of union of opposites that falls apart if scrutinized too closely. We can now recall our earlier discussion of the ideological operation of reconciling oppositions. We argued that in the transition from late-Modernism to postmodernism, what used to constitute non-reconciliation becomes itself a reconciliatory gesture—one that is perceived as a reaffirmation of one's unconscious beliefs, rather than a challenging of them. *The Smile of the Lamb* is an instance of precisely such non-reconciliatory-reconciliation: the effectiveness of "the occupation" as an ideologeme is reaffirmed by its fusion with a crisis of mediation (or the unbridgeable alienation of subject from social world). It is in this sense that Grossman's political novel is just as "postmodern" as the works of Orly Castel-Bloom and Yehudit Katzir that we discussed in the previous chapter—demonstrating once again that postmodernism was never simply a style to be adopted or dropped at will. A quick thought experiment easily demonstrates that Grossman's novel indeed offers one such postmodern reconciliation. One only has to try to imagine a novel in which Uri's personal effort to usher in Israeli-Palestinian peace fails, but his project itself is reaffirmed as beneficial (which is, of course, an adaptation of a popular "genre" plotline). That would of course necessitate imagining all manner of material connections between Israelis and Palestinians that *Smile of the Lamb* never addresses. Such a novel, had it existed, would surely have been greeted with contempt in the 1980s—in this case a sure sign that it is this resolution that actually expresses some kind of resistance to hegemonic sensibilities.

Infiltration, or, the Postmodern Soldier

Yehoshua Kenaz's *Infiltration* will offer a very different point of entry into 1980s "serious" literature than Grossman's political novel. What becomes of crucial importance in the case of *Infiltration* is that it belongs to a genre inaugurated by late-'40s and '50s writers, including the works by Yizhar, Shaham, and Mossinsohn that we discussed in previous chapters, whose subject matter has to do with military experience. As we argued in the '50s chapters, the soldier takes the place of the settler as a leading figurative device. Now, at the outset we should emphasize that the works belonging to this genre are not really about war. With the exception of some of the *Palmach* generation's writing, influential novels that narrate the experience of Israeli soldiers do not revolve around the lived experience of war, as the latter is usually represented in literature since the First World War. Yizhar's *Khirbet Khizeh*, with its very un-war-like Israeli conquest of a Palestinian village, is a good example. And so is the very little attention given to actual battle in Shaham's work—whose condemnation by 1960s "New Wave" critics revolves precisely around its social dimension as we have seen. More recent novels such as Yuval Shimoni's *A Room* (1999) or Ron Leshem's *Beaufort* (2005) can serve as additional exemplars of this genre, which has everything to do with soldiers but almost nothing to do with war.[28] That means that we are not dealing here with war stories in any generic or formal sense. Rather, the appropriate name for these narratives is the rather cumbersome one of "genre of soldiers' experience," a genre from which some war novels, such as Yizhar's formidable *Days of Tsiklag* (1958) or Kaniuk's *Himmo King of Jerusalem* (1966), are excluded.[29]

Now, to claim the status of a genre for a group of literary texts is to do more than simply assert thematic or formal commonalities. Rather, I will take up here Phillip Wegner's notion of a genre:

> The dialectical model I propose here views genre as akin to other collective institutions—languages, cultures, nations, classes, bureaucracies, corporations, and so forth—in that it too possesses what Martin Heidegger names *Dasein,* or "being-in-the-world." As with the particular embodiments of these other institutional forms, the works composing any genre make palpable, in the course of their narrative realization, a self-interpreting "awareness" of what it means to be part of this institution and its history. Such a self-interpretation becomes evident both in the ways each participant in the generic institution engages with the possibilities and potentialities of its predecessors—the existence or being-in-the-world of the individual text placed in a background of shared social practices that are sometimes referred to by the abstraction "generic conventions"—and also in its particular remaking of the institution in response to the desires and interests of its unique historical context.[30]

We can thus see *Infiltration* as performing precisely such reflection on the genre inaugurated by Yizhar and others, in which the social transformations that fuel '80s Israeli "postmodernism" feature prominently. In Yizhar's or

Shaham's late '40s works, this genre was used, as we have seen, to express the repressed break or discontinuity between the Zionist utopian collective project and the establishment of a capitalist nation-state. A failure of narration was used to figure this repressed historical break—the demise of radical social transformation as a project and a descent into welfare-state capitalism. It is precisely this narrative failure as a generic convention that is reworked in *Infiltration*, rethinking the institutional role of the genre in response to its moment, to use Wegner's definition.

Infiltration's reception, exhaustively described by Dror Mishani, will prove an important starting point for us here, for it charts the main coordinates of the novel's national-allegorical interpretation—an interpretive framework on which most critics of the novel focus.[31] Since Kenaz's soldiers are not busy fighting battles—the whole novel follows a group of soldiers through their basic training period—critical commentary is not focused on attitudes to Palestinians. Rather, the national-allegorical interpretation is focused on problems internal to Israeli society. Of those, the discussion of the novel's relation to national allegory seems to revolve around two main arenas. The first is the one which we have already discussed extensively: the emergence of Israeli "postmodernism" in the 1980s. The second has to do with the representation of Mizrachi Jews in the novel.[32] The two questions, usually discussed separately, are in fact strongly related to each other, as we will see in what follows.

Infiltration is not structured around a single event or a noteworthy historical moment, such as the 1948 war and the occupation of the Palestinian village in Yizhar's novella. Rather, it is precisely the expandability or non-importance of Kenaz's soldiers that unifies them, as many critics note.[33] The soldiers in the group were all deemed physically unfit for combat positions, which immediately disrupts any attempt to locate their subjectivities within any heroic nationalist military narrative. Of the novel's many characters, four become more central than the rest: Avner, a Jerusalem-born Mizrachi romantic; Micky, a professional soccer player from an urban background, with strong individualist or liberal streaks to his character; Alon, who grew up on a kibbutz to be a true believer in the national ethos; and Melabes, the narrator throughout most of the novel, whose character is much harder to pin down than that of the others, for reasons that will become clear.

Two more complicating factors have to be taken into consideration. The first is that the novel functions as something like a coming-of-age novel: the reader expects the young protagonists to undergo personal transformation as a result of their encounter with the allegorized national group. Within the context of the national allegory, the coming-of-age aspect of the novel cues the reader to expect to see nothing less than the formation of national subjects—a cultural figurative operation that by the '80s has been thoroughly reified and satirized. But that leads us to the second factor: while Kenaz's novel was published in the 1980s, its plot is taking place in 1950s Israel. What the reader expects is therefore a new understanding of the '50s from the perspective of the '80s, generating something like a renewal of national historicity. Both of these are, of course, a result of the genre's institutional role in figuring the national collective—the soldier, since the late '40s, functioning as the figure of the Israeli "everyman." The cueing of the reader to expect a becoming of national subject to take place is therefore something like the content carried by the very form of the genre into this later iteration.

Yet it is narrative failure as an inherited convention that comes, slowly but surely, to sabotage the becoming of the national subjects. But in the context of the 1980s this disturbing failure ceases to be disturbing. An indeterminacy of the subjects' process of transformation characterizes this "failure" throughout *Infiltration*. Thus, for example, very early in the novel, Melabes betrays Avner's trust while they are on guard duty together, letting Avner get caught smoking on duty. Melabes finds a sense of self-defining freedom in committing the act of betrayal:

> It was now clear to me that he would be caught and punished. Just as on similar occasions I had known what was about to happen with an uncanny certainty and vividness. I was overcome by the sensation that I was losing the possibility of hesitation and choice and control over my actions, and operating within the framework of some grand plan, step by step [. . .] Thanks to this sensation, I had been enabled, on these very rear occasions, to taste the taste of freedom, and to realize that it was not simply a wish and a promise, but a real and actual event.[34]

The unity of freedom and necessity here seems pregnant with the possibilities of a successful convergence of personal desire and collective need, thereby advancing the coming-of-age narrative and that of national allegory. Yet, a few pages later, rather than a milestone of national coming-of-age story, the act of betrayal is suddenly completely drained of its meaning for Melabes:

> . . . the act I myself had committed now seemed very disappointing to me. Almost meaningless. After the fading of the

> sense of power and freedom that I had experienced in myself [. . .] I no longer felt any desire for the act. All it had left in me was a feeling of dreariness, lowness, and wretchedness. No transformation had taken place in me or my surroundings.[35]

What is insinuated in the text is that the act itself had been the object of Melabes's desire all along (rather than its possible implications); he has enjoyed taking the position of the traitor to his friend, rather than being that traitor. For now, what is important to notice is the indeterminacy generated by these "almost-moments" of a national coming-of-age story: the reader is cued to expect some dramatic development toward some renewed self-understanding, which is every time deferred. If the initial reason for the soldiers' uneasiness is that they are prevented from imagining themselves taking part in a more heroic national narrative, as we argued above, this uneasiness receives here a more permanent cause: this indeterminacy of meaning, this constant failure to narrate, in which every cueing up of the reader to expect some allegorical understanding immediately undoes itself, becomes a permanent cause of disorientation Kenaz's soldier's restlessness and disorientation.

This indeterminacy is present throughout the novel, repeating countless times for all its main protagonists. Thus, for example, Avner's romantic pursuit of women is reignited over and over again, even though at the end of each episode he seems to have changed in a way that would break the endless cycle. After his pursuit of Ziva seems to have failed, for example, Avner suddenly turns his attention to her friend Miri, who he had rejected in the past:

> She gives him a look calculated to show that she can see right through him, that his motives are crystal clear to her, and that she has no intention of falling into his trap again. He knows that to get her cooperation he must be sincere, speak with humility that bears the stamp of truth. But the need to go beyond the truth, to test other possibilities, is stronger than he is [. . .] "Look, don't think I'm stupid. You came to ask where Ziva is. Why don't you come straight to the point?" "No," he says, "I have no chance with Ziva. That was just a dream. I've woken up. I know she's making a fool out of me [. . .] once I thought I knew all there was to know about girls. Now I've come to realize that I don't know the first thing about them." [. . .] He

nods. Gradually the lies and the empty words are becoming true: He desires this ironic girl, not as means of reaching Ziva, not as substitute to fill the loneliness of the evening ahead of him, he desires her in truth, for what she is.[36]

Lies become truths as the performance of desire generates true desire; and one final twist: performing desire includes a denial of its nature as performance for Avner, who sounds in this passage as if he is inspired by Althusser's account of the workings of ideology, in which practice precedes belief.[37] Avner's romantic pursuits are thus always reborn, and their rebirth depends on his avowal of the opposite, and his restlessness is precisely the result of not being able to distinguish transformation from repetition. The novel explores all possible valences of what must be seen as inescapable antinomy of transformation and sameness: The turning of means into ends in themselves (as in Melabes's example above, in which the act becomes its own purpose); which is also the becoming aesthetic of the functional and vice versa, recalling the Kantian bourgeois definition of art, but also its Lyotardian reworking, which is simultaneously that dizzying distinction between temporal perspectives: contingent acts losing their very contingency when viewed retrospectively, as in the Hegelian Ruse of Reason.[38] And since, in Avner's case, the confusion has a temporal sense, Avner ends up confessing to a temporal feeling of disorientation, which complements Melabes's feeling of spatial disorientation.[39] Both spatial and temporal disorientations echo the meaning of the novel's Hebrew name, which denotes a military exercise in which lone soldiers need to orient themselves in unfamiliar surroundings.

It is this indeterminacy that leads to what Hannah Herzig sees as a complicated threading of thematic and ideological oppositions, in which each "value" tends to be destabilized narratively countless times.[40] For example, power or strength seem at moments to be associated for the narrator with both collectivity and beauty, particularly during some of the group drills the soldiers perform, expressing some "marvelous logic, uniform, economical, and spectacular [. . .]" culminating in a feeling that the other soldiers "were feeling the same thing [Melabes] felt, and what has been up to now surrender and renunciation turned into love. It flowed among [them] like repressed weeping, contagious and electrifying and full of beauty."[41] Yet, in other instances strength, power, and beauty becomes associated with evil—for example through the soldiers' fascination that exercise of arbitrary power has for the soldiers—and with individualism—through one of the soldier's notion of the artist's need of autonomy from the world, in which artistic creation is seen as a powerful act—or through another soldier's admiration for strong political leaders.[42] Finally, Beauty is associated several times with weakness in Melabes's mind, and strength with ugliness, especially in Melabes's conversations with his friend.[43] The dizzying play of associations thus ends up collapsing in roundabout ways, one pole of each opposition into its opposite: beauty turns into ugliness, collectivity into individual mania, strength into weakness, and vice versa. Indeed, if Herzig's attempt to map some of the threading of thematic and ideological oppositions in the novel is indicative of anything, it is the fact that Kenaz's novel definitely puts to the test the limit of readers' cognitive ability to hold the unstable thematic and ideological relations in their minds. The narrative thus ends up deconstructing, in a well-nigh Derridean sense, any attempt at closure or at stable meaning, through this continuous process in which opposite valences of meaning are never able to "defeat" each other in the battle for interpretive supremacy.

Thus, whenever Kenaz's narrative leads its readers to believe that an important revelation or discovery has finally happened, it is immediately followed by the cancellation of this effect: just as Melabes's betrayal turns out to be meaningless, so does the spectacular collective drill that we just mentioned end with the sudden death of a soldier. Avner's almost-allegory seems to have precisely the same point:

> My father knows all kinds of legends and stories [. . .] one of the stories is about a gypsy and a bear. Once there was a gypsy and he had a bear, and he would appear with it at circuses and fairs. Once the gypsy lay down to sleep on the roadside, or maybe it was the forest, and suddenly some murderers fell on him, or maybe they were wild animals, I don't remember. And anyway it was always changing. In any case the bear jumped on them and killed them. And the gypsy was saved [. . .] The gypsy hugged and kissed the bear, but the bear turned his head and said: *your breath stinks*. The gypsy said to him: "*It's a pity you saved my life*." "I don't understand the moral." "There is no moral. It's just a story. You can read anything you like into it."[44]

One should keep in mind the strictly temporal quality of these narrative failures: this is not an anti-allegorical position that is as it were outside the logic of failed attempts to understand reality. Such stable anti-allegorical position could lead to the formation of a new allegory out of a rejection of older ones. *Infiltration*, however, does not even permit us this certainty: allegories constantly seem to work, only to prove false or useless at a later point in the process of narration. In other words, the anti-allegorical position is given the same treatment as the different allegorical clues and false starts themselves. It is precisely this indeterminacy that Herzig and other critics celebrate as *Infiltration*'s fundamental ambivalence toward national ideology, not allowing any collective allegorization to develop, and favoring a decentered individuality over the "illusion" of a cohesive self.[45]

We should now, however, note that even if the novel sabotages any attempt to grant stable meaning to the ideologemes it conjures, it is still possible to map the novel formally. As mentioned above in the cases of Melabes's betrayal and Avner's performance, the novel's objects of reflection seems to be not only collectivity and individuality themselves, but also, "postmodernly" perhaps, the aesthetic processes through which these are themselves imagined. Thus, the novel not only tries to imagine a national coming-of-age story, but also reflects on the various modalities available for such plot. Accordingly, we can see each of the four characters as standing for one possible outcome of the encounter between individual and collective: Micky stands for successful adjustment and transformation (even if in his case as well it is not clear how transformation takes place); Avner stands for repetition with no adjustment; Alon stands for a rejection of both adjustment and repetition as narrative resolutions (his suicide constituting a refusal to recognize the fact that he cannot live up to his imagined ideals, and at the same time a refusal to abandon these ideals); and Melabes stands for a unity of both repetition and adjustment (which is the reason for his relatively weak or loose characterization, being the only one which makes such "unity" possible).

If we read the novel in this way—as reflecting on the different modalities of the coming-of-age narrative—we can use a Greimassian rectangle to chart the four positions. In Fredric Jameson's use of it, the Greimassian rectangle offers a spatial metaphor for the workings of dialectical thinking.[46] The rectangle is defined by two types of opposition: the top horizontal line of the internal square connects two contraries, to use Jameson's term. These are two terms that exclude each other logically, while being positive concepts in their own right. The diagonal lines in the internal square connect each of the main contraries with its negation, or a term that receives its significatory power first by negating the term with which it is diagonally connected, only later becoming endowed with positive content. Thus, the following is a rectangle representing the four different narrative options represented by the four main characters of *Infiltration*:

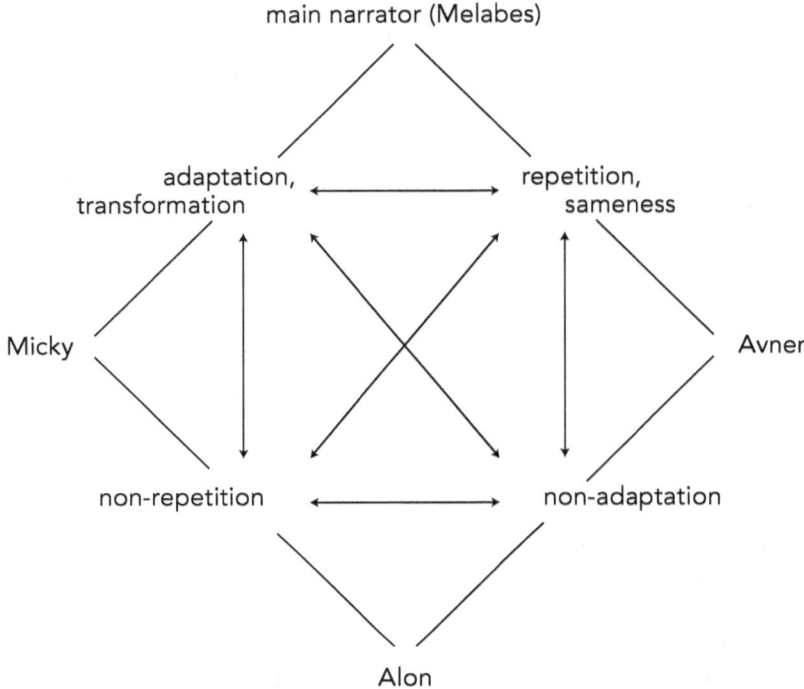

Now, by mapping the novel in this way, we seem to have finally generated a stable reading of the novel: while Melabes constitutes what Jameson calls the ideological pole of the novel (ideologically reconciling adaptation and repetition), Alon can be seen as the "neutral" or utopian term in the schema.[47] This interpretation is seemingly a strong social one: each of the four main protagonists represents a certain 1950s "social type," as Herzig suggests,[48] and their fates seem to foresee the novels future: the decline of the kibbutz and its associated ideals symbolically captured in Alon's suicide, and the rise of urban individualism and suspicion of Zionist ideals, captured in Micky's successful adjustment: a narrative that one finds reproduced by almost all historical accounts of the 1950s.[49]

This interpretation, however, is problematic. For it must here be finally observed that *Infiltration* does not simply recast 1950s content into a new form. Rather, as was the case in the '80s works in the previous chapter, it pastiches the '50s own self-representation: Ashkenazi racism toward Mizrachi characters, and the social neglect of the '50s notorious transit camps (*ma'abarot*) is very similar, for instance, to its representation in '50s and

'60s literature (for example in Hanoch Bartov's *Each has Six Wings* that we discussed in a previous chapter); the oppositional incredulity toward some reified national metanarrative echoes its portrayal in the literature leading up to the 1980s, as we have seen, for example. Nathan Shaham's *Always We* can be seen as some kind of a '50s urtext here: together with the staging of national ideology's failure, *Infiltration* also adopts Shaham's signature sudden leaps between narrative perspective (of which Dan Miron complains when they are pastiched in Kenaz's novel);[50] the oppositions between individualist urban subjects and rural True Believers of the kibbutz (Alon) draws on a long representational tradition, on which we have touched, beginning in the realist literature of the 1920s and ending up in its reification and satirization in, for example, Aharon Megged's *Hedva and I*.[51] Nor are the fates of the characters and their mapping against each other new: think, for example, of Uri's death in *He Walked Through the Fields*, also a tragic result of some perverted adherence to kibbutz values. *Infiltration* does not inject its social oppositions with new social content even where it is certainly available. For example, the Ashkenazi-Mizrachi opposition has by the 1980s become much more mediated by capitalism than the direct state discrimination and overt racism of the 1950s. The rise Israeli Black Panthers movement, as well as the results of the election campaigns of 1977 and 1981, attest precisely to this transformation. Thus, all of these self-representations of the 1950s are served up by *Infiltration* as food for thought *as representations*, rather than as active social signifiers.

The Greimassian rectangle presented above therefore rehearses oppositions whose social relevance is already gone in the 1980s, becoming instead only important *as representations*. The representation of Mizrachis in the novel is not exactly some great coming of a great multicultural corrective to older representations, as Hirschfeld claims.[52] Nor does it exactly recast Mizrachi Israelis as the bearers of that old ideologeme of Jewish (European) diasporic bodily degeneration, as Dror Mishani claims in his critique of Hirschfeld—a reified representation devoid of social content by the time the 1980s come around.[53] Rather, the Mizrachi characters are somehow fused European diasporic degeneration simply because this is one of the ways in which they were represented in '50s literature. The pastiching tendencies that we traced in the cases of Castel-Bloom's and Katzir's more playful novels become in *Infiltration* a kind of encyclopedic historicism, a pastiche of all 1950s representational forms. The surreal Mizrachi dance scenes in the novel—in which threats to normative sexuality as well as Ashkenazi cultural hegemony are recreated—are here comparable to those surreal musical numbers from David

Lynch's *Blue Velvet*, which as Jameson argues enact precisely this recreation of dead ideologemes in the postmodern nostalgia film.[54]

It is in this way that *Infiltration* is a "postmodern" novel, regardless of its sincerity. Even though critics such as Herzig deny that *Infiltration* should be read as a postmodern novel, critical commentary certainly tends to ascribe postmodern characteristics to it.[55] Chief among these is the critics' celebration of novel's explosion of any notion of a collective metanarrative or centered subjectivity,[56] or in a less abstract vain, that it explodes Ashkenazi hegemonic ideology in the name of marginalized identities, particularly Mizrachi ones.[57] All of these tend to be celebrated by the critics, for which hegemonic ideology was always fictional anyway: the Israeli " 'melting pot' an unrealizable fantasy from the moment of its inception";[58] and more generally informing us that alienation is actually part of human nature: "the existential paradox that Kenaz expresses is that human beings are essentially placeless and homeless."[59] Critics thus tend to see Kenaz's novel as justifying their own ideological beliefs, a stance we have already problematized. More to the point: the demonstration of *Infiltration* dependence on pastiche or postmodern historicism should by now put its "postmodern-ness" beyond any doubt—as long as we remember that this explosion of the historical imagination is a result of the Palestinian proletarianization after 1967. The critical confusion about the novel's postmodern-ness can be easily attributed to the impossibility of distinguishing in any absolute sense postmodern works from their late-modern predecessors on the grounds of formal qualities alone, as we have already discussed.[60]

A final reflection is in order on *Infiltration*'s own commentary on its genre or its institutionality, to adopt Wegner's conception that we quoted in the beginning of this section. I argued that the encyclopedic historicism or pastichization of the novel has to do with considering past representations *as* representations, rather than as bearers of social content. What these were charged with is historical consciousness itself, or historicity—that mapping of the present and its thinking in terms of some ongoing process. *Infiltration* stages a kind of allegorical juxtaposition of these historicity-laden representations with a present bereft of these, highlighting not only the dissolution of past historical imaginary of the nation but also a more generalized crisis of the historical and social imagination. *Infiltration* thus invokes its generic history allegorically, expressing its own inability to generate historicity through this invocation of older moments and the fullness and determinateness of their historical imagination (in which some version of a good social existence versus a bad one is still very much alive). Institutionally, therefore, *Infiltration* comments on its own genre's diminished capacity for mapping social space or historical movement (which comes down to the same operation—a synchronic system inevitably implying some historical trajectory). It is precisely this institutional crisis to which the next section, on the rise of the detective novel, speaks.

The Detective Returns: Batya Gur and Social Totality

The consideration of genre and its self-reflecting transformations with which we ended the previous section will now provide for us the basis for discussing another generic phenomenon of 1980s Israeli literature: the return of the detective novel. About fifty years separate this '80s revival from the previous and brief appearance of Israeli or Hebrew-Zionist detective in Palestine in the 1930s and 1940s.[61] That previous moment coincides perfectly with the much-maligned flourishing of realism in Hebrew writing from Palestine that we discussed in the first chapter. This coincidence of the detective with the brief realist hegemony is not coincidental, as I will argue below, having to do with something like the institutional role of genres that Phillip Wegner describes in the quote above. But before we discuss the detective's relation to the early realist dominant we should complicate the puzzle a little further, by adding the genre of Soldier's Experience to the mix, noticing that it, too, has enjoyed a revival in the 1980s, after having no significant exemplars in the 1960s and 1970s. Charting the rise and fall of the three genres would then look like this:

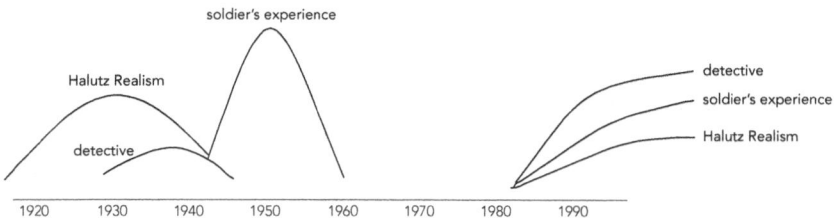

The graph is of course not an accurate numerical representation of the occurrence of works in each genre, but simply an attempt to map the activity in each genre in terms of the appearance of canonical or influential works. It should however be emphasized that the return of the detective is the more dramatic of the three 1980s trends, in terms of quantitative change but also in terms of literary earnestness—a measure that has hitherto functioned as leitmotif of this book's two 1980s chapters, and can become more conceptual now. For the *halutz* novels of the late '80s are the clearly playful ones of Meir Shalev's works or the impressionistic ones of Yizhar's return to literary production, the works of both hardly qualifying as realist.[62] That the novels of soldiers' experience do not display the same formal or thematic playfulness was indeed the reason for separating the works of this chapter from those of the previous one. Yet, as our discussion of *Infiltration* demonstrated, the work itself comments on the erosion in the capacity of its own genre to provide working figurations of social reality and its contradictions. Other important works in the genre, such as, partially, Grossman's *Smile of the Lamb*, and Shimoni's 1999 novel *A Room* can easily be shown to provide the same reflective content about the social status of the genre. Thus, theirs is an earnestness that simply registers its own failure to provide usable social figures.[63]

We can now finally suggest an explanation for the appearances and disappearances of the detective story from Hebrew letters—one that is much more decisive and pronounced than the fluctuations in the other two genres. For it becomes possible now to posit the existence of a whole economy of literary social figuration, whose ebb and flow is registered in the chart. The detective in the earlier moment can be seen as the urban counterpart to *halutz* realism, keeping in mind the latter genre's difficulties in producing a mapping of urban spaces. Thus both genres can be considered to complement each other: the high-literary *halutz* genre engaging the process of social figuration in the countryside, while the popular detective genre, emerging only after urban experience became common enough, providing the process of social figuration or mapping in the urban space. We argued before that the invention of the genre of soldiers' experience becomes a much more effective literary device for social allegorizing, in the transition from utopian collective project to national imaginary. We can now further expand this claim, arguing that the soldier replaces not only *halutz* realism, but also the early detective, very effectively subsuming both of these in a single figure of the soldier or group of soldiers, one whose subjects are much more useful for imagining a national space—in which urban and rural must somehow be reconciled (and capitalist social relations asserted). The genre of soldiers' experience, as Žižek puts it in a different context, is in this sense the most perfect realization of its two "institutional" predecessors, even as it is already a distinct genre in its own right.[64]

Yet now we come to the '80s reemergence of the three genres, of which the detective's is the most dramatic. Our discussion of these genres in terms of their role as so many "institutions" that are in charge of producing social mapping will now make it possible for us to provide an account of this reemergence that is much more comprehensive than other ones. One such account is Dan Miron's moralistic explanation—linking it to a deep sense of guilt of an increasingly consumerist and nationalist Israel (but it should be noted that nationalism was certainly not on the rise in the 1980s, but rather is something that belongs to Miron's later moment of writing, projected for some reason on the earlier period).[65] Miron is here echoing Ziva Shamir's much earlier linking of the '30s detective with the late-'80s one, arguing that both arise in the context of "unease, violence and a loss of morality."[66] That this explanation does not really provide a good reason for why it is that the detective story is particularly well-suited to address moral bankruptcy should be obvious (one would wonder, for instance, if moral allegories would not be better at "displacing the drama of crime and punishment, from its true space, that of the social order towards the false one of universal morality").[67] It should be clear here that Miron's account remains a moral one, as long as it sees the detective story's return as a result of some deep sense of guilt whose not-very-clear cause is "bourgeoisification" or nationalist values—even if he opposes the detective story's own moral stance. Other accounts, such as Dvir Abramovich's, in which the rise of the detective is simply a filling of a vacancy, as if the detective genre is some natural development of all literatures, and it is therefore its absence rather than presence, is some abnormality to be cured or explained. Explanations such as these are of course circular—they assume that the existence of detective fiction is a natural or normal state in order to explain its emergence.[68]

We can now suggest a different explanation for the reemergence of the detective story, one that does not annul the more moral one, but rather includes this ethical mediation as one of its levels. The reemergence of detective fiction is in our account a result of a renewed need for social mapping, for figuring the social. That the genre of soldier's experience returns to life in this period too, commenting on its own inability to figure social reality—as is the case with *Infiltration*, attests precisely to growing sense social disorientation whose origin, we argued, was the incorporation of Palestinians into Israeli capitalism after 1967. At the heart of the detective's return thus lies an unconscious impulse to map social space, to generate what Jameson calls a "totality effect"—a sense that we have somehow contained the entire social realm in the represented world. The fourfold characterological typology of *Infiltration* achieves precisely this effect, in its appeal to all four possible outcomes of the coming-of-age novel (and their mapping onto four social types that as if "cover" all of Israeli society).

The return of the detective novel should be understood in opposition to *Infiltration* and the formerly "high" attempt to figure the social whole that it carries with it. The detective novel, in other words, seeks to demonstrate that it is much more up to this task than the old institutional figurative devices of the genre of soldier's experience. It is for this reason that Gur's detective seems at times to encroach at the realm of what used to be "high" literature and its functions—a sure sign of precisely this inter-genre antagonism, rather than a weakness of Gur's writing. That Gur's detective, Michael Ohaion, was formerly an academic historian (much like the academic protagonists of Oz and Yehoshua), is yet another sign of claiming the vocation of social mapping for the reborn detective:

> But here he sensed that he had to proceed with the greatest possible delicacy, the only way to get onto the wavelength of the person sitting opposite him and pick up those ostensibly trivial things. The things people said between the lines and sometimes never said at all, that in the last analysis provided the master key to solving the mystery. And there was also what he privately referred to as "my historical need." In other words, the historian's need to obtain a full picture, to see everything concerning human beings as part of an overall process, like a historical process possessing laws of its own which—he never tired of explaining—if only we are able to grasp their meaning, provide us with the tools for going right to the heart of the problem.[69]

It is in moments like this that the detective novel perceives its role precisely in tackling the problem that was once reserved to other genres in the Israeli context—the exhaustive mapping of a sociohistorical situation. It is precisely this vocation that distinguishes Gur's detective and which makes him particularly interesting. The trespassing of Gur's detective onto the social realm reserved for "high literature" (a concept whose coherence is lost today anyway) is therefore its greatest strength, and the reason for the genre's reappearance in the first place—rather than constituting a weakness of Gur's novels, as Miron claims.[70] Of paramount significance in this respect is the confrontation between the police detective and the high-ranking military officer in Gur's first novel, *The Saturday Morning Murder*, which stands in for the very confrontation between the genres of the soldier and the police-detective. The officer is almost ritualistically subdued and humiliated during his interrogation by the detective.[71] This confrontation between police and military will find its echoes in the much later detective novels of Dror Mishani, which we will not have an opportunity to discuss in this book.

The reemergence of the detective novel is thus a result of a renewed need for social mapping. So our argument will revolve around the ways in which social totality is mapped in Gur's first novel. We need not work very hard to notice Gur's fascination with closed social groups and their internal workings. Her first three novels focus on precisely three such social spaces: the psychoanalytic institute of *Saturday Morning Murder*, the university Literature Department of *Literary Murder*, and the eponymous social group of *Murder on a Kibbutz*. Each of these will therefore supply the reader with a logical division for some social structure, a whole hierarchy of different positions, each of them holding specific function within the whole. We should be wary however of adopting Gur's own ideology of her fascination with these micro-systems, according to which "to a large extent, every system is fascist," erasing individuality before the demands of the system itself.[72] The clear relation of this ideology to the sense that one is penetrating a hidden, closed social order in the first three novels should be clear, the characters of *Saturday Morning Murder* expressing some basic resistance to the detective's questioning gaze, refusing subconsciously to cooperate with an outside authority—a reflex that has to do with the psychic libidinal investments, as we will soon see. For, now, it is only important to mention that we need not adopt the liberal ideological anti-utopian fear of systematicity and authority to notice that in the novel, this ideology provides an excuse for the attempt to provide some figuration for social totality itself—no matter how ideologically distorted the resultant "totality" might be.

A further note about the relation between the detective novel's ideological underpinnings and the role of social mapping that I am ascribing to it in the Israeli context is in order. We should resist a too-hasty dismissal of the detective genre in general as simply reaffirming bourgeois ethics, a position taken by many critics, including Miron, but also Ernest Mandel.[73] One should rather insist that the ethical is merely one interpretive register of the detective novel; allegorically, the cognitive effort demanded by the genre is aimed precisely at the opposite of this reaffirmation of familiar ethical positions—the allegorical projection of some social whole and its contradictions. Yet we must remember that this whole is ultimately unrepresentable, and that therefore this whole is to be constructed out of a logical division into several oppositional types, a typology whose exhaustion must somehow be endowed with a sense of wholeness. When one speaks of the cognitive effort demanded by the detective novel, as in Brecht's account, one should distinguish between two such efforts.[74] The first, and very much the more conscious and explicit of the two, has to do with the familiar movement from clues to the reconstruction of the crime. The second and far more interesting one has to do with the generation of a "totality effect": how antagonistic social types are encoded, and the way in which this logical typology is charged with a sense of wholeness.

In *Saturday Morning Murder*, the logical structuring of the social is clearly provided by the Psychoanalytic Institute's own intricate hierarchical structure, one that includes three major groups: candidates, associate members, and full members, in which the division between candidates and members is by far the most significant one. Candidates work under the supervision of members, and must undergo psychoanalysis at their hands. The process of promotion and the rites of passage that it includes are under the control of the Institute's Training Committee, composed of a select group of full members. The division between candidates and members also has a spatial expression: while the former must see their patients at the Institute, members are free to receive patients in their home office. Crucial is the fact that the Institute functions not only as some non-reflexive social order, but as an autonomous and self-reinforcing libidinal and cognitive unit: the hierarchy of social roles is fortified through Gur's ingenious use of Freudian transference inevitably taking place in the analytic process, described early in the novel:

> The patient, [Hildesheimer] added, spoke about the therapist, too, but never saw him as he really was. In the patient's mind the therapist took on many different guises. At one and the same time he was all the significant figures in the patient's life: his mother, his father, his brothers and sisters, his teachers, friends, wife, children, boss—all in accordance with the projections of his own personality structure.[75]

The social structure is thus held in place by libidinal investments carried by the therapist-patient relation between members and candidates and the transferences it inevitably entails. That Neidorf (the victim) and Hildesheimer function as symbolic parents to so many of the other candidates and members is strongly suggested throughout the novel—even senior members such as Joe Linder hold some kind of Oedipal grudge toward the couple. To the transferred libidinal investments one has to add the selective or reflexive role of the analytical situation within this social structure—psychoanalysis performing the role of gatekeeper or police to the social structure, of revealing whatever inner desires candidates harbor and thus selecting out those that might infringe on the strict laws of the institute. The sense that that their world has been irrevocably shattered, or that Neidorf's murder signals some terminal fault in the system designed to be fool-proof, expressed by many of the institute's members, has precisely to do with this probing function of the autonomous social unit and its failure.

It is important that we notice that detective Ohayon is never some purely external observer to the drama internal to the institute. First, the analogy between the detective and the analyst in the novel suggest a kind of a positional affinity, which puts the detective in danger of becoming absorbed into the institution that he is investigating. That Ohayon displays the same fear of hermeneutical failure is clear in his comments about the movie *Alien*, which he watches with his child: the movie evoking in him the fear of not being able to distinguish the corrupt from the innocent.[76] Yet it is perhaps better to see Gur's novel treatment of the detective-analyst analogy more in terms of mediation or transcoding—a switching between codes—rather than as an analogical structure. For the detective is seen as the providing an external complement to the psychoanalyst's internal or psychological hermeneutic—which become one and the same in the interrogation/therapy situation, in both of which the mode of symptomatic reading is necessary for the hermeneutical process to advance. It is also important that Ohayon becomes entangled in the web of libidinal transference: several times in the novel he struggles to not let his own transferences influence the course of his investigation.

Yet, setting up the analogy between detective and analyst, and Ohayon's libidinal entanglement in the drama, should not be seen as revelations about the detective story in their own right. Indeed, one should notice how tangential they are to the solving of the crime, which as in most of Gur's narrative does not depend on the detective's logical skills in putting together the puzzle, but rather on incidental witnesses that appear toward the end of the novel (in the case of *Saturday Morning Murder*, it is a medical student who, toward the end, provides the missing piece of the puzzle).[77] Thus it is not the detective's psychoanalytical powers nor his personal psychology that are the point. Rather, these are part of a larger imaginative effort in the novel. For the connection between public and private that both of these make possible is part of Gur's novel's setting up of a structure of mediation between public and private spheres, or between individual and collectivity—precisely that which we said becomes impossible or at least very problematic in the case of *Infiltration*, *Smile of the Lamb*, or indeed the other '80s novels that we discussed.

It is here that we can finally address the way in which the novel generates closure or its "totality effect." We should resist the impulse to identify the solving of the crime as the moment of narrative closure, as Eden Tzivoni does in the case of Gur's novel.[78] Rather, as Jameson notes, the solving of the crime should be taken as a sign or mark of closure rather than the enactment of closure itself—which demands a much more complex narrative operation (and which of course allows for the cognitive effort's splitting in two, as mentioned above).[79] In the case of Raymond Chandler, whose novels are Jameson's object, the sense of wholeness is generated first, through the construction of a logical ordering of the social itself, a typology whose options are completely exhausted by the novel (populating each of the logical options with characters). This more logical order is then endowed with a sense of wholeness by its textual juxtaposition to nature and landscape—an operation made possible by Los Angeles's unique relation to landscape, according to Jameson. Reformulating Roman Jakobson's argument about the formal operation of poetry, Jameson argues that

> Closure in Chandler's novels is achieved by something like the projection of the axis of geography or nature onto that of society; and that the intermeshing of these two systems allows for the transfer of closure as such from the vaster totality of the natural landscape to the far more questionable and purely logical systematization of the social order.[80]

In Gur's novel, the two orders or codes are completely different. The logical typology of the social is provided for us, as noted, by the Institute's social structure that provides us with a social typology that has to do with rank, initiation rites, and a libidinal economy that aligns with the social hierarchy (and in which, fittingly, the subjectivity of the ones at the top of the chain function much like the Lacanian Big Other that folds within it those models of Ideal-Ego and the Ego-Ideal—both role model and never-satisfied punitive instance that must always remain hidden, whose subjectivity must always remain hidden, as Hildesheimer says).[81] Indeed, desire and recognition in Gur's novel replace the function of spatial coding of the typology in Chandler.

Yet the crucial difference of Gur's novel is the way in which a sense of wholeness is as if conferred on this arbitrary logical social structure. What replaces Chandler's natural order in Gur's work is no other than the national order as such, represented mostly by all kinds of subjectivities semiotically related to the fate of the nation. What seems like mere gossipy details turns in our reading to be crucial for the novel: be it the sideways mention of Neidorf's relation to big business, or that Dana Silver's husband is a prominent judge, or that Elisha's father is a high-ranking diplomat. The unlikelihood of so many allegorically laden subjects being related to the investigation even becomes something of a joke to the police detectives, one of whom commenting that the case has "so many important people. Judges, military governors, psychologists, you name it!"[82] Even some kind of historical connection to Zionism is not missing from these small asides. Describing the Institute's history, Hildesheimer describes the atmosphere in the Institute's first days as "*halutzic*," saying that:

> Life was very hard, from every point of view: the analytical training was extremely arduous, and they earned hardly any money. Deutsch insisted that they treat the children and adolescents sent out of Germany without their parents, wards of the Youth Aliyah, and they, of course, could not pay. In fact, Deutsch supported them, all the—he searched for the right word—the candidates, that's what they really were, he and the Levines, and Fruma and Litzie, candidates for the as yet nonexistent institute.[83]

Crucial for us here is that the institute's history becomes implicitly aligned with or juxtaposed to Zionist nation-building—the struggles of the first analysts to establish the institute, and the relation to "aliya" (a term that associates Jewish immigration to Palestine with the nation-building cause) are here used to associate the institute with the nation.

It is therefore through the juxtaposition of the institute's social logic with the nation and its codes, which possess a sense of wholeness, that closure is conferred on the institute's social structure itself. It is in this respect that the questioning of the high-ranking officer that we have previously mentioned becomes important, functioning as a red herring in the novel—the reader expecting the officer to be the killer, only to find out that his involvement stopped at trying to keep secret his therapy sessions. The investigation we claimed functions as a symbolic marker of the detective genre's claim to stage social totality better than other genres, in particular the genre of soldiers' experience. If soldiering is the strongest "code" for national social figuration, it must of course appear in the background of Gur's novel, a background that provides the nation's "wholeness" to be juxtaposed to the institute. But the soldier itself must lose to the detective in order to "prove" the detective genre's superiority, and the barring of the soldier from providing the figure of national or historical subject must also be somehow registered. It is for this reason that the officer must register a tension or a contradiction: both its potential strength and also an impotence or a falling-short. It is for this reason that the military governor ends up being something like an impotent monster: his impotence a personal manifestation of the conundrum of his position within the system: to be a military governor in the occupied territories is to be the direct oppressor of Palestinians (a lesson that emerges in full force in Grossman's *Smile of the Lamb* as well), or in the officer's words: "no one can be a liberal military governor; those are two mutually contradictory terms."[84] The officer's sexual impotence thus becomes the nagging personal manifestation of the his public impotence, and his secret therapy sessions are therefore seen by the novel as an attempt to take care of a symptom rather than a cause. The soldier is thus neutralized as the ultimate figure for a national subject, yet is ingeniously still used, among other such sideways evocation of national code, to infuse the psychoanalytic institute with national wholeness.

Gur's first detective novel is thus an attempt to produce a new social mapping, at a moment in which the "institutions" or genre that were usually entrusted with this task—such as the genre of soldiers' experience—can produce only expressions of their failure to do so, as was the case for *Infiltration*. What remains now is to remind ourselves again that postmodernism, in the sense of the deeper social and economic transformation on which it rests, is not a matter of personal choice or aesthetic preference (which would lead us to distinguish between postmodernism and postmodernity, the latter denoting the socioeconomic level explicitly rather than the cultural one). In the previous chapter I argued that Israeli postmodernism is a result of the proletarianization of Palestinians at the hands of Israeli capital after 1967, and the crisis of social imagination that followed. No literary work, however seriously it takes upon itself the task of social mapping, can avoid this crisis in the last analysis—even if it is the attempt, rather than the failure, that interests us here. One should distinguish between two kinds of failure here. First there is the more general failure to "correctly" map social space. This failure seems unavoidable, since the process of figuration it entails requires a reductive operation that must always simplify (a novel that tries to encompass the truly global reach of social relations under multinational capitalism is as dependent on this reductive operation as more locally focused works, Indeed, Christian Thorne has recently suggested that the novel form itself might be ill-suited to the task of productively reducing this global multiplicity).[85]

Yet there is a second kind of failure, which has to do with the more localized attempt to produce a positive figure for some collectivity, a condensation of multiple perspectives and conditions into one historical agent—an operation that we discussed in the introduction to this book and that depends to some extent on the existence of some collective political project. The soldier had been the latest such figure in Israeli literature of course. This type of failure has more to do with the failure of imagination associated with postmodernism—an inability to imagine futurity or any determinate historical trajectory becoming a failure to imagine its agent. Now, the literary detective was never much of a figure for collective action (although this possibility is not completely unrealized, as attested by some attempts at producing a socialist detective novel).[86] Yet the existence of a single unified perspective that made it possible to somehow imagine social totality and its dynamics can at least imply the possibility of the figure of such an agent. What is important is to notice that in Gur's case the detective's perspective never actually single-handedly solves the crime. The intervention of marginal perspectives is crucial to signify closure: not only that of the medical student that we already mentioned, but countless other ones, which become for a short interval the narrative focalizing perspective: that of Dr. Gold that opens the novel, or that of the nosy neighbor, or that of the Palestinian gardener—all of which make essential (if small) contributions to the process of social figuration, in a very straightforward way (the detective does not need to interpret their narrative contributions in any significant way). Gur's fidelity to the importance of these minor perspectives remains somewhat of a constant throughout her detective novels: the point of view of the little girl whose disappearance is crucial to the solving of the crime in *Murder in Jerusalem* (2001) can serve as a good example.[87]

For our purposes, it is important to notice that the second type of failure that we associated with postmodernism appears in Gur's narrative in the guise of an absence of a unified figure for collective action or perception: Ohayon is barred from being that subject, nor is there a group of protagonists that constitutes such a figure for agency—the marginal perspectives vanish just as they disappear, never joining the detective in some kind of symbolic union. The crisis of the social imagination thus makes its appearance in Gur's novel as well, despite the novel's efforts to provide some kind of social mapping in the face of a fading social imagination.

6

Time in Hiding

Israeli Fiction and Neoliberalism

If there is any newness to contemporary Israeli fiction, one that would distinguish it from its 1980s and 1990s predecessors, it has to do with a return to questions of history and temporality, as I will show in this chapter. Whether it is through the invocation of the everyday (or its absence) implied by Einat Yakir's 2012 *Sand* (whose Hebrew title's literal translation is "days of sand," a Hebrew expression denoting non-weekend and non-holiday time), or to Ofir Touché-Gafla's speculative literary reflections on death and temporality in *The Day the Music Died* (2010) and *The World of the End* (2004), or even Eshkol Nevo's *Neuland* (2011), whose title evokes Herzl's *Altneuland* and its projection of a utopian future—all of these touch in some very serious way on the presence of time in Israeli reality.[1] Yet as the discussion of Israeli postmodernism in the previous two chapters should have made clear, that mere presence of representations of time and history is not enough to claim that literature offers us a new understanding of history—as the discussion of historical pastiche in the previous chapter should have amply demonstrated. The following two chapters therefore will argue that these newer literary temporal imaginations are in some decisive way different from the pastiches or historical simulacra that dominated '80s and '90s literature.

But here inevitably surfaces a much larger problem of periodization implied by the claim to the literary return of time, namely, whether postmodernism as such is over. Compounding this problem is that Israeli postmodernism as I theorized it is different in its historical coordinates than its western counterpart—beginning in the late 1970s as a result of the dramatic proletarianization of Palestinians into Israeli capitalism after the 1967 war. But if for a moment we bracket this additional complicating factor, we can address very briefly several attempts to argue that postmodernism is over, as in Jefferey Nealon's *Post-Postmodernism* or Mark Fisher's attempt to posit "capitalist realism" as a new cultural dominant.[2] I argue, with others, that none of these constitutes some determinate break with postmodernism (as both Fisher and Nealon would agree to some extent). Fisher's organizing theme, the total elimination of our ability to imagine an alternative to life under capitalism, or Nealon's emphasis of neoliberalism's financialization as more immediately and tightly bound to every realm of life (which we might think of as some real subsumption of every realm of life under neoliberal regimes of accumulation, where only their formal subsumption existed before, to use Marx's terms)—are already present in our conception of postmodernism: that elimination of historical and temporal thinking, and capitalism's colonization of every realm of life (both spatially across the globe, but also of subjectivity and the unconscious).[3] Following Fredric Jameson and Mathias Nilges, I suggest that we distinguish between postmodernism and postmodernity—the former designating a style, and the latter naming a historical period in more economic and social terms.[4] To argue that postmodernism is not a matter of aesthetic choice but some inescapable condition, as I did in the previous chapters, should thus be understood as a claim about postmodernity rather than postmodernism. This conceptual distinction makes it possible for us to see postmodernism as the early stage of postmodernity, thus allowing us to theorize cultural transformations internal to postmodernity itself (or conceive of mutually antagonistic cultural "phases" internal to postmodernity, the first of which is postmodernism proper).[5]

The importance of Nilges's intervention is precisely not that it makes it possible for us to argue that postmodernism is still with us (which would be to insist that nothing has changed—a conservative position *par excellence*), but rather that we should rethink the conceptual apparatus undergirding our periodization so that postmodernism would now occupy the position of an "old-new," or of a historical trajectory that must itself be scrapped for some new conceptualization of the new and the future. postmodernism thus becomes the past or the background actor, to a much larger and more ominous postmodernity which postmodernism has confused with itself. From this new perspective, the prognostication force of Jameson's older conceptualization of postmodernism becomes visible again—that it is presciently understood that postmodernism's claiming for itself a temporality of liberation (from grand narratives, for instance), contained its own imminent negation, namely the utter collapse of our historical imagination and ability to imagine futurity. For it is the latter that suddenly makes its appearance in so many cultural assessments of the present: in Amir Eshel's *Futurity*, in Jonathan Crary's *24/7*, in Fisher's *Capitalist Realism*, and in Eric Cazdyn's *The Already Dead* (the latter will become important for us later in this chapter), to name just a few instances.[6]

Yet what characterizes many of these positions is that they breathe new life into the possibility of resistance, for a strained effort to once again find where literature (and culture) can oppose this reduction to a permanent present. Thus, for instance, Eshel sees literature's renewed engagement with questions of temporality a challenging of the present's blockage of our historical imagination;[7] Nilges, for his part, sees the novel itself as inherently antagonistic to the immediacy or absolute contemporaneity imposed by neoliberal material regimes.[8] It is important to distinguish these approaches from that of Jameson: for the latter, the work of the literary critic is that of the detective, unearthing the resistance to capitalism unconsciously expressed by all contemporary texts, regardless of their more explicit "messages." These newer approaches are in contrast marked by a certain voluntarism, a much more explicit sense of agency in a certain effort to resist postmodernity's effects. As Fisher puts it,

> [E]ven if it is now evident that the credit crisis will not lead to the end of capitalism all by itself, the crisis has led to the relaxing of a certain kind of mental paralysis. We are now in a political landscape littered with what Alex Williams called 'ideological rubble'—it is year zero again, and a space has been cleared for a new anti-capitalism to emerge which is not necessarily tied to the old language or traditions.[9]

At first sight, this claim to agency might seem like a collapsing of the Jamesonian levels of interpretation: erroneously presenting as a matter of choice and willed effort what is essentially a textual "resistance" that takes place in a completely unconscious register, in Jameson's model (which has always been the strength of the Jamesonian system of interpretation—showing us how the most non-committed texts subconsciously and inevitably express the contradictions of capitalist society). What however must be insisted upon is the following: that this renewed sense of possible agency or at least of new openings, rifts in history that hold revolutionary potential, has to do, as Fisher puts it in the quote above, with some kind of transformation in the makeup of objective reality and not with the writer's preference.

The literary readings that follow all explore this new transformation. Rather than constituting a smooth continuity or intensification of their predecessors, as I hope to show, contemporary Israeli literary texts display a kind of becoming-problematic of what was a resolution for postmodernism—therefore designating an antagonistic break from these. Israeli literature's new engagement with temporality in the contemporary moment will thus have to do with the production of problems—very serious problems, in many shapes and forms, that all revolve around temporality in some way.

So our readings will link Israeli literature with neoliberalism and thus to the global economic order, which exerts pressure to eradicate anything that somehow comes to oppose it. The specificities of the Israeli situation must then be considered from that perspective. If the post-1967 situation, in which Palestinians became part of Israeli (still relatively autonomous) capitalism, it is important that we stress the briefness of this arrangement: after the first *Intifada* (armed Palestinian resistance) began in the late 1980s, Israeli has steadily decreased its dependency on Palestinian labor in favor of the global alternatives—cheap labor imported from eastern Europe and the Far East, as many show.[10] If the crisis of the social imagination caused by the inclusion of Palestinians was somehow still potentially surmountable, this latter transformation—one that coincides with Israel's joining the neoliberal Washington Consensus—only further heightens this crisis. It should be noted that Israel is the state that has the highest ratio of migrant laborers to citizens among OECD members, making the purchase of national imaginary less and less relevant. Indeed, at what point does one declare one's national culture a museum exhibit? Despite the absence of Marxist research, one can indicate that the real-estate bubble in Israel, in the coastal areas and Jerusalem, is a mediation of the contradictions of global capitalism into Israeli reality: it is global capital's rent extraction on which the Israeli housing market completely depends. Soaring housing prices have made large swathes of the country unlivable for most Israelis. Indeed, as Daniel Gutwein, Eran Kaplan, and others argue, it is this impoverishment of the Israeli middle class that pushed so many Israelis to live in West Bank settlements.[11] As I argue elsewhere, the 1990s peace process between Israel and the Palestinians should be seen, from an Israeli perspective, as a vanishing mediator, an old goal whose renewed, vigorous pursuit made possible the weakening of the welfare state and the universalization of neoliberal subjectivity.[12]

Yet as I have already hinted, the Israeli displacing of capitalism's contradictions geographically—seeking refuge in West Bank housing—makes for a hybrid situation rather than some total subsumption under neoliberal order. We can divide what is under the Israeli state control today into three general parts: The first is Israel without the occupied territories, in which neoliberalism is indeed pervasive and the dissolution of the Israeli welfare state is almost complete. The second would be the Israeli population that is living in the occupied territories. Here, surprisingly perhaps, state social mediation is still dominant. The welfare state is not dead in Israel, but has rather moved to the West Bank, as others argue.[13] The third is the Palestinians who live under Israeli control, for which not even basic subsistence is guaranteed by Israel, let alone citizenship rights. This third area can be said to be internally externalized by capitalism; it is included in the system by being mostly outside of the circulation of capital (that some of it is propped up in some vague semblance of social order by non-productive capital should not mislead anyone in this sense: Israel is in complete control over the cycles of "development" and destruction of Palestine). It is important to emphasize that while the separation between the first and second parts is a geographical or a spatial one, the separation between the second and the third is not geographical, or at least not spatial in the same sense: both of these coexist in the same space, even if they are slowly being separated from each other on the level of social infrastructure (segregated system of roads, water and sewage, etc.). We must also remember that these three areas do not together form an economic whole—it is no longer Palestinian labor that is exploited by capitalism in Israel (the expression "Israeli capital" has of course become increasingly misleading), nor is middle-class settlers' labor its engine. Even though Palestinian labor is still to some degree exploited in the settlements, foreign labor has been slowly integrated into the settlements wage-labor as well.[14] That importing cheap labor is taking place while 40 percent of all wage earners make less than minimum wage, and in which over 30 percent work only part-time because of the growing job precarity, is of course one of the paradoxes which would surprise no one familiar with the global economy.

This hybrid structure can no longer be wholly subsumed under what we think of as neoliberalism. However reductive, this division into three distinct parts makes it possible for me to advance the following hypothesis: the representation of social experience would include three general temporalities, or three different subjective relations to time. To pursue this hypothesis is beyond the scope of this work, and not only because it would require a reading of Palestinian literature. It would also require a study of what one can call the "settlement novel," or contemporary literature whose main subject matter is Israeli settlements in the occupied territories, or literature that moves back and forth between Israel and the territories, and would thus have to juxtapose these two different temporalities, if my hypothesis is correct. Several novels in recent years have started to map such connections, including Liad Shoham's *Oversight*, Assaf Gavron's *The Hilltop*, and Yonatan Berg's *Five more Minutes*.[15] Yet this very recent and small body of works should signal to us that Israeli settlement culture has not been chiefly mediated through novels, and that the development of the latter has to do with the commodified literary production (commodification being the first sign of production for an alienated other, or for exchange value)—or again neoliberalism—creeping into the settlement as well. We will come back to the effects of commodification on Israeli literature. For now, it is important for me simply to note the possibility of such future comparative study, based on the specific hybridity of Israeli space under neoliberalism, one that must remain beyond the scope of this book, in which I will only discuss literature from the first part—non-settlement Israel.

One last comment is in order before I begin the literary readings themselves. Those familiar with Marxist cultural studies would perhaps think that there is an important concept missing from my exposition so far, namely, the notion of uneven development—on which we had more to say in the introduction to this book. This latter conception has been used to designate precisely the persistence of the old within or alongside the new, older hierarchies or systems of domination stubbornly still alive right next to late-capitalist social formations, as the Warwick Collective puts it.[16] But, of course, there is a causal connection here that used to deliver a kind of shock to our sense of time: if one used to think of underdeveloped societies as "behind" the developed world, or as straining to catch up economically to the more advanced-capitalist world. Thus geography was imagined temporally. Uneven development challenged this temporal arrangement, as it posited the simultaneity of the less developed with the advanced, or noticed that capitalism *produced* underdevelopment as the necessary flipside to the developed world. The Warwick Collective takes its cue for the material theorization of uneven development from Immanuel Wallerstein's world-systems analysis; but more importantly they turn to Jameson's insistence on seeing modernity as a single process as the cultural basis of their conception. It is this shock of contemporaneity that Jameson uses for his argument in *A Singular Modernity*, suggesting that the same process (the formation of global capitalism) produces the advanced and the underdeveloped, and that each of their cultures should be read as responding to this singular process, in its many manifestations.[17] Nicholas Brown's *Utopian Generation* is here another good example for this approach—seeing African independence writers and European modernists as responding to the same process of "modernization."[18]

It thus seems that we should use the concept of uneven development to describe the tripartite schema through which I argued we should see contemporary Israel. There is one major problem with this approach—that the linear temporality of development to which uneven development was opposed has itself disappeared with the coming of postmodernity (or, in material terms, with the collapse of the modernization and development schema in underdeveloped countries, neoliberal "structural adjustment" programs that dismantle all social protections replacing state-planned development), replaced by an eternal present bereft of futurity as already mentioned. But it is important here to use Emilio Sauri's specific understanding of this crisis of temporality, in which "the illusion of temporal simultaneity of the first world and third world is ultimately revealed as the disappearance of time itself."[19] The advantage in Sauri's formulation is that simultaneity here takes the place of the hegemonic ideology of time, rather than being an imposition of capitalist realism behind which some real temporality still lives. In this situation, the uneven development's substitution of simultaneity for development's linear temporality loses all its critical power (instead, any imagination of a sense of non-simultaneity would be resistant, under this new hegemony of simultaneity or contemporaneity). Nor would the settlements' "welfare state" be a necessary flipside to the rest of Israel's neoliberal reality, since global capitalism's abode of production is now truly global.

This short detour through uneven development makes it possible for us to make the following argument: we should not see the three parts as existing on an imagined axis of linear development; but we should neither think of them as each other's absolute contemporaries—since this latter is precisely how these relations are viewed from within neoliberalism. Instead, the question of their temporal relation should remain open, a matter of the return of historicity rather than some empirical investigation—to be determined by the development of capitalism or an exit from it. We would thus do well to mine the existing material for what kinds of time still exist within it, for each fleeting spark of temporal imagination might very well be the seed of time to come.

Searching for Time in a Neoliberal Landscape: Einat Yakir's *Sand*

What is surely missing from the above discussion is literary criticism and what it has to say about contemporary Israeli literature. We should also not forget the question that remained open at the end of the two 1980s chapters, namely, why has Israeli literary criticism abandoned postmodernism as a periodizing term, arguing that it is not particularly useful (as in Peleg's case) or outright denying that it ever existed as a substantial period in Israeli literature (as in Shifman's case). We will return to this question toward the end of this chapter, in which we will also discuss the effects of neoliberalization on literary criticism itself. This last issue cannot be ignored, for it accounts for the near-absence of critical writing about the contemporary novels I discuss in what follows (with the exception of the movie version of Ron Leshem's *Beaufort*), despite their relative importance. As we will see, the decline of Israeli literary criticism has to do with exactly the same situation to which literature is responding.

But there is no doubt that it is literature that is better equipped to positively represent the subjective experience of neoliberal Israel. Einat Yakir's *Sand* will begin our literary discussion precisely for its most direct engagement with neoliberal reality. The family of immigrants at the center of the novel—probably belonging to the massive wave of immigration to Israel of Russian Jews that took place around the collapse of the Soviet Union—moves to southern Tel Aviv from a peripheral Israeli town, to which it returns at the conclusion of the novel. The representation of Tel Aviv in *Sand* is by all means new—it has nothing to do anymore with the national-allegorical "white city in the sand," nor with its representations of the 1970s. Yakir's Tel Aviv is that of refuse and garbage, of discarded items that confront the reader almost visually as an enormous pile of civilization's useless leftovers, smothered in dust—a sense that is strongly heightened in the novel's beginning.[20] Yakir's Tel Aviv is thus closely related to that of Orly Castel-Bloom's post-apocalyptic urban landscape. Yet, if in the latter, the free-floating objects were a source of enjoyment and play, this is no longer the case in *Sand*, in which the rubble is rather a problem or something to be overcome, even if only imperfectly and temporarily, as we will see. The personage of the novel—which we can no longer call protagonists or anti-heroes in any way—appear just as broken and placeless as their setting, their displacement from social role again no longer a source of utopian potentiality and play, but rather characterized as placeless and damaged, a chasm preventing them from fulfilling any social role, to adopt Yakir's own description in an interview.[21] Again: we have grown accustomed to intellectual celebrations of placelessness and damaged subjectivity to such an extent that the more literal meaning of these as pressing problems has to be brought up again and again. Not in some ethical sense, but in that their main function in the novel stems from these more literal and mundane meanings, rather than their appropriation by our utopian imagination. This inversion of the 1980s and 1990s playfully disordered representation of Tel Aviv is very important in Yakir's novel, as we will see below.

So here we already encounter the novel's first problematization of temporality. The novel's Hebrew title, as already mentioned, denotes the mundane and habitual—in particular the workaday repetitive time. Or precisely what is completely absent from lives of the four main characters: Hannah, her son Peter and daughter Leah, and Sebastian, the children's father, who is hardly a father figure in the novel. It is this absence of the everyday or the routine which defines the characters, emphasized with behaviors that outlive their usefulness, such as in Alexandra's case, who "dresses up and begins her day, which is actually empty."[22] Such sentences have to do with the status of such obsolete gestures as events or as little performances of time, but this is a point to which we will return later. For now, I simply wish to register the stark contrast between *Sand* with a 1950s novel such as *Each had Six Wings* that we discussed in a previous chapter should be obvious—the latter could be said to create something like the habitual or the mundane by the telling the story of the immigrant family, providing a figuration of petit-bourgeois and proletarian life under capitalism. The false opposition between the allegorical and realism should be apparent: the 1950s realist (or, actually, naturalist as I argued) novel's point is precisely to provide an allegory of everydayness, to generate reality itself and the subject's place within it. The debris or destruction encountered by the immigrants is all totalized by the family's action into a coherent project. In Yakir's 2012 novel, in contrast, everydayness itself and its time seems to have contracted into singularities, as I will argue in what follows, and the object world is completely untotalizable. Any subjective transformation is completely indecipherable in this perspective—perhaps most emphatically demonstrated by Leah's sudden entry into the symbolic order, her shedding the silence that characterizes her through most of the novel, which is never narrated or explained, her family members hardly even registering the sharp transformation.

Thus we have in *Sand* a strong assertion of life under neoliberal capitalism and the destruction of habitual middle-classness, which is wholly antagonistic to the playful utopian mess of Castel-Bloom's Tel Aviv, or that of Katzir. Yet the hopelessly dilapidated reality of Yakir's characters is not without its oppositions, namely, its animation by desire. It is important to notice that the reader's encounter with Yakir's character produces the same effects as when one notices crows collecting shiny debris, or the visual effect of filthy third-world settings in which are nestled cheap, plastic, brightly colored toys that capture the attention of the crowd. The same contrast between filth and beauty or its idea is countless times repeated in the novel, for example: "Peter stopped in front of a picture of a ship at sea that was cut out of some newspaper, framed, and hung on the wall above the TV. In vain he tried to read the Latin script under the picture. The blue faded into green, and gave the picture some bitter force."[23] Then, a couple of pages later:

> And then she saw a Japanese fan in the store across the street, and her legs carried her. Inside a selection in two sizes was laid out. She had a hard time deciding. She left empty-handed, but a few moments later she returned and bought two, a large one and a small one for the daughter, and a couple of white teacups with handles and matching saucers and small cups . . . with an emperor and geishas and a peacock and a fawn facing a princess in a kimono, rosy-cheeked. On some of the cups the paint was peeling off the china.[24]

One would at first sight blame some kind of unsubtlety of taste as what activates a reflex of being repelled from such fascination with such cheap and imperfect beauty. One immediate such implication is the folding of utopian impulses dialectically back into the reality that produces them, or as Yakir herself puts it, these are not people who "fail but still have a utopian horizon, but rather characters that move around like cockroaches in this world."[25]

Yet the repulsion that these moments generate, and that Yakir reproduced with the metaphor of cockroaches, is in the novel a strong marker of time and its presence, and leads us back to what uneven development once was. Yet we must peel off a couple of interpretive layers first. For, what we have here is already a failure of beauty as a form of resistance to the effects of capitalism—an ideology whose most well-known advocate is perhaps Oscar Wilde, for whom the conquest of Victorian squalor by beauty was one of revolutionary socialism's most urgent tasks.[26] Yet, in the case of

Yakir's novel, the cheaply beautiful no longer fulfils that function for the reader but rather only for the characters themselves, whose desires remain stubbornly opaque for us, a strong sign of the failure or the falling apart of national mediation of subjectivity (or, in other words, that we cannot understand the characters' desires as our own).

Yet another valence here is something like the function of utopian compensation itself, which could be said to be one of causes of shock. It seems that for the characters these objects do somehow compensate for the dissolution that dominates every other part of their lives. Yet the more dialectical understanding of such compensation, as in Adorno's thinking about the culture industry in general and popular music in particular, proves useful here. Adorno traces the need to *hide* the canned factuality of such gratification beyond a façade of newness in culture meant to reproduce repetitive and exhausting life under Fordist capitalism.[27] This hiding of repetition, which is a highly creative act in Adorno's analysis, can be said to be equivalent (in moralistic terms, but also in terms of cognitive effects), to the hiding of the garbage itself—the refuse produced by capitalism displaced to the Third World, so that its middle-class consumers can avoid seeing it. The shock of such passages in Yakir's novel is thus precisely the result of the crumbling of the Fordist reproductive pact into post-Fordism or neoliberalism—in which not only garbage reappears in all its menacing glory, but we also no longer need to be tricked into mistaking sameness for complexity. The compensatory function of capitalism's culture thus becomes starkly visible again in Yakir's third-worldly Tel Aviv, which proves unnerving to our unconscious tendency to hide it.

It is here that time surprisingly reappears in Yakir's novel, in this chafing of welfare-state universe and that of neoliberalism, which has its mirror image in Adorno's consideration of the entry into fully industrialized cultural production that we just mentioned. We have already considered images of the Third-World market as delivering a shock-effect equivalent to the one produced by the novel's characters' attachment to objects (for which the novel's ultimate figure is the character of "Nahum the kid" and his childish attachment to his miniaturized Book of Psalms).[28] To this we should now add another parallel, one that would bring us surprisingly closer to the subjects populating the novel. For these attachments to immediate compensation are much like those of East Germans' first encounter with "tasteless" capitalist cultural commodities (pornography, fast food, etc.), thoroughly documented in films such as *Good Bye Lenin!*, but no less present in the short-lived rush of Israelis to American fast-food restaurants when those first appeared in Israel. It is here that the chafing of two systems, two antagonistic forms of life, is expressed formally in the film: that of the former Soviet Union and that of the capitalist West. What is important for us is to notice that Yakir's ex-soviet immigrant family is precisely a subject position that brings back this friction between the systems, that revives again the sense of an alternative system, or the presence of time—their carrying with them of underdevelopment or "childishness" providing some glimmer of time which has disappeared from our geopolitical imagination, as argued above. Perhaps another way of saying the same thing is the following: that the subjective sense that this form of consumption is somehow childish or naïve has to do with the transition to postmodernity itself. For, as Jameson puts it, in postmodernity we consume not only commodities themselves for their usefulness, but a developed ideology that accompanies every commodity (Žižek's often-invoked example of so-called "fair-trade coffee" is a clear example of this).[29] What is missing from the pursuits of Yakir's character is precisely this ideological extra baggage, which evokes a form of consumption of a not-yet-postmodernized social order. By embodying an earlier form of consumption, Yakir's immigrants bring back time to a reality from which it has disappeared.

The temporal world of uneven development is thus made sensible again through the figures of the immigrants. We should briefly notice another effect that their full-of-time presence generates, which is that of the certain magical-realist character of the novel—sudden flotations in mid-air, the mother's experiences of fortunetelling (to which I will return below), all kinds of unexplained certainties and sensations. As the Warwick Collective argues following Jameson's argument about Latin American magical realism, this doubling is precisely again the result of the coexistence of capitalism with previous social forms.[30] In the absence of a sense of time, this magic-realist form and its attachment to the immigrants does not act to shatter our sense of time. Rather, the immigrant characters of *Sand* are precisely the locus or signifiers of lost temporality as such.

I thus argue that *Sand* should be read as an allegory of a search for time itself, for which the immigrants are used as trackers or detectors. This search takes place spatially, which is why a quick typology of spaces is in order. Two kinds of places present themselves to us in Yakir's novel. The first is those spaces of mediation between private and public (or that somehow stand in for public space itself): the windows, doors, the seaside promenade, but above all balconies and street- or park-benches—all of which function as potential openings into the public sphere and collectivity.[31] The appearance of such places in *Sand* is very common—not usually very noticeable but rather part of the background:

> "There was one, a gentile, cleaned for work, in our building." [The old man] told [Leah], turning his gaze to her. "This was once a building that was all families, six families." In the sun's merciless glare, in the thickness of the summer air that descended, she saw a grey spark in his eyes. "Maybe twenty people we were in families in the building," he told her. Her hands were sticky from egg yolk, and she rubbed her fingers to drive away the glue. "[A]nd there was once, she saw the door open, and entered." He turned his eyes forward again, towards her mother who was in the balcony in the building across from them, who meanwhile turned inside with the man in the military coat. "She went to the bedroom, where my wife slept." Leah got up with the plate. "She came in, saw, understood what happened, called me, and I came—they took her away." He was dripping with sweat. Leah wanted to tell him to get out of the balcony, but he preferred to stand there and talk to her. "She went like that, all at once, on the floor." She thought that if she'll go into the apartment he will come after her, but the old man stayed in the balcony, and only turned his back to the railing . . .³²

So balconies (but also park benches and other openings) convey a certain public recognition and affirmation of a state of affairs, a testimony and an assessment, fulfilling this function countless times in the novel—most conspicuously at the end of chapters, where some character's being in the balcony is mentioned as if to affirm that something has taken place.

We should recall here Karen Grumberg's discussion of the function of balconies in Castel-Bloom's writing to again notice a certain inversion at work in *Sand*. In Castel-Bloom's work, as Grumberg argues, balconies are used only to subvert their mediating role: they are there to help one witness extreme violence (but one intentionally empty of allegorical significance), and the playful deterioration of public space generally.³³ In Yakir's novel, on the other hand, the balconies function as a kind of ontological affirmation or hinge, a kind of Cartesian guarantee of existence by collectivity itself, but a collectivity which is in advance barred from being the older national one, of which there is hardly any mention or even semiotic invocation, as Esty Shoshan argues.³⁴ Thus, one type of place in *Sand* acts as the strong presence of what remains of public-ness and collectivity (and these places become less and less inhabitable in the novel: as Sebastian notes, the public benches on which he sleeps are slowly replaced by a kind of bench on which an additional railing in the middle prevents anyone from sleeping on it—a real measure adopted by municipalities to drive away the homeless). This very politicized return of public space is significant here, even if it not yet part of a new collective entity.

Yet it is the second type of place in Yakir's novel that is even more important for our purposes. The balcony in the following passage functions in a different manner than in the cases just discussed:

> And all of a sudden, after months have gone by, they are again four people in an apartment. Family. Peter plays and [Hannah] goes to make dinner, the daughter goes into the closet with the cat, and Sebastian takes a cardboard box and flips it to form a table. And when they all meet in the balcony to eat eggs they sit close together and look at each other with an awkward innocence, as if their time is all wrong. As if a different time had been handed them, an hour of wholeness, of some real while, that they couldn't even imagine.[35]

What is significant here is of course the surprising reemergence of time, which is not at all unique to the balcony in this case, but to a second set of places in the novel: bedrooms (the old man's bedroom, but also that of Hannah, and that of the dead carpenter's apartment), the carpentry in which Peter works briefly, and the ballet studio—between all of which our characters keep moving. The return of temporality in each of these places is clearly subordinated to place itself, and its mode of appearance is that of what Fredric Jameson calls singularity—time reappears as a result of an event that cannot be repeated.[36] In the quote above, it is the whole combination of characters, action, and setting which suddenly makes the time of the family appear and become felt again—a paradoxical presence of that time with all of its developmental implications, in one moment that cannot be reproduced ("that they couldn't even imagine").

The sleeping together of Hannah and the old man should be seen in the same way: the ritualized bedroom encounter as if evoke for the old man his life with his wife—again a time whose presence is brought about by an event.[37] Another example is the dance studio's effect on Leah—the dancing itself making possible for her a kind of return to a childhood cut short (for her mother used to be a ballet instructor). The dance studio provides Leah with a surrogate maternal and sisterly figure of identification (Nastia), which then makes it possible for her to "grow up"—if the term can be applied to such sudden and unacknowledged transformation—as signified by the end of her muteness, or entry into the Symbolic, in Lacanian terms. Also important here is the carpentry and that time of work which it evokes. The literary lineage here is important: one should recall how in Bartov's 1950s *Each had Six Wings* the petit-bourgeois small workshop was a convenient ideological solution for imagining both the city dwellers' complex interdependence and a sense of one's control over one's life, as argued in one of the previous chapters. The small workshops of the '50s novel thus strongly becomes a point of mediation between personal time to that of the nation. But then the Tel Aviv carpentry of Castel-Bloom's *Where am I?* is also evoked here, aimed at sabotaging precisely this past possibility of mediation—the identity of the carpenter undeterminable: soldier on leave, assassin for hire, carpenter. It is this history and its close association of urban workshops with this temporal mediation that is significant for the appearance of carpentry in Yakir's novel. Here, the carpentry is precisely a place of importance because of the temporality that it contains—Morris the carpenter acting briefly as father-figure for Peter, so that some possibility of familiar temporal development is combined with the repetitive time of work itself. Work here generates temporal singularity—an event that summoning briefly into existence the time with which it is associated.[38]

Yet the most important of these singular appearances of time is of course Hannah's fortunetelling, which almost always takes place in her bedroom (and the evocation of prostitution is very much intentional). It is easy to see in the fortunetelling the complete transition to privatized history—not only in the sense of its commodification (insofar as various narratives are available to consumption on the market), but also in the transition from a the nation's mediated narrative (the national subject is somehow a figure that allows everyone to see their own selves and histories in it), to a particularized historical narrative whose relation to its subject is immediate—it tolerates no process of figuration or condensation of the multiplicity into a single subject). Hannah's very ritualized fortunetelling, however, has another function:

> [Hannah] said: "Bad tidings indeed." The mother started weeping. "What do you mean?" [the son] snapped at her. "I see grief," she said. "And that's it?" His eyes wide open. "She leaned towards

the cup's left side. "The past is unclear, sir, there's a struggle here [. . .]" "So you're saying he has no chance." She stayed silent for a minute, "now he is in grave danger." "[A]nd on the right side, what do you see on the right?" his wife called from behind [. . .] "The future is open," she said. "There are both good and bad possible outcomes." "Do you see patterns?" Asked the son. She looked at him. "What do you see?" he asked. I'm sorry, I don't say what I see. "What do you see!" he aggressively persisted. She said, "A crow." "Are you sure?" he asked. "could it be a dove?" tried his wife. "A crow," she said. "nothing to be done?" the son tried." She looked again. For them. "It could still be good at home, for the kids. I see you moving to another place, closer to the sea, open." "Now?" he asked. "Soon." "[A]nd will it help him?" his voice begged. "You had once a bad experience with him. The move. He's been sick a long time now. He's very sensitive to light, to sunlight. Now there's something not good. Inside and out. You need to be by his side." "Will he get better?" she said nothing else. "Will he?"[39]

Several points should be pointed out about this moment of a singular emergence of futurity, which is repeated (but always in some way different) throughout the novel. First, that the clients' main question about the future is never explicitly answered by Hannah in any decisive way, but at the same time one has the feeling that the clients' wish was nonetheless satisfied. That, with the valence of prostitution that we already mentioned, seems to indicate that one has to do with something like the Lacanian dialectic of desire, in which, as Žižek puts it, desire's ultimate goal is its reproduction, or the continuous deferral of some final satisfaction.[40] Hannah thus knows better than her clients what they need, since what she gives them is a kind of space of possibilities that ties their present to a future—something like a historical scaffolding through which it becomes possible to imagine a past, preset, and future that have some causal relation between them. It is the possibility of the latter that is of course resistant to the neoliberal illusion of permanent present or the absence of time.

But there is a more crucial point for our purposes, one that is related to the tendency of this future to be only immediately and privately understandable that we mentioned above. In the quote, the clients seem to understand something that the reader cannot—the significance of the crow. The future and temporality itself thus become understandable only to those who take part in the singular event, making language useless outside an immediate relation to the event (and here a certain ideology of what is available only to the knowledge of the lower classes is certainly at work in Yakir's writing). The singularity of the future-telling event is thus strongly affirmed here, its symbols and meanings limited in their efficacy to the immediate context only—lacking precisely the possibility of being mediated or transmitted and understood by any bigger imagined collectivity such as that of the nation.

Language itself thus becomes another realm in which *Sand* marks its difference from its 1980s predecessors. The material project of manufacturing a unified national language, of which Benedict Anderson's *Imagined Communities* is perhaps the most well-known study, is strongly related to processes of figuration of national subjectivity and its relation to the history of collectivity.[41] The unification of many dialects into a unified language has always a matter of a balancing act in which localized or ethnic linguistic particularities could never be completely effaced in the process of constructing the new language. Rather, the previous groupings must always be able to recognize themselves in some part of the new language (much as in the Gramscian conception of hegemony's operation). National language thus stands as a realm of mediation *par excellence*—national institutions making sure to "condense" multiplicity into a single figure. Hebrew is of course no exception to this, and the state's dominant role in the fields of publishing and communication was, of course crucial, to this project. The privatization of all kinds of communication in Israel in the '80s and early '90s of course spelled the end of this project.[42] Yet the collapse of national language and symbolic hegemony was already visible in '80s literature: not only in its satirization becoming non-threatening, but also in more complex cases such as the novels of Grossman discussed earlier. In Grossman's novels, the hollowing out of national language is of course liberating, ineffective abstraction that comes to be substituted by a personal and almost embodied linguistic production whose authenticity must always be renewed.[43] The breaking of high and low, ethnic and class inflections, are all seen as more authentically reflexive—as new, if temporary—guarantors of language's communicative success.

Important for our purposes is the altogether different attitude in Yakir's novel. Here Grossman's ideology of the private as some guarantor of the possibility of authenticity is completely gone. Language is rather like the rest of the character's environment—so much dysfunctional debris, bric-a-brac and wreckage to which they must nonetheless resort in communicating. This is no longer a playful operation or one of postmodern assertion of new mode of authenticity. The prevalence of colloquial language and Englishisms, the sudden appearance of this or that remnant of some official jargon (such as the "bad tidings indeed" at the beginning of the quote above), the use of deictic phrases and context-based references as replacement for longer descriptive expressions—all of these speak to some inexorable deterioration of language as a medium of mediation of social relations—but which is no longer presented as liberating, as it was in the case of Grossman. That language becomes a matter of singular events, as in the fortunetelling example, is of course a much darker end of language as useful collective abstraction than that of Grossman, signaling the possible end of literature itself (which might already be with us, considering that Yakir's novel is already a novel of only a part of Israel—the neoliberalized space in the tripartite division we mentioned earlier). This terminal decomposition of language as mediation is expressed also in the new role of the other arts in the novel, which act as if to compensate for language's failure: dance as a mediator for Leah's coming-into adulthood (and into language itself), music as a form of communication, and perhaps most strongly the role of photography for Peter, which he uses "as if to decipher" reality—all of which appear as substitutes for language in the novel.[44]

I would like therefore to suggest that Yakir's novel should be read as an allegory for a search for temporality and time as such—the novel's characters move between different singular sparks of time. If the novel's titular worry is the absence of everydayness and the routine, it is this everydayness that returns in surprising singular moments, such as in one of the quotes above, and several other moments in which a sudden sense of everydayness and repetition is produced, paradoxically in a way that makes their repetition impossible. Sebastian and Leah's day together suggests this regular repetitiveness that is never actually repeated,[45] and so are the Hanna's visits to the old man's house, and Peter's work in the carpentry. In all of these a "sudden sensation of a strange routine" is evoked in some unreproducible way.[46]

We can now address the way in which *Sand* constitutes a response to its historical context, which will allow us to finally distinguish it from '80s literature. Yakir herself mentions the 2011 mass protests in Israel as what inspired in part the writing of the novel.[47] The protests, erupting overnight over the price of housing in Tel Aviv, are strongly related to the dissolution of the Israeli state's institutions of social mediation. The immigrant family's perspective is here precisely such an attempt to capture how a life from which those familiar marks of temporality have been taken away is to be lived. This experience gradually become that of the newly impoverished middle class: existing somewhere between the new Tel Avivi elite of financial and real-estate speculation and the "third-world" reality, to use Yakir's words, of a growing population of foreign workers that has developed at the margins of the city.

So the immigrant family provides a kind of way to live this neoliberal life, and that is already a significant revision of the problematic and imaginary projected by the dissolution of national hegemony in the 1980s. This latter was finally couched in terms of a new freedom—the dissolution of hegemonic reality was here celebrated as its own resolution, to recall my formulation in the previous chapter. In contrast, *Sand* suddenly recognizes this dissolution as a problem that has to be solved or contained. That the immigrants sniff out time and its experience is precisely an allegorical attempt to solve the absence of time, which economic reality has turned into a problem. A quick look back at those passages in which the eponymous everydayness is found in the novel plainly reveals this new reflex to search for time rather than dissolve it—each is offered to the reader as a moment of imaginary closure or achieved balance, however localized or singular it is. It is this closure that is now the sought-after achievement, rather than the dissolution and pastiche of '80s and '90s literature. It is precisely this sudden awareness to the dissolution of time as a problem, rather than a solution, that animates *Sand* and the other novels that I discuss in this chapter and the next one.

Death and Temporality in Ofir Touché Gafla's *The Day the Music Died*

Our final literary example in this chapter for contemporary Israeli literature's exploration of questions of time has to do with the birth of Israeli science fiction, an event that one can trace back to the early 2000s. The explosion of SF in Israeli fiction (ignoring older singular appearances, such as Amos Kenan's *The Road to Ein Harod*, or Yehoshua Bar Yossef's *Utopia in Blue and White*) merits a much lengthier study than my quick commentary here, despite what Israeli literary criticism's total silence about it seems to entail—a topic on which we will have more to say in what follows.[48] It should be stated at the outset that Gafla's 2010 *The Day the Music Died*, my main literary object in this section, is not quite SF, nor Fantasy exactly—its proximity to our present reality prevents the strong distancing effect of these latter genres. Rather, it is more accurately described as what Bruce Sterling called "Slipstream" in the 1990s, the rise of which he sees as a result of a certain reification and exhaustion of SF's energies and possibilities. In contrast to SF, "Slipstream tends not to 'create' new worlds, but to *quote* them, chop them up out of context and turn them against themselves."[49] Important in Sterling's account is Slipstream's challenging of current reality and of capitalism's "categories," echoing an agenda of disruption and shock reminiscent of modernism. The feeling of "weirdness" that this practice of quoting generates (that of a text like Gogol's "The Nose" rather than of Jules Verne's inventions), according to Sterling, very strongly characterizes Gafla's novel, whose imaginary town of Ignoville residing not on some distant planet but at the heart of western Europe, not in the near or distant future, but in the early 2000s.

But before we delve into the novel, a few more comments about genre are in place. It is first important that we problematize Sterling's view of Slipstream as resistant to capitalism, at least in terms of its contemporary cultural location. For whatever resistant impulse animated Slipstream in the 1980s, defying its clear categorization, is surely today gone, as the new genre (if it can be called that) has been completely absorbed into the capitalism which Sterling opposes. Gafla's novels, whatever their shock value, are received warmly by readers, judging by brief newspaper critical pieces and sales figures. Nor is the crossing of realism with SF inherently anti-capitalist, even if it does contain some newness. Actually, as Andrew Hoberek and Nicholas Brown argue in different ways, works that strictly follow generic conventions tend to resist much more readily capitalism's demands of cultural commodities today.[50] Brown's criticism is particularly poignant here: if commodification is that production-for-the-other (or that dominance of exchange-value over use-value, to use Marxist terminology), then the sure sign of the heightened commodification of cultural production means the breakup of whatever internal coherence or conventions to satisfy some perceived consumer demand. This is much clearer in the movie industry, with its much closer dependence on capital than in literary production. For example, capitalism demands of new Hollywood superhero movies that they do not follow some generic formula, but rather adhere to a host of demands that strain their internal structure—ones that dictate how many minutes each character is seen on screen, what kinds of scene should be included (and how many of each and at what length), etc. Thus, what might have originated as an act of defying of generic divisions that exist solely to facilitate consumption (Sterling's proverbial "rackspace"), gives birth to a much more dense commodification of culture (or what can be named a transition from formal to real subsumption, using the Marxist vocabulary again).

We can now finally approach the appearance of the genre in Israeli literature as precisely the result of the complete commodification of the cultural realm, following the early privatization of anything that had to do with cultural production—from publishing houses to television and film production. It is only in this context that a genre that has almost nothing to do with the nation as an imagined collectivity can develop. The 1980s detective fiction of Batya Gur, as we have seen, is still defined by its attempt to figure national collectivity—her detective novels implicitly arguing that they figure the nation better than other genres. With Gafla's novels, the nation as a social totality that literature attempts to imagine disappears altogether (even though it lives on in other literary cases, as I will argue in the next chapter). The surest sign of this development is Gafla's treatment of Hebrew. In Yakir's case, as we have seen, the loss of the possibility of linguistic mediation was problematized through all that linguistic debris and desiderata, a problem and hindrance rather than playful linguistic chaos. For Gafla, however, the falling apart of Hebrew is not charged with meaning at all—the ample use of English phrases and words, as well as the use of Hebrew structures that are clearly of recent English origin is done completely un-ironically and free of any judgment, as Arik Glasner notes.[51] Gafla is not alone: other contemporary Israeli Slipstream novels, such as Ruby Namdar's *The House that was Destroyed*, also deterritorialize the relation between Hebrew and national collectivity.[52] This normalization of Hebrew's receding status in Gafla's novel is mirrored in the generally minor role that anything Israeli has in *The Day the Music Died* (with one exception, which we will discuss in what follows).

The appearance of Israeli Slipstream should therefore be seen as an important development, whose meaning is for the moment stubbornly ambivalent: on the one hand, it registers the final subsumption of the novel by the commodity, as the latter's mediation is no longer performed by state institutions, but rather by those of the market. On the other, this state of affairs opens up the way dialectically to an unexpected reappearance of autonomous art, as Emilio Sauri argues, even though it is a dark return: national collectivity does not weigh heavily on literature's mind, nor can the author's livelihood depend on producing literature (so many Israeli authors remind their readers in interviews that one cannot make a living writing novels).[53] Novels are thus still commodities, to the degree that print publication and distribution still depend on the market, but writers can develop an indifference to both nation and market, as neither are essential for writing—neither the writer's material reproduction can depend on them, nor do they necessarily inflect the writer's subject matter. Gafla's novel and Israeli Slipstream in general, I argue, occupy precisely this cultural location of a dubious new literary autonomy, which in addition to Slipstream is not unrelated to the genre of "Settlement Novel," which we have posited earlier in this essay, whose existence also depends on this new autonomy (and the surprising points of intersection between Slipstream and Settlement Novel, as in Gavron's *The Hill*, can provide a good starting point for exploring their mutual reinforcement).[54] One can thus predict that new Israeli Slipstream is no longer related, even negatively, to the older literary project of national figuration—it is at worst a commodity whose form is decided directly by the market or at best the new seeds of a new collectivity, one that cannot as yet be named or conceptualized.

Gafla's *The Day* has a simple enough otherworldly premise: every resident of Ignoville knows the date on which he or she will die, thanks to a visit to the town by a mysterious stranger who can tell when a person's death will come by looking into that person's eyes. Yet it is not as simple as that: the stranger—to whom we will return in what follows—visited the town in 1984, so only the people that were in the town during his visit (and went to meet the stranger) know the date of their death. All those born after the visit, for example, do not. As well as those who choose not to find out when they will die (for the dates are stored in a special institution)—for the knowledge is not forced on a person. Rather, after one turns eighteen, one can choose to find out the death-date that the stranger read in their eyes. Which ends up being the great majority of the townspeople—and those who for some reason do not know their dates are considered somewhat external to the town's social order, labeled either "ignorant by will" (those who choose not to know their expiration date) or "ignorant by necessity" (those for whom that knowledge is denied, such as everyone born after the visit). To this state of affairs Gafla adds one other twist to drive his plot: After turning eighteen, Dora Mater, the novel's protagonist, sets out to find out the date of her death, only to discover a blank page—the mysterious stranger has not recorded her death-date for some unknown reason.

This deceptively simple initial premise turns *The Day* immediately into something like a utopian novel (in which Dora is like that alien visiting a strange new society), with the genre's familiar division into two: detailed social descriptions juxtaposed to the narrative of Dora's personal life. Yet the utopians are not people who have gained some superior form of existence, but are rather seen as truly abject: Dora is full of contempt for "the living dead," as they are colloquially known, for their tendency to plan their lives according to their death-date, for what she sees as the banishment of unknown possibilities and complete existence within the realm of the known. Knowing the date of one's death produces a certain insensitivity in the Ignovillians, according to Dora, their eyes covered with "a strange film, like in those of a tired person at the end of a workday," which produces "an indifferent gaze" that sees "only what one needs to see, nothing else."[55] Yet the similarity to the form of utopian novel is reproduced not only in Dora's externality to the unfamiliar social structure, but also in the novel's detailed exploration of new social institutions and practices. A good example would be the Municipal Center for Life Planning, presided over by one Mr. Diderot, who urges the townspeople to consult the Center in order to lead a "satisfying life without regret," and on the back of their brochure one sees "a salt figure of a weeping women. 'Do Not Look Back with Anger,' shouts the big black print on the letterhead."[56] The invocation of Diderot and Lot's wife urge one to read such passages as humoristic ones, but this is a deeply ambivalent laughter: it gives off a whiff of postmodern playfulness, but also of that Freudian kind of jokes in which laughter inadequately covers something terrifying.

To the Center one should add the Carpe Diem Parties, which take place a few days before one dies, and which provide a quasi-religious cathartic outlet and organized farewell; the Tour de Force, a trip around the world that all Ignovillians take at least once in their lives; the funerals and Farewell Ceremonies that take place in conjunction with them—meticulously planned by the deceased themselves, in which they choose the music that will be played (with the help of the municipal Farewell DJ, an official city post that Dora takes after a while); the custom of wearing black on the anniversaries of one's death; The Death Exchange, in which bets are placed on a person's cause of death; a special hospital section for those who wish to be hospitalized when their time of death approaches; the division of the cemetery into the plots of "living dead," and the various kinds of "ignorants" (and the living dead, of course, choose their grave plots and headstones in advance and visit them often).[57] The planning of life does not only deal in positivities, but extends to something like Donald Rumsfeld's "known unknowns," through what Gafla calls the principle of mishap or accident, trying to plan for the unpredictable.[58] Yet here we are already moving dialectically in the direction of the novel's resolution, on which we will have more to say in what follows.

So Dora initially finds herself dislodged from this social order, one that seems to frustratingly resemble ours yet to be completely different at the same time. The novel constitutes something like her coming-of-age story, in which she will finally become reconciled to a society from which she is biologically estranged (for it is not possible for her to actually overcome the difference—the date of her death remains unknown, while theirs remain known). Yet the initial opposition must be stressed in all its severity: the problem of subjective transformation is itself something like the problem of death itself—recalling here Freud's death-drive in its precise meaning as a drive for renewal and becoming-other (its object being loss itself, as Žižek puts it).[59] Drive here stands in opposition to desire's striving to fulfill a perceived lack in the current subject (and therefore including a certain working toward the death of one's current self—a problem whose core is wholly temporal)—whose opposite number is not existence as such but rather reproduction (and its relation to sexual instincts and pleasures for Freud).[60] Thus Dora initially stands in for such "death drive," or for partial and unknown possibilities, for the ephemeral and necessarily temporary—and precisely against the pleasures (or, more precisely, the collective organization of enjoyment) of the townspeople.

Dora's reconciliation with the social order takes place in two ways. First, she finds work as Ignoville's Farewell DJ, in which her attraction to the unplannable and unique is fortuitously combined with the townspeople's planning of life and death. Music for Dora is strongly related to the inimitable—her mind associates a song with each one of her close friends, in a completely irrational and irreproducible way, "and no two people get the same song," she declares.[61] It is for this reason that Dora is happy to become the town's Farewell DJ, who specializes precisely in matching each person with their unique soundtrack. It is important here that music is a purely temporal art, one that does not exist outside its temporal taking-place. If one's life is a singular event, as Dora would have it against the town's penchant for planning, it is only music that allows something like a reproduction of the irreproducible—or rather a re-enactment of something that can only attained ontologically. Each musical piece as if makes it possible to re-experience this singular event that is paradoxically already gone, or irreproducible:

> . . . You know me well enough to know that for me, just like you, music is a calling, and that nothing excites me more than

> the connection between a person and a soundtrack, especially when it's a life and death matter. The song that you played, for example, in Brodin's ceremony. I know exactly why you chose it, and how it serves the memory of the living person. It's the essence. Five minutes that capture a whole life. This deep silence all around, when the crowd is listening to the music. I understand how the choice is supposed to act on those present. I understand that the same song will never sound the same again . . .[62]

Within the novel's ideology, therefore, it is only through music that the unique can be re-experienced, in what should already remind us something like what we discussed above as postmodern singular temporality. Here, too, songs become like so many Proustian Madeleines—allowing an experiential return to some moment associated with its hearing (but, significantly, here the madeleine moment is engineered in advance—the soundtrack performatively associating the song with the person, so that the ceremony itself will be evoked by it). We will discuss further in what follows the role of music in the novel and its treatment of temporality. For the moment, it is only important that we notice that Dora's reconciliation with society is made possible through this postmodern notion of music.

Yet it is not only music that helps Dora find her place in the social order. Her four romantic relationships are also important in her transformation. Central to their relationships is something that limits them to potentiality alone, to unrealized possibilities that must remain unrealized for attraction to exist in the first place. This is true of all her relationships, but the strongest articulation of it comes after her affair with Radon, a married man, whom she meets in a motel. As Dora puts it,

> As early as the second time he called me and asked if I want to see him I already knew that I'm about to learn an unusual lesson in the theory of unrealized relationships. Every time I dared imagine going out of room 34 into the open spaces of the future I saw him in my mind's eye . . . performing some reassuring hand gesture, as if trying to alert me to the story's known boundaries . . . They say that people who admit their addiction are in some advanced stage on the road to defeating it. Nonsense. In the second month I already realized that I'm addicted to the short phone calls, to the unplanned drive to the motel, to the unique feeling that whenever the door opens, I enter a new time-space that no one except for me could understand,

> to the happy second in which Radon floods my senses, to the miraculous hours together, to the pause before opening the door, to the shock when it shuts behind me, to the drive home feeling empty, to the euphoria that comes after that, and to the loss that followed that . . .[63]

It is the strong investment of the relationship with its own definite finality that suddenly raises its head here, creating a clear analogy with the townspeople's known future. The sense of unrealized possibilities here dialectically reappears as itself an exclusion of possibility or a definiteness that negates the flight from definiteness from which it initially sprang. And it is this "certain knowledge that our mutual future is an abstract contradiction" that drives Dora to end the relationship (and the irony of ending something that has its end built into itself does not go unrecognized by her).[64]

The final step toward reconciliation with society, or the development of Dora's desire for a certain future, takes place through her final relationship, with Sebastin. His abrupt disappearance after meeting Dora only once constitutes what she calls an "act of reverse creation," in which he disappears into something like an inscrutable Lacanian Real before she even has time to form a desire for a stable future.[65] The radical fragmentariness of their acquaintance manages to negate any temporality or finality from being part of the relationship. It is only after learning that Sebastin knew he was about to die, and that their relationship was something like an ultimate exercise in pre-planned timelessness that she finds herself jealous of those that know the date of their death and enjoy a certain certainty about the future. When she finds out that she is pregnant with Sebastin's baby, the pregnancy becomes for her symbolically charged with stable futurity, making possible a complete identification with the townspeople.

Yet the reconciliation through pregnancy and child-bearing is strongly ambivalent: at once seeming to belong to a previous age in which the family and its values bore a strong ideological charge. But at the same time evoking the contemporary renewal of such ideology in a far more immediate relation to capitalism. And this alone should propel us to reread the novel in terms of its relation to its historical background. In terms of content, the novel has very few historical markers—the period of time in which events take place (the mid-'80s to mid-2000s) seems almost arbitrary, the novel not mentioning anything like the collapse of the communism or the attack on the World Trade Center, or any other historical event. I would like to suggest that music itself, or rather the form of its consumption, is what gives us a specific generational marker, if only a very weak one: the transition from vinyl LPs to cassettes and CDs and finally to downloading music online. The disappearance of the record store and the particular mode of socialization that it implies—one that is very important to the young Dora, who bemoans it just as Gafla himself does in an interview—is what in the novel stands in for transformation of collectivity and something like an inexorable movement of history.[66] The disenchantment of the world or fall out of naïveté into adulthood, implied in the novel's titular reference to Don McLean's song, helps mediate between the more collective dimension and the personal coming-of-age narrative. I argue here that this more cultural transformation provides an occasion for an unconscious exploration of Israel's neoliberalization, which of course takes place in the same period (its beginning usually traced to the Market Stabilization Program of 1985).

I would therefore like to suggest the following: that Gafla's novel's organizing principle is the staging of an allegorical encounter between neoliberal temporality and a more Fordist or pre-postmodern one. It should be clear by now time and temporality themselves are central to the novel, but it is for now far less clear at this point how this thinking about death and endings in general are related to the temporality of neoliberalism discussed at the beginning of this chapter. Eric Cazdyn's writing can be of help here, thematizing the neoliberal end of temporality through death or finality themselves. For his version of thinking through neoliberal temporality, Cazdyn coins the term "chronic time," to designate a temporality from which both cure and death have been removed:

> If the possibility of death is removed, if the terminal cannot be even considered or risked, we effectively rule out certain courses of action in the present whose ends cannot be known in advance (precisely because we cannot know if they will end in death or the death of the present system). To remove the possibility of death and settle for the new chronic is to choose the known limits of the present over the unknown freedom of the future.[67]

Important here is that what was once the death of metanarratives turns in Cazdyn's formulation into a clear limitation: the exclusion of radical transformation and unknown possibilities from the stamping of everything with the sign of the present. Cazdyn's "new chronic" is thus a strong articulation of neoliberal permanent present, the absenting of futurity, or the illusion of absolute contemporaneity.

Cazdyn's formulation makes it possible for us to relate Gafla's novel to our contemporary problem of the absence of time, but in what seems to be a deeply ambivalent way. For, surprisingly, the townspeople's lives can now finally assume for us the appearance of a utopian existence, in which death has been reintroduced into time, as it were, negating neoliberalism's chronic time (or absenting of death, as Cazdyn has it). Indeed, to know one's death-date is not only an affirmation of subjective life's necessary end. It is at the same time dialectically a removal of the worries of survival from one's life until that date, a kind of guarantee of basic existence (which is, of course, the basic premise of any utopian state of affairs). It now becomes possible to understand the existence of the townspeople as itself an "unknown possibility of the future" that is removed from our (and Dora's) neoliberal chronic time—and thus our view of Dora is now reversed. Instead of representing infinite potentialities from which the townspeople are excluded, it is her state that is degraded or less rich in potentialities. The calm and apathy of the townspeople (which Dora's mother strongly represents) is in this interpretation the result of a successful construction of desire, as it were, the successful turning of reality into Lacanian fantasy-space. Planning is precisely the success of this construction: the reduction implied by Dora's accusation that the townspeople see only what they need to see (quoted above) is here turned on its head: this reduction is precisely the necessary operation of "reduction" of desire itself, producing reality as an ordered space in which one's desire can be pursued. Yet rather than a future utopian state, the townspeople seem to represent the immediate past (to whom access to newer generations is blocked—of which Dora is an exceptionally early case). If Dora stands for neoliberal chronic time, what emerges here is a kind of allegorization of the transformation from a more Fordist social form to the neoliberal one, in which the utopian state is simply an estranged version of the immediate past's Fordist social security or guarantee of relatively comfortable existence.

Here enters the ambivalence: the life planning and calculation associated with the townspeople seems many times to belong also to the immediate future—to the commodification and objectivization of possibilities; a future intensification of the known and expected. What we have here is a kind of folding of temporality or future trajectory into objects themselves. Not only people's end becomes a matter of calculation and prediction (recall Ignoville's Death Exchange, in which bets are placed on people's cause of death), but also everyday objects are charged with a specific future trajectory. One striking example is Ignovillians' dismissive attitude when presented with a map of the town's cemetery, on which specific grave plots are marked:

One of the visitors sneered in contempt and asked "And what about all the new dead? The "ignorant by necessity"? "And those who know," another continued the line of thought, "but don't yet have a headstone?" Virl [. . .] answered "this is the map as of this moment. Any change or update, after tomorrow, will appear as a blinking red dot on the identical map that you can find on the cemetery's website, courtesy of Ignoville's municipality.[68]

The visitors' contempt is a result of the fact that the map does not somehow contain the projected future of the cemetery, rather only its present. Even future surprise and accident become paradoxically planned, as in Gafla's striking imagining of "condoms that self-destruct during sex, a means for raising the birthrate in backwards countries" or "the principle of malfunction" through which life-planning accounts for unforeseen turns in one's life—planning for known unknowns.[69] And here, too, we can recall the reverse Proustian-madeleine-effect moment discussed above—in which a song is consciously invested with the life trajectory of a specific person (rather than a song surprisingly taking one back to a moment in time, here the song is intentionally invested with this moment). In this way, Ignovillians stand for an even greater future degree of penetration of capitalism into everyday life, rather than for the older Fordist social form.

So we have two options through which to read the contrast between Dora and the townspeople in relation to their context, and the larger historical transformation in which it exists. I would like to suggest now that this ambivalence is not a result of some conceptual unclarity or innocent mistake—it is rather the novel's imaginative problem-solving in action. For the confusion of the older Fordist stable life with the newer folding of pre-known temporality into objects depends on not noticing the main difference between the two: the ephemerality and spatial particularity of the newer temporalities or certainties, as opposed to the all-encompassing or totalizing one of Fordist life (and the latter's dialectical mediation into a collective "metanarrative" or telos, as in the narratives of modernization that we mentioned above). The newer temporal trajectories, folded into individuals and objects, are also subject to sudden change from one moment to the next: each history is a history that a specific present allows one to tell, as Dora herself puts it (paradoxically making each person ultimately unknowable).[70] That this ephemerality of temporalities is of course a result of neoliberal reality is perhaps best captured in that financial instrument we call the derivative—which should be seen as producing precisely such fleeting temporalities) or expectations for the future based on past events), as Jameson argues, based on Dick Bryan and Michael Rafferty's work.[71] These should remind us of those fleeting appearances of time in Yakir's *Sand* that we discussed earlier. These fleeting "times" are altogether different from the older totalizing temporality—in the singular—of Fordism, in which the single, stable, time of one's existence transformed everything in one's life.

A certain mapping of corresponding utopian openings and possibilities accompanies the novel's unification effort of older Fordist (or welfare state) time and that of neoliberalism. Those of the older way of life include, for example, those constitutive fantasies—those goals that are not really to be achieved, since they fulfil their function precisely in remaining possible future undertakings. Dora's father's wish to travel extensively around the world is a good example, and so is Dora's friend's unchanging love for a married man.[72] The surprising and the contingent belong here too, designating a sort of sudden end of the planned. But more interesting are the utopian temporal openings that the novel relates to the neoliberal absence of time. One such example is the "waiting, without knowing for what"—a reimagining of the sense of accident and contingency, but in a situation from which all time has been robbed.[73] Put in this way, time sneaks back in: as if holding an empty space for a future perspective that would provide the aimless waiting (ultimately an oxymoron) with its yet unimaginable purpose (a position whose great defender is Walter Benjamin), for which spatial or architectural equivalent is something like doors that lead nowhere). If, as Cazdyn argues, neoliberal chronic time robs such waiting for not-yet-known of radical openness, the novel reintroduces this sense of openness—at least temporarily—to the timelessness of Dora's life.[74] In this way, again, the novel suggests a kind of unity or reconciliation of welfare-state temporality with that of emerging neoliberal reality.

It is, of course, useless to try to decide which of these options—welfare-state secure life, or neoliberal folding of temporalities into singular events, people, and objects—is finally the "correct" referent of Ignoville's townspeople. The point is rather precisely the novel's allegorization of these two social forms (through each of their experiences) speculative identity or unification. It is important to note that the achievement of closure is here precisely contained in Dora's perfectly impossible reconciliation with a society from which she will never truly be part—if only because she is barred from the security of knowing her own death-date. Thus Dora becomes the perfect ideological inheritor to her welfare-state predecessors—constituting a paradigmatic affective laborer under neoliberal capitalism—one that knows to empathize with the elderly, despite their belonging to a social order from which the younger generation is excluded. One might even mention that the formal equivalence created between Dora's story and that of the death-date-prophet (delivered to us in the last fifty pages of the novel) is another such attempt at imaginary reconciliation between the two social forms. The prophet David Fuchs does know his own death-date, and his sudden disappearance from his wife's life establishes him as a stand-in for Dora's Sebastin—their symbolic union is of course affirmed in Dora's pregnancy. For the new empathetic Dora, closure or containment are given symbolic affirmation through Fuchs's death: "the unique opportunity to know [one's death-date] was torn away from life, flooding me with a feeling of freedom."[75] The important point for our purposes is not the operation of ideological reconciliation itself, but that there is a drama of containment at all. In the late-'80s works that we discussed, non-reconciliation was pastiched (along with reified past representations), or turned into a new form of reconciliation. In contrast, in *The Day the Music Died*, literary subject matter must again reconcile living social contradictions. It is in this shift that the difference between the two periods reside—one that I will explore in the next chapter as well.

Contemporary Israeli Literary Criticism and Neoliberalism

The two 1980s chapters of this book began with positing of three questions about the appearance of Israeli postmodernism. I have answered two of them—those that were concerned with the existence of Israeli postmodernism itself and its material conditions. I would like now to finally address the third question, namely, why has postmodernism fallen out of grace as a periodizing term in Israeli literary criticism? In our previous discussion, we noted that the turn away from postmodernism as a periodizing concept—in the work of Shifman, Peleg, Uri Cohen, and others—leads to a failure to distinguish between literature there is a general failure to distinguish between the literature of the 1980s and 1990s and its predecessors.[76] The alternative periodizing concepts to postmodernism suggested by these authors, I argued, were generally very unstable, easily collapsing into the interpretive frameworks of the previous generation of critics (dominated by Shaked and Miron): Peleg's suggestion of seeing '90s literature in terms of an emphasis on romantic coupledom and a rejection of politics, for example, clearly echoes Shaked much earlier periodization of the '60s turn: an abandonment of overtly politicized literature for more individual affairs. Peleg's new period is thus at most an intensification of previous trends, rather than a break from them. Similar arguments for the other cases too. Even Yigal Schwartz, who complains about contemporary critics' inability to form an understanding of literary history antagonistic to that of their predecessors, ends up failing to posit an alternative critical or historiographical understanding of Israeli literature, as I tried to show in the beginning of the 1980s discussion. On the one hand, postmodernism is abandoned as a periodizing concept; on the other, all suggested alternatives easily collapse into earlier distinctions.

I argue that the last three chapters have finally equipped us not only to understand this weakness of the imagination of Israeli literary criticism; they can also help us explain another curious development: the near-absence of literary-critical writing about contemporary novels. The five works that I explore in these last two chapters are good examples: despite including works and writers that have enjoyed considerable appreciation (and not only that of sales figures, but also from the literary critical establishment). Einat Yakir's work is a good example here: her work now extends over a decade and a half, winning considerable attention, but has never been the subject matter of "serious" (or, simply, academic) literary-critical study. Ofir Touché-Gafla's work has received the same treatment, and so is Lilach Netanel's (which we will discuss in the next chapter). Most new novels that are still discussed are those of novelists who were already established in the 1980s—including of course Amos Oz and A. B. Yehoshua, but also Orly Castel-Bloom and Ronit Matalon. Literary criticism whose focus is more identity oriented has tended to fare a bit better: Adia Mendelson-Maoz's survey of Israeli literary multiculturalism, for instance, includes discussions of more recent works, and so does Lital Levy's work on Israeli-Palestinians literary relationships (it should however be clear that the critical paradigms evoked in these are very much still those of the '80s and '90s, even if their subject matter is newer).[77] But these are clear exceptions. The overall trend is clearly one of turning inward or of a failure to address these new literary developments, preferring instead renewed reflection on familiar topics.

I would like to suggest now an explanation for both of these developments—that absence of generational "break" or rebellion and the dearth of critical writing on new literature. Both should be seen as the effects of the neoliberal disintegration of the relation between academic humanities work and social form which used to be mediated by the nation-state. Neoliberalization here is expressed not as some simplistic death or withering away of the state, which many have shown to be inaccurate.[78] Instead, for our purposes, neoliberalization means a more immediate (or non-mediated) relation to market forces—as Mathias Nilges puts it. What is lost here is the state's institutions providing a sort of distance or mediating force-field between academic work and the market. The Israeli national academy's ideological role, however one judges it ethically, has before neoliberalism created a kind of space for a project of constructing collectivity that is set apart from market forces. The rapid decline of the literary expert corresponds here to her loss of place within a neoliberal order—in which the functions of the humanities academia have been relegated to the market. It is easy to uncover the straightforward relation between the death of stable interpretation and the neoliberalization of literature and interpretation: literature simply turns into a commodity here—its use value (in the case of literature, its interpretation) becomes completely subjective, while exchange-value (sales figures) become an objective measure. The historical movement that we have here follows the logic of Hegel's ruse of reason: what is initially perceived as a liberation from national canon and expertise turns out to be mere unwitting pretext for neoliberalization.

And thus literary experts lose their social role and reason for existing in the first place, and the humanities academy shrinks and becomes older. A star-system comes to dominate the emaciated ranks of younger academics (since only those that have gained market fame outside of academia will sell well as academics). The two points that we sought to explain almost explain themselves now. With neoliberalization's erosion of the role of the humanities academic, there is very little reason for academics to write about new authors, or to start new struggles over interpretation—the changed conditions brought about by neoliberalism make these operations lose their larger significance, becoming instead a matter of sandbox disputes. Even the aversion to postmodernism as a periodizing term becomes demystified here: literary postmodernism was usually identified among Israeli literary critics with playfulness. This initial stage is precisely that transition period in which a new freedom seemed to be in sight. It is only later, through the work of that ruse of reason that this playfulness disappears—leaving in its place a decimated humanities to which no one pays attention. Little wonder, then, that postmodernism as a periodizing concept, and the playfulness it connoted are suddenly eyed as suspicious or a naïve dead-end.

7

In Search of New Time

Renarrating Soldier, Pioneer, and the Tel Aviv Subject-to-Come

In this last chapter I will enlarge the scope of the previous chapter's argument about contemporary Israeli literature and its difference from that of the 1980s and 1990s. What the '80s and '90s Israeli postmodernists were representing as the liberating dissolution of national imaginary and temporality suddenly becomes a generalized problem of the absence of time and social mapping in the contemporary texts. One should not fail to see the chasm and even antagonism separating the two moments, even if both exist within postmodernity: while the falling apart of national time and social imagination is itself a form of ideological reconciliation in the 1980s, it suddenly poses a threat and a problem for the newer texts by Yakir and Gafla that I explored. In the newer literature, one wakes up into a nightmare, as it were, in which life itself depends on the desperate possibility of generating new social temporalities—the absence of futurity and accompanying illusion of absolute contemporaneity become conditions to be solved or contained—but without yet having some other collective horizon, which makes the reconciliatory moments as inherently localized, ephemeral, and aesthetically unsatisfactory (such as the turn to motherhood in Gafla's novel, or those fleeting productions of time in Yakir's).

In this chapter I will chart this new moment in three other novels: Ron Leshem's 2005 *Beaufort*, Lilach Netanel's 2008 *The Hebrew Condition*, and Yiftach Ashkenazi's 2014 *Fulfillment*. The reason I have chosen these novels from among many other possibilities is that all constitute instances, however impurely, of genres that exist since pre-statehood: the *halutzic* settlement novel (Ashkenazi), the soldier's experience novel (Leshem), and the Tel Aviv picaresque or voyeur (Netanel). In a more strictly historically comparative framework, each should be contrasted with its '80s and '90s generic predecessors: Kenaz's *Infiltration* and Shimoni's *A Room* in Leshem's case; Meir Shalev's postmodern settlement novels (for example, *Loves of Judith* and *The Blue Mountain*) in Ashkenazi's case; and Orly Castel-Bloom's writing and that of Etgar Keret and others in Netanel's case.[1] I will not engage here in this type of comparative analysis in any systematic way, even if I have cursorily done so for some of the 1980s works that were discussed in the previous chapters. Rather than this more explicit comparative method, the reader's familiarity with the analysis of these '80s and '50s predecessors that was performed in previous chapters will be assumed, so that quick references to these will suffice in my attempt to tease out the newness of the more recent novels.

It is important to emphasize that the analysis of each work will not simply be a repetition of the previous chapter's analysis of Gafla's and Yakir's works. Rather, one of the reasons for choosing these five contemporary novels (the two discussed in this chapter and the three of the previous one) is that each offers a different and very original novelistic figuration of the social contradictions of its moment—making for surprising mediations of social and aesthetic. Indeed, to rehearse yet again a defense of Marxist literary analysis from the knee-jerk accusation of reductionism, one should insist that this is not at all the case that Marxist cultural or literary criticism is reductive—or that it ignores an inherently complexly varied field of cultural expressions by seeing all of them as basically identical, or as expressing the same social contradictions. Opposite this misconception it should be stressed that the creative moment of each work is not at all lost in Marxist criticism—for the imaginative vehicles each work uses to capture social forces are not at all known in advance; each (interesting) novel has to reinvent it, given the novelistic "codes" or genres that exist, which are like so many tools with which the novelist can work, and which are themselves reworked and reinterpreted in the process (which can finally be recognized as a dialectic of form and content). And this creativity is visible only through considering the relation of a work to its context and larger historical placement—as stressed in Walter Benjamin's view of allegory as the creator of preconceptual imaginary newness, rather than as the boring vehicle for reiterating old conceptual or ethical dogmas.[2] Thus, each novel's way of capturing (both consciously and unconsciously) its social subject matter is new and surprising, as I hope to show, and does not in any way follow some formula. The grand organizing thematic of these two last chapters—Israeli literature's dawning realization that the dissolution of temporality and historicity are a problem to be overcome—should be seen as a key to addressing creative newness rather than a reduction to the old and familiar. It allows us to see the present moment in Israeli literature as an age of new allegories, of so many attempts—no matter how minor and localized at this moment—to imagine solutions for this problem of temporality and restart the movement of history in the realm of our collective imagination. The problem of each work's creative imagination in all its intransigence thus turns out to be, in this Marxist account, always-already an inherently social and historical problem, rather than being dispelled or ignored (or "reduced" away) by the latter instances. And it is in this way that the following chapter should be read: as trying to make visible the inventive newness, the purely contingent creative intervention that each text constitutes in the way it inevitably confronts the social reality in which it finds itself.

Beaufort, or, Utopia against Neoliberalism

Beaufort is the last text of the only genre that I have been following in each of three moments explored in this book—the genre of soldiers' experience. As I argued earlier, Kenaz's *Infiltration* had turned the utopian content carried by the genre from the 1950s into that all-encompassing narrative failure that we related to postmodernism. As I hope to show, *Beaufort* presents us with yet another reworking of this utopian content. At the outset it is easy to see that Leshem's *Beaufort* constitutes a sharp repoliticization of its genre (the novel's very strong political dimension is to a large degree minimized in the novel's film adaptation). The 2005 novel, published under a Hebrew title that translates literally as "If there's Heaven," narrates the story of a group of Israeli soldiers in the Beaufort outpost in southern Lebanon, just before Israel's withdrawal from the area in 2000. The political debates that took place in Israel just before the withdrawal and the conflict between Israel and Hezbollah serve as background to the events of the novel. Of the three texts that belong to the soldiers' experience genre discussed in this book, *Beaufort* is the one in which military violence is most directly present, although even in this novel the space devoted to actual military action is not considerable. The novel is also distinguished by its reception—becoming well-known because of its place in bestsellers lists rather than critical appreciation, a phenomenon which I have tried to relate to neoliberalization. It is true that *Beaufort* has received more critical attention than the other contemporary texts discussed in these two last chapters. But in comparison to, for example, Yizhar's and Kenaz's texts, it has drawn very meager critical attention. The overt political stance of the novel's soldier-protagonist—Israeli political center-Right—has here been an additional repellent to critics, as Israeli literary critics, who tend to be associated with the other side of the political map.

We can use what can be seen as a common leftist response to the novel as a starting point for our discussion of the protagonist's restlessness. In this account, *Beaufort* presents "a critique of the [Israeli] security and political establishment, particularly of its policies dealing with the occupation of southern Lebanon, which nonetheless reinforces the social convention according to which military service should be undertaken and military orders obeyed."[3] Although this critique is aimed at the film version of *Beaufort*, it might as well have been written about the novel. What must be asserted about this critical position is that it reads literary and filmic narratives too quickly as if they were badly written policy papers—comparable to Adorno's "culture haters'" attitude toward cultural production.[4] That *Beaufort* is a novel with a nationalist political horizon is self-evident; what is easily ignored is what it has to conjure in order to reassert that nationalist horizon. Another critical response that elides what undergirds the overt political commitment is the one that sees the novel as simply translating older national values into more contemporary understandings, the novel finally "serv[ing] up patriotism with a twist more palatable for a Post-Zionist or postnational age."[5] As we will see, it is precisely the utopian valences that are carried by the figure of the soldier (after his late '40s literary birth) that are repurposed in *Beaufort* to figure new social contradictions, and whose recognition is crucial for a dialectical understanding of the novel.

The national coming-of-age narrative arc of the novel is very clear: the initial alienated state of the soldier is overcome by an ideological reconciliation of the soldier to the nation. Passages that stress the protagonist's alienation from Israeli society abound—in what has become, of course, a staple of war novels (the alienated soldier's visit home in Remarque's *All Quiet on the Western Front* can serve as a good contrast here). Going on leave back into Israel, for example, the narrator constantly emphasizes that "there is no way they can understand us."[6] For example:

> Finally, we reach the meeting point, where the Safaris pick us up. Our shivering turns to goose bumps of excitements that Israel

is getting closer, along with a feeling of relief that this insane thing is ending without incident. By the time the border gate opens and we cross through, and bolt from the vehicles on the whitetop at Ha'egel base, we can see the first light in the sky. Take in a deep breath of Air, I gesture to River. Look at the sky and calm yourself. There's nothing like entering Israel at this hour, when everyone is waking up along with you, a new day. They have no idea where you're coming from and no clue what you've been through. Milk trucks unload their wares at Itzik Zagouri's grocery in Kiryat Shmona, and the bakery puts out its first tray of croissants, and the paperboys deliver their newspapers [. . .] and people are out jogging, waving hello to you. It's a different planet. Such sweet moments, like from a movie, and at first glance everything seems so innocent. Just a village filled with calm people, smiling at one another, unaware of what's happening a few feet away from their lives, right under their noses.[7]

What "at first glance" seems to possess a familiar habituality to it—just like those school field trips invoked by Yizhar's narrator in one of the passages quoted above—turns out later to be a false appearance. This constancy has a peculiar syntactic structure, which is as if a result of self-generating text, associated with it: the repeating "and . . . and . . ." structure (evidenced in the passage above), itself borrowed from Yizhar. What is important to notice is the association of this structure in *Beaufort* with something like a welfare-state everyday life and its familiar cyclical rhythms (or what I called Fordist temporality in the discussion of Gafla's *The Day the Music Died*). At the same time, however, this repetitiveness seems symptomatically signaling to us that there is something not so agreeable under the thin veneer of everydayness. We will have more to say on Leshem's use of repetitive structures below. For now, however, we should simply note that the protagonist's inability to communicate his experiences of the military outpost thus constructs, through the first half of the text, an opposition between the narrator and Israeli society. It is this communicative failure that raises its head with regard to the protagonist's girlfriend, friends, family members, and the narrator's commanding officers—everyone except the other soldiers in the Beaufort outpost.[8] The kernel of protest in this stubborn insistence on the incommunicability of his experience is mediated into the protagonists' rebellious demand that the outpost will never be evacuated by the military, even as withdrawal from Southern Lebanon becomes imminent as the novel progresses.

The moment of ideological reconciliation between soldier and nation is equally clear. It occurs during a visit by an older high-ranking officer, Kaplan, to the outpost. Only after Kaplan's demonstration that he understands the soldiers' experience—expressed in his participation in their rituals and in his emotionally charged narration of the conquest of the Beaufort outpost in 1982 in which he participated—does the narrator's defiance begin to dissipate, paving the way to the ideological conclusion of the coming of age narrative. Kaplan's response to one of the soldier's questions is what finally permits the transition, and it is worth quoting, if only to demonstrate the contradictory emptiness of all such moments of ideological reconciliation:

> [Kaplan said] "I'm one of those squares who think that the only way to protect Israel's northern settlements from the growing threat that is Hezbollah is by maintaining a security zone in southern Lebanon. And control of Beaufort, with its topographical superiority, is exactly what makes the difference [. . .] But who knows? Maybe afterward, when this whole thing is over, we'll ask ourselves how we didn't think of this withdrawal a few years earlier." [. . .] I asked him, "Is there a chance you weren't even supposed to conquer the Beaufort that day, but you stormed anyway?" Kaplan took a deep breath, and his small, sad smile nearly disappeared, "Yes there is," he answered. "There was apparently some sort of order like that—not to attack—but it never reached us. To this very day it's not clear where exactly it got stopped."[9]

Israel should stay in Lebanon, but it should also withdraw from it; Israel needs to hold the Beaufort, but it is there by mistake—the incoherence of Kaplan's answer, which nonetheless paves the way for the protagonist's reconciliation with Israeli society, is probably the best evidence that *Beaufort*'s figurative work is performed elsewhere.

We can now finally take note of the fact that the strong opposition that the novel constructs between Israel and the Beaufort outpost is not merely a ploy for the coming-of-age narrative. For the Beaufort outpost functions as something like utopian enclave in the novel, a space set apart so that a utopian thought experiment can take place in it.[10] Crucial to this process is what Louis Marin calls utopian neutralization, namely, the process by which the ideological and material determinants of the Israeli context are rendered ineffectual. This process is evident not only in the parodying of political positions—both left and right—but also in slowly canceling the divide between religious and secular soldiers, and between Ashkenazi and Mizrachi soldiers.[11] It is important to emphasize that this is not a process of reconciliation of opposites, but of each pole's cancelation: the religious becoming not-religious, while the secular becoming not-secular in some way. One can parallel this process to the journey to the remote island of the protagonist and his friend in Herzl's *Altneuland*, before arriving at the utopian society. The sojourn on the island is imagined to neutralize the effects of European society on them, preparing them for the utopian social order.

Second, and more importantly for our purposes, the utopian neutralization process opens up the way for new structures to be set in place. This is true not only in the trivial sense of having all material aspects of life governed and controlled, but also in the sense of mapping individual roles into a larger imagined goal (suggested in the brief passage in which the outpost commander maps their individual roles into the larger logic of the goal of the military's presence in southern Lebanon).[12] The detailed descriptions of the different kinds of military operations, stakeouts, and ambushes that the group of soldiers undertakes discloses a fascination with cooperative functioning itself: each soldier is trained for a particular role in each of these contexts, and each role fulfils some necessary collective function.[13] What the utopian enclave revives, then, is a sense of social cognitive mapping—having a clear place within a known social order—or even something like what Sartre calls a group-in-fusion, in which the purpose of each part of a totality is clearly reflected in the functioning of all others.[14] The outpost's soldier society is thus surprisingly similar to Gafla's living-dead of Ignoville.

This functional mapping of the utopian enclave is paired with new positive freedoms and individual play: from linguistic inventiveness, culinary experiments, and playing makeshift musical instruments, to the (plainly apparent yet constantly disavowed) homoeroticism among the soldiers, to filmmaking.[15] And reciting Shakespeare's *Henry V* in a passage foreshadowing the moment of ideological reconciliation:

> "*We few, we happy few, we band of brothers,*" he said [. . .] "*And gentlemen in England shall think themselves accursed they were not here.*" [. . .] "You think they'll make a show about us one day?" I asked. "A Play?" he said, correcting me. "No, I don't think so" [. . .] He drank his tea. "They weren't even supposed to conquer this hill, they didn't mean to" [. . .] "The next morning Ariel Sharon arrived [. . .] with a whole entourage and a TV crew.

There were still puddles of blood on the ground. He proclaimed it a historical achievement."[16]

What is important for our purposes in this passage is not, again, the feeble historical revisionism. Rather, in this rudimentary representation of artistic activity in the outpost, Leshem revives something like the utopian imagination's allegorical structure, or like a precapitalist situation in which symbolic institutions have not yet been abstracted from their social context and functioning: making and interpreting art clearly become in this passage a vehicle for mediating between individual existence and that of a collective. What Phillip Hollander sees as an exploration of the limits of Israeli masculinity, one that challenges the Israeli status quo, in the film version of *Beaufort* it is precisely a result of the constructive utopian logic of the outpost.[17] It is this weaving together of art and function in the utopian enclave that makes the Beaufort outpost seem like a mysterious space "that follows its own logic," as one critic comments, and highlights its fragility and ultimate impossibility or ephemerality, as all utopian spaces tend to be.[18]

Meanwhile, Israeli society itself must be the utopian enclave's opposite: it is what the social imagination cannot order, thoroughly torn by contradictions (the existence of which is made clear through the process of neutralization itself). It is at this point that the contrast between Leshem's and Yizhar's *Khirbet Khizeh*, which we discussed in an earlier chapter, becomes suggestive. For what we have in *Beaufort* is an inversion of what we called above the narrative foreground and background in *Khirbet Khizeh*. In the latter, as I argued, the narrative background consisted of a stable utopian transformative imaginary (that of the *halutz*), while the narrative foreground—the military conquest plot—registered an irresolvable narrative crisis. In contrast, in *Beaufort* military experience is precisely where utopia resides, and the narrative background is where social imagination is in complete disarray. We can thus see in *Beaufort* a textbook example of Adorno's ingenious formulation according to which literary form is nothing but sedimented content. It is precisely the charging of the military experience with utopian energies—in Kenaz's novel, for example, following transformations outside literature[19]— that makes this formal inversion possible by the time *Beaufort* is published.

Why, then, does *Beaufort* end with a reconciliation between soldier and nation, a reconciliation refused by all other texts belonging to its genre? If the soldiers of both *Khirbet Khizeh* and *Infiltration* are never cured of their utopian restlessness, *Beaufort*'s utopian enclave must be evacuated and contained—something made imaginatively possible only through the inversion of Yizhar just mentioned. To answer this question, one should understand in what sense Israeli society is represented as the outpost's opposite. The utter social disorientation associated with Israeli society should be reread now in terms of neoliberalization and the dismantling of the Israeli welfare state, discussed in more detail in the previous chapter. In other words, here my argument is going to be that imagined reconciliation with Israeli society is in the novel precisely a reconciliation with neoliberal social reality and the falling-apart of welfare-state temporalities.

To illustrate how this falling-apart of welfare-state social form and its time, we can now finally return to that first quote from the novel and its use of the "and . . . and . . . and . . ." construction in its description of Israeli life outside the outpost. Above, I suggested that this construction expressed both a stable and habitual everydayness associated with welfare-state middle-class life, and at the same time functioning as an excessive pastiche of this everydayness, a symptom of something disturbing hidden behind this everydayness. It is here that we can quote a similar use of an additive construction: whenever a soldier dies in *Beaufort*, his friends play a game called "What He Can't Do Anymore," in which the soldiers take turns in completing the sentence:

> Yonatan can't take his little brother to the movie anymore. Yonatan can't watch Hapoel bring home the soccer trophy anymore. Yonatan can't listen to the latest disc by Zion Golan anymore. He can't see Tom with the ugliest slut in Nahariya anymore [. . .] He'll never know how great it is when your mother's proud of you getting accepted to college. Even a community college. He won't be at his grandfather's funeral. He won't know if his sister gets married . . . .[20]

This passage, which opens the novel, continues in the same fashion for two pages (and the game is played several more times in the novel). Here, too, the additive structure allows for something like an anxious inventory-taking of familiar life-moments, relating both to the present of the 20-year-old soldiers, but also to what seems like a middle-class future adulthood. The ritual is the soldiers' way of coping with death. But here we can give these passages—whose form makes them stand out in the novel—a social interpretation that rewrites this more ethical and psychological one. For, what better figure for neoliberalism's dissolution of welfare-state middle class existence than these passages, in which these life's moments are literally torn out of any ordered temporality, to simply float next to each as so many independent "experiences." The parceled moments, which appear as the content of the different statements, are precisely what is abstracted by neoliberal capitalism, becoming a commodity rather than some ordered national common experience (a common experience that is the condition of possibility for any collective figuration). It is in this way that the reality outside the Beaufort outpost—Israeli society—is an anxiety-ridden pastiche of some social experience, all broken down into separate "experiences," abstracted from a concrete social project, ready to be commodified (something like a Lacanian Real that requires "cutting down" by a Symbolic order).[21] We have, indeed, come very far from Yizhar. In the latter's work, as we have seen, the reality outside the experience of the soldier was the stable imaginary of Zionist utopian vanguardism, complete with its sense of historicity and its allegorization in ideas of individual transformation. In Leshem's novel, in contrast, the outside to outpost is associated with the complete lack of social orientation, and with a desperate clinging-on to the pastiche of middle-class social experience, to a social existence that is quickly eroding by the time *Beaufort* is published.

What *Beaufort* does, therefore, is register the Israeli crisis of social imagination *as a problem*, in contrast to the late'80s works (such as *Infiltration*), in which this crisis is regarded as a new freedom to be playfully explored, as we have seen in the previous chapters. The novel's ending with the reconciliation of the soldier to Israeli nationhood is an imaginary solution to precisely this problem: it is an attempt at reconciliation with neoliberal reality, an attempt to contain the felt social anxiety and revolutionary impulse awakened by neoliberal destruction of anything that ever evoked, in however reified a manner, a collective project. In this reading, therefore, the true imaginative effort of *Beaufort* is not in its superficial return of the soldier to the bosom of the nation or legitimating Israeli policies (for the social experience related with nationhood as a collective project is completely gone by the time the novel is published). Rather, *Beaufort*'s ideological operation—that infamous Althusserian reconciliation of contradictions—is in its attempt to imagine a non-anxious existence under neoliberal capitalism.

The Hebrew Condition and the Art of Failure

Lilach Netanel's first novel *The Hebrew Condition* will here constitute a kind of final moment for that genre of Tel Aviv mapping subjectivity, whose earlier instances are the works of Castel-Bloom, Etgar Keret, and others (but that undoubtedly stretches back to S. Y. Agnon's 1930s, and Brenner's even earlier works). Here, again, we are confronted with a near-absence of critical commentary on the novel, despite in the seven years that have passed since its publication. As I argued at the end of the previous chapter, this is the result of the same neoliberal "condition" to which the novel tries to speak. The novel recounts events in the life of the novel's four main characters: Zvi, a historian who is attempting to write a history of Israel; his life partner Mina, who seems not to have a life outside the rural house she inherited; and Zvi's parents, who meet for the first time in the 1930s in a kibbutz, and are not identified in the novel by their first names. The majority of the novel revolves around two historical times: one takes place across several days in the 1980s, in which Mina is informed that she has miscarried, and in which Zvi realizes that he is failing to write a coherent historical narrative. The other temporal coordinate takes place in the 1930s, bringing together Zvi's father immigration to Palestine and his meeting with Zvi's mother in a rural settlement, which takes place around the time of the murder of Haim Arlosoroff, a Zionist leader.

What we should note at the outset is that even at this preliminary literal level the novel seems to be thematically centered on failure, as Amotz Giladi notes.[22] The novel creates an allegorical parallel between at least three failures: the first is Zvi's father's failure to become part of Zionist "history" in the kibbutz, captured most generally in his alienation from kibbutz life.[23] The second one has to do with a failure to write or recount history itself, a failure that drives Zvi to the brink of madness at the end of the novel. This failure is related many times in the novel to something like a failure to signify of language itself, a Hebrew that lives "on sound alone" as Netanel repeatedly puts it.[24] The third is the failure of Mina's pregnancy, which coincides a general feeling that Zvi's and Mina's relationship is at a dead end.[25] The symbolic connection between these three failures is constantly highlighted in the novel, reminiscent of the failures of the author-protagonists of early twentieth-century literature from Palestine—both realist and modernist—to both find their place in *yishuv* society and to write about it.[26] That early Hebrew writers (mostly modernists, but not entirely) is where Netanel finds the models for her characters is clearly evident from her extensive quoting of them—many of the novels chapter begin with a quote from Brenner, Gnessin, Agnon, and other writers.

What is important at this point is simply to note that by conjuring both a 1930s failure and 1980s one, a structure of equivalence begins to emerge: the failure of Zvi's parents to relate to history in the '30s is made equivalent with a failure in the '80s—which in *The Hebrew Condition* seems to stand for everydayness or mundaneness, standing in opposition to the historical significance attached to the '30s. This alignment of the '80s with the structures and institutions of everyday life under a welfare state is clear in the novel's second part, which wholly focuses on the '80s. The passages dealing with Zvi's mother's lost identity card and her obsessive going through her other forms of identification (Senior Citizen identification card, Tel Aviv resident card, etc.), the long section dealing with the office of the Ministry of the Interior, and other sections are indicative of precisely this identification of the '80s with everydayness and its rhythms and institutions.

That this everydayness is suddenly thrown into crisis and thus made equivalent to the '30s is where Netanel begins to diverge from previous "postmodern" representations of the Zionist past, in which the '80s are usually not included as an object of representation alongside the earlier period. What is, however, invoked by this representation of the '80s is precisely the '80s and '90s (Tel Aviv) urban picaresque of Orly Castel-Bloom, Etgar Keret, and others, in which everydayness falls apart into sheer chaos—a kind of indivisible chaos of the Lacanian Real, which we discussed at length.[27] The difference between these and *The Hebrew Condition*'s portrayal of the Israeli urban 1980s is that the latter is far less celebratory and playful in its approach to the dissolution of middle-class everyday life. Both the failure of the 1930s and that of the 1980s is clearly a source of distress for the characters, who keep sensing that they have lost something ineffable—a sense of distress that is also expressed in the novel's form, as we will soon see (which aligns Netanel strongly with Yakir's writing, discussed in the previous chapter). The content of Netanel's novel thus brings together two previous representations of the past: the 1930s pre-state Zionist past, as it was represented by the early Hebrew modernists, and the 1980s' representation of its own urban present, and sees both in terms of a loss, or a failure that we have yet to define.

The novel's present moment is not entirely absent from it. It is registered in the novel's form rather than its content, or in the way the novel presents its subject matter. Now, Netanel's novel is very ambitious in terms of the formal devices it invents and utilizes—radical fragmentation and repetition being dominant among theses. We will address repetition in what follows. As for radical fragmentation, it is not new in Hebrew letters, particularly in texts which take their formal inspiration from (or even, clearly imitate) the modernist masters—Agnon, Gnessin, Brenner, and others—under whose spells *The Hebrew Condition* certainly falls. Yet Netanel's novel displays a heightening of the tendency toward fragmentation, a greater density of brokenness than in any of her predecessors. This heightening is what surely should give pause to any attempt to see Netanel as merely pastiching the early twentieth-century Hebrew modernists, as one would expect from a postmodern novel.[28] No matter which Agnon or Brenner novel one opens, fragmentation is never as dense as in *The Hebrew Condition*. Yet, to the degree that fragmentation itself is a form of utopian compensation in postmodernism, as Jameson notes, its heightening still does not make the novel break the spells of the older cultural mode.

The reason for which fragmentation is important to our discussion is that it holds the key to other formal characteristics of Netanel's novel. In the first part of the novel, it makes possible a constant contrasting of unimportant details and with historically significant events. For example:

> In the days after Arlosoroff's death the word grief was on every tongue. In the heavens death throes of blue light were mourning death. Words of lament were written on a piece of paper and then spoken out loud. Beautiful words were these words and they bespoke a new vibrant Hebrew. Meanwhile summer was over and the trees greened and the nights came early and when they came they found the fields awake with heartbeat. To the toolshed a bird came and said "tsa. Tsa." A humble ceremony was held to commemorate Arlosoroff's death. At night holiday clothes were worn and everyone walked to the dining hall. White shirts flapping in the wind. Tzvi's father was sitting at the end of one of the wooden benches in the dining hall, near a window, wearing his only white shirt.[29]

This juxtaposition of meaningless detail and significant historical events repeats throughout the first part of the novel, highlighting Zvi's parents sense of alienation from history happening around them. This tension between detail and history, or between subject and historical agency, is precisely one of the ways of thematizing a problem of narration, or that of totality, to paraphrase Georg Lukács.[30] What is important for our purposes is that rather than celebrate a sort of equality of random details and personal experience with historical events—as can be expected from a more properly postmodern or deconstructive sensibility—Netanel's novel insists on seeing the relation between personal and historical, or detail and system, as a real problem to be solved narratively.

This becomes evident when we consider a different formal element: that of closure. If in in postmodernism proper a failure of closure is always triumphantly enacted (or, the problem of closure becoming dialectically its own imaginary solution), Netanel's novel always makes a sincere attempt at closure—an attempt that nonetheless fails. Thus, for example, the first part begins and ends with a heightened feeling of disorientation, which is precisely the result of the failure to mediate small detail or private subjective experience with overarching Zionist history. The "question that freezes in Zvi's face" at the end of the first part, echoing the same "freezing" in Hinda's face in the quote from Brenner that opens that part of the novel, poses the question of closure in all its sincerity, demanding a solution for it.[31]

The second and third parts use the heightened fragmentation—taken in Netanel to be an objective condition of existence to be fought against—for similar purposes. If the emphasis of the first part seems to be more historical or to stress a diachronic problem of relating detail to history, the second part deals with a more synchronic thematization of this problem: mediating between subject and an invisible yet omnipresent system, the one that governs '80s everydayness. Invisible urban systems are treated with suspicion, a kind of nominalistic distrust of the intangible that is nonetheless aware of something at work beyond the sensible: "space is realized in the gaze and ends in the invisible [. . .] one does not deal with that which one does not see." The invisible social system appears under many figures here: The sewage system's "pipes that are hidden in the walls pumping water and emptying water . . . draining into the sinkhole meeting something down there" are one example, as well as the phone network's similarly mysterious connections, are some of the more infrastructural images of this hidden, yet omnipresent, system; while the offices of the ministry of the interior stand in for the more properly social-institutional system of the state itself; and finally language standing for yet another unrepresentable system.[32] Even the body itself loses its systemic Kantian organicity under the narrator's nominalistic gaze, reverting instead to a fragmentation whose source is Cartesian doubt as to the unity of subjectivity—both in time ("[. . .] her skin changed color, but nonetheless she is always called by the same name, and nonetheless she is always herself"), and in space ("Zvi's father is sitting on the edge of the bed. His hands feel that the mattress is as warm as his body").[33] Zvi's mother's losing her identity card—standing obviously for a loss of identity itself[34]—is thus in this part a result of a failure to mediate between subject and system, an inability to grasp one's place in a whole.

In the third part, fragmentation makes it possible to capture formally something like a dialectic of identity and otherness, through the use of characters' names as titles for short sections that deal with them. The system makes its appearance here through the impossibility of separating completely one person's thoughts and history from others that stubbornly appear in their narrative. No matter how strictly the text tries to observe the distinction between individuals—through the name-titles of the short sections—the monads never stay entirely separate, giving a formal figure to the texts' insistence that "everyone is anyway connected to each other so that they become indistinguishable," expressed also in the "persontopersontoperson" construction.[35] Literary form—the section titles—seem here to be an external imposition on a chaotic reality. Surprisingly, however, it is reality itself that is actually trying to give itself form (rather than form being some alien imposition on it), as intimated at moments like this one:

> And he suggests, "why won't you rest for a little while. Slow. Slow," and she does not pay him any attention [. . .] because she is interwoven with a song of life that he does not know, because she is
>
> THE MOTHER
>
> Standing at the other side. Looking at him [. . .][36]

What is crucial here is that the section title "THE MOTHER" appears as possibly being part of the text itself, rather than some external imposition. It is impossible to tell, in Netanel's novel, if form is considered an external constraint on an essentially unruly text, or an internal effort by the text itself toward self-understanding, a kind of textual "agency" over itself.

The struggle to give text and temporality a form brings us to what can be seen as a larger over-determination of the novel's form as a whole. First, lyrical poetry is strongly evoked by Netanel's capacity for estranging the most mundane activities and sensations. As in lyrical poetry in general, affect is extremely heightened through Netanel's linguistic mastery: her mobilization of a rich vocabulary and constructions (borrowed, as others comment, from early twentieth-century Hebrew), which are undoubtedly untranslatable; and her uncompromising insistence on highlighting the figurative dimension of language, creating new similes, metaphors, and symbols every second sentence. Yet not only lyrical poetry is evoked through this preference for the affective and timeless ("for there is no early or late in poetry"),[37] but also the epic and in particular orally transmitted myths of origin. The latter are evoked by the constant repetition-with-variation that the novel enacts, with slight modification in each version. The novel's opening is a good example: the scene of Zvi's mother leaving her home for the market, and then cooking, intertwined with Zvi's meeting of his parents' neighbor on his way to their apartment, is narrated over and over again, with slight variation in emphasis, perspective, and tense.[38] Both of these, of course, are completely in line with the heightening of affect and the deterioration of temporal imagination that are completely in line with postmodern aesthetic, whose origin—particularly in terms of the decline of temporal narration and the rise of free-floating affect—can be traced historically to the rise of the culture industry or the commodification of culture.[39]

Yet, it is perhaps on the grounds of temporality itself that Netanel's formal experimentation is at its boldest. For the breaking of linear temporality is not only present in Zvi's failure to reconstruct ordered history, or in the novel's fragmentation. Rather, the incessant, almost compulsive repetitions should be seen as so many attempts to give order to the narrative (the novel's three parts are named "versions," also implying a process of rewriting). In many cases, the reader simply ends up not knowing the order of events, as the narrator keeps rearranging them through repetitions and slight variations in what is surely a literary attempt to do film better than film itself—to show how the meaning of images is modified when they are arranged differently. The short opening of the third part of the novel provides a good illustration for this puzzling formal effect. The three "images" here—Zvi walking with his friend the professor; them sitting at a café; and a student interrupting their walk to address the professor—are put in different temporal relations to one another through several narrative repetitions.[40]

Here we can begin again to see the difference between Netanel's novel and her postmodern predecessors. These attempts at ordering—much like Zvi's own attempts at reconstructing history—are not celebrated in the novel as pure play, or as intimating that any stable order must be an illusion or lie. Rather, they betray the presence of a loss, or of a problem, one on whose solution historical agency and identity ultimately hinge. Constructing a "polyphonic" history, as Zvi and her students try to do in the novel, does not end up constituting an attempt to rid history of all narrativity (as if the latter is only some externally imposed constraint that can be stripped away), since the witnesses' "recordings" at the end of the second part again betray an impulse to narrate their experiences, no matter how feeble and unsuccessful it is. Rather than ridding history of narrativity, their project betrays a search for a new historical narrative, recognizing a loss of relation to history. Netanel's choice of presenting the researcher's work as a search for utopia—framed as such by the quote from Leah Goldberg's *And This is the Light* (invoking a whole utopian Hebrew tradition through Goldberg's title's referencing of Ibn Ezra's utopian poem)—is of course very telling in this respect.[41] It is this genuine search for a new historical narrative which distinguishes *The Hebrew Condition* from its postmodern predecessors.

The Hebrew Condition ends up adopting something like an aesthetic and historical ideology of incompleteness with which to contain the failure or the loss of relation to history that it invokes. This is not only evident in the continuous process of re-writing that the novel's form emphasizes (disclosing of course, very "un-postmodernly," that there is something to be completed), but also on the level of sentence structure—the novel is full of incomplete sentences (for example, "History that doesn't coalesce into a."). Periods are used by Netanel to make present the problem of closure almost as often as they are used to end actual sentences. And it is precisely with incompleteness that the novel unconvincingly tries to enact closure in its last sentences: Zvi's father, living once again the moment of his arrival at Palestine and travel to the rural settlement, remembering that

> On the beach a man waited for me and took me to the valley. Thorns and plants and pieces of wood cutting. Making way through. And menacing on the way. And very tired [. . .] Managing despite it all to say a couple of words to her. And I become scattered in all directions. I went beyond the beyond and to the dwellers of the beyond and in this unfinished sense of the word I am Hebrew.[42]

The state of incompleteness becomes something like a narrative solution here. It explains the novel's obsession with fragmentariness, and the repeated attempts at narrating both history and everydayness as a developing, unfinished process, or as disclosing a state of transition. The historical failure around which the novel is structured thus becomes part in a chain of unrelenting attempts to "fix" history. What is important to emphasize here is again the distance generated by this stance from the novel's postmodern predecessors:

the dissolution of the possibility of narration, the becoming-disjointed of time, and the dissolution of the Zionist project as well, as if Israeli everydayness is not treated triumphantly as the playful falling apart of ideological illusion. Rather, they are posed as objective problems that demand some kind of solution. This shift does not simply mark a static change from a negative view of the Zionist "metanarrative" in the 1980s to a less negative one today. Rather, a complete dialectical transformation of the ground of thinking history takes place between these two moments. In the 1980s, Israeli literature celebrated the dissolution of the Zionist "metanarrative." In Netanel's novel, in contrast, the same dissolution is perceived as a general crisis of historicity. The former implies the end of "grand" historical narratives; the latter revolves around the utter absence of the possibility to imagine a relation between personal agency and a history that nonetheless still moves. The former implies a solution; the latter implies a problem. Thus, the failures on which the novel focuses are not these of the older historical imaginary (e.g., Zionism favoring Ashkenazi men, marginalizing to others, teleological, etc.), but rather of the new one—the failures to mediate between subject and history, and between detail and system.

Fulfillment as an Allegory of a Representational Crisis, or, the Parable of the Donkey and the Fruit Soup

Yiftach Ashkenazi's *Fulfillment* (2012) will provide for us a good counterpart for Netanel's novel in this chapter, not only because it constitutes another example the new historical sensibility that I have been describing, but also because it is at the same time the opposite of Netanel's novel. If the latter draws its inspiration from the more "anti-generic" or modernist heroes of early twentieth-century Hebrew literature—reworking the form as well as the common subject matter of novels by Agnon, Brenner, and others—Ashkenazi's novel evokes a tradition of writing usually considered to be the Modernists' chief cultural antagonist—"genre" writers with their far more realist aesthetic tastes and their thematic focus on rural collectivist settlement life, and conscious national-allegorical dimension (which is not to say that the novel's grounding realism prevents it from exploring all manner of postmodernist formal features, as we will see).[43] It thus develops the new historical imaginary in a different branch of Israeli literature than Netanel's novel. The modernists evoked by Netanel had always championed the perspective of an outsider—that alienated consciousness whose efforts to belong always falter and for whom the failure of the collective project only somehow affirmed what they suspected all along to be true. *Fulfillment*, on the other hand, takes up the perspective of the insiders, for whom being part of the collective effort was always an ongoing transformative trial (as in the work of 1930s realists such as Yisrael Zarchi or Yosef Aricha), and who expressed a sense of collective crisis when kibbutz life could no longer be held as some political ideal (as in Mossinsohn's 1950s work, or Oz's 1960s short stories and novels). If in the 1980s and afterwards the kibbutz and its archetypes became just another setting or dead "style" to be playfully pastiched by postmodern historicism (as in Shalev's *The Blue Mountain*) or explored for its completely new social realities (as in Batya Gur's *Murder on a kibbutz*), that have nothing do to anymore with the kibbutz's utopian past,[44] Ashkenazi's novel, as we will see, marks the emergence of a different literary imagining of the kibbutz and its history as figurative devices.

Fulfillment presents us different moments in the lives of its group of protagonists, spanning a period of time that stretches from the 1960s to 2011. The group is part of a special state program that replaced the pre-state Zionist settlement vanguard—helping establish and populate rural collectivist settlements, which by the 1960s are simply the different kibbutzes. Of course, by the '60s the utopian effort that drove the founding of the rural collectives was all but reified and made completely non-threatening to capital by its absorption into the state apparatus (which was precisely of course the cause for of Nathan Shaham's '50s protagonist's frustration, expressed in his realization that "pioneering will from now on be a game for children who haven't grown up").[45] In any case, Ashkenazi's novel sheds light on different moments in the lives of the members of the group or collective, toward which the narrator initially takes the position of something like an archival detective: each chapter is made up of documents obtained by the narrator (journal entries, book segments, letters, interviews, etc.) that pertain to one or more of the protagonists' lives. The chapters are not arranged chronologically, or by character, but rather function more like dissociated fragments, each with its own "style" and content.

It is on the success of synthesizing the fragments of the protagonists into a coherent narrative that the novel hinges, a cognitive puzzle-solving effort in which both narrator and reader take part. What should now be clear is that what Ashkenazi's novel tries to revive is a national allegory, in which the narrative arc of the private lives of the protagonists stand in some important figurative relation to the life of the nation itself—a relation which does not have to be one of simple reflection (such as, the triumph of an individual or a group does not have to coincide with that of the nation, as the '20s and '30s realist allegories of Yisrael Zarchi and Ever Hadani demonstrate). This allegorical dimension is emphasized by, first, that the group members all become different "types" of the Israeli bourgeoisie: from higher-ups at the Ministry of Finance and the banking system, to construction moguls, academics and successful artists. Second, this allegorical dimension is strengthened by the ubiquitous yet peripheral presence of important historical events in what is mostly personal narratives (such as the Yom Kippur War, the second Palestinian *Intifada*, the protests against the massacres in the Palestinian refugee camps Sabra and Shatila during Israel's 1982 invasion of Lebanon, and other events).[46] The novel thus urges us to read it as a national allegory, despite the narrator's rejection of this allegorical function, treating it as simplistic or stupid.[47] We will touch further on the role of the narrator and his denials in the novel in what follows.

Important for us in this juncture are two points. First, that Ashkenazi's return to allegory should be seen as a counter-movement to the postmodern or late-modernist rejection of national allegories (articulated strongly in Kenaz *Infiltration*, for example), or even the possibility of allegorization generally—either through the taking up of a Derridian deconstructive textual philosophy in which allegories constantly undo themselves, or through an unrelenting effort to debunk allegorical signification, busting myths to uncover some underlying truth. It is important to notice in this respect that Ashkenazi's allegorization does not constitute a return to older national allegories, which to be sure are no longer satisfactory as imaginary devices. Rather, Ashkenazi's allegory is a new one, demonstrating precisely what allegory's postmodern critics always missed: as noted earlier in this chapter, living allegories (as opposed to reified older ones) never simply reiterate what is already known; rather, they constitute a pre-conceptual working-through of a narrative for which we do not yet have a concept or a name, and which only in hindsight will seem like superfluous illustrations of familiar narratives or concepts.[48] The brilliance of Ashkenazi's novel is precisely in rediscovering allegory's potential for exploring new narrative possibilities, for probing its subject matter for new patterns and temporalities. It is for this reason that the novel goes through many of its protagonists' life-moments, attempting to detect the beginnings of a new narrative trajectory in them. Bringing together the different life "fragments" poses here the problem of their cohesion into a totalizing narrative in all its seriousness, as a problem that must be solved even if at this initial state the fragments of Ashkenazi's novel do not yet coalesce into a narrative.

The second point to be emphasized is that the allegorical effort resides in juxtaposing the personal and the national, thus highlighting the problem of mediating between the protagonists' personal experiences and the larger history taking place. It is here that Ashkenazi's masterful pastiching of literary and representational "styles"—each of them evoking specific subjectivities as well as having the familiar postmodern historicist underpinnings—comes into play. Rather than the playful evocation of dead styles, each pastiched form connotes a specific way of juxtaposing the personal to the historical. A good example is one of the chapters narrated through the consciousness of Yoav—a member of the group who is a military officer. The chapter narrates his participation, with other members of the group, in a historically significant demonstration protesting the Israeli military's involvement in the massacre of Palestinians in the Sabra and Shatila refugee camps in southern Lebanon in 1982. This is how the chapter begins:

> Yoav decided to go to the demonstration in *Malkhei Yisrael* plaza (get those commanders over here. Did you think we're not gonna have a briefing before the op?). Avshalom told him, we can't be silent about what happened in Sabra and Shatila, and promised that the entire group will be there (the target, a FATAH command center that was rebuilt right under our eyes). Yoav said he'll think about it. Avshalom said, what is there to think, murder is murder is murder. Yoav said, true (our forces: the brigade, artillery. Radio code: greedy. They will cover us only in emergency. We have enough firepower in the brigade even without those artillery pussies).[49]

Throughout the chapter, then, Yoav's participation in the demonstration against the Israeli military's involvement in Lebanon is curiously interlaced with another text—one that narrates in military jargon the events of a military operation that he commanded in Lebanon. As if this tension is not enough, we quickly learn that Yoav's true motivation for attending the protest was meeting Nira, one of the women in the group, with whom he ultimately strikes up a love affair. The dominant formal feature here—the military operation's narrative given to us in segments in parentheses—is borrowed from Yuval Shimoni's novel, *A Room*, only one among many literary works whose form and content Ashkenazi pastiches in the novel.[50] This form constantly suggests to the reader that the events of the bracketed narrative are figuratively related to those of the unbracketed one, making each a potential interpretive code for the other—but with the postmodern or Borges-like twist that the "code" is as wide and detailed as the text to be deciphered. The reader is thus confronted with three narrative levels (historical protest, military operation, love interest) that seem to demand that we mediate between them, or that we determine how each is related to the others. Yet, there are no such easy connections. In fact, the disconnect itself, the glaring absence of an explanation for the seeming incompatibility—participating in the military operation and participating in the protest against it—is what ends up being foregrounded by the chapter's form.

It is in this way that the absence of mediation between the personal and the historical is constantly made to appear in *Fulfillment*. It is here that we can start finding patterns in Ashkenazi's sprawling allegory. For, its unresolved contradictoriness is the only thing that seems to tie together the different organs of our allegory. Central to Rotka's story, for example, is the evocation of a threatening exilic European Jew—sexually deviant, weak, anti-Zionist—an otherness pastiched from much earlier Hebrew literature (used by '30s and '40s realists to signify a threat to the Zionist project, and later taken up again by '60s authors such as Amos Oz to signify a zone of forbidden desires, as in *Elsewhere, Perhaps*).[51] Here, too, Ashkenazi presents us with several levels of narrative, each constituting an interpretation of other ones. Hans—the figure of the European Other—takes advantage of Rotka's mother's traumatic loss of her boyfriend in the '48 war and abuses her sexually. Rotka herself interprets her mother's story about Hans as a warning sign—she wants to make sure that she does not repeat her mother's (fatal) pattern. Thus, she tries to make secure her boyfriend (Avshalom, the group's unofficial leader) from the threat of death in military operations, and she tries to take revenge on Hans. It transpires, however, that instead of exacting revenge, she ends up falling for Hans's charms herself, half-admitting toward the end of her story that she might have been simply seeking sexual thrills all along.[52] What happens here is, of course, that the most recent level of interpretation fails to mediate the previous ones, to create out of them determinate meaning for the lives of its protagonists: it is unclear if, for Rotka, Hans functions as a threat to be contained (as his figure functioned in '30s and '40s literature), as a forbidden object of desire (as in Oz's '60s literature), or somehow as both of these together. Thus, Hans's figurative status becomes unclear in Rotka's own story—the layering of the two different "levels" of interpretation (Rotka's mother's story, and Rotka's own story), as in Yoav's example above—only ends up highlighting an absence of clear process of national figuration.

Now, if our analysis were to end at this point, Ashkenazi's novel would be no different than its postmodern, anti-allegorical counterparts in the literature of the '80s and '90s, in which the possibility of any clear figurative relation between protagonist and nation is evoked only to be negated or mocked.[53] However, we must take into consideration a final dialectical twist that will turn things surprisingly on their head. As we mentioned above, each of Ashkenazi's chapters are presented as found material—as representations produced by the members of the group themselves. Rotka's letters (which are interspersed with others' letters) end with the narrator's following comment: "I would like to thank Michal Peled that helped me reach Avner's letters. Without her, I would most likely unable to decipher Rotka's small handwriting. It is important maybe to comment that certain details in the story found in Rotka's letters [. . .] seem to hint at the possibility that at least part of the story is made up."[54] We will come back to the narrator's personal relation to the group. What is important for our purposes is that if pastiche of historical "style" is the imitation of a historical self-representation, of a style of a period's representation of itself, then Ashkenazi here returns pastiche to its status as someone's (or some period's) self-representation: the different pastiched styles are constantly exposed as a group member's self-representation at a given moment.[55] Thus, the failure of figuration—the disconnect between different narrative levels that takes place in the two examples above and throughout the novel—is not the narrator's doing, but a failure of the members of the group themselves. It is they who constantly avoid relating their actions to larger historical frameworks—and who many times revel in this avoidance.

The overarching pattern in Ashkenazi's grand allegory is thus the group members' failure to relate their actions to larger history, which can now transform the way we view the beginning of the novel, and also can now be seen as some kind of "creation myth" of the group members' blindness to this failure. For, the obvious contradiction running through the early part of the novel is the one hinted at in Shaham's conviction quoted above: a thin veneer of a collectivist game constantly chafes here against the sensibilities of the young group members, which are much more in line with those of a consciousness forged under capitalism. The debates about private belongings and money, the plainly visible fact that joining the collective is the adolescents' way of rebelling against their parents or finding excitement, and the use of collectivist tropes ("the benefit of the group") as weapons in petty political power struggles—all hint that it is not the collectivist "game" that actually determines the group's lives, but rather the capitalist realities that lay invisible beyond it.⁵⁶ It is this moment of blindness toward, or repression of, the glaring contradiction between reified collectivist ideology and capitalist existence that can be seen as an inaugural moment—one that gives birth to the group members' continued inability to mediate between the personal and the historical, as in the two examples we discussed above.

This generational representational failure is also very strongly felt in the event that concludes the history of the group—a sudden financial collapse in 2003, in which Avshalom's financial speculation causes major losses to many investors, including members of the group, despite his and his friends' expertise as bankers and finance experts.⁵⁷ Avshalom is then supposedly killed in a car accident following his attempt to escape the police. Yet, what would have otherwise constituted a narrative that blames Avshalom and his friends for national financial crisis—thus successfully mediating personal events and national history—ends up failing as well. We find out that Mendelbaum, who was in the car with Avshalom, keeps changing his story about Avshalom's last moments to suit his needs, preventing in this way any sense of closure that would have resulted from a clear admission of guilt, or an attempt to deny it. A stable relation between the personal and historical thus fails to form once again.

Fulfillment's tracing of the group's history up to the financial crisis and the supposed death of its leader is therefore not exactly an allegorization of the financial collapse itself, but of that generation's inability to relate personal events to larger history. Indeed, Avshalom's repeated joking that he understands money just "as well as a donkey knows his way around fruit soup," (a once-common Israeli expression) turns out to be ironically true, even as he misrecognizes the true object of his blindness: it is not exactly money, but the historical forces that truly shape his life. It is at this point, however, that the narrator's own character becomes important. Toward the end of the novel, it becomes clear that the narrator is Avshalom's son, who grew up attending many of the group's reunions, never completely separating himself from his father's social world. He confesses that what attracted him to it was a "double feeling," or "a feeling of being at home and not being at home, of being a good boy who belongs with them and at the same time being the bad kid that blew it and disappointed his dad."⁵⁸ This passage indicates that the narrator had inherited the group members' penchant (or chronic disease of) for representational failure, being simultaneously part of the group and breaking away from it, in contrast to the more temporal arrangement of a Freudian schema of generational relationships. The narrator's reproduction of this failure is further strengthened, by the last section of the novel in which he seems to both distance himself from the novel (claiming that it was actually someone else's manuscript) but at the same time insinuates that he's lying, and that he is, after all, the text's true author.[59] The suspicion that his father, Avshalom, is not dead after all also contributes to the narrator's inability to relate determinately to history. For, Avshalom's symbolic death would have constituted a kind of Freudian killing of the father, or a symbolic attempt to break away from the previous generation—which the narrator ends up denying by hinting that Avshalom is actually alive. The tone of this final gesture of representational failure is one of frustration at this inability to determine his own relation to history.

Thus, what *Fulfillment* leaves its readers with is an allegory of representational failure itself—in which a postmodern inability to mediate personal and historical is seen as originating with a generation that came into adulthood in the 1970s, and which still plagues the narrator, despite his belonging to a different generation. This generational logic is, of course, where the novel's closure effect lays: it provides something like an origin story for representational failure itself in the Israeli context. Again, it is important to emphasize the way in which the historical imaginary of Ashkenazi's novel dialectically subsumes and neutralizes the previous one of the postmodern moment of the 1980s or 1990s: what was previously seen as a liberating death of grand narratives is here not denied but rather recognized as a loss of the possibility of relating personal experience to history, made strongly evident in the novel's form. The loss of historicity that has been all along the unconscious content of the postmodern "end of history" thus floats into consciousness in Netanel's and Ashkenazi's novels, and in many other ones that we will not be able to discuss here.

Note Toward the Future

I began this chapter by declaring that its purpose is to strengthen the thesis that I posed in the previous chapter about contemporary Israeli literature: that its growing preoccupation with time and history signal a kind of deeper change, in which the what has previously been perceived as a new freedom—from national time and forms of knowledge—tends to be seen now as a problem to be solved—a more general absence of temporality and social imagination. Yet in the same breath it should be added that this is not merely a problem of perceptions or aesthetic preference. Rather, it is a matter of an objective condition—that loss of historicity—that gradually floats into literary consciousness. What has been completely unconscious for the postmoderns thus emerges, at least partially, into literary consciousness as a problem to be solved and contained in some positive way (as opposed to that dialectical turning of problems into their own solutions that so characterized the earlier Israeli postmodernists, as I attempted to show). Literature thus wakes up from history's end to find out that it is moving again—even if it has not formed a very stable conception of which seed of time will grow, and which will not. The different strategies of imaginative containment that each novel articulates are still unconvincing. They seem to belong to that space between the Lacanian "Two Deaths," as theorized by Phillip Wegner and others. This is a time in between two ends, a Real one and a Symbolic one, in which the ideological (and material) desiderata of the past float about, no longer able to generate that strong sense of totalizing closure with which they were once endowed—a situation which bears a strong relation to the post-apocalyptic, as Evan Calder Williams forcefully argues.[60] It is in a time such as this that contemporary Israeli literature seems to exist at the moment, in which the older functions of social mapping and a stable temporality become once again necessary, but the different past solutions thrown up by our imaginations seem never to be quite up to the task. The different localized moments of containment offered up by the contemporary novels that we discussed all seem to be of this order of figurative devices. It is for this reason that so many times one feels betrayed by these novels—they manage to make all these problems perceivable again but never quite manage to resolve them without collapsing the new problems themselves back into the realm of the known. Yet one cannot blame literature for not finally being smarter than its historical moment; left to us is simply to note that the old postmodern blockage of our temporal imaginations is now finally threatening to break. And that future historicity is to be found among the different twisted and unsatisfactory amalgamations of older imaginations that this literature throws up for our consideration and evaluation.

Whether this state of historical opening would end up in an exit from capitalism altogether, or would reveal itself to be simply a transition into yet another form of capitalism is an open question. What should be stressed, however, is that the old theoretical attacks on teleology and historical continuity or narrative themselves—those articulated by Lyotard and Foucault but also by the more sophisticated theoreticians of Post-Zionism such as Adi Ophir (which were discussed in the introduction)—are now to be considered historically conservative rather than progressive. For it is easy to observe that the new fascination with temporality in Israeli literature means also a revival of utopian thinking—a move from older anti-history to newer anti-anti-history. "Anti-anti-history" here is not quite a positive new history—they do not yet offer us explicit visions of a future better society (even if Gafla's work comes close to that), but it should be clear beyond any doubt, after our survey of these five novels, that this position involves resistance to the blockage of our historical imagination. A renewed effort of historical narration is thus on the side of the promising and threatening; and the explosion of narrativity as such has become a conservative position, in a textbook example of history's dialectical movement. It is this taking up of a search for new time that is at the heart of contemporary Israeli fiction.

We should thus resist the claim according to which the post-Zionist explosion of metanarratives—(which belongs only to a specific branch of post-Zionism, that of Adi Ophir and Hannan Hever) was somehow always wrong or delusional, as scholars such as Daniel Gutwein and Eran Kaplan have argued (and which seems to be the subtext of literary-historical revisionism such as Smadar Shifman's, which we discussed in the previous chapter).[61] Rather, the anti-historical post-Zionists were as right as one could be in their historical moment—since only through taking on the task of exploding the old narratives that our current moment can come about. The Israeli imagination's current search for new historical time (one that clearly drives Kaplan's intellectual project, as well as Gutwein's more explicit national one) would thus have been impossible without the intervention of Post-Zionism. It should be clear, however, that the historical role of anti-historical post-Zionism is over, and that any new such writing has become what Benny Morris once called new old history: new instances of what is essentially an older historiographical project (taking the place of new old national historians on which Morris was originally commenting, such as Anita Shapira). To the degree that they reproduce the explosion of national historiography (or some theoretical anti-narrativity generally), these new old post-Zionisms hold very little value for the search for new time that animates, as I tried to show, contemporary Israeli literature. The more materialist and dialectical view of the post-Zionist stance is that it was right, and precisely for that reason it should now be now abandoned: it has performed its historical role in evacuating our historical imagination; and it is the search for new time and historicity, one that contains a new political struggle, to which we should turn our attention now.

Notes

Introduction

1. A good example (if not the inaugural one) of this use of "The West" can be found in Edward Said's work. See his Said, *Orientalism*; Jameson, "Third World Literatures in the Age of Multinational Capitalism."

2. Sauri, "Autonomy after Autonomy, Or, The Novel beyond Nation: Roberto Bolaño's 2666."

3. Lazarus, "The Fetish of 'The West' in Postcolonial Theory"; Brown, *Utopian Generations: The Political Horizon of Twentieth-Century Literature*, 6–9.

4. Brenner, *The Economics of Global Turbulence: The Advanced Capitalist Economies from Long Boom to Long Downturn, 1945-2005*; Wallerstein, *World Systems Analysis: An Introduction*.

5. Marx, *Grundrisse: Foundations of the Critique of Political Economy*, 408.

6. Warwick Research Collective, *Combined and Uneven Development: Towards a New Thoery of World Literature*, 10–12.

7. Kang, *Aesthetics and Marxism: Chinese Aesthetic Marxism and Their Western Contemporaries*.

8. Jameson, *A Singular Modernity: Essay on the Ontology of the Present*, 13.

9. Brown, *Utopian Generations: The Political Horizon of Twentieth-Century Literature*, 12.

10. Parry, "Aspects of Peripheral Modernisms," 32; Warwick Research Collective, *Combined and Uneven Development: Towards a New Thoery of World Literature*, 71.

11. Jameson, "On Magic Realism in Film," 311.

12. Moretti, "Conjectures on World Literature," 63.

13. Schwarz, *Misplaced Ideas: Essays on Brazilian Culture*, 22–24.

14. For a discussion of the contemporary return of realism in American culture, see La Berge and Shonkweiler, *Reading Capitalist Realism*.

15. Adorno, "On Popular Music."

16. Benn Michaels, "Model Minorities and the Minority Model—the Neoliberal Novel," 1024.

17. Brown, *Utopian Generations: The Political Horizon of Twentieth-Century Literature*, 12.
18. Jameson, *The Ideologies of Theory*, 309–43.
19. Jameson, 330–32.
20. Žižek, *For They Know Not What They Do: Enjoyment as a Political Factor*, 183.
21. Žižek, 189.
22. Harry Harootunian, Marx after Marx: History and Time in the Expansion of Capitalism (New York: Columbia University Press, 2015).
23. Sauri, "Autonomy after Autonomy, Or, The Novel beyond Nation: Roberto Bolaño's 2666," 403.
24. Esty and Lye, "Peripheral Realisms Now," 284–85.
25. Thorne, "The Sea Is Not a Place; Or, Putting the World Back into World Literature," 2013; Deckard, "Peripheral Realism, Millennial Capitalism, and Roberto Bolaño's 2666."
26. Schwartz, *Ma Shero'im Mikan*, 19.
27. Laor, *Anu Kotvim Otach Moledet: Masot Al Sifrut Yisra'elit*, 118–19.
28. Mishani, *Bechol Ha'inyan Hamizrakhi Yesh Eize Absurd*; Gluzman, *Haguf Hatsiyoni: Leumiyut, Migdar Uminiyut Basifrut Ha'ivrit Hahadasha*.
29. Feldman, *No Room of Their Own: Gender and Nation in Israeli Women's Fiction*.
30. Marx, *A Contribution to the Critique of Political Economy*, 3.
31. For an example of the difference between a Marxist approach and historicist relativism, see Jameson's review of Hayden White's work Jameson, "Figural Relativism, or the Poetics of Historiography."
32. Lukács, *History and Class Consciousness: Studies in Marxist Dialectics*, 1971, 151.
33. Adorno, *Aesthetic Theory*, 5.
34. Jameson, *A Singular Modernity: Essay on the Ontology of the Present*, 29.
35. Nir, "Towards a Renewal of Israeli Marxism, or Peace as a Vanishing Mediator."
36. For an extensive survey of the antagonism between the two narratives, see Silberstein, *The Postzionism Debates*.
37. Likhovski, "Post-Post-Zionist Historiography."
38. Nir, "Towards a Renewal of Israeli Marxism, or Peace as a Vanishing Mediator."
39. Cohen, *Hanusakh habitkhoni*.
40. Morris, "The New Historiography: Israel Confronts Its Past."
41. Hever, *Producing the Modern Hebrew Canon*; Ophir, "She'at Ha'efes"; Hever, "The Post-Zionist Condition."
42. Ginsburg, *Rhetoric and Nation: The Formation of Hebrew National Culture, 1880–1990*, 6.

43. Gozansky, *Hitpatkhut hakapitalism bepalestina [The Formation of Capitalism in Palestine]*, 1986.
44. Sand, *The Invention of the Land of Israel: From Holy Land to Homeland.*
45. Nir, "Towards a Renewal of Israeli Marxism, or Peace as a Vanishing Mediator."
46. McGowan, "Subject of the Event, Subject of the Act: The Difference between Badiou's and Žižek's Systems of Philosophy."
47. Lebovic, *Tziyonut Umlenkolia: Hakha'im Haktzarim Shel Israel Zarchi*, 11.
48. Za'it, *Halutzim Bamavoch Hapoliti [Pioneers in the Maze of Politics: The Kibbutz Movement, 1927–1948]*; Margalit, *"Hashomer Hatza'ir"—Me'adat Ne'urim Lemarksizm Mahapchani (1913–1936)*; Neumann, *Tshukat Hahalutzim.*
49. Shaked's well-known inauguration of the new period of Israeli letters was perhaps most famously articulated in his Shaked, *Gal khadash basiporet ha'ivrit*. The resultant periodization of Israeli literature is evident in each one of his five-volume survey of Hebrew literature, which as I argued above, is still widely accepted among critics.
50. One example of such attempts to reject postmodernism as a periodizing term, see Shifman, *Dvarim Shero'im Mikan: David Grossman, Orly Castel Bloom Vemeir Shalev: Me'ever Lamodernism?*; Peleg, *Israeli Culture between the Two Intifadas: A Brief Romance.*
51. Shabtai, *Past Continuous.*
52. Harvey, *A Brief History of Neoliberalism.*
53. This is of course, in general lines, Harvey's account of the transformation (Harvey; Brenner, *The Economics of Global Turbulence: The Advanced Capitalist Economies from Long Boom to Long Downturn, 1945–2005.*
54. Weizman, *Hollow Land: Israel's Architecture of Occupation.*
55. Žižek, *For They Know Not What They Do: Enjoyment as a Political Factor*, 181.

Chapter 1

1. Shaked, *Modern Hebrew Fiction*, 44.
2. Gertz, *Sifrut Ve'ideologia Be'eretz Yisreal Beshnot Hashloshim*, 31.
3. Gertz, 175.
4. Laor, *Anu Kotvim Otach Moledet: Masot Al Sifrut Yisra'elit*, 118–19.
5. Hasak Lowy, *Here and Now: History, Nationalism, and Realism in Modern Hebrew Fiction*, xiv–xxix.
6. Shaked, *Modern Hebrew Fiction*, 69.
7. For a good collection of the debates around realism and modernism by Bloch, Lukács and others, see the collected essays in Jameson, *Aesthetics and Politics.*
8. Wegner, *Imaginary Communities: Utopia, the Nation, and the Spatial Histories of Modernity*, 2002.

9. Wegner, 15.
10. Marin, *Utopics: Spatial Play*, 1984, 163.
11. Althusser, *For Marx*, 233–34.
12. Gluzman, *Haguf Hatsiyoni: Leumiyut, Migdar Uminiyut Basifrut Ha'ivrit Hahadasha*, 34–66.
13. Herzl, *Old-New Land*, 6.
14. Gluzman, *Haguf Hatsiyoni: Leumiyut, Migdar Uminiyut Basifrut Ha'ivrit Hahadasha*, 36–37.
15. Boyarin, "Neshef Hamasechot Hakoloniali: Tziyonut, Migdar, Khikuy," 125.
16. For discussions of the influence of socialism ideas on Herzl's thought, see Penslar, *Zionism and Technocracy: The Engineering of Jewish Settlement in Palestine*, 49; Boyarin, "Neshef Hamasechot Hakoloniali: Tziyonut, Migdar, Khikuy," 130.
17. Melamed, "Ma Asita Li Herzl?"
18. Boyarin, "Neshef Hamasechot Hakoloniali: Tziyonut, Migdar, Khikuy"; Khalidi, "Utopian Zionism or Zionist Proselytism? A Reading of Herzl's Altneuland."
19. Wegner, *Imaginary Communities: Utopia, the Nation, and the Spatial Histories of Modernity*, 2002, 9.
20. Lukács, "Realism in the Balance," 1980, 28–59; Jameson, *The Political Unconscious: Narrative as a Socially Symbolic Act*, 1981, 17–102; Jameson, *Archaeologies of the Future: The Desire Called Utopia and Other Science Fictions*, 4–5.
21. Suvin, *Metamorphoses of Science Fiction: On the Poetics and History of a Literary Genre*, 61; Jameson, *Archaeologies of the Future: The Desire Called Utopia and Other Science Fictions*, 4–9; Jameson, *Postmodernism, Or, The Cultural Logic of Late Capitalism*, 1991, 279–96.
22. Shaked, *Hasiporet Ha'ivrit 1880–1980*, 1993, 4:16.
23. Neumann, *Tshukat Hahalutzim*, 16–20.
24. Neumann, 16–17. All quoted passages from the novel in this chapter were translated by me, O.N.
25. Marx, *The Economic and Philosophical Manuscripts of 1844 and the Communist Manifesto*, 69–84.
26. Za'it, *Halutzim Bamavoch Hapoliti [Pioneers in the Maze of Politics: The Kibbutz Movement, 1927–1948]*, 13–24; Za'it, "Bein Realism Le'utopia: Konstruktivism, Kolektivizatzia, Vedu-Le'umiyut Behitpatkhut Hashomer Hatsair (1926–1942) [Between Realism and Utopia]," 22.
27. Gorny, *Zionism and the Arabs 1882–1948: A Study of Ideology*, 154–55; Margalit, *"Hashomer Hatza'ir"—Me'adat Ne'urim Lemarksizm Mahapchani (1913–1936)*.
28. Za'it, *Halutzim Bamavoch Hapoliti*, 20–28.
29. Za'it, 59–60.
30. Za'it, 102; Bernstein, *Constructing Boundaries: Jewish and Arab Workers in Mandatory Palestine*.
31. Zarchi, *Yamim Yekhefim*, 1934, 17–18.
32. Zarchi, 10–11, 88.

33. Zarchi, 10, 62–63.
34. Zarchi, 10–11.
35. Zarchi, 114.
36. Zarchi, 80.
37. Zarchi, 57, 150–60.
38. Zarchi, 145.
39. Zarchi, 46.
40. Zarchi, 107–09.
41. Jameson, *The Modernist Papers*, 2007, 157.
42. Zarchi, *Yamim Yekhefim*, 1934, 165.
43. Zarchi, 42.
44. Zarchi, 191.
45. Zarchi, 208.
46. Lebovic, *Tziyonut Umlenkolia: Hakha'im Haktzarim Shel Israel Zarchi*.
47. Aricha, "Lekhem Vekhazon."
48. Aricha, 156.
49. Aricha, 157.
50. Chernyshevsky, *What Is to Be Done?*; Lenin, *What Is to Be Done? Burning Questions of Our Movement*.
51. Aricha, "Lekhem Vekhazon," 169.
52. Hadani, *Tzrif Ha'etz*.
53. Neumann, *Tshukat Hahalutzim*, 21.
54. Hadani, *Tzrif Ha'etz*, 25–26. All the quotes from the novel in this chapter were translated by me, O.N.
55. Gertz, *Khirbet khizah vehaboker shelemakharat*, 1983, 43.
56. Shaked, *Hasiporet Ha'ivrit 1880–1980*, 1983, 1:266.
57. Gertz, *Sifrut Ve'ideologia Be'eretz Yisreal Beshnot Hashloshim*, 176–80.
58. Hadani, *Tzrif Ha'etz*, 28.
59. Gertz, *Sifrut Ve'ideologia Be'eretz Yisreal Beshnot Hashloshim*, 177.
60. Hadani, *Tzrif Ha'etz*, 67.
61. Hadani, 35, 81.
62. Hadani, 150.
63. Hadani, 92–95, 121.
64. Hadani, 137–38.
65. Hadani, 165.
66. Hadani, 34.
67. Hadani, 194.
68. Žižek, *Looking Awry: An Introduction to Jacques Lacan through Popular Culture*, 1991, 7. Emphases in the original.
69. Nevo, *Neuland*.
70. Jameson, "Third World Literatures in the Age of Multinational Capitalism."
71. Yizhar, *Khirbet Khizeh*, 2014.

72. Shaked, *Hasiporet Ha'ivrit 1880–1980*, 1993, 4:15–21; Gertz, *Khirbet khizah vehaboker shelemakharat*, 1983, 16–44.

73. See for example Dror Mishani's reproduction of Shaked's distinction between the "generists" and the "anti-generists" in Mishani's own discussion of the national-allegorical dimension of Yehoshua Kenaz's *Infiltration* (Mishani 2006, 58–9).

74. Za'it, *Halutzim Bamavoch Hapoliti*, 70–81, 126–43.

75. In addition to Zait's analysis, see, for example, Deborah Bernstein, *Constructing Boundaries: Jewish and Arab Workers in Mandatory Palestine*; Gozansky, *Hitpatkhut hakapitalism bepalestina*, 1986; Shafir, *Land, Labor, and the Origins of the Israeli-Palestinian Conflict, 1882–1914*.

76. Meletz, *Ma'agalot*; Mossinsohn, *Derekh Gever*.

77. Shamir, *Hu halach basadot*, 2010.

78. Pappe, *The Ethnic Cleansing of Palestine*, 45.

79. Yizhar, *Khirbet Khizeh*, 2014, 3.

80. Yizhar, 3–5.

81. Yizhar, 12.

82. Yizhar, 74.

83. Kna'ani, *Beinam Leven Zmanam*, 96.

84. Yizhar, *Khirbet Khizeh*, 63.

85. Yizhar, *Khirbet Khizeh*, 87–8.

86. Nagid, "Mavo," 16–17.

87. Yizhar, *Khirbet Khizeh*, 82–83.

88. Ibid., 97–107.

89. Oz, "Khirbet Khizeh Vesakanat Nefashot"; Shapira, "Hirbat Hizah: Between Remembrance and Forgetting," 40–41; Laor, *Anu Kotvim Otach Moledet: Masot Al Sifrut Yisra'elit*, 115–70.

90. The military actions against Palestinians were not themselves at all repressed, but rather a hot political topic during the war. A famous example of their appearance in literary production is Nathan Alterman's poem, "On That." For a more detailed survey, see See Laor's detailed analysis (1995, 115–31).

Chapter 2

1. Shaked, "Tamid Anakhnu Guf Rishon Rabim? (Al Yetzirato Shel Natan Shaham)," 176–86; Shaked, *Hasiporet Ha'ivrit 1880–1980*, 4:270–77.

2. Mossinsohn, *Be'arvot Hanegev*.

3. Feldman, "Shel Mi Hakorban Haze La'azazel? Aliyato Unefilato Shel Avraham Ha'oked Beshnot Hakhamishim," 131.

4. Shaked, *Hasiporet Ha'ivrit 1880–1980*, 4:276.

5. Ben David, *Mipleshet Ad Ziklag: Iyunim Beroman Milkhemet Ha'atzma'ut*, 170–73; Ben David, 83; Holtzman, "Hasiporet Shel 'dor Ba'aretz,' " 266–70; Mahalo, *Vekhi Erom Ata?!: Emet Umitos Besipurei Dor Hapalmach*, 157; Govrin, *Kri'at Hadorot: Sifrut Ivrit Bema'agaleha*, 2:132.

6. Mahalo, *Vekhi Erom Ata?!: Emet Umitos Besipurei Dor Hapalmach*, 30.

7. Mossinsohn, *Derekh Gever*; Rozin, *Khovat Ha'ahava Hakasha: Yakhid Vekolektiv Beyisrael Beshnot Hakhamishim*.

8. Nathan Shaham, *Ha'elim Atzelim* (Merkhavia: Sifriyat Po'alim, 1949); Nathan Shaham, *Tamid anakhnu* (Merkhavia: Sifriyat Po'alim, 1952); Yudit Handel, *Street of Steps*, trans. Rachel Katz and David Segal (New York; London: Herzl Press, 1963 [1955]).

9. Arbell, "Gavriyut Venostalgia," 53; Miron, *Arba Panim Basifrut Ha'ivrit Bat Yamenu*, 194–97.

10. Shaked, *Hasiporet Ha'ivrit 1880–1980*, 1988, 3:259.

11. Quoted in Mahalo, *Vekhi Erom Ata?!: Emet Umitos Besipurei Dor Hapalmach*, 13.

12. Arbell, "Gavriyut Venostalgia," 62.

13. Shaked, *Hasiporet Ha'ivrit 1880–1980*, 4:269–76.

14. Mossinsohn, *Derekh Gever*, 30–36.

15. Shaked, *Hasiporet Ha'ivrit 1880–1980*, 4:275.

16. See for example in Shaham, *Dagan Ve'oferet*.

17. Shimoni, *Kheder*; Kenaz, *Infiltration*, 2003.

18. Positing subjectivity as a new interpretive level of the text corresponds to a certain degree to Fredric Jameson's "ethical" interpretive level in his discussion of the ways in which mediation works in Marxist cultural interpretation. See Jameson, *The Political Unconscious: Narrative as a Socially Symbolic Act*, 1981.

19. Mossinsohn, *Derekh Gever*, 164–65. All quotes from the novel were translated by me, O.N. Change of font in the original.

20. Žižek, *Looking Awry: An Introduction to Jacques Lacan through Popular Culture*, 1991, 3–17.

21. Mossinsohn, *Derekh Gever*, 7–16.

22. Mossinsohn, 86; Mossinsohn, 104; Mossinsohn, 27.

23. Mossinsohn, *Derekh Gever*, 100.

24. Mossinsohn, 185; Mossinsohn, 186–87; Shaked, *Hasiporet Ha'ivrit 1880–1980*, 4:278.

25. Mossinsohn, *Derekh Gever*, 48.

26. Mossinsohn, 71.

27. Althusser and Balibar, *Reading Capital*.

28. Mossinsohn, *Derekh Gever*, 76–164.

29. Mossinsohn, 165–272.

30. Mossinsohn, 217–18.

31. Mossinsohn, 206.
32. Mossinsohn, 267–72.
33. Mossinsohn, 271.
34. Jameson, "Reification and Utopia in Mass Culture."
35. Hever, "Mapa Shel Khol," 172.
36. Feldman, "Shel Mi Hakorban Haze La'azazel? Aliyato Unefilato Shel Avraham Ha'oked Beshnot Hakhamishim," 131–33; Mossinsohn, *Be'arvot Hanegev*.
37. Shaked, *Hasiporet Ha'ivrit 1880-1980*, 4:275 n.17.
38. Robinson, *The Years of Rice and Salt*.
39. Shaked, "Tamid Anakhnu Guf Rishon Rabim? (Al Yetzirato Shel Natan Shaham)," 181.
40. Gurfein, *Le'or Hakatuv*, 88.
41. Shaked, *Hasiporet Ha'ivrit 1880-1980*, 4:177.
42. Jameson, *The Political Unconscious: Narrative as a Socially Symbolic Act*, 1981, 215; Thorne, "The Sea Is Not a Place; Or, Putting the World Back into World Literature," 2013.
43. Shaham, *Tamid anakhnu*, 51.
44. An extreme example would be Kurtzweil, "Boser Snobisti Ve'efes Me'upas"; Shaked, "Tamid Anakhnu Guf Rishon Rabim? (Al Yetzirato Shel Natan Shaham)," 180–81.
45. Shaham, *Dagan Ve'oferet*, 11–18.
46. Shaham, *Tamid anakhnu*, 29–30.
47. Shaham, 52.
48. Shaham, 61.
49. Shaham, 53.
50. Shaham, 137.
51. Shaham, 30.
52. Shaham, 93.
53. Shaham, 31.
54. Lukács, *History and Class Consciousness: Studies in Marxist Dialectics*, 1971.
55. Shaham, *Tamid anakhnu*, 153–54.
56. Gurfein, *Le'or Hakatuv*, 88.
57. Shaked, "Tamid Anakhnu Guf Rishon Rabim? (Al Yetzirato Shel Natan Shaham)," 178.
58. Shaham, *Tamid anakhnu*, 51.
59. Shaham, *Ha'elim Atzelim*; Yizhar, "Ephraim Khozer La'aspeset."
60. Miron, *Arba Panim Basifrut Ha'ivrit Bat Yamenu*.
61. Shaham, *Tamid anakhnu*, 192.
62. Williams, *Combined and Uneven Apocalypse*, 2010, 1–13.
63. Marin, *Utopics: Spatial Play*, 1984, 163. This point is of course central to Walter Benjamin's thinking about allegory, as Phillip Wegner and others point

out (Wegner, *Life between Two Deaths: US Culture in the Long Nineties* (Durham, NC; London: Duke University Press, 2009), 6–7).

Chapter 3

1. Bartov, *Shesh Knafayim Le'achad*; Handel, *Street of Steps*. Hendel's last name is spelled "Handel" in the translated version of her novel, and it is under this spelling that she appears in the bibliography. Since, however, all commentators use the "Hendel" spelling, this is the one I will use throughout our discussion.
2. Shaked, *Hasiporet Ha'ivrit 1880-1980*, 4:16.
3. Shamir, *Hu halach basadot*, 2010; Megged, *Ruakh Yamim*.
4. Laor, "Ha'aliya Hahamonit Ketokhen Venose Basifrut Ha'ivrit Bishnot Hamedina Harishonot," 1989.
5. Ukhmani, "Gidulo Shel Mesaper"; Gurfein, "Sefer Khadash, 'Shesh Knafaim La'echad' Lehanoch Bartov."
6. Laor, "Ha'aliya Hahamonit Ketokhen Venose Basifrut Ha'ivrit Bishnot Hamedina Harishonot," 1989, 171. It is important to mention that Laor contrasts Bartov's work to the satire of Ephraim Kishon, whose work, according to Laor, avoids precisely the national imaginary reconciliation of contradictions. We will not here be able to address Kishon's work in any detail, but we should put forth the hypothesis that the social contradictions that animate Kishon's satire are no longer threatening or socially active at the time Kishon depicts them, and therefore are less "anti-ideological" as Laor would have them be.
7. Gertz, "Hatziyonut, hakibutz, veha'ayara"; Shayat, "Lo 'margish aizen' "; Shimony, "Hamakom she'elav halev kameha."
8. Bartov, *Shesh Knafayim Le'achad*, 16–24.
9. Bartov, 26–29.
10. Bartov, 42–45, 134, 62.
11. Bartov, 82–100.
12. Gertz, "Hatziyonut, hakibutz, veha'ayara," 501; Shimony, "Hamakom she'elav halev kameha."
13. Shaked, *Hasiporet Ha'ivrit 1880–1980*, 4:70–71.
14. Gertz, "Hatziyonut, hakibutz, veha'ayara," 503.
15. Bartov, *Shesh Knafayim Le'achad*, 26, 18. All quotes from the novel in this essay were translated by me, O.N.
16. Lukács, *History and Class Consciousness: Studies in Marxist Dialectics*, 1971, 92–110.
17. Gertz, "Hatziyonut, hakibutz, veha'ayara," 500–01.
18. Bartov, *Shesh Knafayim Le'achad*, 26.
19. Bartov, *Shesh Knafayim Le'achad*, 113.

20. See for example Bartov, 115.
21. Gertz, "Hatziyonut, hakibutz, veha'ayara," 507–08.
22. Shamir, *Hu halach basadot*, 2010.; Yigal Mossinsohn, *Aforim Kasak* (Merkhavia: Sifriyat Po'alim, 1946); See Arbell's analysis for the gendered aspect (Arbell, "Gavriyut Venostalgia." We should also not confuse Gitl's "imperfect" femininity with the properly feminist impulses towards liberating women from their reproductive roles in the "genre" literature (*The Wooden Cabin*, which we discussed in a previous chapter, can serve here as a good example). In Bartov's novel, the transgressions against bourgeois femininity are a matter of necessity (need to earn money) or a historical scar (surviving the holocaust and exile in general), rather than part of a transformative project.
23. Bartov, *Shesh Knafayim Le'achad*, 218; It is here and in other places that Bartov's novel takes up the theme of bureaucratic corruption, which as we have seen comes up as a thematization of contradiction in the work of Shaham and in many others novels in the period.
24. Gertz, "Hatziyonut, hakibutz, veha'ayara," 500; Laor, "Ha'aliya Hahamonit Ketokhen Venose Basifrut Ha'ivrit Bishnot Hamedina Harishonot," 1989, 170–71.
25. Bartov, *Shesh Knafayim Le'achad*, 233.
26. Handel, *Street of Steps*, 168.
27. Miron, *Hakoakh Hakhalash: Iyunim Basiporet Shel Yehudit Hendel*.
28. Miron, 32–35.
29. Miron, 35–36.
30. Ratok, "Nashim bemilkhemet ha'atzma'ut: mitos vezikaron," 291.
31. Makov-Hasson, "Oedipus' Sister: Narrating Gender and Nation in the Early Novels of Israeli Women"; Marin, "Lisdok et Hamar'a: Melankolia Ke'intertertu'aliyut Baroman Rekhov Hamadregot Me'et Yehudit Hendel"; Shirav, *Ktiva lo tama*.
32. Mossinsohn, *Kazablan*.
33. Handel, *Street of Steps*, 80–149.
34. Handel, 85.
35. Shamir, *Hu halach basadot*, 2010, 57–76; Megged, *Ruakh Yamim*.
36. Miron, *Hakoakh Hakhalash: Iyunim Basiporet Shel Yehudit Hendel*, 37–41.
37. Marin, "Lisdok et Hamar'a: Melankolia Ke'intertertu'aliyut Baroman Rekhov Hamadregot Me'et Yehudit Hendel."
38. Miron, *Hakoakh Hakhalash: Iyunim Basiporet Shel Yehudit Hendel*, 37.
39. Lukács, "Realism in the Balance," 1980, 38–39.
40. Jameson, *Postmodernism, Or, The Cultural Logic of Late Capitalism*, 1991, 16.
41. Handel, *Street of Steps*, 220–21.
42. Handel, 163.
43. Handel, 223.
44. Handel, 278.
45. Handel, 283.

46. Handel, 324.
47. Miron, *Hakoakh Hakhalash: Iyunim Basiporet Shel Yehudit Hendel*, 41.
48. Ratok, "Nashim bemilkhemet ha'atzma'ut: mitos vezikaron," 291.
49. It is important to add that seeing the novel as exposing the essence of the Mizrachi characters that populate the Street of Steps as passive or over-emotional can resemble a racist assertion, as in Miron's claim that "the sea symbolizes the heritage of the Street of Steps that lies deep within Avram's soul, and which makes him stumble again and again—a heritage that brings together passivity and a quick temper, frustration and a tendency to give up." Miron, *Hakoakh Hakhalash: Iyunim Basiporet Shel Yehudit Hendel*, 30.
50. Handel, *Street of Steps*, 273–74.
51. Handel, 358.
52. Handel, 206.
53. Handel, 66.
54. Handel, 251–55.
55. Žižek, *Looking Awry: An Introduction to Jacques Lacan through Popular Culture*, 1991, 3–17.
56. Žižek, *The Sublime Object of Ideology*, 21–22. See Philip Wegner's discussion of the development of collective structure of enjoyment and their relation to the nation-state Wegner, *Imaginary Communities: Utopia, the Nation, and the Spatial Histories of Modernity*, 2002, 48–50.
57. Handel, *Street of Steps*, 336.
58. Marin, "Lisdok et Hamar'a: Melankolia Ke'intertertu'aliyut Baroman Rekhov Hamadregot Me'et Yehudit Hendel," 155–58.
59. Arbell, "Gavriyut Venostalgia," 53–54; Shirav, *Ktiva lo tama*, 64.
60. Shaham, *Ha'elim Atzelim*; Shaham, *Tamid anakhnu*.
61. Mossinsohn, *Be'arvot Hanegev*.
62. Jameson, "Cognitive Mapping," 1988.
63. Althusser, *On The Reproduction of Capitalism*, 2013, 171–208.
64. Hever, *Sifrut Shenikhtevet Mikan*, 19; Ratok, "Nashim bemilkhemet ha'atzma'ut: mitos vezikaron," 289; Miron, *Hakoakh Hakhalash: Iyunim Basiporet Shel Yehudit Hendel*, 40–41.
65. Miron, *Hakoakh Hakhalash: Iyunim Basiporet Shel Yehudit Hendel*, 41.
66. Gertz, *Khirbet khizah vehaboker shelemakharat*, 1983, 31.
67. For a survey the of Marxist debates about realism, modernism and their relation to capitalism see *Aesthetics and Politics* Jameson, *Aesthetcis and Politics*.
68. Lukács, "Realism in the Balance," 1980, 36–37.
69. Lukács, 38–40.
70. Even though will not be able to discuss this topic in any detail here, it could be argued that the "solution" that Hendel finds for the contradictions that *Street of Steps* conjures—the becoming "human nature" of alienation and failure—is proto-postmodern. That, since in its later role as hegemonic literary ideology (in

the hands of Shaked, Miron, Oz, Yehoshua, and others), it makes possible the institutionalization of previously resisting modernisms.

71. Lukács, "Realism in the Balance," 1980, 43.
72. Žižek, "Introduction: The Spectre of Ideology," 3.
73. Lukács, *The Meaning of Contemporary Realism*, 13–46.
74. Bloch, "Discussing Expressionism"; Benjamin, "Against Georg Lukács."
75. Lukács, *The Meaning of Contemporary Realism*, 26–39.
76. Thorne, "The Sea Is Not a Place; Or, Putting the World Back into World Literature," 2013, 62.
77. Jameson, "Cognitive Mapping," 1988. Jameson has written extensively on the realism/modernism divide and its relation to the development of capitalism, particularly in relation to the development of postmodernism. See in particular his "The Ideology of the Text" (2008), and *The Modernist Papers* Jameson, *The Modernist Papers*, 2007.
78. Toscano and Kinkle, *Cartographies of the Absolute*, 2014, 36.
79. Gozansky, *Hitpatkhut hakapitalism bepalestina*, 1986, 82–93.
80. See Lukács, *History and Class Consciousness: Studies in Marxist Dialectics*, 85–87; Marx and Frederick, *Karl Marx, Frederick Engels: Collected Works*, 34:426.
81. Jameson, "Cognitive Mapping," 1988, 353.

Chapter 4

1. Gurevitz, *Postmodernism: Tarbut Vesifrut Besof Ha'mea Ha'esrim*; Bartana, *Shmonim: sifrut yisra'elit ba'asor ha'akharon*.
2. Peleg, *Israeli Culture between the Two Intifadas: A Brief Romance*, 2.
3. Jameson, *Postmodernism, Or, The Cultural Logic of Late Capitalism*, 1991.
4. Jameson, 4.
5. Jameson, *Postmodernism, Or, The Cultural Logic of Late Capitalism*, 1991.
6. Jameson, "Cognitive Mapping," 1988.
7. For her more recent attempt to deny any substantial existence of Israeli postmodernism, see Shifman, *Dvarim shero'im mikan: David Grossman, Orly Castel Bloom vemeir Shalev: me'ever lamodernism?*, 19–24; For her only slightly older characterizing of Castel-Bloom as a watershed postmodernist of Israeli letters, see Shifman, "Ha'im Ani Nimtzet: Sipur Hakhanicha Hanashi Etzel Tsruya Shalev Veyehudit Katsir," 126.
8. Peleg, *Israeli Culture between the Two Intifadas: A Brief Romance*, 3.
9. Eran Kaplan traces the appearance of consumerism Israel to the late '60s and early '70s (Kaplan, *Beyond Post-Zionism*).
10. Peleg, *Israeli Culture between the Two Intifadas: A Brief Romance*, 6.
11. Mendelson Maoz, *Multiculturalism in Israel: Literary Perspectives*, 3.
12. Abramovich, *Back to the Future: Israeli Literature of the 1980s and 1990s*, 1–13.

13. Schwartz, *Ma Shero'im Mikan*, 19.
14. Schwartz, 21.
15. For attempts to distinguish the critique of national narratives of '80s writers from that of earlier writers, see for example Peleg, *Israeli Culture between the Two Intifadas: A Brief Romance*, 10–13; Abramovich, *Back to the Future: Israeli Literature of the 1980s and 1990s*, 11; Hasak-Lowy, "Postzionism and Its Aftermath in Hebrew Literature: The Case of Orly Castel-Bloom," 89. In all of these cases, '80s authors' writing (Orly Castel-Bloom, Meir Shalev, and others) is said to be post-Zionist, rather than simply reiterating the older critiques of national ideology of Oz or Yehoshua. Yet, all fall back to notions of postmodernism-as-style to enforce the distinction (e.g., the claim that Castel-Bloom's critique of national ideology is performed through postmodern flattening or lack of meaning), which then leaves the critique itself untouched, seeing the difference mostly as a stylistic matter (and of course reinserts postmodernism as a periodizing term through the back door, against the initial impulse to rid the periodization of the term).
16. Jameson, *A Singular Modernity: Essay on the Ontology of the Present*, 179.
17. Wegner, *Life between Two Deaths: US Culture in the Long Nineties*, 20.
18. Gertz, *Khirbet khizah vehaboker shelemakharat*, 1983.
19. Oz, *Elsewhere, Perhaps*; Oz, *My Michael*.
20. Gurevitz, *Postmodernism: Tarbut Vesifrut Besof Ha'mea Ha'esrim*, 303; Ophir, "Al ktiva postmodernit ve'efsharut hatzdakata hamusarit," 117.
21. Cohen, *Likro et Orly Castel Bloom*, 26–29.
22. Cohen, 26; Shifman, *Dvarim Shero'im Mikan: David Grossman, Orly Castel Bloom Vemeir Shalev: Me'ever lamodernism?*, 111–12; Peleg, *Israeli Culture between the Two Intifadas: A Brief Romance*, 18–19; Hasak-Lowy, "Postzionism and Its Aftermath in Hebrew Literature: The Case of Orly Castel-Bloom," 88–89.
23. Castel-Bloom, *Heichan Ani Nimtzet?*, 1990, 34–35. [All translations from the novel are mine, O.N.]
24. Rudin, "Orly Castel Bloom's Perception of Coupledom and Women's Oppression in Light of Impressionist Features and Intertextual Connections in the Novel Where Am I," 262.
25. Hess, "Kvar Ein La 'Ikuvim: Kri'a Feministit Belikro La'atalefim Lekhana Bat Shakhar 'Ubeheichan Ani Nimtzet Le'orly Castel Bloom," 389–90.
26. Hess, 383–86; Shifman, *Dvarim Shero'im Mikan: David Grossman, Orly Castel Bloom Vemeir Shalev: Me'ever Lamodernism?*, 127.
27. Jameson, *Postmodernism, Or, The Cultural Logic of Late Capitalism*, 1991, 15.
28. Rudin, "Orly Castel Bloom's Perception of Coupledom and Women's Oppression in Light of Impressionist Features and Intertextual Connections in the Novel Where Am I," 264.
29. Oz, *My Michael*, 209–10.
30. Miron, "Mashehu Al Orly Castel-Bloom."
31. Oz, *My Michael*, 214.

32. Kahana Carmon, *Veyare'akh Be'emek Ayalon*, 30.
33. Žižek, *For They Know Not What They Do: Enjoyment as a Political Factor*, 181–82.
34. Jameson, *The Political Unconscious: Narrative as a Socially Symbolic Act*, 1981.
35. Grumberg, *Place and Ideology in Contemporary Hebrew Literature*, 77–83.
36. Castel-Bloom, *Heichan Ani Nimtzet?*, 1990, 46–47. My translation.
37. Castel-Bloom, 63–65.
38. Oz, *My Michael*, 190–92.
39. Peleg, *Israeli Culture between the Two Intifadas: A Brief Romance*, 21–23.
40. Freud, *The Psychopathology of Everyday Life*.
41. Derrida, *Of Grammatology*, 61.
42. Castel-Bloom, *Heichan Ani Nimtzet?* [*Where Am I?*], 1990, 16.
43. Oz, *My Michael*, 209.
44. Wegner, *Life between Two Deaths: US Culture in the Long Nineties*, 6; Benjamin, *The Origin of German Tragic Drama*.
45. Examples of critics who tend to share Castel-Bloom's postmodern (or modernist) distrust of allegory in general include Cohen, *Likro et Orly Castel Bloom*.
46. Shamir, "Sefer Khadash Mishmeret Khadasha," 7; Herzig, *Hakol ha'omer: ani: megamot basiporet hayisraelit shel shnot hashmonim*.
47. Žižek, "Introduction."
48. Lukács, "Realism in the Balance," 1980, 38–40.
49. Katzir, *Closing the Sea*, 44–45.
50. Herzig, "Efsharuyot Akherot Besogrim et Hayam Leyehudit Katzir," 299.
51. Katzir, *Closing the Sea*, 6–7.
52. Zertal, *Israel's Holocaust and the Politics of Nationhood*.
53. Shamir, "Sefer Khadash Mishmeret Khadasha."
54. Katzir, *Closing the Sea*, 97–98.
55. Žižek, *Looking Awry: An Introduction to Jacques Lacan through Popular Culture*, 1991.
56. Mossinsohn, *Aforim Kasak*, 102; Shamir, *Hu halach basadot*, 2010, 214.
57. Oz, *My Michael*, 175–76.
58. Kenan, *Sefer Hata'anugot*.
59. Oz, *Elsewhere, Perhaps*, 273.
60. Katzir, *Closing the Sea*, 121–22.
61. Katzir, 64.
62. Jameson, *Postmodernism, Or, The Cultural Logic of Late Capitalism*, 1991, 279–96.
63. Herzig, "Efsharuyot Akherot Besogrim et Hayam Leyehudit Katzir."
64. Jameson, "Cognitive Mapping," 1988; Toscano and Kinkle, *Cartographies of the Absolute*, 2014, 6–20.
65. Bichler and Nitzan, *The Global Political Economy of Israel*, 3–9.

66. Shalev, "Have Globalization and Liberalization 'normalized' Israel's Political Economy?"
67. Bichler and Nitzan, *The Global Political Economy of Israel*, 121.
68. Farjoun, "Hapoalim Hafalastinim—Tzva Milu'im Kalkali."
69. Grossman, *Khiyuch Hagdi*, 65.
70. Matalon, *Zarim Babayit*.
71. Keret, *Missing Kissinger*, 2007, 11–14.
72. Cohen, *Likro et Orly Castel Bloom*, 28. [my translation, O.N.]

Chapter 5

1. Gur, *The Saturday Morning Murder: A Psychoanalytic Case*; Kenaz, *Infiltration*, 2003; Grossman, *The Smile of the Lamb*.
2. Adi Ophir's is perhaps the most well-known case of arguing that there are too many pressing problems in Israeli reality for postmodernism to develop (see Zemach, "Hapost-Modernizm: Rav-Si'akh"). This view has unfortunately been reproduced in later writing by Smadar Shifman and others.
3. Brown, "Close Reading and the Market."
4. See for example Annie McClanahan, *Dead Pledges: Debt, Crisis, and Twenty-First-Century Culture*, 143–84.
5. Wegner, "Greimas Avec Lacan: From the Symbolic to the Real in Dialectical Criticism."
6. Grossman, *See Under—Love*; Grossman, *The Book of Intimate Grammar*.
7. Peleg, *Israeli Culture between the Two Intifadas: A Brief Romance*, 12.
8. Barma, "Kmo Milim Al Khut Tayil," 83.
9. Yehoshua, "Facing the Forests."
10. Grossman, *The Smile of the Lamb*, 6.
11. Grossman, 13.
12. Lipsker-Elbak, "Hadibur Vehaktav"; Gluzman, "Sfat Haguf Besefer Hadikduk Hapnimi," 338.
13. Lipsker-Elbak, "Hadibur Vehaktav," 215.
14. Grossman, *The Smile of the Lamb*, 99. Translation modified, O.N.
15. Grossman, 265–66. Translation modified, O.N.
16. Laor, "Ha'aliya Hahamonit Ketokhen Venose Basifrut Ha'ivrit Bishnot Hamedina Harishonot," 1989.
17. Grossman, *The Smile of the Lamb*, 33–34.
18. Morahg, "New Images of Arabs in Israeli Fiction," 147–50.
19. Oppenheimer, *Me'ever Lagader: Yitzug Ha'aravim Basiporet Ha'ivrit Vehayisraelit (1906–2005)*, 311.
20. Žižek, "Introduction," 8.

21. Oppenheimer, *Me'ever Lagader: Yitzug Ha'aravim Basiporet Ha'ivrit Vehayisraelit (1906–2005)*, 233.

22. Hever, "Minority Discourse of a National Majority: Israeli Fiction If the Early Sixties."

23. Yehoshua, "Facing the Forests," 375–76.

24. Grossman, *The Smile of the Lamb*, 276–78.

25. Grossman, 318–19.

26. Grossman, 236.

27. Oppenheimer, *Me'ever Lagader: Yitzug Ha'aravim Basiporet Ha'ivrit Vehayisraelit (1906–2005)*, 315–16.

28. Shimoni, *A Room*; Leshem, *Beaufort*.

29. Yizhar, *Days of Tsiklag*; Kaniuk, *Himmo, King of Jerusalm*.

30. Wegner, *Imaginary Communities: Utopia, the Nation, and the Spatial Histories of Modernity*, 2002, 5.

31. Mishani, *Bechol Ha'inyan Hamizrakhi Yesh Eize Absurd*, 41; Herzig, *Hakol ha'omer: ani: megamot basiporet hayisraelit shel shnot hashmonim*, 182.

32. Hirschfeld, "Zehut Nigmeret Umatkhila Akheret"; Herzig, *Hakol ha'omer: ani: megamot basiporet hayisraelit shel shnot hashmonim*, 20–30; Mishani, *Bechol Ha'inyan Hamizrakhi Yesh Eize Absurd*, 39–79.

33. Ben Dov, "Sparta Veyeladeyha Ha'avudim," 115; Ben Yair, "Shigaon Utvuna Behitganvut Yekhidim," 18.

34. Kenaz, *Infiltration*, 2003, 47.

35. Kenaz, 51.

36. Kenaz, 527–29.

37. Althusser, *On The Reproduction of Capitalism*, 2013, 171–208.

38. Žižek, *For They Know Not What They Do: Enjoyment as a Political Factor*, 239.

39. Kenaz, *Infiltration*, 2003, 380–85, 439.

40. Herzig, *Hakol ha'omer: ani: megamot basiporet hayisraelit shel shnot hashmonim*, 187–98.

41. Kenaz, *Infiltration*, 2003, 66.

42. Kenaz, 174, 127, 370.

43. Kenaz, 193.

44. Kenaz, 502. Emphasis in the original.

45. Herzig, *Hakol ha'omer: ani: megamot basiporet hayisraelit shel shnot hashmonim*, 185; Ben Dov, "Sparta Veyeladeyha Ha'avudim," 115.

46. Jameson, *The Political Unconscious: Narrative as a Socially Symbolic Act*, 1981, 166; Wegner, "Greimas Avec Lacan: From the Symbolic to the Real in Dialectical Criticism."

47. Jameson, *The Political Unconscious: Narrative as a Socially Symbolic Act*, 1981, 167.

48. Herzig, *Hakol ha'omer: ani: megamot basiporet hayisraelit shel shnot hashmonim*, 187.

49. For a recent example, see Rozin, *The Rise of the Individual in 1950s Israel: A Challenge to Collectivism*.

50. Miron, "Min Hashulay'im El Hamerkaz Ubekhazara."

51. Megged, *Hedva Ve'ani*.

52. Hirschfeld, "Zehut Nigmeret Umatkhila Akheret."

53. Mishani, *Bechol Ha'inyan Hamizrakhi Yesh Eize Absurd*, 75.

54. Jameson, *Postmodernism, Or, The Cultural Logic of Late Capitalism*, 1991, 279–97.

55. Herzig, *Hakol ha'omer: ani: megamot basiporet hayisraelit shel shnot hashmonim*, 29.

56. Ben Dov, "Sparta Veyeladeyha Ha'avudim," 117–18; Shifman, "Mehitganvut Yekhidim Lehaolam Ktzat Akhar Kach: Kur Hituch O Hitganvut Rav Tarbutit?," 60.

57. Hirschfeld, "Zehut Nigmeret Umatkhila Akheret"; Ben Yair, "Shigaon Utvuna Behitganvut Yekhidim."

58. Shifman, "Mehitganvut Yekhidim Lehaolam Ktzat Akhar Kach: Kur Hituch O Hitganvut Rav Tarbutit?," 60.

59. Ben Dov, "Sparta Veyeladeyha Ha'avudim," 115.

60. Herzig, *Hakol ha'omer: ani: megamot basiporet hayisraelit shel shnot hashmonim*, 29.

61. Eshed, *Mitarzan Ve'ad Zbeng*.

62. Yizhar, *Mikdamot*; Shalev, *The Loves of Judith*; Shalev, *The Blue Mountain*, 1991.

63. In this respect, one should also problematize any attempt to see these '80s novels—both the soldiers' experience and the *halutz* ones—as historical novels in any meaningful way. The strong tendency in these later works towards pastiching the past's representations of itself means that their only "historicity" they create has to do with registering the very lack of historicity, rather than dialectically producing some positive imagined relation between past and present, like older historical novels (see in this respect Jameson, *Postmodernism, Or, The Cultural Logic of Late Capitalism*, 1991, 284–87.

64. Butler, Laclau, and Žižek, *Contingency, Hegemony, Universality: Contemporary Dialogues on the Left*, 94.

65. Miron, "Komeriya Be'israel: Kama He'arot Al Hasipur Habalashi Vemekomo Batarbut Hayisraelit," 126.

66. Shamir, "Habalash Ha'ivri Make Shenit."

67. Miron, "Komeriya Be'israel: Kama He'arot Al Hasipur Habalashi Vemekomo Batarbut Hayisraelit," 120.

68. Abramovich, "Israeli Detective Fiction: The Case of Batya Gur and Shulamit Lapid," 147–49.

69. Gur, *The Saturday Morning Murder: A Psychoanalytic Case*, 51.

70. Miron, "Komeriya Be'israel: Kama He'arot Al Hasipur Habalashi Vemekomo Batarbut Hayisraelit," 104.

71. Gur, *The Saturday Morning Murder: A Psychoanalytic Case*, 177–79.

72. Katzman, "Slicha, Yesh Od Gviya Bamarak Sheli," 36.

73. Mandel, *Delightful Murder: A Social History of the Crime Story*, 135.

74. Brecht, "On the Popularity of the Crime Novel."

75. Gur, *The Saturday Morning Murder: A Psychoanalytic Case*, 60.

76. Gur, 112.

77. Gur, 188.

78. Tzivoni, "Haroman Habalashi—Tekes Gilui Hagufa/Misdar Hakhashudim," 60.

79. Jameson, *Raymond Chandler: The Detections of Totality*, 40.

80. Jameson, 51.

81. Žižek, *How to Read Lacan*, 79–80.

82. Gur, *The Saturday Morning Murder: A Psychoanalytic Case*, 224.

83. Gur, 54.

84. Gur, 256.

85. Thorne, "The Sea Is Not a Place; Or, Putting the World Back into World Literature," 2013.

86. Braham, *Crimes against the State, Crimes against Persons: Detective Fiction in Cuba and Mexico*, 20–32.

87. Gur, *Murder in Jerusalem*.

Chapter 6

1. Touché Gafla, *The World of the End*; Touché Gafla, *Bayom shehamusika meta*; Nevo, *Neuland*; Yakir, *Yeme khol*.

2. Nealon, *Post-Postmodernism, or The Cultural Logic of Just-in-Time Capitalism*; Fisher, *Capitalist Realism: Is There No Alternative?*

3. Nealon, *Post-Postmodernism, or The Cultural Logic of Just-in-Time Capitalism*, 26, 150; Fisher, *Capitalist Realism: Is There No Alternative?*, 2.

4. Jameson, "The Aesthetics of Singularity," 104; Nilges, "The Presence of Postmodernism in Contemporary American Literature," 6.

5. Nilges, "The Presence of Postmodernism in Contemporary American Literature," 10–11.

6. Eshel, *Futurity: Contemporary Literature and the Quest for the Past*; Crary, *24/7: Late Capitalism and the Ends of Sleep*; Cazdyn, *The Already Dead: The New Time of Politics, Culture, and Illness*.

7. Eshel, *Futurity: Contemporary Literature and the Quest for the Past*, 11.

8. Nilges, "Neoliberalism and the Time of the Novel," 372.

9. Fisher, *Capitalist Realism: Is There No Alternative?*, 78.

10. Kemp and Raijman, *Ovdim vezarim: hakalkala hapolitit shel Hagirat avoda beyisrael*, 67–94; Bichler and Nitzan, *The Global Political Economy of Israel*, 120 n.11.

11. Gutwein, "He'arot al hayesodot hama'amadi'yim shel hakibush"; Kaplan, *Beyond Post-Zionism*.

12. Nir, "Towards a Renewal of Israeli Marxism, or Peace as a Vanishing Mediator."

13. Shehada, "Dokh mekhkar: medinat harevakha shel hamitnakhlim."

14. For more information (in English and Hebrew) about trends in employment of foreign labor, see the Israel Democracy Institute website: https://www.idi.org.il/parliaments/11099/11108.

15. Shoham, *Lemar'it a'yin*; Gavron, *Hagiva*; Berg, *Od khamesh dakot*.

16. Warwick Research Collective, *Combined and Uneven Development: Towards a New Thoery of World Literature*, 10–15.

17. Jameson, *A Singular Modernity: Essay on the Ontology of the Present*, 13.

18. Brown, *Utopian Generations: The Political Horizon of Twentieth-Century Literature*.

19. Sauri, "Autonomy after Autonomy, Or, The Novel beyond Nation: Roberto Bolaño's 2666," 403.

20. Yakir, *Yeme khol*, 5.

21. Sela, "Sefer: Be'azuva tel avivit khaya la mishpakha shkufa." All excerpts from the interview were translated by me, O.N.

22. Yakir, *Yeme khol*, 258. All translations from the novel are mine, O.N.

23. Yakir, 50.

24. Yakir, 52.

25. Sela, "Sefer: Be'azuva tel avivit khaya la mishpakha shkufa."

26. Wilde, *The Soul of Man Under Socialism*.

27. Adorno, "On Popular Music."

28. Yakir, *Yeme khol*, 44–45.

29. Jameson, "The Aesthetics of Singularity," 111.

30. Warwick Research Collective, *Combined and Uneven Development: Towards a New Thoery of World Literature*, 7.

31. Adivi Shoshan, "Psanter bli bayit."

32. Yakir, *Yeme khol*, 210.

33. Grumberg, *Place and Ideology in Contemporary Hebrew Literature*, 80–82.

34. Adivi Shoshan, "Psanter bli bayit."

35. Yakir, *Yeme khol*, 196.

36. Jameson, "The Aesthetics of Singularity," 111–13.

37. Yakir, *Yeme khol*, 146–47.

38. Yakir, 33, 41.

39. Yakir, 31–32.

40. Žižek, *Looking Awry: An Introduction to Jacques Lacan through Popular Culture*, 1991, 4.

41. Anderson, *Imagined Communities: Reflections on the Origin and Spread of Nationalism*.

42. Kaplan, *Beyond Post-Zionism*, 34.

43. Gluzman, "Sfat haguf besefer hadikduk hapnimi."

44. Netanel, *Hamatzav ha'ivri*, 2008, 91.

45. Yakir, *Yeme Khol*, 149.

46. Yakir, 200.

47. Sela, "Sefer: Be'azuva Tel Avivit Khaya La Mishpakha Shkufa."

48. Bar Yossef, *Utopia Bekachol-Lavan*; Kenan, *Haderech Le'ein Kharod*.

49. Sterling, "Slipstream."

50. Brown, "Close Reading and the Market"; Hoberek, "Introduction: After Postmodernism."

51. Glasner, "Hamavet Eino Mekhusar Ta'arich: Al 'bayom Shehamusika Meta' me'et Ofir Touché Gafla."

52. Namdar, *Habayit Asher Nekherav*.

53. Sauri, "Autonomy after Autonomy, Or, The Novel beyond Nation: Roberto Bolaño's 2666," 404–06.

54. Gavron, *Hagiva*.

55. Touché Gafla, *Bayom Shehamusika Meta*, 231.

56. Touché Gafla, 191.

57. Touché Gafla, 220, 181, 212, 232–233, 109.

58. Touché Gafla, 192.

59. Žižek, *The Parallax View*, 65.

60. Freud, *Beyond the Pleasure Principle*.

61. Touché Gafla, *Bayom Shehamusika Meta*, 94.

62. Touché Gafla, 225.

63. Touché Gafla, 268.

64. Touché Gafla, 270.

65. Touché Gafla, 308, 317.

66. Cohen, "Musikat Hamikre: Re'ayon Im Ofir Touché Gafla"; Touché Gafla, *Bayom Shehamusika Meta*, 105, 189.

67. Cazdyn, *The Already Dead: The New Time of Politics, Culture, and Illness*, 6.

68. Touché Gafla, *Bayom Shehamusika Meta*, 304.

69. Touché Gafla, 192–93, 286.

70. Touché Gafla, 391.

71. Jameson, "The Aesthetics of Singularity," 122; Bryan and Rafferty, *Capitalism with Derivatives*.

72. Touché Gafla, *Bayom Shehamusika Meta*, 127.

73. Touché Gafla, 183, 188.

74. Cazdyn, *The Already Dead: The New Time of Politics, Culture, and Illness*, 43.

75. Touché Gafla, *Bayom Shehamusika Meta*, 397.

76. Shifman, *Dvarim Shero'im Mikan: David Grossman, Orly Castel Bloom, Vemeir Shalev: Me'ever Lamodernism?*; Peleg, *Israeli Culture between the Two Intifadas: A Brief Romance*; Cohen, *Likro et Orly Castel Bloom*; Mendelson Maoz, *Multiculturalism in Israel: Literary Perspectives*.

77. Levy, *Poetic Trespass: Writing between Hebrew and Arabic in Israel/Palestine*; Mendelson Maoz, *Multiculturalism in Israel: Literary Perspectives*.

78. Gilbert, "What Kind of Thing Is Neoliberalism?," 8–9; Harvey, *A Brief History of Neoliberalism*, 27.

Chapter 7

1. Shalev, *The Blue Mountain*, 1991; Shalev, *The Loves of Judith*.
2. Benjamin, *The Origin of German Tragic Drama*, 162.
3. Benziman, "'Anachnu Hayinu Bayam': Habikoret Hame'asheret Besirtei Mikre Levanon Hayisra'eli'im She'achrei Milkhemet Levanon Hashniya [We Were at the Beach]," 314. My translation, O.N.
4. Adorno, "Cultural Criticism and Society."
5. Peleg, "Beaufort the Book, Beaufort the Film: Israeli Miilitarism under Attack," 399–40.
6. Leshem, *Beaufort*, 143.
7. Leshem, 153–54.
8. Leshem, 167.
9. Leshem, 304.
10. Suvin, *Metamorphoses of Science Fiction: On the Poetics and History of a Literary Genre*, 5.
11. Leshem, *Beaufort*, 21, 129–30, 62–65, 132.
12. Leshem, 53, 58–60.
13. Leshem, 80–83.
14. Sartre, *Critique of Dialectical Reason*, 1:375.
15. Leshem, *Beaufort*, 21, 57, 132–32.
16. Leshem, 250–51.
17. Hollander, "Shifting Manhood: Masculinity and the Lebanon War in Beaufort and Waltz with Bashir," 347.
18. Kh., "Im Yesh Gan Eden, Hu Nimtza Belevanon Veyesh Bo Rak Gvarim."
19. Even though we will not be able to extensively discuss this here, it is important to mention that following the establishment of Israel, the Israeli military itself was imbued with utopian energies (the "melting pot" allegory being the expression of social transformation through military service, aimed at fighting poverty, providing access to education, and other welfare-state programs.
20. Leshem, *Beaufort*, 2.

21. It was of course Georg Lukács, following Marx, who highlighted capitalism's tendency to abstract everything in human experience as it increasingly penetrates existing social formations (Lukcás, *History and Class Consicousness*, 89–91)

22. Amotz Giladi, "Sipur hakishalon hatzioni derekh kishalon hasafa ha'ivrit," Ha'aretz, May 29, 2008, http://www.haaretz.co.il/literature/1.1327789.

23. Netanel, *Hamatzav ha'ivri*, 23, 54.

24. Ibid., 12, 202–05, 157, 164–65.

25. Ibid., 129–34.

26. The most well-known example is perhaps the narrator-protagonist of Brenner, "Mikan Unmikan"; Zarchi, *Yamim Yekhefim*, 1934. C. Y. Brenner, "Mikan Unmikan," in *Kol Kitve Y. C. Brenner*, vol. 4 (Warsaw: Shtibel, 1926), 105–247; Yisrael Zarchi, *Yamim Yekhefim* (Tel Aviv: Sefer, 1934). C. Y. Brenner, "Mikan Unmikan," in *Kol Kitve Y. C. Brenner*, vol. 4 (Warsaw: Shtibel, 1926 [1911]), 105–247. The same tendency to focus on protagonists that were also ambitions writers with historical projects is also evident in the work of U. N. Gnessin. A lesser known fact is that the much-maligned realists or "genre" writers also commonly used author-protagonists that mostly fail in their enterprises. See for example Yisrael Zarchi, Yamim Yekhefim (Tel Aviv: Sefer, 1934).

27. Castel-Bloom, Heichan Ani Nimtzet?; Etgar Keret, Missing Kissinger (London: Chatto & Windus, 2007).

28. Fredric Jameson, *Postmodernism, Or, The Cultural Logic of Late Capitalism* (London; New York: Verso, 1991), 20.

29. Netanel, *Hamatzav ha'ivri*, 65. [All quotes from the novel were translated by me, O.N.]

30. Georg Lukács, "Realism in the Balance," in *Aesthetics and Politics*, ed. Fredric Jameson (London; New York: Verso, 1980), 36–37.

31. Netanel, *Hamatzav ha'ivri*, 9; ibid., 64. Of course, that "Zvi" is the masculine Hebrew translation of the Yiddish "Hinda" only further strengthens the analogy.

32. Netanel, *Hamatzav ha'ivri*, 79; ibid., 87; ibid., 100–06.

33. Ibid., 84–86.

34. Ibid., 106.

35. Ibid., 196.

36. Ibid., 192.

37. Ibid., 163.

38. Ibid., 11–23.

39. Theodor Adorno and Max Horkheimer, Dialectic of Enlightenment (London: Verso, 1949).

40. Netanel, *Hamatzav ha'ivri*, 161–63.

41. Netanel, 123; Leah Goldberg, *And This Is the Light* (New York: Toby Press, 2011 [1946]).

42. Netanel, *Hamatzav ha'ivri*, 204–05. Zvi's father is invoking here the etymological roots of the word "Hebrew" in Hebrew, which does in fact refer to

"being beyond" or in a state of transition, as Amotz Giladi notes ("Sipur hakishalon hatzioni derekh kishalon hasafa ha'ivrit," Ha'aretz, May 29, 2008, http://www.haaretz.co.il/literature/1.1327789).

43. See Shaked's work for the distinctions and antagonisms between the Hebrew Modernists and realists (Gershon Shaked, *Hasiporet Ha'ivrit 1880–1980*, vol. 4 (Tel Aviv: Hakibutz Hame'ukhad, 1993), 14–188.)

44. Batya Gur, *Murder on a Kibbutz* (New York: HarperCollins, 1994); Meir Shalev, *The Blue Mountain* (New York: HarperCollins, 1991).

45. Nathan Shaham, *Tamid anakhnu* (Merkhavia: Sifriyat Po'alim, 1952), 50.

46. Yiftach Ashkenazi, *Haide lahagshama* (Tel Aviv: Khargol, Modan, 2014), 228; ibid., 254; ibid., 151.

47. Ashkenazi, *Haide lahagshama*, 333.

48. Louis Marin, *Utopics: Spatial Play* (London; Atlantic Highlands, NJ: Macmillan; Humanities Press, 1984), 163.

49. Ashkenazi, *Haide lahagshama*, 228. [All passages from the novel that appear in this essay were translated by me, O.N.]

50. Yuval Shimoni, Kheder (Tel Aviv: Am Oved, 1999)

51. See for Yigal Schwartz, *The Zionist Paradox: Hebrew Literature and Israeli Identity* (Baltimore, MD: Project MUSE, 2014), 280. Schwartz's discussion of the way in which Oz reverses what Schwartz calls "the vector of desire," in which the representations of the exilic Jew as abject or degenerate are reversed, recoding him as an object of desire.

52. Ashkenazi, *Haide lahagshama*, 91–122; ibid., 269.

53. For the tendency to explode figurative hermeneutical schemas in Israeli postmodernism, see Avraham Balaban, *Gal akher basiporet ha'ivrit* (Jerusalem: Keter, 1995), 37.

54. Ashkenazi, *Haide lahagshama*, 122.

55. For an account of "historical" pastiche as originating in other period's self-representation, see Jameson, *Postmodernism, Or, The Cultural Logic of Late Capitalism*, 279–96.

56. Ibid., 34–78.

57. Ashkenazi, 353–66.

58. Ibid., 333.

59. Ibid., 378–79.

60. Williams, *Combined and Uneven Apocalypse*, 2010, 9.

61. Gutwein, "He'arot al hayesodot hama'amadi'yim shel hakibush"; Kaplan, *Beyond Post-Zionism*.

Bibliography

Abramovich, Dvir. *Back to the Future: Israeli Literature of the 1980s and 1990s.* Newcastle, UK: Cambridge Scholars Publishing, 2010.

———. "Israeli Detective Fiction: The Case of Batya Gur and Shulamit Lapid." *Australian Journal of Jewish Studies* 14 (2000): 147–79.

Adivi Shoshan, Esty. "Psanter Bli Bayit." *Ha'aretz*, August 8, 2012. http://www.haaretz.co.il/literature/safrut/list/1.1796579.

Adorno, Theodor. *Aesthetic Theory.* London: The Athlone Press, 1997.

———. "Cultural Criticism and Society." In *Prisms*, 17–35. Cambridge: MIT Press, 1983.

———. "On Popular Music." *Studies in Philosophy and Social Sciences* 9 (1941): 17–48.

Adorno, Theodor, and Max Horkheimer. *Dialectic of Enlightenment.* London: Verso, n.d.

Althusser, Louis. *For Marx.* London: Allen Lane, 1969.

———. *On The Reproduction of Capitalism.* London; New York: Verso, 2013.

Althusser, Louis, and Etienne Balibar. *Reading Capital.* New York: Pantheon, 1970.

Anderson, Benedict. *Imagined Communities: Reflections on the Origin and Spread of Nationalism.* London: Verso, 1983.

Arbell, Michal. "Gavriyut Venostalgia." *Madaei Hayahadut* 39 (1999).

Aricha, Yosef. "Lekhem Vekhazon." In *Ktavim: Mivkhar Sipurim*, 1:7–169. Tel Aviv: Niv, 1967.

Ashkenazi, Yiftach. *Haide lahagshama.* Tel Aviv: Khargol, Modan, 2014.

Balaban, Avraham. *Gal akher basiporet ha'ivrit.* Jerusalem: Keter, 1995.

Bar Yossef, Yehoshua. *Utopia Bekachol-Lavan.* Tel Aviv: Sifriyat Ma'ariv, 1990.

Barma, Yisrael. "Kmo Milim Al Khut Tayil." *Moznayim* 58, no. 1–2 (1984): 82–84.

Bartana, Ortsion. *Shmonim: sifrut yisra'elit ba'asor ha'akharon.* Tel Aviv: Agudat hasofrim ha'iryim be'israel, 1993.

Bartov, Hanoch. *Shesh Knafayim Le'achad.* Tel Aviv: Am Oved, 1973.

Ben David, Mishka. *Mipleshet Ad Ziklag: Iyunim Beroman Milkhemet Ha'atzma'ut.* Tel Aviv: Tarmil, 1990.

Ben Dov, Nitza. "Sparta Veyeladeyha Ha'avudim." *Aley Si'akh* 33 (1993): 113–19.
Ben Yair, Itamar. "Shigaon Utvuna Behitganvut Yekhidim." *Moznayim* 87, no. 1 (2013): 16–19.
Benjamin, Walter. "Against Georg Lukács." In *Aesthetics and Politics*, edited by Fredric Jameson, 68–85. London; New York: Verso, 1980.
———. *The Origin of German Tragic Drama*. London: New Left Books, 1977.
Benn Michaels, Walter. "Model Minorities and the Minority Model—the Neoliberal Novel." In *The Cambridge History of the American Novel*, edited by Leonard Cassuto, Clare Virginia Eby, and Benjamin Reiss, 1016–30. Cambridge, UK: Cambridge University Press, 2011.
Benziman, Yuval. "'Anachnu Hayinu Bayam': Habikoret Hame'asheret Besirtei Mikre Levanon Hayisra'eli'im She'achrei Milkhemet Levanon Hashniya [We Were at the Beach]." *Teoria Ubikoret* 41 (2013): 313–25.
Berg, Yonatan. *Od Khamesh Dakot*. Tel Aviv: Am Oved, 2015.
Bernstein, Deborah. *Constructing Boundaries: Jewish and Arab Workers in Mandatory Palestine*. Albany, NY: State University of New York, 2000.
Bichler, Shimshon, and Jonathan Nitzan. *The Global Political Economy of Israel*. London: Pluto Press, 2002.
Bloch, Ernst. "Discussing Expressionism." In *Aesthetics and Politics*, edited by Fredric Jameson, 16–27. London; New York: Verso, 1980.
Boyarin, Daniel. "Neshef Hamasechot Hakoloniali: Tziyonut, Migdar, Khikuy." *Teoria Ubikoret* 11 (1997): 123–44.
Braham, Persephone. *Crimes against the State, Crimes against Persons: Detective Fiction in Cuba and Mexico*. Minneapolis: Minnesota University Press, 2004.
Brecht, Bertolt. "On the Popularity of the Crime Novel." *The Irish Review* 31 (2004): 90–95.
Brenner, C. Y. "Mikan Unmikan." In *Kol Kitve Y.C. Brenner*, 4:105–247. Warsaw: Shtibel, 1926.
Brenner, Robert. *The Economics of Global Turbulence: The Advanced Capitalist Economies from Long Boom to Long Downturn, 1945–2005*. London; New York: Verso, 2006.
Brown, Nicholas. "Close Reading and the Market." In *Literary Materialisms*, edited by Emilio Sauri and Mathias Nilges, 145–65. New York: Palgrave Macmillan, 2013.
———. *Utopian Generations: The Political Horizon of Twentieth-Century Literature*. Princeton, NJ: Princeton University Press, 2006.
Bryan, Dick, and Michael Rafferty. *Capitalism with Derivatives*. London: Palgrave, 2005.
Butler, Judith, Ernesto Laclau, and Slavoj Žižek. *Contingency, Hegemony, Universality: Contemporary Dialogues on the Left*. London: Verso, 2000.
Castel-Bloom, Orly. *Heichan Ani Nimtzet?*. Tel Aviv: Zmora Bitan, 1990.
Cazdyn, Eric. *The Already Dead: The New Time of Politics, Culture, and Illness*. Durham, NC: Duke University Press, 2012.

Chernyshevsky, Nikolay. *What Is to Be Done?* Ithaca, NY: Cornell University Press, 1989.
Cohen, Boaz. "Musikat Hamikre: Re'ayon Im Ofir Touché Gafla." *Nrg*, May 21, 2010. http://www.nrg.co.il/online/47/ART2/108/936.html.
Cohen, Uri. *Hanusakh Habitkhoni*. Tel Aviv: Mosad Bialik, 2017.
———. *Likro et Orly Castel Bloom*. Tel Aviv: Akhuzat ba'it, 2011.
Crary, Johnathan. *24/7: Late Capitalism and the Ends of Sleep*. London; New York: Verso, 2013.
Deckard, Sharae. "Peripheral Realism, Millennial Capitalism, and Roberto Bolaño's 2666." *Modern Language Quarterly* 73, no. 3 (2012): 351–72.
Derrida, Jacques. *Of Grammatology*. Baltimore, MD: Johns Hopkins University Press, 1976.
Eshed, Eli. *Mitarzan Ve'ad Zbeng*. Tel Aviv: Bavel, 2002.
Eshel, Amir. *Futurity: Contemporary Literature and the Quest for the Past*. Chicago: University of Chicago Press, 2013.
Esty, Jed, and Colleen Lye. "Peripheral Realisms Now." *Modern Language Quarterly* 73, no. 3 (2012): 269–88.
Farjoun, Emanuel. "Hapoalim Hafalastinim—Tzva Milu'im Kalkali [The Palestinian Workers – An Economic Reserve Army]." *Dapim Adumim* 5 (1978).
Feldman, Yael. *No Room of Their Own: Gender and Nation in Israeli Women's Fiction*. New York: Columbia University Press, 1999.
———. "Shel Mi Hakorban Haze La'azazel? Aliyato Unefilato Shel Avraham Ha'oked Beshnot Hakhamishim." *Mikan* 9 (2008): 125–57.
Fisher, Mark. *Capitalist Realism: Is There No Alternative?* Winchester, UK ; Washington: Zero Books, 2009.
Freud, Sigmund. *Beyond the Pleasure Principle*. Mineola, NY: Dover, 2015.
———. *The Psychopathology of Everyday Life*. New York: Norton, 1965.
Gavron, Assaf. *Hagiva*. Tel Aviv: Aliyat hagag; Miskal, 2013.
Gertz, Nurit. "Hatziyonut, hakibutz, veha'ayara." *Iyunim bitkumat yisrael* 8 (1998): 498–519.
———. *Khirbet khizah vehaboker shelemakharat*. Tel Aviv: Hakibutz Hame'ukhad, 1983.
———. *Sifrut Ve'ideologia Be'eretz Yisreal Beshnot Hashloshim*. Tel Aviv: The Open University Press, 1988.
Giladi, Amotz. "Sipur hakishalon hatzioni derekh kishalon hasafa ha'ivrit." *Ha'aretz*. May 29, 2008. http://www.haaretz.co.il/literature/1.1327789.
Gilbert, Geremy. "What Kind of Thing Is Neoliberalism?" *New Formations* 80–81 (2013): 7–21.
Ginsburg, Shai. *Rhetoric and Nation: The Formation of Hebrew National Culture, 1880–1990*. Syracuse, NY: Syracuse University Press, 2014.
Glasner, Arik. "Hamavet Eino Mekhusar Ta'arich: Al 'bayom Shehamusika Meta' me'et Ofir Touché Gafla." *Nrg*, June 2, 2010. http://www.nrg.co.il/online/47/ART2/112/300.html.

Gluzman, Michael. *Haguf Hatsiyoni: Leumiyut, Migdar Uminiyut Basifrut Ha'ivrit Hahadasha*. Bnei brak: Hakibutz Hame'ukhad, 2007.

———. "Sfat Haguf Besefer Hadikduk Hapnimi." In *Sifrut Vekhevra Batartub Ha'ivrit Hakhadasha*, edited by Yehudit Bar El, Yigal Schwartz, and Tamar Hess. Hakibutz Hame'ukhad; Keter, 2000.

Goldberg, Leah. *And This Is the Light*. New York: Toby Press, 2011.

Gorny, Yosef. *Zionism and the Arabs 1882–1948: A Study of Ideology*. Oxford; New York: Clarendon Press; Oxford University Press, 1987.

Govrin, Nurit. *Kri'at Hadorot: Sifrut Ivrit Bema'agaleha*. Vol. 2. Tel Aviv: Gvanim, 2002.

Gozansky, Tamar. *Hitpatkhut hakapitalism bepalestina*. Haifa: University of Haifa Press, 1986.

Grossman, David. *Khiyuch Hagdi*. Tel Aviv: Hakibutz Hame'ukhad, 1983.

———. *See Under—Love*. New York: Farrar, Straus and Giroux, 1989.

———. *The Book of Intimate Grammar*. New York: Farrar, Straus and Giroux, 1994.

———. *The Smile of the Lamb*. New York: Farrar, Straus and Giroux, 1990.

Grumberg, Karen. *Place and Ideology in Contemporary Hebrew Literature*. Syracuse, NY: Syracuse University Press, 2011.

Gur, Batya. *Murder in Jerusalem*. New York: HarperCollins, 2007.

———. *Murder on a Kibbutz*. New York: HarperCollins, 1994.

———. *The Saturday Morning Murder: A Psychoanalytic Case*. New York: Aaron Asher Books, 1992.

Gurevitz, David. *Postmodernism: Tarbut Vesifrut Besof Ha'mea Ha'esrim*. Tel Aviv: Dvir, 1997.

Gurfein, Rivka. *Le'or Hakatuv*. Tel Aviv: Hakibutz Hame'ukhad, 1972.

———. "Sefer Khadash, 'Shesh Knafaim La'echad' Lehanoch Bartov." *Al Hamishmar*. October 8, 1954.

Gutwein, Dani. "He'arot al hayesodot hama'amadi'yim shel hakibush." *Teoriya ubikoret* 24 (2004): 203–11.

Hadani, Ever. *Tzrif Ha'etz*. Jerusalem; Tel Aviv: Mitzpe, 1930.

Handel, Yudit. *Street of Steps*. Translated by Rachel Katz and David Segal. New York; London: Herzl Press, 1963.

Harvey, David. *A Brief History of Neoliberalism*. Oxford; New York: Oxford University Press, 2005.

Hasak Lowy, Todd. *Here and Now: History, Nationalism, and Realism in Modern Hebrew Fiction*. Syracuse, NY: Syracuse University Press, 2008.

Hasak-Lowy, Todd. "Postzionism and Its Aftermath in Hebrew Literature: The Case of Orly Castel-Bloom." *Jewish Social Studies: History, Culture, Society* 14, no. 2 (2008): 86–112.

Herzig, Hannah. "Efsharuyot Akherot Besogrim et Hayam Leyehudit Katzir." *Siman Kri'a* 21 (December 1990): 293–99.

———. *Hakol ha'omer: ani: megamot basiporet hayisraelit shel shnot hashmonim*. Tel Aviv: Open University Press, 1998.

Herzl, Theodor. *Old-New Land*. Haifa: Haifa Publishing Company, 1960.
Hess, Tamar. "Kvar Ein La 'Ikuvim: Kri'a Feministit Belikro La'atalefim Lekhana Bat Shakhar 'Ubeheichan Ani Nimtzet Le'orly Castel Bloom." In *Eshnav Lekha'yehen Shel Nashim Be'khevrot Yehudiyot*, edited by Yael Atzmon, 375–94. Jerusalem: Merkaz Zalman Shazar, 1995.
Hever, Hannan. "Mapa Shel Khol." *Teoria Ubikoret* 20 (n.d.): 165–90.
———. "Minority Discourse of a National Majority: Israeli Fiction of the Early Sixties." *Prooftexts* 10, no. 1 (1990): 129–47.
———. *Producing the Modern Hebrew Canon*. New York: NYU Press, 2001.
———. *Sifrut Shenikhtevet Mikan*. Tel Aviv: Yedi'ot akharonot sifre khemed, 1999.
———. "The Post-Zionist Condition." *Critical Inquiry* 38, no. 3 (2012): 630–48.
Hirschfeld, Ariel. "Zehut Nigmeret Umatkhila Akheret." *Politika* 33 (1990): 48–54.
Hoberek, Andrew. "Introduction: After Postmodernism." *Twentieth Century Literature* 53, no. 3 (2007): 233–47.
Hollander, Philip. "Shifting Manhood: Masculinity and the Lebanon War in Beaufort and Waltz with Bashir." In *Narratives of Dissent: War in Contemporary Israeli Arts and Culture*, edited by Rachel S. Harris. Detroit, MI: Wayne University Press, 2012.
Holtzman, Avner. "Hasiporet Shel 'dor Ba'aretz.'" In *Ha'asor Harishon: 1948–1958*, edited by Zvi Tzameret and Hannah Yablonka, 263–80. Jerusalem: Yad ben tzvi, 1997.
Jameson, Fredric. *A Singular Modernity: Essay on the Ontology of the Present*. London; New York: Verso, 2002.
———, ed. *Aesthetcis and Politics*. London; New York: Verso, 1980.
———. *Archaeologies of the Future: The Desire Called Utopia and Other Science Fictions*. London; New York: Verso, 2005.
———. "Cognitive Mapping." In *Marxism and the Interpretation of Culture*, edited by Cary Nelson and Lawrence Grossberg, 347–60. Urbana: University of Illinois Press, 1988.
———. "Figural Relativism, or the Poetics of Historiography." *Diacritics* 6, no. 1 (1976): 2–9.
———. "On Magic Realism in Film." *Critical Inquiry* 12 (1986): 301–25.
———. *Postmodernism, Or, The Cultural Logic of Late Capitalism*. London; New York: Verso, 1991.
———. *Raymond Chandler: The Detections of Totality*. London; New York: Verso, 2016.
———. "Reification and Utopia in Mass Culture." *Social Text* 1 (1979): 130–48.
———. "The Aesthetics of Singularity." *New Left Review* 92 (2015): 101–32.
———. *The Ideologies of Theory*. London; New York: Verso, 2008.
———. "The Ideology of the Text." In *The Ideologies of Theory*, 20–76. London; New York: Verso, 2008.
———. *The Modernist Papers*. London; New York: Verso, 2007.
———. *The Political Unconscious: Narrative as a Socially Symbolic Act*. Ithaca, NY: Cornell University Press, 1981.

———. "Third World Literatures in the Age of Multinational Capitalism." *Social Text* 15 (1984): 65–88.
Kahana Carmon, Amalia. *Veyare'akh Be'emek Ayalon*. Tel Aviv: Hakibutz Hame'ukhad, 1971.
Kang, Liu. *Aesthetics and Marxism: Chinese Aesthetic Marxism and Their Western Contemporaries*. Durham, NC; London: Duke University Press, 2000.
Kaniuk, Yoram. *Himmo, King of Jerusalem*. New York: Atheneum, 1969.
Kaplan, Eran. *Beyond Post-Zionism*. Albany, NY: State University of New York, 2015.
Katzir, Yehudit. *Closing the Sea*. New York; San Diego; London: Harcourt Brace Jovanovich, 1992.
Katzman, Avi. "Slicha, Yesh Od Gviya Bamarak Sheli." *Ha'aretz*, March 24, 1989.
Kemp, Adriana, and Rebeca Raijman. *Ovdim Vezarim: Hakalkala Hapolitit Shel Hagirat Avoda Beyisrael*. Tel Aviv: Hakibutz Hame'ukhad, 2008.
Kenan, Amos. *Haderech Le'ein Kharod*. Tel Aviv: Am Oved, 1984.
———. *Sefer Hata'anugot*. Tel Aviv: A Levin-Epstein, 1970.
Kenaz, Yehoshua. *Infiltration*. South Royalton, VT: Steerforth Press, 2003.
Keret, Etgar. *Missing Kissinger*. London: Chatto & Windus, 2007.
Kh., P. "Im Yesh Gan Eden, Hu Nimtza Belevanon Veyesh Bo Rak Gvarim [If There Is Heaven, It Is in Lebanon, and It Has Only Men]." *Ha'aretz*, January 1, 2006. http://www.haaretz.co.il/literature/1.1073541.
Khalidi, Muhammad Ali. "Utopian Zionism or Zionist Proselytism? A Reading of Herzl's Altneuland." *Journal of Palestine Studies* 30, no. 4 (2001): 55–67.
Kna'ani, David. *Beinam Leven Zmanam [Between Them and Their Time]*. Merkhavia: Hashomer Hatsa'ir Press, 1955.
Kurtzweil, Baruch. "Boser Snobisti Ve'efes Me'upas." *Ha'aretz*. July 1, 1949.
La Berge, Leigh Claire, and Alison Shonkweiler, eds. *Reading Capitalist Realism*. Iowa City, IA: University of Iowa Press, 2014.
Laor, Dan. "Ha'aliya Hahamonit Ketokhen Venose Basifrut Ha'ivrit Bishnot Hamedina Harishonot." *Hatziyonut* 14 (1989): 161–75.
Laor, Yitzhak. *Anu Kotvim Otach Moledet: Masot Al Sifrut Yisra'elit*. Tel Aviv: Hakibutz Hame'ukhad, 1995.
Lazarus, Neil. "The Fetish of 'The West' in Postcolonial Theory." In *Marxism, Modernity, and Postcolonial Studies*, edited by Crystal Bartolovich and Neil Lazarus, 43–65. Cambridge: Cambridge University Press, 2002.
Lebovic, Nitzan. *Tziyonut Umlenkolia: Hakha'im Haktzarim Shel Israel Zarchi*. Jerusalem: Carmel, 2015.
Lenin, Vladimir Ilich. *What Is to Be Done? Burning Questions of Our Movement*. New York: International Publishers, 1969.
Leshem, Ron. *Beaufort*. New York: Random House, 2008.
Levy, Lital. *Poetic Trespass: Writing between Hebrew and Arabic in Israel/Palestine*. Princeton, NJ: Princeton University Press, 2014.
Likhovski, Assaf. "Post-Post-Zionist Historiography." *Israel Studies* 15, no. 2 (Summer 2010): 1–23.

Lipsker-Elbak, Avinadav. "Hadibur Vehaktav." *Ot: Ktav et Lesifrut Uleteoriya* 2 (2012): 211–21.
Lukács, Georg. *History and Class Consciousness: Studies in Marxist Dialectics.* Cambridge: MIT Press, 1971.
———. "Realism in the Balance." In *Aesthetics and Politics*, edited by Fredric Jameson, 28–59. London; New York: Verso, 1980.
———. *The Meaning of Contemporary Realism.* Translated by John Mander and Necke Mander. London: Merlin, 1963.
Mahalo, Aviva. *Vekhi Erom Ata?!: Emet Umitos Besipurei Dor Hapalmach.* Be'er Sheva: Ben Gurion Univeristy Press, 2008.
Makov-Hasson, Hadar. "Oedipus' Sister : Narrating Gender and Nation in the Early Novels of Israeli Women." New York University, 2009.
Mandel, Ernest. *Delightful Murder: A Social History of the Crime Story.* Minneapolis: University of Minnesota Press, 1985.
Margalit, Elkana. *"Hashomer Hatza'ir"—Me'adat Ne'urim Lemarksizm Mahapchani (1913–1936).* Tel Aviv: Hakibutz Hame'ukhad, 1971.
Marin, Louis. *Utopics: Spatial Play.* London; Atlantic Highlands, NJ: Macmillan; Humanities Press, 1984.
———. *Utopics: Spatial Play.* London; Atlantic Highlands, NJ: Macmillan; Humanities Press, 1984.
Marin, Tamar. "Lisdok et Hamar'a: Melankolia Ke'intertertu'aliyut Baroman Rekhov Hamadregot Me'et Yehudit Hendel." *Ot* 2 (2012): 149–73.
Marx, Karl. *A Contribution to the Critique of Political Economy.* Moscow: Progress Publishers, 1977.
———. *Grundrisse: Foundations of the Critique of Political Economy.* New York: Penguin, 1993.
———. *The Economic and Philosophical Manuscripts of 1844 and the Communist Manifesto.* New York: Prometheus Books, 1988.
Marx, Karl, and Engles Frederick. *Karl Marx, Frederick Engels: Collected Works.* Vol. 34. New York: International Publishes.
Matalon, Ronit. *Zarim Babayit.* Hasifriya hakhadasha, 1992.
McClanahan, Annie. *Dead Pledges: Debt, Crisis, and Twenty-First-Century Culture.* Stanford, CA: Stanford University Press, 2016.
McGowan, Todd. "Subject of the Event, Subject of the Act: The Difference between Badiou's and Žižek's Systems of Philosophy." *Subjectivity* 3, no. 1 (2010): 7–30. https://doi.org/doi:10.1057/sub.2009.31.
Megged, Aharon. *Hedva Ve'ani.* Tel Aviv: Hakibutz Hame'ukhad, 1954.
———. *Ruakh Yamim.* Tel Aviv: Hakibutz Hame'ukhad, 1950.
Melamed, Ariana. "Ma Asita Li Herzl?" *Yedi'ot Ahronot*, September 7, 2002. http://www.ynet.co.il/articles/0,7340,L-2103414,00.html.
Meletz, David. *Ma'agalot.* Tel Aviv: Am Oved, 1945.
Mendelson Maoz, Adia. *Multiculturalism in Israel: Literary Perspectives.* West Lafayette, IN: Purdue University Press, 2014.

Miron, Dan. *Arba Panim Basifrut Ha'ivrit Bat Yamenu*. Tel Aviv: Shoken, 1975.
———. *Hakoakh Hakhalash: Iyunim Basiporet Shel Yehudit Hendel* [*The Weak Strength*]. Tel Aviv: Hakibutz Hame'ukhad, 2002.
———. "Komeriya Be'israel: Kama He'arot Al Hasipur Habalashi Vemekomo Batarbut Hayisraelit." *Ho!* 3 (2006): 99–128.
———. "Mashehu Al Orly Castel-Bloom." *Al Hamishmar*, August 16, 1989.
———. "Min Hashulay'im El Hamerkaz Ubekhazara." *Haolam Haze*. February 11, 1987.
Mishani, Dror. *Bechol Ha'inyan Hamizrakhi Yesh Eize Absurd*. Tel Aviv: Am Oved, 2006.
Morahg, Gilead. "New Images of Arabs in Israeli Fiction." *Prooftexts* 6, no. 2 (1986): 147–62.
Moretti, Franco. "Conjectures on World Literature." *New Left Review* 1 (2000): 54–68.
Morris, Benny. "The New Historiography: Israel Confronts Its Past." *Tikkun* 3, no. 6 (1988): 19–23, 99–108.
Mossinsohn, Yigal. *Aforim Kasak*. Merkhavia: Sifriyat Po'alim, 1946.
———. *Be'arvot Hanegev*. Tel Aviv: Or Am, 1989.
———. *Derekh Gever*. Tel Aviv: Tverski, 1953.
———. *Kazablan*. Tel Aviv: Or Am, 1989.
Nagid, Chaim. "Mavo." In *S. Yizhar: Mivkhar Ma'amarim Al Yetzirato*, edited by Chaim Nagid, 7–37. Tel Aviv: Am Oved, 1972.
Namdar, Ruby. *Habayit Asher Nekherav*. Or Yehudah: Kineret, Zmora Bitan, 2013.
Nealon, Jeffrey. *Post-Postmodernism, or The Cultural Logic of Just-in-Time Capitalism*. Stanford, CA: Stanford University Press, 2012.
Netanel, Lilach. *Hamatzav ha'ivri*. Tel Aviv: Bavel, 2008.
Neumann, Boaz. *Tshukat Hahalutzim*. Tel Aviv: Am Oved, 2009.
Nevo, Eshkol. *Neuland*. Or Yehuda: Kineret, Zmora Bitan, Dvir, 2011.
Nilges, Mathias. "Neoliberalism and the Time of the Novel." *Textual Practice* 29, no. 2 (2015): 357–77.
———. "The Presence of Postmodernism in Contemporary American Literature." *American Literary History* 27, no. 1 (2015): 186–97.
Nir, Oded. "Towards a Renewal of Israeli Marxism, or Peace as a Vanishing Mediator." *Under consideration*.
Ophir, Adi. "Al Ktiva Postmodernit Ve'efsharut Hatzdakata Hamusarit." *Mikan* 1 (2000): 115–33.
———. "She'at Ha'efes." *Teoria Ubikoret* 12–13 (1999): 15–32.
Oppenheimer, Yochai. *Me'ever Lagader: Yitzug Ha'aravim Basiporet Ha'ivrit Vehayisraelit (1906–2005)*. Tel Aviv: Am Oved, 2008.
Oz, Amos. *Elsewhere, Perhaps*. New York: Harcourt Brace Jovanovich, 1973.
———. "Khirbet Khizeh Vesakanat Nefashot." *Davar*, February 17, 1978.
———. *My Michael*. New York: Alfred A. Knopf, 1972.

Pappe, Ilan. *The Ethnic Cleansing of Palestine*. Oxford: One World, 2006.
Parry, Benita. "Aspects of Peripheral Modernisms." *Ariel* 40, no. 1 (2009): 27–55.
Peleg, Yaron. "Beaufort the Book, Beaufort the Film: Israeli Militarism under Attack." In *Narratives of Dissent: War in Contemporary Israeli Arts and Culture*, edited by Rachel S. Harris, 336–45. Detroit, MI: Wayne State University Press, 2013.
———. *Israeli Culture between the Two Intifadas: A Brief Romance*. Austin: University of Texas Press, 2008.
Penslar, Derek. *Zionism and Technocracy: The Engineering of Jewish Settlement in Palestine*. Bloomington: Indiana University Press, 1991.
Ratok, Lily. "Nashim bemilkhemet ha'atzma'ut: mitos vezikaron." *Sadan* 5 (2002): 287–303.
Robinson, Kim Stanley. *The Years of Rice and Salt*. New York: Bantam, 2002.
Rozin, Orit. *Khovat Ha'ahava Hakasha: Yakhid Vekolektiv Beyisrael Beshnot Hakhamishim*. Tel Aviv: Am Oved, 2008.
———. *The Rise of the Individual in 1950s Israel: A Challenge to Collectivism*. Waltham, MA: Breindeis University Press, 2011.
Rudin, Shai. "Orly Castel Bloom's Perception of Coupledom and Women's Oppression in Light of Impressionist Features and Intertextual Connections in the Novel Where Am I." *Hebrew Studies* 52 (2011): 259–77.
S., Yizhar. *Days of Tsiklag*. Tel Aviv: Am Oved, 1958.
Said, Edward. *Orientalism*. New York: Pantheon, 1978.
Sand, Shlomo. *The Invention of the Land of Israel: From Holy Land to Homeland*. London: Verso, 2014.
Sartre, Jean Paul. *Critique of Dialectical Reason*. Vol. 1. London; New York: Verso, 1990.
Sauri, Emilio. "Autonomy after Autonomy, Or, The Novel beyond Nation: Roberto Bolaño's 2666." *Canadian Review of Comparative Literature* 42, no. 4 (2015): 396–409.
Schwartz, Yigal. *Ma Shero'im Mikan*. Or Yehuda: Kineret, Zmora Bitan, Dvir, 2005.
Schwarz, Roberto. *Misplaced Ideas: Essays on Brazilian Culture*. London; New York: Verso, 1992.
Sela, Maya. "Sefer: Be'azuva Tel Avivit Khaya La Mishpakha Shkufa." *Ha'aretz*, June 29, 2012. http://www.haaretz.co.il/1.1743212.
Shabtai, Yaakov. *Past Continuous*. Philadelphia: Jewish Publication Society of America, 1985.
Shafir, Gershon. *Land, Labor, and the Origins of the Israeli-Palestinian Conflict, 1882–1914*. Cambridge: Cambridge University Press, 1989.
Shaham, Nathan. *Dagan Ve'oferet*. Merkhavia: Sifriyat Po'alim, 1948.
———. *Ha'elim Atzelim*. Merkhavia: Sifriyat Po'alim, 1949.
———. *Tamid anakhnu*. Merkhavia: Sifriyat Po'alim, 1952.

Shaked, Gershon. *Gal khadash basiporet ha'ivrit*. Merkhavia: Sifriyat Po'alim, 1971.
———. *Hasiporet Ha'ivrit 1880–1980*. Vol. 1. Tel Aviv: Hakibutz Hame'ukhad, 1983.
———. *Hasiporet Ha'ivrit 1880–1980*. Vol. 3. Tel Aviv: Hakibutz Hame'ukhad; Keter, 1988.
———. *Hasiporet Ha'ivrit 1880–1980*. Vol. 4. Tel Aviv: Hakibutz Hame'ukhad, 1993.
———. *Modern Hebrew Fiction*. Bloomington: Indiana University Press, 2000.
———. "Tamid Anakhnu Guf Rishon Rabim? (Al Yetzirato Shel Natan Shaham)." In *Lesaper et Hakibutz: Mechkar Uvikoret*, edited by Shimon Shur and Lea Hadomi, 176–204. Tel Aviv: Sifriyat Po'alim, 1990.
Shalev, Meir. *The Blue Mountain*. New York: HarperCollins, 1991.
———. *The Loves of Judith*. Hopewell, NJ: Ecco Press, 1999.
Shalev, Michael. "Have Globalization and Liberalization 'normalized' Israel's Political Economy?" *Israel Affairs* 5, no. 2–3 (1998): 121–55.
Shamir, Moshe. *Hu halach basadot*. Tel Aviv: Am Oved, 2010.
———. *Hu halach basadot*. Tel Aviv: Am Oved, 2010.
Shamir, Ziva. "Habalash ha'ivri make shenit." *Ma'ariv*, May 26, 1989.
———. "Sefer khadash mishmeret khadasha." *Iton 77* 123 (April 1990): 7.
Shapira, Anita. "Hirbat Hizah: Between Remembrance and Forgetting." *Jewish Social Studies* 7, no. 1 (2000): 1–62.
Shayat, Heddy. "Lo 'margish aizen.'" *Mikan* 9 (2008): 158–82.
Shehada, Amtanes. "Dokh Mekhkar: Medinat Harevakha Shel Hamitnakhlim." *Teoria Ubikoret* 47 (2017).
Shifman, Smadar. *Dvarim Shero'im Mikan: David Grossman, Orly Castel Bloom Vemeir Shalev: Me'ever Lamodernism?* Jerusalem: Carmel, 2007.
———. "Ha'im Ani Nimtzet: Sipur Hakhanicha Hanashi Etzel Tsruya Shalev Veyehudit Katsir." *Mikan* 2 (2001): 125–41.
———. "Mehitganvut Yekhidim Lehaolam Ktzat Akhar Kach: Kur Hituch O Hitganvut Rav Tarbutit?" *Hador* 3 (2009): 60–67.
Shimoni, Youval. *A Room*. Champaign, IL: Dalkey Archive Press, 2016.
Shimony, Batya. "Hamakom she'elav halev kameha." *Dapim lemekhkar besifrut* 16/17 (2008): 294–310.
Shirav, Pnina. *Ktiva lo tama*. Tel Aviv: Hakibutz Hame'ukhad, 1998.
Shoham, Liad. *Lemar'it A'yin*. Or Yehuda: Kineret, Zmora Bitan, Dvir, 2016.
Silberstein, Laurence. *The Postzionism Debates*. New York; London: Routledge, 1999.
Sterling, Bruce. "Slipstream," 1989. https://w2.eff.org/Misc/Publications/Bruce_Sterling/Catscan_columns/catscan.05.
Suvin, Darko. *Metamorphoses of Science Fiction: On the Poetics and History of a Literary Genre*. New Haven, CT: Yale University Press, 1979.
Thorne, Christian. "The Sea Is Not a Place; Or, Putting the World Back into World Literature." *Boundary 2* 40, no. 2 (2013): 53–79.

Toscano, Alberto, and Jeff Kinkle. *Cartographies of the Absolute*. Winchester, UK; Washington, USA: Zero Books, 2014.
Touché Gafla, Ophir. *Bayom Shehamusika Meta*. Jerusalem: Keter, 2010.
———. *The World of the End*. New York: Tor Books, 2013.
Tzivoni, Eden. "Haroman Habalashi—Tekes Gilui Hagufa / Misdar Hakhashudim." *Resling* 4 (1998): 60–70.
Ukhmani, Azriel. "Gidulo Shel Mesaper [A Storyteller's Growth]." *Al Hamishmar*. February 18, 1955.
Wallerstein, Immanuel. *World Systems Analysis: An Introduction*. Durham, NC: Duke University Press, 2004.
Warwick Research Collective. *Combined and Uneven Development: Towards a New Theory of World Literature*. Liverpool: Liverpool University Press, 2015.
Wegner, Phillip. "Greimas Avec Lacan: From the Symbolic to the Real in Dialectical Criticism." *Criticism* 51, no. 2 (2009): 211–45.
———. *Imaginary Communities: Utopia, the Nation, and the Spatial Histories of Modernity*. Berkeley; Los Angeles; London: University of California Press, 2002.
———. *Life between Two Deaths: US Culture in the Long Nineties*. Durham, NC; London: Duke University Press, 2009.
Weizman, Eyal. *Hollow Land: Israel's Architecture of Occupation*. London; New York: Verso, 2007.
Wilde, Oscar. *The Soul of Man Under Socialism*. London: Porcupine Press, 1948.
Williams, Evan Calder. *Combined and Uneven Apocalypse*. Winchester, UK; Washington, USA: Zero Books, 2010.
Yakir, Einat. *Yeme khol*. Tel Aviv: Keter, 2012.
Yehoshua, A. B. "Facing the Forests." In *Three Days and a Child*. Garden City, NY: Doubleday, 1970.
Yizhar, S. "Ephraim Khozer La'aspeset." In *Hakhorsha Asher Bagiva*. Tel Aviv: Hakibutz Hame'ukhad, 1947.
———. *Khirbet Khizeh*. New York: Farrar, Straus and Giroux, 2014.
———. *Mikdamot*. Tel Aviv: Zmora Bitan, 1992.
Za'it, David. "Bein Realism Le'utopia: Konstruktivism, Kolektivizatzia, Vedu-Le'umiyut Behitpatkhut Hashomer Hatsair (1926–1942)." MA thesis, Tel Aviv University, 1984.
———. *Halutzim Bamavoch Hapoliti*. Jerusalem: Yad ben tzvi, 1993.
Zarchi, Yisrael. *Yamim Yekhefim*. Tel Aviv: Sefer, 1934.
Zemach, Adi. "Hapost-Modernizm: Rav-Si'akh." *Iton 77* 138–139 (1991): 25–36.
Zertal, Idith. *Israel's Holocaust and the Politics of Nationhood*. Cambridge, UK ; New York, NY: Cambridge University Press, 2005.
Žižek, Slavoj. *For They Know Not What They Do: Enjoyment as a Political Factor*. London; New York: Verso, 1991.
———. *How to Read Lacan*. New York; London: W. W. Norton & Company, 2006.

———. "Introduction." In *Mapping Ideology*, edited by Slavoj Žižek, 1–34. London; New York: Verso, 1994.

———. *Looking Awry: An Introduction to Jacques Lacan through Popular Culture*. Cambridge, MA: MIT Press, 1991.

———. *The Parallax View*. Cambridge, MA; London, England: MIT Press, 2006.

———. *The Sublime Object of Ideology*. London; New York: Verso, 1989.

Index

1948 War, 58, 66–67, 76, 78, 85, 87, 88, 90, 95, 101, 113, 119, 133, 152, 158
1967 War, 5, 6, 16, 34, 139, 141, 143, 149, 167, 169, 176, 180, 182

Abramovich, Dvir, 113–15, 169
Adorno, Theodor, 17, 25, 36, 104, 106, 189, 216, 220
African literature, 12–13, 185
Agnon, S.Y., 40, 96, 223, 225, 230
allegory: of breakdown of historicity, 7, 103, 136, 162, 230, 237; national, 5, 90, 158–59, 231–32; of search for time, 187, 190, 196, 234, 235; theory of, 86, 128, 133, 162, 163, 187, 214, 232
Althusser, Louis, 28, 42, 73, 102, 123, 144, 161, 222
Altneuland. *See* Herzl, Theodor
Always We. *See* Shaham, Nathan
Anderson, Benedict, 195
Anti-genre. *See* genre
Arab Spring, 19
Arabs, representation of, 115, 126, 138, 150–54
Arbell, Michal, 67–68, 84, 101
Aricha, Yosef, 47, 51, 231; *Bread and Vision*, 51
Ashkenazi, 89, 95, 99, 164–66, 219, 230

Ashkenazi, Yiftach, 7, 213, 214, 230, 231–37; *Fulfillment*, 7, 230–37
Assis, Machado de, 15

Balaban, Avraham, 5
Bar Yossef, Yehoshua, 197
Barefoot Days. *See* Zarchi, Yisrael
Barma, Yisrael, 146
Bartana, Ortsion, 109
Bartov, Hanoch, 4, 85, 87–93, 165, 193; *Each Has Six Wings*, 88–93, 95, 165, 187, 193
Beaufort. *See* Leshem, Ron
Ben Yehuda, Netiva, 67, 80
Benjamin, Walter, 32, 84, 86, 128, 135, 208, 214
Benn Michaels, Walter, 17
Berg, Yonatan, 184
Bichler, Shimshon, 138–39
Big Other, 119, 174
Bildungsroman. *See* coming of age
Black Panthers, the Israeli, 165
Bloch, Ernst, 41, 104
Borochov, Ber, 46
Bourgeois, 37, 46, 49, 68, 81, 90, 91, 93, 95, 98, 112, 117, 120, 121, 125, 154, 161, 169, 171, 187, 193, 232
Bourgeoisification, 112, 169
Brazilian literature, 13–15
Bread and Vision. *See* Aricha, Yosef

278 Index

Brenner, Robert, 10
Brenner, Y. H., 40, 41, 48, 49, 61, 116–17, 223, 225, 226, 230
Brown, Nicholas, 12–13, 18, 19, 144, 185, 198
Burla, Yehuda, 40, 47

Calvin, John, 20
capitalism, 7, 20, 82, 84, 85, 104, 108, 123, 144, 180–81, 187, 188, 189, 198, 204, 235, 238; and fascism, 37; formation of, 19–20, 21, 22; global, 7–13, 16, 18–19 21, 28, 35–36, 49, 104, 107, 137, 177, 182, 185; late, 34, 108; and literature, 104–108, 153; monopoly, 49, 158; in Palestine/Israel, 16, 29, 31–32, 34, 36, 65, 76, 78, 82–83, 85, 139, 153 165, 169, 180, 182, 183; peripheral, 13, 19, 184, 190; and totality, 31, 88, 106. *See* neoliberalism
Castel-Bloom, Orly, 5, 6, 109, 111, 112, 115, 117, 118–28, 129, 136–37, 140–41, 144, 156, 165, 186, 188, 191, 193, 210, 214, 223–24; *Where am I?*, 117, 118–28, 193
Cazdyn, Eric, 181, 205–206, 208
Chandler, Raymond, 174–75
Chernyshevsky, Nikolai, 52
China, 11, 18, 19
class, 58, 68, 81, 90, 91, 95, 123, 139, 182, 183, 189, 195, 197, 221–24
closure, 28, 57, 119, 120, 141, 162, 174, 175, 177, 197, 208, 209, 226, 229, 236, 237, 238
cognitive mapping, 102, 107, 108, 110, 136, 137, 138, 141, 142, 219
Cohen, Uri, 27, 118, 140, 141, 209
collectivity, 24, 51, 69, 75, 77, 85, 90, 91, 112, 123, 138, 161, 162, 163, 174, 177, 190–92, 195, 199, 200, 205, 211
colonialism, 9, 10, 14, 18–20, 138
coming of age, 158–60, 163, 170, 202, 205, 216, 218
consumerism, 112, 131–35, 137, 140, 169, 189, 198
contemporaneity, 7, 9, 11, 22, 23, 181, 185, 205, 213
Crary, Jonathan, 181

Deckard, Sharae, 23
Derrida, Jacques, 120, 127, 162, 232
development, 7, 9, 10, 11, 22, 185; under, 138, 184–85, 190; uneven, 7, 10, 12–13, 20, 22, 23, 138, 184–85, 188, 190
diaspora, 43, 117, 131–32, 234

Each Has Six Wings. *See* Bartov, Hanoch
economic base, 15, 19, 20, 25, 66
economic infrastructure. *See* economic base
enjoyment, 100, 102, 131, 133–35, 137, 202
Eshel, Amir, 181
Esty, Jed, 23

Farjoun, Emmanuel, 139
Feldman, Yael, 24, 66, 76, 77
Fordism, 6, 189, 205–208, 217
Foucault, Michel, 30, 123, 238
Frankfurt School, 18, 22, 37
Freud, Sigmund, 18, 40, 62, 85, 101, 121, 126 140, 147, 152, 172, 201–202, 236–37
Fulfillment. *See* Ashkenazi, Yiftach

Gavron, Assaf, 184, 200
General Federation of Labor (the *Histadrut*), 46–47, 57

genre, 35, 157–58, 214; 20s and 30s realism, 44–57; detective, 6, 136, 167–78; "genre" and "anti-genre" literature, 32, 41, 66, 72, 77, 84, 87, 90, 93–94, 95, 96, 102–104, 108, 152, 156, 230; naturalism, 104–108; Science Fiction, 197–209; Settlement Novel, 184, 200; Slipstream, 197–200; of soldiers' experience, 85–86, 156–59, 166–67, 215, 220; of utopian literature, 41–44
Gertz, Nurit, 39, 40, 53, 55, 57, 90, 91, 116
Giladi, Amotz, 223
Ginsburg, Shai, 28, 31
Glasner, Arik, 199
Global North/South, 9
Gluzman, Michael, 24, 42–43
Gnessin, U.N., 48, 116, 117, 223, 225
Gogol, Nikolai, 198
Goldberg, Leah, 229
Govrin, Nurit, 66
Gozansky, Tamar, 229
Gramsci, Antonio, 36, 114, 195
Greimas, Algirdas Julien, 145, 163–65
Grossman, David, 6, 117, 137, 140, 156, 168, 176, 195, 196; *Book of Intimate Grammar*, 145, 148; *See Under—Love*, 145; *Smile of the Lamb, the*, 6, 140, 144, 145–56, 168, 174, 176
Grumberg, Karen, 124, 191
Gur, Batya, 6, 117, 136, 145, 167–78, 199, 231; *Literary Murder*, 171; *Murder in Jerusalem*, 177; *Murder on a Kibbutz*, 171, 231; *Saturday Morning Murder*, 144, 167–78
Gurevitz, Yossi, 109, 118
Gurfein, Rivka, 78, 83, 88
Gutwein, Daniel, 182, 239

Hadani, Ever, 40, 52, 232; *Wooden Cabin*, 52–55
halutz, 41, 44–47, 51, 52, 55, 57–58, 60–62, 65, 66, 68, 71, 72, 76, 77, 78, 82–85, 87–91, 97, 99, 100–103, 107, 108, 133, 167, 168, 175, 220
Harootunian, Harry, 21
Harvey, David, 34
Hasak-Lowy, Todd, 40–41, 118
Hebrew Condition, the. *See* Netanel, Lilach
Heffner, Avraham, 140
Hegel, G.W.F., 20, 25, 28, 55, 122, 161, 211
Hendel, Yehudit, 4, 5, 67, 85, 87, 89, 93–104, 105–107, 133, 149–50; *Street of Steps*, 4, 67, 87, 93–104, 133, 149
Herzig, Hannah, 130, 136, 161–64, 166
Herzl, Theodor, 3, 42–43, 179, 219; *Altneuland*, 3, 42–43, 57, 179, 219
Hess, Tamar, 120, 122
Hever, Hannan, 27, 76, 152, 239
Hirschfeld, Ariel, 165
histadrut. *See* General Federation of Labor
historicism, 32, 36, 165, 166, 231
historicity, 4, 5, 6, 7, 32, 35, 45, 68, 75, 76, 77, 78, 83, 108, 111, 136, 141, 144, 159, 166, 185, 215, 222, 230, 237, 238, 239
Hobbes, Thomas, 67
Hoberek, Andrew, 198
Hoffman, Yoel, 140
Hollander, Phillip, 220
Holocaust, the, 130–31, 133, 137, 155

idealism, 19, 20, 25, 31, 33, 48, 102
identity politics, 12, 17, 18, 118, 210
ideologeme, 113, 156, 163, 165, 166

immigration: of Jews to Palestine/ Israel, 88, 175, 223; from former USSR, 186
imperialism, 10
Infiltration. See Kenaz, Yehoshua
intifada, 112, 141, 182, 232
irrealism, 13
Israeli military. *See* military

Jakobson, Roman, 174
Jameson, Fredric: on Greimassian square, 163–64; on historicization, 26; on interpretation, 17, 57, 123, 144, 153, 169, 174, 181; on magic realism, 13, 190; on modernism and modernity, 11, 13, 49, 76, 107, 108, 116, 117, 184–85; on postmodernism and postmodernity, 34, 110–11, 114, 116, 120, 122, 127, 136, 144, 166, 180, 190, 208; on utopia, 44. *See* cognitive mapping, historicity, vanishing mediator

Kahana-Carmon, Amalia, 117, 120, 122
Kang, Liu, 11, 18
Kaniuk, Yoram, 157
Kaplan, Eran, 182, 239
Katzir, Yehudit, 5, 6, 109, 117, 128–37, 140, 144, 156, 165, 188; *Closing the Sea*, 117, 128–37
Kenan, Amos: *The Book of Pleasures*, 132–33; *The Road to Ein Harod*, 197
Kenaz, Yehoshua, 6, 7, 69, 117, 129, 137, 141, 143, 144, 145, 156–67, 214, 215, 216, 220, 232; *Infiltration*, 6, 69, 129, 141, 144, 156–67, 168, 169, 170, 174, 176, 214, 215, 220, 222, 232
Keret, Etgar, 112, 140, 156, 214, 223, 224
Khirbet Khizeh. *See* Yizhar, S.

kibbutz, 52, 57, 58, 68, 69, 70, 71, 72, 73, 74, 75, 76, 78, 79, 80, 81, 82, 132, 133, 158, 164, 165, 171, 223, 231
Kna'ani, David, 60
Kurtzweil, Baruch, 79

labor, 13, 47, 50, 53, 60, 81, 91, 138, 139, 154, 182, 183, 208; transformative, 44–46, 51, 53, 54, 58, 61, 77, 82; wage, 13, 29, 46, 48, 51, 58, 84, 85, 90, 102, 108, 138, 153
Labor Brigade, 46
Labor Unity, 46
Lacan, Jacques, 18, 43, 56, 71, 90, 100, 101, 109, 123, 132, 174, 193, 194, 204, 222, 224, 238
Laor, Dan, 88
Laor, Yithak, 24, 40
Lebanon, 113, 215, 216, 217, 218, 219, 232, 233
Lebovic, Nitzan, 31, 32, 51
Lenin, Vladimir, 31, 49, 52
Leshem, Ron, 7, 157, 186, 213, 214, 215–22; *Beaufort*, 7, 157, 186, 213, 215–22
Lipsker-Elbak, Avidav, 148
Lukács, Georg, 18, 22, 25, 44, 48, 82, 97, 104–108, 123, 129, 225
Lye, Coleen, 23
Lynch, David, 166

ma'abarot. *See* transit camps
Macherey, Pierre, 18, 144
Mandate, the British, 69, 75
Mandel, Ernest, 34, 171
Margalit, Elkana, 32
Marin, Louis, 42, 56, 86, 218
Marin, Tamar, 101
Marx, Karl, 10, 21, 25, 46, 85, 108, 180

Marxism, 3, 8, 10–12, 17–38, 42, 46, 49, 70, 88, 104, 107–108, 123, 144, 180, 182, 184, 198–99, 214–15
Matalon, Ronit, 140, 210
materialism, 29, 31, 32, 33, 102, 239
Megged, Aharon, 96; *Hedva and I*, 165; *Sea Winds*, 88
melancholia, 5, 101
Meletz, David, 58
melting pot, 166
Mendele Mocher Sforim, 91, 92
Mendelson-Maoz, Adia, 113, 115, 210
military, 4, 45, 58, 60, 61, 78, 79, 80, 81, 82, 119, 121, 146, 155, 156, 158, 161, 170, 171, 175, 176, 191, 215, 216, 217, 219, 220, 233, 234
Miron, Dan, 5, 67, 94, 96, 99, 101, 102, 103, 104, 106, 115, 121, 165, 169, 170, 171, 209
Mishani, Dror, 24, 158, 165, 171
Mizrachi, 17, 24, 27, 89, 95, 99, 114, 115, 138, 158, 164, 165, 166, 219
mode of production, 29, 123, 137
modernism, 12, 13, 16, 33, 41, 49, 94, 104–108, 110, 111, 116, 122, 137, 138, 145, 198; Hebrew, 16, 111, 117, 118, 121; late, 114, 116, 117, 140, 156
modernity, 10, 107, 184–85; alternative, 10, 11
Moretti, Franco, 13
Morhag, Gilead, 151
Morris, Benny, 27, 239
Moshava, 47, 50, 51
Mossinsohn, Yigal, 4, 58, 65, 66, 67, 68–77, 78, 79, 83, 84, 85, 86, 89, 92, 93, 95, 101, 102, 103, 107, 122, 124, 132, 156, 231; *Grey as Sack*, 92, 132; *In the Negev Prairies*, 66, 76, 77, 102; *Kazablan*, 95; *Way of a Man*, 58, 68–78

multiculturalism, 2, 17, 113, 114, 115, 165, 210

Namdar, Ruby, 199
nation, 4, 15, 18–19, 20, 24, 27, 29, 31, 32, 33, 35, 40, 42, 46, 52, 53, 55, 57, 78, 79, 95, 107, 108, 111, 117, 133, 149, 158, 175, 189, 193, 195, 199, 210, 211, 222; ideology of the, 4, 23, 35, 62, 66, 69, 76, 77, 87, 88, 89, 95, 101, 102, 103, 104, 113–17, 119, 120, 121, 123, 125, 126, 127, 132, 134, 138, 146, 150, 151, 152, 153, 159, 163, 165, 166, 169, 175, 182, 197, 199, 213, 216, 237; literature of, 4, 5, 85, 88–89, 90, 92, 93, 94, 120, 121, 127, 131, 132, 137, 140, 148, 149, 158, 159, 160, 163, 176, 186, 216, 218, 220, 230, 231, 232, 233, 234, 235; national narrative, 3, 4, 11–20, 21, 22, 23, 26, 28, 30, 46, 76
naturalism, 33, 66, 87, 88, 104–108, 129, 149
neoliberalism, 1, 7, 16, 23, 32, 34, 35, 37, 139, 142, 144, 179, 181–87, 189, 194, 196, 197, 205, 206, 207, 208, 209–11, 215, 216, 221, 222, 223
Netanel, Lilach, 7, 210, 213, 214, 222–30, 237; *The Hebrew Condition*, 7, 213, 222–30
Neumann, Boaz, 32, 44, 45, 52
Nevo, Eshkol, 57, 179
New Wave, 2, 4–5, 14, 113, 145, 157
Nilges, Mathias, 180, 181, 211
Nitzan, Jonathan, 138, 139
nostalgia, 32, 67, 68, 83, 84, 93, 101, 102, 129, 130, 131, 133, 135, 136, 166

objet petit-a, 56

occupied territories, 16, 34, 35, 60, 89, 176, 183, 184
Ophir, Adi, 27, 28, 29, 30, 31, 181, 137, 238, 239
Oppenheimer, Yochai, 151
Oz, Amos, 62, 115, 116, 117, 121–27, 132, 133, 136, 139, 140, 141, 146, 147, 170, 210, 231, 234; *Elsewhere, Perhaps*, 117, 121, 125, 133, 234; *My Michael*, 117, 121, 125, 132, 147

Palestine, 3, 16, 29, 32, 39, 42, 46, 47, 57, 58, 65, 75, 81, 89, 155, 167, 175, 183, 223, 229
Palestinian, 5, 16, 27, 29, 32, 34, 35, 43, 46, 47, 58, 60, 62, 89, 139, 140, 141, 143, 146, 150, 151, 152, 154, 155, 156, 157, 158, 166, 169, 176, 177, 180, 182, 183, 184, 210, 232, 233
Palmach, 4, 66, 67, 68, 77, 78, 79, 80, 81, 82, 83, 84, 85, 133, 156
Pappé, Ilan, 58
parody, 69, 218
Parry, Benita, 13
Pastiche, 6, 15, 69, 95, 120, 122, 123, 124, 125, 126, 127, 128, 129, 132, 133, 136, 137, 140, 141, 144, 145, 149, 150, 164, 165, 166, 179, 197, 209, 221, 222, 225, 231, 233, 234, 235
peace, 156; process, 182
Peleg, Yaron, 109, 112, 118, 145, 186, 209, 210
Periodization, 2, 5, 8, 16, 26, 33, 34, 35, 36, 109, 111, 112, 113, 115, 116, 137, 179, 180, 186, 209, 210, 211
peripheral literatures, 8, 9, 11, 13, 18
petit-bourgeois, 91, 93, 117, 187, 193
post-apocalyptic, 85, 186, 238

postcolonial, 9, 138
post-Fordism. *See* Fordism
postmodernism, 2, 5, 6, 7, 8, 16, 28, 30, 33, 34, 35, 43, 69, 86, 104, 109–18, 120, 122, 127, 128, 129, 130, 131, 136, 137, 138, 139, 141, 142, 143, 144, 145, 146, 156, 157, 158, 163, 165, 166, 176, 177, 179, 180, 181, 182, 186, 190, 195, 201, 203, 205, 209, 210, 211, 213, 214, 215, 224, 225, 226, 228, 229, 230, 231, 232, 233, 234, 235, 237, 238
postmodernity, 6, 34, 180, 181, 185, 190, 213
post-Zionism, 3, 4, 18, 26, 27, 28, 29, 30, 32, 113, 115, 216, 238, 239
Protestantism, 20
Psychoanalysis, 101, 106, 114, 126, 171, 172, 173, 176

realism, 2, 16, 23, 33, 87, 96, 104–108, 120, 187, 198, 230; 20s and 30s Hebrew, 2, 39–63, 66, 71, 87, 88, 93, 95, 97, 100, 102, 103, 104–108, 155, 167, 168; capitalist, 180, 181, 185; Magic, 13, 190; Socialist, 16
reductionism, 17, 18, 26, 29, 101, 107, 150, 181, 206, 214, 215
Remarque, Erich Maria, 216
Revolution, 9, 19, 46, 52, 54, 65, 68, 72, 76, 77, 78, 84, 85, 91, 108, 133, 153, 154, 182, 188, 222
Robinson, Kim Stanley, 77
Rudin, Shai, 120

Sand. See Yakir, Einat
Sand, Shlomo, 29
Saturday Morning Murder. See Gur, Batya
Sauri, Emilio, 9, 22, 185, 199

Schwartz, Yigal, 23, 24, 33, 114, 115, 210
Schwarz, Roberto, 13–15
science fiction, 35, 44, 197–209
settlements, in occupied territories, 35, 182, 183, 184, 185, 200
Shabtai, Yaakov, 33, 139, 143
Shaham, Nathan, 4, 65, 66, 67, 69, 70, 78–86, 89, 93, 101, 102, 103, 107, 124, 133, 156, 157, 158, 165, 231, 235; "Always We," 67, 69, 78–86, 165; *The Gods are Lazy*, 67, 83; *Hay and Lead*, 79
Shaked, Gershon, 4, 5, 24, 33, 39, 40, 41, 44, 50, 51, 53, 55, 57, 66, 67, 68, 69, 73, 77, 78, 80, 83, 84, 94, 102, 103, 113, 115, 127, 145, 209
Shakespeare, 219
Shalev, Meir, 140, 168, 214 231
Shalev, Michael, 139
Shalom Aleichem, 91, 92
Shamir, Moshe, 58, 87, 92, 95, 96, 122, 132; *He Walked through the Fields*, 58, 87, 92, 96, 122, 132, 165
Shamir, Ziva, 131, 169
Shifman, Smadar, 111, 115, 118, 120, 186, 209, 239
Shimoni, Yuval, 69, 157, 168, 214, 233
Shofman, Gershon, 53
Shoham, Liad, 184
Shoshan, Esty, 191
Shternhall, Ze'ev, 24
singularity, 192, 193, 195
Slipstream, 197–200
Smile of the Lamb. See Grossman, David
Socialist, 16, 20, 24, 32, 43, 68, 177, 188
socioeconomic infrastructure. *See* economic base

Soviet Union, 6, 7, 9, 11, 16, 19, 186, 190
state, 3, 4, 27, 29, 30, 31, 32, 33, 34, 40, 46, 52, 55, 57, 62, 67, 68, 72, 75, 76, 78, 80, 83, 102, 103, 104, 111, 133, 152, 158, 165, 182, 183, 185, 195, 196, 199, 210, 211, 214, 226, 231, 232; failed, 22; Generation (*Dor Hamedina*), 3; welfare, 16, 34, 35, 131, 142, 158, 183, 185, 189, 195, 208, 217, 221, 224, 226
Stendhal, 146
Sterling, Bruce, 197–98
Street of Steps. See Hendel, Yehudit
subject, 4, 15, 20, 26, 29, 33, 36, 45, 46, 49, 56, 67, 68, 69, 70, 73, 75, 76, 78, 79, 81, 83, 84, 85, 88, 90, 101, 105, 106, 107, 108, 120, 122, 123, 124, 125, 126, 127, 132, 133, 134, 138, 140, 151, 151, 152, 153, 154, 156, 158, 159, 168, 174, 175, 177, 184, 187, 189, 190, 193, 195, 202, 206, 211, 222, 226, 227, 233; dissolution of, 110, 166; of history, 32, 40, 41, 47, 52, 75, 78, 84, 85, 106, 176, 177, 193, 225, 226, 230; neoliberal, 16, 183, 186
symptom, 1, 28, 62, 66, 70, 73, 79, 80, 93, 106, 110, 126, 127, 132, 133, 147, 173, 176, 217, 221

temporality, 6, 7, 10, 22, 95, 97, 98, 99, 102, 131, 146, 152, 153, 179, 181, 182, 185, 187, 190, 192, 193, 194, 196, 203, 204, 205, 206, 207, 208, 213, 215, 217, 222, 227, 228, 237, 238, 239
third world, 138, 185, 188, 189, 197
Thorne, Christian, 23, 107, 177
totality, 7, 10, 11, 16, 28, 31, 35, 36, 37, 88, 105, 106, 107, 108, 167,

totality *(continued)*
    169, 171, 172, 174, 175, 177, 199, 219, 225
Touché Gafla, Ophir, 6, 179, 197–209, 210, 213, 214, 217, 219, 239; *The Day the Music Died*, 6, 179, 197–209, 217; *World of the End*, 179
transit camps, 164
Tzivoni, Eden, 174

uneven development. *See* development
USSR. *See* Soviet Union
utopia, 2, 3, 6, 31, 32, 33, 36, 37, 41–44, 46, 47, 48, 49, 50, 52, 53, 54, 55, 57, 58, 65, 68, 72, 76, 77, 78, 84, 85, 86, 87, 90, 93, 95, 97, 99, 100, 101, 102, 108, 112, 113, 114, 133, 135, 145, 152, 153, 158, 164, 168, 171, 179, 185, 186, 187, 188, 189, 197, 200, 201, 206, 208, 215, 216, 218, 219, 220, 222, 225, 229, 231, 239

vanishing mediator, 2–3, 29, 32, 33, 44, 65, 116, 18
Verne, Jules, 198

Wallerstein, Immanuel, 10, 184
war, 27, 75, 101, 113, 150, 157; Cold, 3, 37; literature of, 85, 86, 87, 156–57, 216; Second World, 75, 78. *See* 1948 war, 1967 war
Warwick Collective, 10, 184, 190
Washington Consensus, 182
Way of a Man. See Mossinsohn, Yigal
Weber, Max, 20, 22
Wegner, Phillip, 42, 44, 116, 128, 145, 157, 158, 166, 167, 238
Weizman, Eyal, 35
welfare state. *See* state

West, the, 8, 9, 12, 33, 111, 112, 113, 117, 118, 129, 132, 138, 139, 143, 180, 190, 198
West Bank. *See* occupied territories
Westernization, 113
Where am I? See Castel-Bloom, Orly
Wilde, Oscar, 188
Williams, Evan Calder, 85, 238
World War II. *See* war

Ya'ari, Meir, 46
Yakir, Einat, 6, 7, 179, 186–97, 199, 208, 210, 213, 214, 224; *Sand*, 6, 179, 186–97, 208
Yehoshua, A.B., 115, 116, 117, 121, 122, 139, 140, 146, 147, 151, 152, 170, 210
yishuv, 223
Yizhar, S., 4, 7, 40, 57–63, 65, 67, 72, 79, 83, 85, 89, 102, 103, 107, 132, 156, 157, 158, 168, 216, 217, 220, 221, 222; *Days of Tsiklag*, 157; "Ephraim returns to the Alfalfa," 67, 83; *Khirbet Khizeh*, 4, 39, 57–63, 83, 157, 220
Young Guard, the, 46, 55, 57

Za'it, David, 32, 46, 57
Zarchi, Yisrael, 3, 47–52, 54, 55, 124, 231, 232; *Barefoot Days*, 3, 47–53, 77, 93
Zionism, 3, 15, 16, 26, 27, 28, 29, 30, 31, 32, 41, 44, 46, 58, 102, 113, 117, 175, 223, 224, 226, 234; antagonism to state of, 27–29, 30, 31, 62, 152, 158; collective transformative project of, 3, 4, 5, 18, 24, 40, 41, 65, 85, 93, 95, 104, 133, 222, 230, 231, 234; in literature, 16, 18, 24, 31, 32, 33, 39, 40, 50, 55, 57, 62, 124, 148,

151, 155, 167; metanarrative of, 4, 23, 44, 50, 66, 87, 94, 102, 106, 115, 230; post-. *See* post-Zionism

Žižek, Slavoj, 21, 29, 37, 56, 71, 100, 105, 106, 129, 151, 168, 190, 194, 202

www.ingramcontent.com/pod-product-compliance
Lightning Source LLC
Chambersburg PA
CBHW020640230426
43665CB00008B/253